Toward the Transformation
of
Secondary
School
Counseling

Editors:
Doris Rhea Coy
Claire G. Cole
Wayne C. Huey
Susan Jones Sears

ERIC Counseling and Personnel Services Clearinghouse
2108 School of Education
The University of Michigan
Ann Arbor, Michigan 48109-1259

and

The American School Counselor Association
A division of the
American Association for Counseling and Development
5999 Stevenson Avenue
Alexandria, Virginia 22304

ERIC Counseling and Personnel Services Clearinghouse
2108 School of Education
The University of Michigan
Ann Arbor, Michigan 48109-1259

ISBN 1-56109-037-9

This publication was prepared with partial funding from the Office of Educational Research and Improvement, U.S. Department of Education under contract no. RI88062011. The opinions expressed in this report do not necessarily reflect the positions or policies of OERI, the Department of Education, or ERIC/CAPS.

Contents

Prologue

High school is a time when students make plans and decisions, develop personal and work habits, and acquire values and attitudes that will shape the rest of their lives. It is a time when secondary school counselors can play a significant role in the developmental years of adolescents. Despite greatly increased student numbers, however, large numbers of secondary school counselors have had to function with the same, or in most cases decreased, staff and resources. And counselors have had to deal with increasing student concerns and problems as they (the students) grapple with the myriad challenges of growing up in today's turbulent society.

The more resourceful and innovative counselors have responded to the challenges facing them by adopting and adapting more effective and efficient counseling procedures. This book provides both a vision of the transformation of school counseling which many counselors are contributing to, as well as a discussion of the practices and programs which school counselors everywhere are using to enhance secondary school counseling. We suggest you use it as both an overview of the transformation which is occurring in secondary school counseling and as a resource for exploration of specific school counseling programs and practices. While the primary focus of the book is on the secondary level, many of the ideas and approaches presented are useful at other levels.

If you are not already aware of it, two companion volumes, *Elementary School Counseling in a Changing World* and *The Challenge of Counseling in Middle Schools,* are excellent sources for gaining an understanding of school counseling K–12. Additionally, ERIC/CAPS' *CounselorQuest* is an ideal resource for broadening your knowledge-ability of 168 specific topics, most of which are relevant to school counseling.

We are sure you will find this book rewarding reading—now and in the future. Perhaps in the next edition it will contain an article by *you* describing what you are doing to facilitate the transformation of school counseling. ERIC/CAPS is forever looking for new ideas and practices. Won't you share your ideas with us?

Garry R. Walz, Ph.D., NCC
Director, ERIC/CAPS and Professor of Education

Foreword

It is my pleasure to introduce the third book in the school counseling series published by ERIC/CAPS in collaboration with the American School Counselor Association. *Toward the Transformation of Secondary School Counseling* is an overview of the field from the past to the not yet seen future. It captures the burdens and blessings of high school counselors as they transform themselves from the "guidance advice-giver" to the "counseling empowerer." This has not been, and will not ever be, an easy journey. Many counseling programs are immobilized because they are unable to escape the expectations of the past or do not have a viable vision of the future. In the process of trying to be all things to all people, secondary school counselors have accumulated a lot of unwanted baggage. In attempting to please everyone, many have actually pleased no one. Overworked counselors are often the recipients of unfair criticism. However, this is not the time for self-pity; rather, it is a time for action! What follows here will provide the tools and resources to transform secondary school counselors into dynamic, empowered counselors.

Nancy S. Perry, NCC, NCSC
1991 President, American School Counselor Association

Preface

Secondary school counselors are people. They are not robots, machines in some cosmic factory, statistics in some report, or programmed functions in a computer. Yet, today many believe that school counseling is like a dry and barren valley without rain, or a person exhausted at high noon in the heat of the summer. In many school districts, school counseling has dried up and is withering away.

School counselors have entered this new decade with the obligation and responsibility to become change agents in the school setting. As we look toward the 21st century, the state of our nation's schools is alarming. Illiterates and a staggering number of dropouts are found in all parts of the system, a system which many feel does not work. We find school counselors trying to cope within an educational system that has become obsolete. Educational reform cannot be achieved without school counselors becoming actively involved in the process. This is not an easy task but, unless we are willing to take on the responsibility, others will take it away from us.

At a recent school administrator's conference, 400 school superintendents listened to a speech by a noted futurist, writer, and consultant to many of the nation's Fortune 500 companies. This man reinforced a belief held by many: The least effective staff members in our schools are the school counselors. They are believed to be the least equipped to meet the needs of students and to help them solve their problems.

We must be able to document the effects of the school counseling program. Our critics seek verification that school counselors can help students make decisions concerning social, personal, educational and career issues. Our critics ask for a product and we answer with a process. They are not addressing the scope of practice of the school counselor, but rather the effect the school counselor has on the school counseling program.

To address the concerns of our critics, these five questions must be answered:

1. What do those we serve expect of *us*?
2. What do *we* expect of those we serve?
3. How will these expectations be met?
4. Where do we find the time, the resources and the training that we need?
5. What are we currently doing that impedes our success?

One of the purposes of this book is to attempt to answer these questions.

Editors:
Doris Rhea Coy
Claire G. Cole
Wayne C. Huey
Susan Jones Sears

About the Editors

Doris Rhea Coy is a secondary school counselor at Whitehall-Yearling High School in Columbus, Ohio. She is the immediate past president of the American School Counselor Association and currently serves as the ASCA liaison to the National Board of Certified Counselors. Ms. Coy has been a consultant, speaker and workshop presenter locally, nationally and internationally, and is the author of many articles for counseling books and journals.

Claire G. Cole, Ed.D., is Director of the Southwest Virginia Assessment and Development Center at Virginia Tech in Blacksburg, Virginia. She is a former high school and middle school counselor. Dr. Cole is currently editor of *The School Counselor*, has written extensively on topics of interest to counselors, and is the author of *Counseling in the Middle School* published by the National Middle School Association.

Wayne C. Huey, Ph.D., is Director of Counseling at Lakeside High School in DeKalb County, Georgia. He is currently Chair of the American School Counselor Association Ethics Committee. In 1982, ASCA named him their Researcher of the Year, and in 1986, their Secondary School Counselor of the Year. Dr. Huey has authored numerous articles and is co-editor of a book on ethical and legal issues in school counseling.

Susan Jones Sears, Ph.D., is an associate professor in the Department of Educational Services and Research at The Ohio State University in Columbus, Ohio. She has written extensively, including articles on secondary school counseling, sex equity, career development, and stress in school-age youth. She has served on the editorial board of *Counselor Education and Supervision* and has worked as an elementary, junior high, and high school counselor.

Contributors

American School Counselor Association, Alexandria, Virginia

Association for Counselor Education and Supervision, Alexandria, Virginia

Roger F. Aubrey, professor of psychology and education, George Peabody College of Vanderbilt University, Nashville, Tennessee

Andrew V. Beale, professor, School of Education, Virginia Commonwealth University, Richmond

Lisa J. Bearden, director, Industrial/Occupational Medicine Department, Montgomery Rehabilitation Hospital, Montgomery, Alabama

Fred Beauvais, research scientist, Department of Psychology, Colorado State University, Fort Collins

Deborah Perlmutter Bloch, assistant professor, Department of Education, Baruch College, City University of New York

Dorothy Tysse Breen, assistant professor of counselor education, University of Maine, Orono

Shirley Gwinn Coffman, counselor, Thompson Valley High School, Loveland, Colorado

Doris Rhea Coy, secondary school counselor, Whitehall-Yearling High School, Columbus, Ohio

James Virgil Cunningham, assistant director, Career and Counseling Services, Alfred University, Alfred, New York

John C. Dagley, associate professor, Department of Counseling and Human Development Services, University of Georgia, Athens

Hannah Dixon, coordinator of guidance and counseling, Springfield City Schools, Springfield, Ohio

Jerry Downing, professor of counseling and educational psychology, University of Nevada, Reno

Linda K. Elksnin, associate professor and coordinator of special education graduate programs, Department of Education, The Citadel, Charleston, South Carolina

Nick Elksnin, school psychologist, Vince Moseley Center, Department of Pediatrics, Division of Developmental Disabilities, Medical University of South Carolina, Charleston

S. Norman Feingold, national director, B'Nai B'rith Career and Counseling Services, Washington, DC; and past-president, American Personnel and Guidance Association.

Dale Fuqua, associate professor of counseling, Department of Counseling, University of North Dakota, Grand Forks

Eldon Gade, professor of counseling, Department of Counseling, University of North Dakota, Grand Forks

Kevin E. Geoffroy, professor of education, College of William and Mary, Williamsburg, Virginia

Valerie D. George, associate professor, Department of Nursing, Cleveland State University, Cleveland

Robert L. Gibson, professor, Department of Counseling and Educational Psychology, Indiana University, Bloomington

Thomas C. Harrison, Jr., assistant professor of counseling and educational psychology, University of Nevada, Reno

Patricia Henderson, director of guidance, Northside Independent School District, San Antonio, Texas

Roger D. Herring, assistant professor of counselor education, University of Arkansas, Little Rock

Glenda T. Hubbard, professor of counselor education, Department of Human Development and Psychological Counseling, Appalachian State University, Boone, North Carolina

Wayne C. Huey, director of counseling, Lakeside High School, DeKalb County, Georgia

Graham Hurlburt, professor of education, Brandon University, Brandon, Manitoba, Canada

Roger L. Hutchinson, professor of counseling psychology, Ball State University, Muncie, Indiana

John Kalafat, director of education, St. Clares-Riverside Medical Center, Denville, New Jersey

Leslie S. Kaplan, director of guidance, York County Public Schools, Virginia

Linda Kelly, substance abuse specialist, Clark County Schools, Ohio

James L. Lee, professor, Department of Counseling Psychology and Counselor Education, University of Wisconsin–Madison

G. Dean Miller, licensed consulting psychologist in private practice, St. Paul, Minnesota

Oliver C. Moles, educational research specialist, Office of Educational Research and Improvement, U.S. Department of Education, Washington, DC

John C. Moracco, professor, Department of Counseling and Counseling Psychology, Auburn University, Montgomery, Alabama

Eugene R. Oetting, professor of psychology, Department of Psychology, Colorado State University, Fort Collins

Michael M. Omizo, associate professor, Department of Counselor Education, University of Hawaii at Manoa, Honolulu

Sharon A. Omizo, junior researcher, Department of Special Education, University of Hawaii at Manoa, Honolulu

Pamela O. Paisley, assistant professor of counselor education, Department of Human Development and Psychological Counseling, Appalachian State University, Boone, North Carolina

Nancy S. Perry, guidance consultant, State of Maine Department of Education, and 1991 president, American School Counselor Association

Charles J. Pulvino, professor, Department of Counseling Psychology and Counselor Education, University of Wisconsin–Madison

Russ Quaglia, assistant professor of educational administration, University of Maine, Orono

Cheryl A. Reagan, English teacher, Goshen Community Schools, Goshen, Indiana

Albert E. Roark, professor, University of Colorado, Boulder

Susan Jones Sears, associate professor, Department of Educational Services and Research, Ohio State University, Columbus

Thomas M. Skovholt, professor, Educational Psychology Department, University of Minnesota, Minneapolis

William A. Spencer, Associate professor, Department of Educational Foundations, Leadership, and Technology, Auburn University, Montgomery, Alabama

Lisa A. Suzuki, doctoral student, University of Nebraska, Lincoln

W. Wesley Tennyson, professor, Educational Psychology Department, University of Minnesota, Minneapolis

M. Donald Thomas, senior partner, Harold Webb Associates, Ltd., Winnetka, Illinois; and former superintendent of schools, Salt Lake City, Utah

Romeria Tidwell, associate professor of counseling psychology, Graduate School of Education, University of California, Los Angeles

Susan C. Whiston, assistant professor, Department of Counseling and Educational Psychology and Foundations, University of Nevada, Las Vegas

R. Craig Williams, assistant professor, Northern Illinois University, DeKalb

Sally Wood, secondary school counselor, Aurora High School, Aurora, Missouri

Chapter 1

The History of School Counseling

It has been said that in order to understand where we are going we must have some understanding of where we have been. As a profession, counseling as a psychological process is in its infancy. Most counseling textbooks date the beginning of the profession to the late 1800s and early 1900s with the founding of vocational guidance by Frank Parsons. However, with the launching of Sputnik in 1957, and the passage of the National Defense Education Act of 1958, guidance headed in a different direction.

Over the years, we have struggled with terminology, role statements, and turf issues but the time has arrived for the profession to take a serious look at the direction in which it is headed. In the past, school counselors have permitted others to delineate this role and function. They have neglected to take the lead in their school counseling program and have, therefore, permitted others to dictate their program, role, and function. Their specialty, counseling, has not been utilized to the fullest in their setting. Instead, tasks that could be relegated to others with less skill and training have become a part of the job description of school counselors.

Roger F. Aubrey in his article "A House Divided: Guidance and Counseling in 20th-Century America," describes the early beginning of vocational guidance with the work of Frank Parsons in Boston and Jesse B. Davis in Detroit. He vividly recounts the struggles the profession went through in those years to find meaning and purpose. He concludes his article with his image of school counseling in the 1980s.

His historical analysis of guidance and counseling from the early 1900s to the 1980s provides the reader with a clearer understanding of the variety of meanings of the words "guidance and counseling." Aubrey states that the wide and varied use of the terms has obscured events that have transformed counseling into a field of its own, competing with guidance in the schools.

However, at this point it needs to be noted that by action of the Governing Board of the American School Counselor Association in 1990, the board unanimously adopted their specialty as "School Counseling" and their program in the school as a "School Counseling Program."

Following this action, a new role statement was adopted which again focused on the **School Counselor** and the **School Counseling Program.** The action of this board demonstrates that school counselors are charting new directions for their profession as they head into the 21st century.

In a second article that chronicles the history of the guidance and counseling movement, S. Norman Feingold describes the past, the present and the future of school counseling in "Perspective of Counseling in the United States—Past, Present, and Future."

History tells us where we have been and delineates the struggles made to get us to our present position, but it is the current members of our profession who will redirect our future. Those risk takers who are willing to stand up and be counted, and those who are willing to take the road less traveled, may be the individuals who will breathe new life into our profession.

We find school counselors trying to cope within an educational system that has become obsolete. However, educational reform offers the opportunity for school counselors to become the change agents in the school setting. The requirements of business and industry have been redefined to go beyond the traditional "3 R's" and today include:

1. Reading, writing, mathematics
2. Influence: organization, effectiveness, leadership
3. Group effectiveness: interpersonal skills, negotiating, teamwork
4. Personal management: self-esteem, goal setting, motivation, personal career development
5. Communication skills
6. Learning to learn
7. Adaptability: creative and critical thinking, problem solving

It is the school counselor who is the professional on the school staff with the skills and expertise to prepare students for what lies ahead in the "real" world. The future is ours in the school setting if we build our programs around the needs of the individuals that we serve.

The past history of our profession cannot be changed, but the visions and dreams of dedicated leaders and members of our profession can redirect school counseling in the future.

A House Divided: Guidance and Counseling in 20th-Century America

Roger F. Aubrey

Historical analysis of guidance and counseling within American public education reveals a house divided by diversity and contradictions.

Guidance and counseling today in elementary and secondary schools is in danger of becoming anachronistic. The work of school counselors entails inordinate amounts of time in clerical and administrative tasks that could just as easily be accomplished by computers or paraprofessionals and at a lower cost. At the secondary level, the college and vocational placement function was seriously challenged in the 1960s by mechanical and technological advancements (Cooley, 1965; Tiedeman, 1968). In the 1970s, computer and systems analysis theory also brought into question traditional counselor approaches to career guidance (Kroll, 1973; Tiedeman, 1972; Vriend, 1971). Finally, and most damningly, carefully researched programs have failed to demonstrate counselor effectiveness in terms of student learning or development (Carkhuff, 1972; Ginzberg, 1971; Kaufman & Lewis, 1969; Kehas, 1975; Miller & Boller, 1975; New York Department of Education, 1974; Tamminen & Miller, 1968).

On balance, many charges leveled at guidance and counseling are unjust or misdirected. Unfortunately, the terms *guidance* and *counseling* convey a variety of meanings and interpretations to lay persons and professionals alike. As a consequence, many criticisms aimed at guidance and counseling reflect disappointments of audiences vastly overrating the potential of school counselors. In addition, the word *guidance* lends itself to many interpretations that result in expectations beyond their legitimate purview.

This history of guidance and counseling is replete with thorny problems centering on terminology and definitions. According to Wrenn (1970), however, this problem did not present itself in the early years of the guidance movement. Prior to 1931, the word *counseling* was rarely used and *guidance* was an umbrella term used for all functions associated with educational and vocational guidance. The central objectives of guidance were to give people help and information in choosing jobs or further education, and these broad aims were readily accepted and acknowledged. It was not until the publication of *Workbook in Vocations* by Proctor, Benefield, and Wrenn (1932), supplementing Proctor's earlier *Educational and Vocational Guidance* (1925), that the concept of counseling as a psychological process was first delineated. Initially, therefore, counseling was viewed as an adjunct process to assist in the presentation of guidance information regarding jobs and educational planning.

Events since the first association between the words *guidance* and *counseling* have broadened considerably both the definitional scope of guidance and the process of counseling. These terms today signify a variety of meanings, including an educational service, a unique process of helping, a theory of psychological intervention, and a conceptual framework. This plethora of meanings has served to obscure significant historical events that have transformed the technique of counseling into a field of its own, competing with guidance for sovereignty in the schools.

One manner of obviating the contradictions among the fields of guidance and counseling has been the use of these terms synonymously. In doing so, the profession has placed emphasis on the distinctiveness of the guidance practitioner by focusing essentially on particular methods and techniques and not on the issue of purposes and objectives (Aubrey, 1980). This perspective has elevated the status of counseling and centered on the situation and audiences school counselors feel best suited to address. That focus has therefore been on alignment of the student with facilitating method or skill. This exclusive emphasis on individuals and idiosyncratic concerns, coupled with a predetermined technology of treatment, has effectively curtailed the development of system-wide guidance purposes encompassing these individual concerns and reaching beyond them in programs designed for universal application.

School Guidance and Counseling: A History of Diversity and Contradiction

Lawrence Cremin (1965) has described the school guidance counselor "as the most characteristic child of the progressive movement" (p. 5). Cremin compliments the school counselor by singling out this individual as the one person most embodying the aims and ideals of progressivism. He also notes, however, that both guidance and progressivism have acquired a heritage of diversity and contradiction. In the case of progressivism, this diversity and contradiction led in time to tremendous internal dissension, eventually culminating in the complete collapse of the Progressive Education Association in 1955 (Cremin, 1961).

The sources of current antagonism within the field of guidance and counseling are similar to those of the progressive movement in that each contains elements of separate movements. The similarity ends there, however. Progressivism from its very inception was widely supported by an audience incorporating segments from business, industry, farm and labor, the clergy, academia, and social work. Guidance has never had such a broad base of support nor has it had a comparable mandate for as many fundamental changes in the process of schooling.

In contrast to the external influences impinging on progressivism, the sources of conflict within the guidance and counseling movement have emanated primarily from either practitioners themselves or their fellow educators in the fields of teaching and school administration. These basic disagreements about the professional purpose of the field have been evident within the guidance and counseling profession since the early founding of vocational guidance by Frank Parsons (1909), and later in educational guidance (Brewer, 1932; Davis, 1941). These two areas alone over a period of 60 years have not been able to reconcile major differences between the pragmatic-economic premises of vocational guidance (Ginzberg, 1971; Hoyt, Evans, Mackin, & Mangum, 1972; Johnson, 1973) and the idealistic-social foundation of educational guidance (Field, Kehas, & Tiedeman, 1963; Tiedeman & O'Hara, 1963).

Diversity and contradiction within the field of school guidance and counseling have not stemmed solely from contending internal ideologies. The guidance movement has also been characterized by a series of competing methodologies (Stefflre & Grant, 1972). As these competing counseling methodologies proliferated, they tended to focus the attention of counselors on technique and process and away from considerations of objectives and content. This is important historically because alterations in counseling methodology sometimes triggered changes in the substance and priority of school guidance programs.

Origins of Guidance in 20th-Century America

Guidance began in American public schools much like any other subject. It was viewed initially as something that could be taught by a teacher in a classroom setting to large numbers of students. Further, guidance was seen as a learning experience enhancing the existing curriculum by specifically addressing areas and topics theretofore ignored or neglected.

Educational historians generally credit Jesse B. Davis with the first effort to systematize guidance into the accepted school curriculum (Brewer, 1942; Miller, 1961). As a school administrator in the rapidly growing industrial city of Detroit between 1889 and 1907, Davis was concerned with the vocational problems and social dilemmas of his students. He carried this concern with him when he accepted the principalship of the Grand Rapids, Michigan, High School in 1907.

Interestingly, Davis selected English composition as the subject most likely to lend itself to the first "guidance curriculum." Shortly after his arrival in Grand Rapids, he developed and introduced the first course in vocational and moral guidance. This unit was to be part of the regular English curriculum with one period per week set aside for vocational and moral guidance.

Coincidental with Davis's recognition of the need for planned guidance programs for students in expanding industrial centers, another guidance pioneer arose in an industrial complex on the eastern seaboard. Frank Parsons, often called the "Father of Guidance," did not begin his career or work in the public schools. Instead, Parsons began as an engineer and later became a social worker in Boston. He was heavily influenced by the example of Jane Adams, and this influence was early reflected by Parsons' work in establishing a settlement house for young adults already employed in labor and industry or in need of a job.

Although the early work of Parsons was focused on out-of-school young people, his hopes centered on a time when vocational guidance would "become a part of the public school system in every community" (Lasch, 1965, p. 157). To this end, Parsons established the Vocation Bureau in Civic Service House in Boston in 1908. A key thrust of the Vocation Bureau was "to serve the armies of child laborers who were leaving the public schools to become wage earners under unfavorable conditions" (Miller, 1964, p. 7).

The founding of the Vocational Bureau by Parsons is generally acknowledged as the first "institutionalization of vocational guidance" (Ginzberg, 1971, p. 23). Even though the bulk of Parsons' work concentrated on underprivileged children and young adolescents about to seek employment, his impact on public schools would be significant in later years.

Vocational Guidance Enters Education

This history of the vocational guidance movement has been exceptionally well covered by Borow (1964) and others (Barry & Wolf, 1962; Brewer, 1942; Super, 1955; Williamson, 1964). Most writers agree that the early beginnings of vocational guidance in schools arose from a concern for individuals "who had moved from rural to urban settings or had been victimized by child labor abuses, and it grew out of a general concern for the job satisfaction of American workers" (McDaniels, 1974, p. 252). The emergence of vocational guidance in public schools was consequently a direct result of rapidly changing conditions in American industry and quite unrelated to the accepted process of schooling known at that time.

The early vocational guidance movement was largely devoid of philosophical underpinnings. The Parsonian model of vocational choice was grounded on simple logic and relied predominantly on observation and analytic skills. Inclusion of this model in the public schools had to be defended on the basis of economic and humanitarian conditions outside the school. With the exception of Jesse Davis and a few others, vocational guidance was not linked to the process of education nor was it viewed as a means of contributing to the development of the individual through a process extending over a number of years.

Although the early years of vocational guidance in the public schools were devoid of strong philosophical or psychological support, this void was soon filled by the growing enchantment with psychometrics. In time, the merger of vocational guidance and psychometrics would set in motion a psychological foundation essentially resting on testing and individual pupil analysis. In Ginzberg's (1971) words, "Vocational guidance became first attracted to and then addicted to testing" (p. 3). This "addiction" would overtake vocational guidance shortly after the conclusion of World War I and continue for at least two decades.

Vocational guidance entered the American public schools during the first decade of the 20th century. As a stepchild, without portfolio, this entrance was marked by diffidence and hesitation. It was therefore not surprising that a movement concerned with individual differences and the callous response of mass industrialization to human needs should embrace the model of Parsons and strengthen it with psychometry and trait and factor psychology. Unfortunately, most of the tools adopted by vocational guidance did not fulfill the hopes and aspirations of its early founders. If anything, these tools worked against the very children and young people it sought to help by rigidly labeling, classifying, categorizing, and sorting students in schools and on leaving school.

Emergence of Educational Guidance

The term *educational guidance* has two distinct meanings. On the one hand, educational guidance can refer to help given to students in selecting courses, adjusting to school, orienting themselves to new surroundings, and deciding on courses of action on completion of schooling. Another meaning of educational guidance is much broader and more intimately related to the total process of education and character building. That definition would see educational guidance as a pervasive force in the curriculum and instructional process itself. Guidance, in this sense, would encompass and embody a set of objectives, methods, and experiences within the total educative process. The push and pull between these two conceptualizations of guidance has long been evident but rarely subjected to examination.

Educational guidance was first described as an educational activity by Truman L. Kelly. In his dissertation, Kelly (1914) advocated this activity as an essential process in helping students to make choices about courses of study and school adjustment problems.

The form of educational guidance promulgated by Kelly owed an early debt to vocational guidance. Conceptually, the extension of guidance from decisions about life after school to life in school was not a big jump. Early advocates of the "new" vocational guidance, such as Proctor (1925) and Koos and Kefauver (1932), felt a need to redefine guidance as not simply an activity appropriate for occupational considerations but for all of a student's educational experiences as well. Their concern was for a broadening of students' horizons through guidance.

Educational Guidance as Pupil Distribution and Adjustment

In actuality, educational guidance was not always seen as promoting new vistas for students. Instead, in many instances, educational guidance was introduced in schools as a process to aid in the distribution and adjustment of pupils. Essentially, this meant that educational guidance was to remedy a number of problems involving students that called for attention beyond that available in most schools. This definition of guidance was first introduced to schools by Proctor (1925) in the 1920s, and by the depression years of the 1930s it vied with vocational guidance for popularity. A number of writers at this time (Kefauver & Hand, 1941; Koos & Kefauver, 1932) expanded this position. As a result, by the 1940s educational guidance as a process of pupil distribution and adjustment was widely accepted by many in the guidance profession (Bratton, 1945; Flory, Allen, & Simmons, 1944; Strang, 1953; Williamson & Foley, 1949).

Educational guidance as a process primarily involving the twin aspects of pupil distribution and adjustment was geared largely to a teacher population. The distributive functions included pupil assistance in such varied life activities as school, home, recreation, vocation, and social pursuits. The adjustive functions included help when the student was unable or unwilling to profit from learning related to school and life goals (Kefauver & Hand, 1941). It was assumed that teachers could by and large perform these functions with little or no formal training. Therefore, the need for school counselors as distinct mental health specialists was not advocated.

Educational Guidance as a Full Partnership

Another form of educational guidance also began to take form in the 1920s and was fully articulated in the early 1930s. It was a far cry from the distributive and adjustive version of guidance. In fact, the leading spokesman for this movement, John Brewer (1932), would repudiate this other view by noting:

> Guidance is neither adjusting nor suggesting, neither conditioning nor controlling, neither directing nor taking responsibility for anyone...the work we do in schools may be described as helping children to understand, organize, extend and improve their individual and cooperative activities.... [This] means guidance. (p. 2)

By expanding the guidance base to include all endeavors engaged in by students, Brewer drastically challenged the previous foundation of guidance. Whereas guidance had earlier been primarily concerned with the choices and decisions of young people regarding the world of work and vocations, Brewer opened up the entire spectrum of education and human development to guidance. This refocus therefore accomplished two ends. First, it encompassed the earlier and narrower version of vocational guidance and blended it into a new model whereby vocational guidance was but one spoke in the wheel. Second, it laid the foundation for a theory of guidance intervention directly linked to the process of education.

Thus, we have seen two early forces in the growth of guidance in public schools. The first guidance movement began at the turn of the 20th century in response to industrialization and changing patterns in American society and educational practice. This movement was vocational guidance, and until the 1940s it played a critical role in influencing guidance practice in public schools. A second guidance movement began in the 1920s. This movement has been called "educational guidance" and was really an admixture of two divergent views. One view arose from the necessity for a distributive and adjustive element in schools due to crowding, shortages of administrators, classroom management, an expanding curriculum, and universal compulsory attendance laws. The second view of educational guidance began as a broadening of earlier schemes of vocational and moral guidance and in time gave rise to a view of guidance relegating vocational aspects to a lesser position. This view would in time evolve into present day theories of developmental and psychological guidance. Concomitantly, vocational guidance would itself undergo a major evolutionary cycle.

From Vocational Choice to Career Development

Super (1956) noted some 25 years ago that "the concept of development has not until recent years been applied to the study of vocational choice and adjustment" (p. 249). Further, he observed that the use of the term *choice* in vocational guidance more frequently than not was used to describe an event, and not a process that is continuous and cumulative. Super concluded with a plea for more inclusion of developmental psychology and self-concept theory in order for vocational guidance to expand its horizons.

The weaknesses mentioned by Super led to the eventual erosion of vocational guidance as a viable theory of intervention with the publication in 1951 of Ginzberg, Ginsburg, Axelrad, and Herma's *Occupational Choice: An Approach to a General Theory*. This publication revealed the fact that vocational guidance had been operating for years without a defensible theory or research base. Although the impact of this volume on the immediate practice of vocational guidance in schools is questionable, the ramifications for the academic community training counselors and teachers were significant (Hummel, 1954).

The challenge of Ginzberg and associates (1951) did not go unheeded. In addition to their own theory, they stimulated a series of responses within the profession resulting in a number of theories of career development (Bordin, Nachmann, & Segal, 1963; Holland, 1959; Roe, 1956; Super, 1957; Tiedeman & Field, 1965). In turn, these theories were influenced by a wave of advances in developmental psychology, learning theory, psychiatry, and sociology (Erikson, 1950; Havighurst, 1952; Inhelder & Piaget, 1958; Lynd & Lynd, 1954; Piaget, 1952; Riesman, 1950; Sullivan, 1953; Warner, Meekr, & Ells, 1949; White, 1960).

Origins of Developmental Guidance

Just as educational guidance followed in the wake of vocational guidance, so did developmental guidance follow the trail of career guidance. Similarly, just as educational guidance attempted to subsume vocational guidance under the larger umbrella of total life experience, so would developmental guidance attempt to engulf career guidance under the theme of human development. In both instances educational and developmental guidance would respond to the disproportionate emphasis on out-of-school and work-related approaches of their protagonists. In turn, educational and developmental guidance would press for intervention measures geared to the day-to-day realities of students and the ongoing process of education. In so doing, educational and developmental guidance would not ignore work and career concerns but would attempt to refocus these under a broader and wider conceptual framework.

Developmental guidance was not given a bridge that allowed for a smooth or logical transition from the earlier framework of educational guidance. Unlike the passage from vocational to career guidance, developmental guidance would find itself without precursors and an eager audience. The justification for developmental guidance would rest primarily on the hopes and ambitions for its originators and not on social or economic grounds. Nonetheless, developmental guidance did capitalize on two factors. First, it inherited none of the barnacles attached to the hull of earlier guidance theories. Second, it sought to utilize the latest advancements in the social and behavioral sciences as applied to education and human development.

Although the lineage of developmental guidance is not easy to trace, some paths can be discerned. A major trail would lead in the same direction as the early beginnings of career guidance and first center on a number of advances in the behavioral sciences in the late 1940s and 1950s. The accumulation of these theories and research findings would provide educators and behavioral scientists with a wealth of operational models, research designs, and testable hypotheses. Further, these findings would seriously challenge existing practices, particularly those with weak conceptual schemes and no substantive underpinnings.

The Pioneering Work of Robert Mathewson

The early ancestry of developmental guidance in schools is traceable to Robert Mathewson (1949, 1962). Even prior to some writings of Erikson (1950), Havighurst (1952), Piaget (1952), and others, Mathewson had stressed the key concept of development as the guiding principle in organizing and implementing programs of school guidance. As early as 1949, Mathewson had written that:

> As an important phase of education, the guidance process moves with the individual in a developmental sequence up to the age of maturity, helping him gain in self-understanding as well as perspective on his surroundings. (p. 29)

Over a period of years, Mathewson would refine and expand this notion of guidance as a process involved in monitoring and aiding human development. He would seriously question the posture that counselors can passively observe the process of development with no active intervention except when this development is arrested or interrupted by external circumstances. Mathewson would also challenge the assumption that teachers alone can provide the experiences required by students in an adequate program of school guidance. As he viewed the changing picture of American democracy, the notion of guidance became a critical factor in utilizing all of education as a means of "furthering and enhancing individual maturation."

Mathewson's work drew heavily on ego psychology and modern conceptualizations of numerous stage theorists. In positing individual development as the keystone in theory building and program elaboration, however, Mathewson was well aware of the lag between theory and practice, propagation and acceptance. Mathewson's appraisal of both the receptiveness of American education to this enlightened view of guidance and the state of the art in guidance practice would prove prophetic for at least a decade or more. In turn, his work would be expanded in the 1960s and 1970s by Kehas (1968, 1970, 1973),

Mosher and Sprinthall (1971), Shoben (1965), and Tiedeman and Field (1965).

An Era of Significant Change

As public school guidance entered the 1960s, a number of significant events brought change to the appearance of guidance in American education. One change was generated by the reaction of the American public to the launching of the Russian Sputnik in 1957. This event, coincidental with the report of James Conant on the state of American schools, brought about the National Defense Education Act of 1958. Within a few years, the number of counselors in secondary schools would triple and the ratio of counselors to students would decrease from 1 to 960 in 1958–59 to 1 to 450 by 1966–67 (Shertzer & Stone, 1971).

The rapid change in counselor-student ratios allowed counselors greater access to more students and created conditions more conducive to a consideration of normal developmental concerns. This decrease in counselor-student ratios and change in guidance focus was also reinforced by 1962 by the publication of C. Gilbert Wrenn's *The Counselor in a Changing World*. Sponsored by the American Personnel and Guidance Association and the Fund for the Advancement of Education, this book reflected the views of a number of outstanding figures in the guidance profession. Wrenn (1962) left little doubt as to one of the central tenets of the book by advocating that:

> Primary emphasis in counseling students be placed on the developmental needs and decision points in the lives of the total range of students rather than upon the remedial needs and the crisis points in the lives of a few students. (p. 109)

The fall of 1962 would see another significant publication advocating change in school guidance and counseling practice. This publication would be a special issue of the *Harvard Educational Review* (Carle, Kehas, Mosher, 1962) devoted to an examination of guidance by leading theoreticians from a number of persuasions. The thrust of the volume was not pragmatic considerations but rather, in the words of the authors, "on a search for theoretical models and substantiating empirical evidence" (p. 371).

The period of the early 1960s would see additional writings whose cumulative effect would bring about serious questioning and reformation of many traditional guidance practices. These writings would span the fields of education, psychology, sociology, anthropology, and economics (Allinsmith & Goethals, 1962; Bloom, 1964; Bruner, 1960; Coleman, 1962; Erikson, 1950; Kohlberg, 1964; Loevinger, 1966; Peck & Havighurst, 1960; White, 1960). Collectively, these writings and many others forced the educational establishment to reappraise the entire scope and sequence of curricular offerings and their suitability for students.

Counseling in 20th-Century America

Counseling, like guidance, has a long history of waiting for a legitimate place under the educational sun. Unlike guidance, counseling in public schools would have a 30-year wait between the first recognition of guidance as a legitimate educational endeavor and the use of counseling as a helping technique. It would not be until Proctor, Benefield, and Wrenn's *Workbook in Vocations* (1932) was published that counseling for the first time would be introduced and encouraged as an adjunct process in furthering the goals of vocational guidance.

Also, unlike guidance, the early history of counseling does not reveal conflict about the purpose or function of counseling within the public school domain. Counseling initially was viewed simply and solely as a convenient tool or technique in accomplishing specific guidance outcomes. Further, the early pioneers of counseling techniques were largely individuals deeply committed to the vocational guidance movement who sought specific tools to aid guidance goals.

The initial impetus for counseling in American education was vocational guidance, and the first technique was trait and factor counseling (Barry & Wolf, 1955; Borow, 1964; Miller, 1961; Super, 1955; Williamson, 1965). The counseling model that evolved under the trait and factor approach in time was known as directive or counselor centered. This model reflected the exactitude and preciseness of the ambitious vocational guidance movement and placed the counselor in a role not unlike that of a teacher. The counselor possessed greater maturity than the student and, in addition, skills and knowledge of benefit to the student. As a consequence, the counselor was seen as the key figure in the counseling process, and this adult figure would take the responsibility for leading the student in areas and directions most helpful to the student.

The erosion of the dominant trait and factor approach to school counseling began in the early 1940s and was complete within a decade. Ginzberg (1971) sees this period as one involving a shift in guidance technique from one of testing to one of counseling. He further speculates that part of the downfall of the trait and factor approach was inevitable "once the academic community in the United States caught up with Freud and Piaget" (p. 32).

The Steamroller Impact of Carl Rogers on School Counseling

Without doubt, the most profound influence in changing the course and direction of the entire guidance movement in the mid and late 1940s was Carl Rogers (1942, 1951, 1954, 1961). The eventual influence of the work of Rogers and his followers was so enveloping and unquestioned that Super (1964) felt the influence inimical to the profession as a whole. For Super, guidance theory at that time was simply too weak to integrate the theory and findings of Rogers without a resultant bandwagon effect.

The concentration on counseling in the field of school guidance opened the doors to many variations on this single theme. Commencing with Rogers, the area of school guidance would be open game for numerous advocates of counseling, ranging from such diverse fields as psychiatry, clinical psychology, psychoanalysis, learning theory, and pastoral counseling. Collectively, the advocates of these approaches offered to school counselors a bonanza of tools and techniques. At the same time, however, they presented to school counselors techniques of questionable utility in school settings (Aubrey, 1969). The net result was the infusion of massive amounts of counseling in the professional training of school counselors and a further segmentation of an already disjointed profession (Aubrey, 1972, 1977).

As guidance enters the 1980s, the proliferation of counseling approaches continues without abatement. What began in the early 1940s as a dialectic between two antithetical views of human behavior and methods of modifying that behavior has resulted not in a synthesis of these views but rather in a steady and constant fragmentation of anything resembling a united position. Instead of striving for some unifying principles or common conceptual framework, the profession of school guidance and counseling has split into camps centering on technique and outcome. The implications of this divorce, or at best separation, between guidance and counseling will be considered in the final section of this article.

Recurring Image of Guidance and Counseling After Eight Decades

Regardless of stated aims and objectives, all school personnel unassigned to regular classroom teaching have traditionally been viewed by teachers as ancillary to the ongoing business of classroom instruction. The point has been noted by Hoyt (1980), Kehas (1968, 1970), Tiedeman and Field (1965), and others. It bears repeating, however, because of its significance to how new forms of knowledge and fresh learning experiences enter the mainstream of schools. The problem in this context is actually a dual question: How are these forms of knowledge and experience to be generated and who is to impart these learnings to students? The stock answer would see university personnel as essentially the suppliers of new content and curricula and teachers as the implementers in classrooms. Nevertheless, this response is overly simple and ignores the complexity with which change and accommodation occurs in schools (Sarason, 1971).

In one sense, the entire history of public school guidance and counseling is a chronicle of individuals and movements attempting to gain acceptance by the gatekeepers of the existing educational order. In some instances what was sought was minor and a logical supplement to the established system. On the other hand, certain forms of guidance and counseling have fought an uphill battle with classroom teachers and the existing structure of education. This was true of the counseling psychology movement and the attempt to promote a voluntary, on-request counseling when determined by students. Teachers and school administrators were quick to notice any infringements on regularly scheduled class time, and counselors were forced to relegate counseling sessions to study hall time, lunch periods, or time before and after school. This is equally true of certain forms of developmental guidance that require discrete time segments in the curriculum. In both instances, the right of access to students for significant experiences beyond that contained in the recognized school curriculum was not sanctioned by the school or supported by the majority of teachers (Aubrey, 1979). Acceptance, therefore, had to be won on a school-by-school or teacher-by-teacher basis. This laborious process effectively curtailed systematic program implementation by a constant dissipation of energy in endless rounds of negotiation.

The real dilemma that guidance and counseling has faced since its inception is that of stating positions and goals in overinflated terms without possessing an adequate framework and technology for delivery. In the case of guidance, this was summarized by Mathewson (1962) as "a search for a system" (p. 73) and in its early days was characterized by myriad statements of objectives and goals. Unfortunately, guidance moved too quickly toward implementing these purposes armed solely with good intentions, a few test batteries, and the Parsonian triad for effective matching of worker and job. The result was a one-shot view of guidance that showed little relation between the process of education and the promise of guidance. At best, the guidance practitioner in the early period was seen as a middle person engaged in sorting out educational products for proper placement in business and industry. At worst, guidance could be accused of being duped by business and industry to serve as their handmaiden in processing and placing young people in labor-scarce jobs (Bowles & Gintis, 1976).

Guidance, in its early stages, did not ask much from the existing educational establishment. Individuals such as Jesse Davis would request a modest one period per week for outcomes related to vocational and moral guidance. Lacking a knowledge base to impart to students, and devoid of a content that was additive or heuristic, guidance had little need for a formal place in the school structure or curriculum.

As the testing movement gained respectability and credibility following World War I, guidance would increase its visibility in schools but retain its image as an adjunct to teaching and instruction. In the next 20 years, the conspicuousness of guidance would continue to grow as trait and factor counseling strengthened guidance and demanded additional time for student contact during the regular school day. At the same time educational guidance would also request time for activities related to testing, pupil appraisal, orientation, placement, data collection, and so on. The sum total of these various guidance activities, however, added up to a very small proportion of student time, and teachers themselves largely regulated these guidance functions.

In the 1940s and 1950s counselors became more ambitious. Fortified with new methods and techniques, they sought greater access to students in need of their services. Yet, with only 4,000 employed counselors in 1945 (Jones & Miller, 1954), and an increase to only 6,780 school counselors in 1951, it is doubtful that the demands of school counselors for access to students proved disruptive to the regular routines of schooling. Events in the late 1950s would dramatically alter this situation and by

1965 the number of school counselors would exceed 30,000 (Armor, 1969).

Even a five-fold increase in the number of school counselors failed to alter the basic rationale for contacts between students and counselors. Students still viewed counselors as persons to see when their current educational or personal experiences were wanting or in need of modification. Students also made contact with counselors at difficult transition points or in cases in school leaving. Of significance, however, is the fact that students still did not maintain ongoing relationships with counselors as an integral part of the total process of education, nor did students look on counselors as individuals with significant learnings to impart on a par with classroom teachers. As a consequence, students and teachers alike continued to view guidance and counseling as a supportive, supplementary, and ancillary activity in public schools. Irrespective of lofty myths and a greatly improved technology, guidance and counseling remained on the periphery of American education, desirous of eminence and influence but hesitant and uncertain.

School Counselor as Chameleon

A thematic view of the guidance and counseling movements in American education resembles a patchwork quilt. This is so because of the number of separate and distinct movements that have marked the history of guidance in American education and the corresponding number of unique movements within the field of counseling. What seems discernible amid the growing confusion between the fields of guidance and counseling is a difference in their regard for schooling as a means of personal growth. Guidance from its early beginnings in vocational and educational guidance has always accorded schools and teachers a large part in the process of individual growth and development. Counseling, however, has not been this receptive. Commencing with the advent of counseling psychology as a distinct specialty, those in this area have increasingly placed themselves out of the mainstream of education and a partnership with teachers.

Thematically, the first four decades of guidance and counseling reveal a rather harmonious relationship between guidance as purpose and direction and counseling as tool and technique. The 1930s, however, would mark the last period in the guidance and counseling movement when counseling would submit to the aims of guidance. Commencing in the 1940s and extending up to the current time, the practice and perpetuation of counseling has become an end in itself. The seeds of this eventual outcome were sown in the 1950s when university trainers of school counselors carried on the heated battles of directive versus nondirective counseling. As Armor (1969) and Sprinthall (1971) have noted, the resolution of this conflict over two distinct counseling models resulted in the adoption by school counselors of a nonmodel, that is, eclecticism.

Eclecticism may well have been the only choice for the harried and harassed school counselor in the late 1950s and 1960s. Caught in the middle of a ceaseless bombardment by proponents of various schools of counseling and therapy, the school counselor was forced to either choose sides or escape the engagement. Conceivably, the school counselor selected the latter course of action because in practice none of these counseling postures were appropriate or operative (Aubrey, 1969).

Finally, school counselors were caught in a triple bind. Guidance and counseling leaders would fight for control over the use of the school counselor's time, while at the same time the agent most in charge of this time did not become involved in the issue at all. Instead, school administrators continued to utilize school counselors in the most advantageous way for the realization of administrative aims and objectives.

Epilogue

As guidance and counseling move through the 1980s, the diversity and contradictions within the profession have seriously endangered any major sense of mission. This purposelessness propels counselors toward a number of glowing lights, but the allure of those many beacons is a poor substitute for one true course of flight.

It is ironic, and perhaps prophetic, that the guidance and counseling movement reached its apex a short time after the dissolution of the Progressive Education Association. It is possible that Cremin was mistaken in describing the school guidance counselor "as the most characteristic child of the progressive movement," or has that child forgotten progenitors and origin?

References

Allinsmith, W., & Goethals, G. (1962). *The role of the schools in mental health*. New York: Basic Books.

Armor, D. J. (1969). *The American counselor.* New York: Russell Sage Foundation.

Aubrey, R. F. (1969). Misapplication of therapy models to school counseling. *Personnel and Guidance Journal, 48,* 273–278.

Aubrey, R. F. (1972). And never the twain shall meet: Counselor training and school realities. *School Counselor, 20,* 16–24.

Aubrey, R. F. (1977). Historical development of guidance and counseling and implications for the future. *Personnel and Guidance Journal, 55,* 288–295.

Aubrey, R. F. (1979). Relationship of guidance and counseling to the established and emerging school curriculum. *School Counselor, 26,* 150–162.

Aubrey, R. F. (1980). Technology of counseling and the science of behavior: A rapprochement. *Personnel and Guidance Journal, 58,* 318–327.

Barry, R., & Wolf, B. (1955). *A history of the guidance-personnel movement in education.* Unpublished doctoral thesis, Columbia University.

Barry, R., & Wolf, B. (1962). *Epitaph for vocational guidance.* New York: Bureau of Publications, Teachers College, Columbia University.

Bloom, B. S. (1964). *Stability and change in human characteristics.* New York: John Wiley.

Bordin, E. S., Nachmann, B., & Segal, S. J. (1963). An articulated framework for vocational development. *Journal of Counseling Psychology, 10,* 107–117.

Borow, H. (1964). Milestones:A chronology of notable events in the history of vocational guidance. In H. Borow (Ed.), *Man in a world of work.* Boston: Houghton Mifflin.

Bowles, S., & Gintis, H. (1976). *Schooling in capitalist America.* New York: Basic Books.

Bratton, D. (1945). Classroom guidance of pupils exhibiting behavior problems. *Elementary School Journal, 45,* 286–292.

Brewer, J. M. (1932). *Education as guidance.* New York: Macmillan.

Brewer, J. M. (1942). *History of vocational guidance.* New York: Harper.

Bruner, J. J. (1960). *The process of education.* Cambridge, MA: Harvard University Press.

Carkhuff, R. R. (1972). New directions in training for the helping professions: Toward a technology for human and community resource development. *Counseling Psychologist, 3*(3), 12–30.

22   TOWARD THE TRANSFORMATION OF SECONDARY SCHOOL COUNSELING

Carle, R. F., Kehas, C. D., & Mosher, R. L. (1962). Guidance: An
    examination. *Harvard Educational Review, 32,* 371–527.
Coleman, J. S. (1962). *The adolescent society.* New York: Fress Press.
Cooley, W. M. (1965). A computer-measurement system for guidance. In
    R. L. Mosher, R. W. Carle, & C. D. Kehas (Eds.), *Guidance: An
    examination.* New York: Harcourt, Brace, & World.
Cremin, L. A. (1961). *The transformation of the school.* New York:
    Knopf.
Cremin, L. A. (1965). The progressive heritage of the guidance move-
    ment. In R. L. Mosher, R. F. Carle, & C. D. Kehas (Eds.), *Guidance:
    An examination.* New York: Harcourt, Brace, & World.
Davis, J. (1941). *Vocational and moral guidance.* Lexington, MA: Ginn.
Erikson, E. H. (1950). *Childhood and society.* New York: W. W. Norton.
Field, F. L., Kehas, C. D., & Tiedeman, D. V. (1963). The self-concept in
    career development: A construct in transition. *Personnel and
    Guidance Journal, 41,* 761–771.
Flory, D. C., Allen, E., & Simmons, M. (1944). Classroom teachers
    improve the personality adjustment of their pupils. *Journal of
    Educational Research, 38,* 1–8.
Ginzberg, E. (1971). *Career guidance.* New York: McGraw-Hill.
Ginzberg, E., Ginsburg, S., Axelrad, S., & Herma, J. (1951). *Occupa-
    tional choice: An approach to a general theory.* New York: Columbia
    University Press.
Havighurst, R. J. (1952). *Developmental tasks and education.* New
    York: Longmans, Green & Co.
Holland, J. L. (1959). A theory of vocational choice. *Journal of
    Counseling Psychology, 6,* 35–45.
Hoyt, K. B. (1980). Contrasts between the guidance and the career
    education movements. In F. E. Burtnett (Ed.), *The school counselor's
    involvement in career education* (pp. 1–12). Falls Church, VA:
    American Personnel & Guidance Association.
Hoyt, K. B., Evans, R. N., Mackin, E. F., & Mangum, G. L. (1972).
    Career education: What it is and how to do it. Salt Lake City:
    Olympus Press.
Hummel, R. (1954). Vocational development theory and guidance
    practice. *Journal of the National Association of Women Deans and
    Counselors, 18,* 13–18.
Inhelder, B., & Piaget, J. (1958). *The growth of logical thinking from
    childhood to adolescence.* New York: Basic Books.

Johnson, L. W. (1973). Out to rekindle the American spirit. *American Vocational Journal, 48,* 44–46.

Jones, A. J., & Miller, L. M. (1954). The national picture of pupil personnel and guidance services in 1953. *The Bulletin of the National Association of Secondary School Principals, 38,* 105–159.

Kaufman, J. J., & Lewis, M. V. (1969). *The potential of vocational education: Observations and conclusions.* University Park: Institution for Research on Human Resources, Pennsylvania State University.

Kefauver, G., & Hand, H. C. (1941). *Appraising guidance in secondary schools.* New York: Macmillan.

Kehas, C. D. (1968). Guidance in education: An examination of the interplay between definition and structure. In V. F. Calia & D. B. Wall (Eds.), *Pupil personnel administration.* Springfield, IL: Charles C Thomas.

Kehas, C. D. (1970). Toward a redefinition of education: A new framework of counseling for counseling in education. In B. Shertzer & S. C. Stone (Eds.), *Introduction to guidance: Selected readings.* Boston: Houghton Mifflin.

Kehas, C. D. (1973). Guidance and the process of schooling: Curriculum and career education. *School Counselor, 21,* 103–113.

Kehas, C. D. (1975). What research says about counselor role. In H. Peters & R. Aubrey (Eds.), *Guidance: Strategies and techniques.* Denver: Love Publishers.

Kelly, T. L. (1914). *Educational guidance.* Unpublished doctoral thesis, Columbia University Teachers College.

Kohlberg, L. (1964). Development of moral character and moral ideology. In M. L. Hoffman & L. W. Hoffman (Eds.), *Review of child development research* (Vol. I). New York: Russell Sage.

Koos, L. V., & Kefauver, G. N. (1932). *Guidance in the secondary schools.* New York: Macmillan.

Kroll, A. M. (1973). Computer-based systems for career guidance and information: A status report. *Focus on Guidance, 10*(10), 1–15.

Lasch, C. (1965). *The new radicalism in America.* New York: Vintage Books.

Loevinger, J. (1966). The meaning and measurement of ego development. *American Psychologist, 21,* 195–206.

Lynd, R. S., & Lynd, H. M. (1954). *Middletown.* New York: Harcourt & Brace.

McDaniels, C. (1974). NVGA: Past, present, and future. *Vocational Guidance Quarterly, 22*, 252–254.

Mathewson, R. H. (1949). *Guidance policy and practice* (1st ed.). New York: Harper & Bros.

Mathewson, R. H. (1962). *Guidance policy and practice*. New York: Harper & Bros.

Miller, C. H. (1961). *Foundations of guidance*. New York: Harper, 1961.

Miller, C. H. (1964). Vocational guidance in the perspective of cultural change. In H. Borow (Ed.), *Man in a world of work*. Boston: Houghton Mifflin.

Miller, G. D., & Boller, J. D. (1975). *Closing the gaps: A study of four counselor education programs and efforts to facilitate role implementation and counselor effectiveness in the school*. St. Paul, MN: Minnesota Department of Education.

Mosher, R. L., & Sprinthall, N. A. (1971). Psychological education: A means to promote personal development during adolescence. *Counseling Psychologist, 2*(4), 3–82.

New York Department of Education. (1974). *An evaluation of the role and function of the guidance counselor*. Albany, NY: Office of Education Performance Review.

Parsons, F. (1909). *Choosing a vocation*. Boston: Houghton Mifflin.

Peck, R. F., & Havighurst, R. J. (1960). *The psychology of character development*. New York: John Wiley.

Piaget, J. (1952). *The origins of intelligence in children*. New York: International Universities Press.

Proctor, W. M. (1925). *Educational and vocational guidance*. Boston: Houghton Mifflin.

Proctor, W. M., Benefield, W., & Wrenn, C. G. (1932). *Workbook in vocations*. Boston: Houghton Mifflin.

Riesman, D. (1950). *The lonely crowd*. New Haven, CT: Yale University Press.

Roe, A. (1956). *The psychology of occupations*. New York: John Wiley.

Rogers, C. R. (1942). *Counseling and psychotherapy*. Boston: Houghton Mifflin.

Rogers, C. R. (1951). *Client-centered therapy*. Boston: Houghton Mifflin.

Rogers, C. R. (1961). *On becoming a person*. Boston: Houghton Mifflin.

Rogers, C. R., & Dymond, R. F. (Eds.). (1954). *Psychotherapy and personality change*. Chicago: University of Chicago Press.

Sarason, S. B. (1971). *The culture of the school and the problem of change*. Boston: Allyn & Bacon.

Shertzer, B., & Stone, S. C. (1971). *Fundamentals of guidance*. Boston: Houghton Mifflin.

Shoben, R. J. (1965). Guidance: Remedial function or social reconstruction? In R. L. Mosher, R. F. Carle, & C. D. Kehas (Eds.), *Guidance: An examination*. New York: Harcourt, Brace & World.

Sprinthall, N. A. (1971). *Guidance for human growth*. New York: Van Nostrand Reinhold.

Stefflre, B., & Grant, W. H. (1972). *Theories of counseling*. New York: McGraw-Hill.

Strang, R. (1953). *The role of the teacher in personnel work*. New York: Teachers College, Columbia University.

Sullivan, H. S. (1953). *The interpersonal theory of psychiatry*. New York: W. W. Norton.

Super, D. E. (1955). Transition: From vocational guidance to counseling psychology. *Journal of Counseling Psychology, 2, 3–9.*

Super, D. E. (1956). Vocational development: The process of compromise or synthesis. *Journal of Counseling Psychology, 3, 249–253.*

Super, D. E. (1957). *The psychology of careers*. New York: Harper & Row.

Super, D. E. (1964). Guidance in American education: Its status and its future. In E. Landy & P. A. Perry (Eds.), *Guidance in American education*. Cambridge, MA: Harvard University Press.

Tamminen, A., & Miller, G. (1968). *Guidance programs and their impact on students: A search for relationships between aspects of guidance and selected personal-social variables*. St. Paul, MN: U.S. Department of Health, Education and Welfare and Minnesota State Department of Education.

Tiedeman, D. V. (1968, March). *Economic, educational and personal implications of implementing computerized guidance information systems*. Information Systems for Vocational Decisions. Project Report No. 13. Cambridge: Harvard School of Education.

Tiedeman, D. V. (1972). Can a machine develop a career? A structure for the epigenesis of self-realization in career development. In J. M. Whiteley & A. Resnikoff (Eds.), *Perspectives on vocational development*. Washington, DC: APGA.

Tiedeman, D. V., & Field, F. L. (1965). Guidance: The science of purposeful action applied through education. In R. L. Mosher, R. F. Carle, & C. D. Kehas (Eds.), *Guidance: An examination*. New York: Harcourt, Brace, & World.

Tiedeman, D. V., & O'Hara, R. P. (1963). *Career development: Choice and adjustment.* New York: College Entrance Examination Board.

Vriend, J. (1971). Computer power for guidance and counseling. In D. R. Cook (Ed.), *Guidance for education in revolution.* Boston: Allyn & Bacon.

Warner, W. L., Meekr, M., & Ells, K. (1949). *Social class in America.* Chicago: Science Research Associates.

White, R. W. (1960). Competence and the psychosexual stages of development. In M. Jones (Ed.), *Nebraska symposium on motivation.* Lincoln: University of Nebraska Press.

Williamson, E. G. (1964). An historical perspective on the vocational guidance movement. *Personnel and Guidance Journal, 42,* 854–859.

Williamson, E. G. (1965). *Vocational counseling.* New York: McGraw-Hill.

Williamson, E. G., & Foley, J. D. (1949). *Counseling and discipline.* New York: McGraw-Hill.

Wrenn, C. G. (1962). *The counselor in a changing world.* Washington, DC: APGA.

Wrenn, C. G. (1970). In B. Shertzer & S. C. Stone (Eds.), *Introduction to guidance: Selected readings.* Boston: Houghton Mifflin.

Perspective of Counseling in the United States: Past, Present and Future

S. Norman Feingold

The Past

While the father of vocational guidance in the United States is considered to be Frank Parsons, there were earlier appraisals of individual capabilities and some indications that this new profession of counseling would emerge.

Prior to 1890

Before the 1890s there was little objectivity in appraisal and in estimation of man's capabilities. Objective means of identifying talents rather than observation and estimation were not available until the late 19th century. Methods of subjective appraisal and observation, as well as "tryout" under master workmen, were the means of identifying capabilities. Objective techniques of testing aptitudes were invented in the psychologists' laboratories. Parsons "borrowed" some of the techniques and demonstrated their use.

Parsons, 1890–1908

In the 1890s, Parsons initiated counseling of underprivileged youth in the Boston area. His methods, as described in his 1909 book, "Choosing a Vocation," consisted of three categories of techniques:

> In a wise choice there are three broad factors: (1) a clear under-
> standing of yourself, your aptitudes, abilities, interests, ambitions,
> resources, limitations, and their causes; (2) a knowledge of the
> requirements and conditions of success in different lines of work,
> and the advantages and disadvantages, the compensation, oppor-
> tunities and prospects in different lines of work; (3) true reasoning
> on the relations of these two groups of facts.

In 1892, Professor Elliot of Harvard spoke of individualized diagnosis. Gilman, in 1892 at Johns Hopkins, made similar proposals. In 1899, Harper in Chicago delivered two addresses outlining the diagnoses of individuals. Harper also at that time predicted that in 50 years there would be specialized counselors in the schools.

In 1905, Parsons established the Breadwinner's Institute in the Civic Service House, a community service agency in the north end of Boston. Its emphasis on counseling and individual help in securing employment and on-the-job training and advancement attracted wide attention in other cities and states. Those who supported it financially viewed it as a substitute for prolonged welfare. Educational leaders saw it as a service that would complement manual training and vitalize education for many, if not most youth.

In 1908, the Vocational Bureau for the City of Boston was established and was supported in part by public funds. The counseling movement started informally in Boston, Massachusetts. Frank Parsons, in addition to his activities at Civic Service House, was also a professor at Boston University. His zeal for social reform and the mental hygiene movement helped spark the development of the guidance movement.

In the decade that followed, many settlement houses and welfare agencies in other big cities employed vocational counselors. The thrust emphasized job-oriented vocational guidance as a means of solving the welfare problem.

The National Vocational Guidance Association was founded in Grand Rapids, Michigan in 1913. Jesse B. Davis helped start the movement in that area and later reinforced the concept as Dean of the School of Education of Boston University. This movement was joined also by psychologists working in psychometrics. At the very time that Frank Parsons began his vocational guidance work in Boston, Alfred Binet published his intelligence scale in Paris.

World War I effected a partial merger of these two groups in the United States. Educators such as John Brewer stressed exploratory experiences in guidance. Psychologists such as Clark Hull had hopes for psychological tests as the basis of vocational counseling.

1913–1930s

After 1915, vocational counselors were employed in increasing numbers in the public schools of the larger cities of the United States. Like their counterparts in social and welfare agencies, these early school vocational counselors concentrated their efforts on job-placement and job-adjustment. There was much talk about keeping "square pegs out of round holes" and vice versa. As the number of high school graduates going to college increased, more and better tests became available. School counselors gave less attention to jobs and more to study of the individual, to academic advisement, and to college placement. When the Smith-Hughes Act of 1917 was passed as a war emergency measure, it established a federally aided program of vocational education of less than college grade. No provision whatever was made for vocational guidance as an ancillary service to vocational education in public schools.

Another breakthrough in vocational guidance originated in France and Germany around the turn of the century. Psychological tests were applied to the identification of workers in various industries who were either accident-prone, or unsatisfactory in meeting employer requirements. Frederick Taylor, in *American Industry*, standardized work units by means of objective observation and studies of time and motion of workers. Until then there was no objective external criterion against which to check and correlate the emerging psychometric tests of aptitudes. Use of an external criterion in validating aptitude tests proved to be significant for the emerging psychology of work and assessment of human capabilities.

In the use of an external criterion of "satisfactoriness" of work tasks, one became cognizant of the reality of "subjective" criteria which deal with "job satisfaction" and interpersonal relationships and other dimensions of personal experience. Early industrial psychologists, according to readings of Viteles and Scott and Clothier, were deeply concerned not only with externally observed work tasks, but also with how the worker felt about work and with feelings of satisfaction.

Next, experimental methods replaced ancient techniques of observation and estimation. Industrial psychology became applied research in its basic methods. The differentiation of "successful" from "unsuccessful" workers in an occupation and differentiation of one occupational group from another were analyzed. This involved basic experimental methods of describing requirements of an occupation. The experimental design of objective differentiation of defined criterion groups first employed in industrial psychology has provided counselors with techniques of individual analysis with regard to aptitudes, interests and personality.

A new kind of occupational information gradually emerged in the occupational ability profile. Work and jobs were described in the same terms in which workers were discussed. New types of scholastic aptitude profiles and differential predictions for school tasks developed into two types of job worker descriptions. The first is exemplified in Munsterberg's experimental comparison of workers using objective tests of aptitudes and skills. The second design, pioneered by Paterson, Viteles, Bingham and others is highlighted, currently, by "estimates" of Worker Trait Requirements, employing trained occupational analysts who "estimated" job-man requirements, including specified aptitudes, temperaments, interests, physical capacities, and working conditions.

Army psychologists, trained in manpower analysis and job descriptions in terms of manpower abilities, turned to the occupation of "studentship" as though it were a vocation, subject to psychometric description by experiment. Correlations with the criterion of grades are less than perfect. They are, however, far better than "estimation" and teacher's ratings of a half-century ago.

The pioneering work of E. K. Strong, Jr., preceded at Carnegie Institute of Technology by B. V. Moore, Jay Bean and Max Freyd, developed objective measurement of that elusive phenomenon called "interest." Methods of psychological research and psychometric measurement were applied to motivational phenomenon. E. K. Strong, Jr. and Frederick Kuder have given us a technical literature which makes possible much improved educational guidance over that based upon self-diagnosis of interests.

A significant contribution is the development of rational reasoning about self in communicable terms. Viteles was one of the early innovators to develop such an instrument. Known as the individual psychograph, it was later adapted by Paterson in the Minnesota Employment Stabilization Research Institute to the guidance of the unemployed adult through objective communicable reasoning about capabilities. Paterson's pioneering work laid the foundation for a new type of employment counseling and placement service in the United States Employment Service and also in the U.S. Office of Vocational Rehabilitation. This new pattern of vocational guidance was adapted to Parsons' step three, "true reasoning" about man and job, and given new meaning and new techniques.

Large-scale unemployment highlighted vocational guidance as a job-placement activity as well as an educational function. The Minnesota Employment Stabilization Research Institute experimented with psychological tests, occupational information, and retraining methods of getting adult workers back into the active labor force. Many private and public vocational counseling centers, together with the United States Employment Service, adapted research and counseling methods developed in this pioneer project. The union of education, of social work, and of psychometrics in the vocational guidance of youth and adults was somewhat more complete, as shown by the strength of the National Vocational Guidance Association and activities of the National Occupational Conference.

Psychology as an organized field this time showed some interest in guidance only through a small group of applied psychologists. In 1937, they organized the American Association for Applied Psychology. While this organization included sections concerned with clinical, consulting, educational, and industrial psychology, none was concerned particularly with vocational guidance.

During the 1930s another movement gathered force. This one was under the auspices of clinical psychology, namely, an interest in psychotherapy. One of the products of this new focus of psychological research and practice was Carl Rogers' book on *Counseling and Psychotherapy* (Rogers, 1942). The years following its publication saw a growing interest in psychotherapeutic procedures. The development soon became even greater than interest in psychometrics. This movement, and numerous research and theoretical contributions which have accompanied it, had its impact on vocational guidance. It made vocational counselors, whether psychologists or otherwise, more cognizant of the unity of personality, and that one counsels *people* rather than *problems*. Problems of adjustment in one aspect of living have effects on other aspects of life. The complexity of the processes of counseling concerning any type of individual adjustment is evident, whether in the field of occupations, of group living, or of personal values.

1940–1970

World War II helped solve the problem of U.S. unemployment almost overnight and accelerated recruitment and training of war production workers. The early 1940s saw the United States involved in a great deal of sophisticated psychological selection techniques to assess, train and employ specialized personnel, both military and civilian. At the close of the War in 1946, much effort was directed to counseling of veterans not only by private agencies but also by the Veterans Administration. Veterans were entitled to counseling under the G.I. Bill. Many thousands effectively utilized the service. The U.S. Employment Service, the Civilian Rehabilitation Service and the Servicemen's Rehabilitation Services similarly expanded their vocational guidance functions.

Vocational counseling and therapy were conducted by psychologists working in various hospital settings in the United States. Private agencies also helped men and women with vocational counseling and selective job placement. This took place while they were still in the hospital and awaiting discharge. The late 1940s, 1950s and early 1960s saw a tremendous growth of rehabilitation counseling. Many terminal and sheltered workshops were opened. Selective job placement for civilian and military handicapped took place in increasing numbers. During the post-war period guidance in the schools drifted away from job-oriented counseling and gave its major attention to personality, emotional problems, and academic advisement.

In 1952, the National Vocational Guidance Association, the National Association of Deans of Women, and the American College Personnel Association were the initiating movers in forming the American Personnel and Guidance Association, the primary professional association of counselors in the United States today. By 1949, about 1,000 colleges and universities offered preparation for counseling.

With the launching of Sputnik in 1957, and the passage of the National Defense Education Act of 1958, education and guidance headed in a different direction. Non-directive guidance was for the most part abandoned. Many counselors turned more to directive counseling in their efforts to recruit bright youth for college. Meantime, many of the non-college bound youth were neglected. By 1962, the counseling profession had become entangled in its own techniques and had apparently lost its way if not its goal. A series of reports by interested groups and laws enacted by Congress did much to bring the guidance movement back to earth again. It incorporated vocational guidance as an essential element in education for employment, job placement, economic development and social welfare.

The 1960s saw the federal thrust pinpointed on the dropout problem. It was aptly called "social dynamite" by educator James Conant. At the same time, there was a growing distance between the world of work and the classroom.

The 1960s were years of powerful value commitments for most people, including counselors. Racism, the Vietnam War, poverty, etc., were powerful issues for most people. Neutrality was passé.

During the 1960s and early 1970s there were demonstrations, blatant racism and marches. Numbers of young people broke away from the traditional mainstream of society. Many of these young people received counseling although the regular institutional programs were unable to reach them. These were times of drug experiences, new sexual styles and an increased rate of births to young people who were not married. The counseling they received, including help for job placement, often came from their own peers.

The Present, 1970–1977

Counseling and guidance in the United States has been responsive to the needs of the community. Currently, the United States labor force is larger than it has ever been. There are more people working and more people looking for work. More people are in college or have college degrees than ever before. For those seeking work, this has led to an increasingly competitive market. A college degree is no longer a guarantee of a suitable job or any job at all.

During the 1960s, and until recently, the emphasis, from the early years of schooling, was to prepare for advanced training for college admission. By the early 1970s in the United States, we had a large pool of students unable to attend college, even unwilling to remain in high school. Thus, we were faced with many school dropouts who were unprepared to enter the labor market or whom business screened out because of the over-supply of candidates.

In an effort to bring counseling and education back to the realities of the world of work, Commissioner of Education Sidney Marland, in the early 1970s, propounded career education and career guidance. With the linking of school training to the skills required for employment, vocational counseling has turned full circle back to the concepts of Parsons, but on a more sophisticated scale.

Technology and urbanization result in new demands upon counseling and provide it with new tools as well. Therefore, I should like to share with you some of these current and emerging trends in counseling in the United States.

Current (1970–1977) and Emerging (1980–2000) Trends in U.S. Counseling

The Counseling Profession Has Begun to Establish Standards for Counselor Educator Programs (CORE), for Counseling Agencies (IACS) and for Counselors (CRCC)

A major problem facing any professional counseling association, and the American Personnel and Guidance Association is no exception, is that of certification and licensing. A further implication, as with other professions, is that counseling may be licensed by one state and not by others. Licensure in one state does not mean reciprocity in another. The counselor who legitimately practiced his profession for 25 to 30 years in the District of Columbia, for example, is unable automatically to practice in Florida, where he may wish to retire; this difficulty may exist even in his home state of Maryland or Virginia, only a few miles from his or her office in the District of Columbia.

Licensing and certification is an issue that, as professionals, counselors will be forced to review and revise constantly. High standards of quality as well as licensing will be enforced so that future generations of counselees will be assured of quality service. Unless consumers feel they are receiving competent service from counselors, they will obtain help from other providers. It is in the self-interest of counselors to enforce high standards of licensing and certification.

Presently, trained counselors will require upgrading and recycling. Counselor education will be forced to account professionally for counselors' training activities. Students today often report that some course content is irrelevant and outdated by the time they enter counseling jobs. Counselor educators will probably be required to work with a caseload either on a full-time basis, for example every third or fourth year, or regularly, on a part-time basis. More full-time counselors probably will teach and supervise interns. Not only do students need practicums, internships, and externships, but counselor educators need "refresher" internships as well.

Selection and methods of educating prospective counselors need further, extensive research and redevelopment. Many employers of counselors in various work settings are concerned about newly-trained counselors and their lack of basic counseling skills. Further study, development and implementation will be necessary for the counseling profession to provide quality services.

High scores on the Graduate Record Examination or Miller Analogies do not necessarily predict counselor potential. There may even be an inverse relationship between high scores on these tests and the warmth and empathy requisite for an effective counseling relationship. Yet, this does not mean that such a person will be incapable of making a contribution to guidance by way of valid perceptions and positive interactions with people. Counselors may have the intellectual ability for academic success, but the work may not be to their liking or relevant to their life styles.

Practicum training or internship experiences will have a wider scope and start earlier in the training process to provide the student greater opportunity to gain intensified on-the-job training. It will also serve as a worthwhile screening device to help weed out those candidates whose abilities and temperaments are not suitable for counseling.

Universities need to take a closer look at supervision provided to students in practicum training. Supervisory concepts and administrative procedures will be more closely scrutinized. At the same time, the practicum experience will more fully prepare counselors to meet their clients' needs. Exchange of ideas and techniques by interns in many work settings, including the school, will be maximized.

Counselors in every work setting will need to be more experienced in and about the world of work.

Maintaining and Upgrading Counselor Competencies

Counselors must be trained to be sufficiently sensitive to lifestyles, attitudes and problems of those members of their client population who come from backgrounds unlike their own. Course work and well-supervised experience may lessen the "communication gap" that now, at times, exists between counselor and counselee.

The work experience of far too many counselors has been narrowly confined to teaching, or other types of professional work. On-the-job training of all kinds will be considered to help bring about a better understanding of their clients' lifestyles. The counselor who is to work with the non-college-bound youth and adults should gain experience in blue-collar work.

Those who intend to work with the disadvantaged may well serve a year in the ACTION program as part of their practicum. A similar type of practicum is needed for those who intend to work with the affluent. Training will also have to help counselors sort out their feelings and adapt to the many changes taking place in the world of work, including efforts by the Feminist Movement.

In the future there will probably be greater use of workshops to help counselors keep up-to-date. Many hundreds of different professional workshops were held during the past year by the American Personnel and Guidance Association, from Value Clarification to Job Skills to Career Life-Planning. In the future, workshops will be multiplied many times. Workshops will cover areas now inadequately covered. It will be essential for a counselor, in order to be licensed and certified, to participate in a specified number of workshops, seminars, or conventions during any current year. This is already true for physicians.

Counselors will have to keep up with recent developments. Some counselors have only a meager working knowledge of the more than 30,000 existing jobs in the United States. They will have to do something about this. Practicing counselors and counselor educators will need continuing experiences in the world of work to update their knowledge about current industrial practices and developments.

One method has been the use of advisory committees of workers and employers for secondary and postsecondary schools. The American Personnel and Guidance Association has taken a step in this direction. It now has cooperative relationships with the National Association for Industry-Education Cooperation, National Alliance of Businessmen, etc. A number of invitational conferences have taken place between top leaders in education and industry. Teachers and counselors may work in industry during the school year and/or during the summer. Industrial leaders have had a new role in helping reform the school curriculum. The exchange of communications and visiting one another in their work settings, as well as in meetings, strengthens the individual counselor. Many of these invitational conferences brought key leaders from industry and education together for the first time on projects of mutual benefit.

It is through these interchanges that counselors may become aware that technological advancement and manpower needs change rapidly. By the time manpower forecasting projections reach professional publications, it may be too late. The job of the counselor becomes more difficult as it becomes increasingly important to keep up with rapid technological change. Youth should be deterred from making specific career choices too early in life. People can be trained in broad areas so as not to become too limited too soon in what may be a disappearing field. They cannot be satisfied with helping a youngster make a "safe" decision about a job or education. Counselors recognize that man can become as obsolete as a machine. Explorer of 1958 is as outmoded as the Model-T Ford.

In addition to keeping abreast of changing manpower needs, counselors will have to keep up-to-date with the increasing number of alternatives to traditional secondary and postsecondary education. Some presently existing are:

- Continuing Education Unit (CEU)
- Correspondence courses at elementary, high school, vocational-technical and college levels
- Advancement based on demonstrated knowledge and skill rather than course enrollment and the passage of time
- Early admission to high school and college
- College credit and degrees by examination
- Elimination of grades based on tests
- Open entrance and open exit
- Credit for independent study
- Home study for college credit
- Flexibility to intersperse academic work with travel, employment and national service
- Increased opportunity for students to design their own majors and curriculum
- Credit for life experiences
- Flexibility of transfer requirements between various types of institutions
- External degree
- Concentrated academic programs for students studying to become lawyers, physicians, or other professionals whose services are in demand
- Voucher system for learning
- Para-curriculum—self-designed major

The great surge in the absolute numbers of women in the labor force and the increasingly diverse occupations which they are entering are conditions with which counselors have to deal. For some counselors this necessitates value clarification as well as more information.

Increasing numbers of women will re-enter or remain in the labor market and combine three careers—wife, mother and careerist. Greater numbers of younger women will return to work and/or school while their children attend day care centers. Greater numbers of women will marry later. Other women will not have children until their careers are established.

Feminist groups have brought to light the job and career issues of women today, and the necessity for initiating accelerated changes in women's life styles. Women now comprise about 40% of the United States labor force. Yet only a small percentage are in professional, technical or managerial occupations. The occupational distribution of women in higher level jobs and careers will be changed, particularly at the professional level. There is no rational explanation for the fact that the percentage of women in dentistry, medicine, engineering, etc., in other countries is five or six times what it is in the United States.

Counselors will need to provide more adequate career information. Special emphasis will be placed on projecting new career opportunities for women. Most media, including printed literature, films and film-strips, are presently geared heavily toward young men in the United States. Counselors will be prepared to help both men and women face the hard realities of stereotyping and sexual discrimination.

As career options change for women there will be changing roles, goals and career patterns for boys and men. In B'nai B'rith Career and Counseling Services programs, professional staff members report that it is exceedingly difficult to find successful male career models in non-traditional male occupations. Counseling men, boys and their parents for changing roles and functions will be required as women's roles change. Thus, some counselors will be confronted with the need for value clarification and new information for boys and men, as well as for girls and women.

Counselors as Models and Change Agents

Future counselors will be much more risk-taking, action-oriented. They will be younger, more creative persons, architects of needed change. Counselors in the United States are running for political office, standing up to the power structure in their work settings and trying new group techniques that are much more risk-taking. The future counselors will move into other areas where their skills are needed in society. They will continue to help their counselees choose wisely among alternatives and in dealing with increasing uncertainties.

In the United States today the increase in social action by professional personnel in the counseling field is a dramatic example of the importance of counselors as living models. "What you do speaks so loudly that I can't hear what you say." Values may often be the hidden agenda, but the skills of human relations remain essential. Most counselors are no longer neutral in the counseling interview or in life itself, nor can they be.

Counselors alone cannot make the necessary behavioral changes but, in cooperation with significant others, they can help. There is and there will continue to be great need for education and training of workers in fields which are grossly undermanned. For example:

- Nursing homes need staffing with social workers, vocational counselors, psychiatrists, foster parents and foster children, or full-time psychologists, specialists in recreation, art, music, etc.
- The growth of day care centers for the very young, the very old, and the recuperating, stresses the need for more nurses, psychologists, counselors, business managers, and other male and female generalists and specialists. These should not be glorified baby-sitting services. They should be places which are both secure and creative, in which those who wish to work, or who must do so, may leave their children, parents, or recovering ill.
- There will be a need for paraprofessionals, aides, physical education teachers, social workers, educational and vocational counselors, and other specialist-educators to assist senior citizens both in special senior citizen housing and senior citizen communities. Geriatrics is a field of increasing importance and rapidly growing career opportunities. With 14% of our population now over 65, this thrust is long overdue.
- Road signs all over the United States are incomprehensible and/or unreadable to many people. Agreement on standards for road signs in the U.S. still seems many decades away. There is a dire need for safety engineers, psychologists, semi-skilled and unskilled people to design and provide better signs and directional markers and safer highways; and there is need for them to make greater use of computers to improve traffic patterns.
- Other needs include acceleration of reform in prisons and other correctional institutions. The likelihood of recidivism among inmates is high. We are not rehabilitating these individuals. More sociologists, psychologists, vocational counselors, teacher aides, inmate aides are needed to ensure that our present system is truly rehabilitative.

- The roles of librarians and libraries should be changed to meet the increasing demands made upon them. Many libraries will be open 24 hours a day, 7 days a week. A few libraries already are increasing their hours, but the vast majority are closed more than they are open. College libraries can be used more effectively and innovatively as learning-resource centers are open longer.
- In the future, education and training for all types of workers, from unskilled to professional, will be offered at a growing number of educational parks. New jobs and careers and the counselor's role in this area will be explored and utilized in depth.

To accomplish these goals of new careers, counselors need competencies and expertise in the areas of social action and legislation. During the past few years in the United States, more counselors than ever before were involved in testimony at the local, state and federal government levels. Counselors were consulted about legislation pertaining to education and guidance, considerably before its introduction in the legislatures. Some counselors have successfully campaigned for public office. Their commitment as policy movers is far greater than ever. Counselor involvement with the power structure of legislatures in the United States will be imperative if counseling is to survive as a separate profession and if counselors are to effect change, both locally and nationally.

Additional Techniques and Tools With Which Counselors Are Becoming Familiar and Which They Need to Know Better

The use of small group methods as part of a comprehensive approach to counseling is one such technique. The notion that there is one best way to counsel all individuals is rapidly becoming passé. Team talents and the skills of many resource people in a wide variety of disciplines is the current thrust. The continuum runs from the counseling aids indigenous to a certain group to the services of a counselor with a doctorate and appropriate post-graduate training and experience.

In some school systems paraprofessionals have been detailed as teacher aides. Where paraprofessionals have been assigned as counselor aides, counselors will use them in more creative and innovative ways. Counselor aides are not to replace counselors, but are to be utilized to supplement and complement them. Many high school counselors in the United States have reported that up to 70% of their time is spent on clerical work. Professional counselors need to maximize their skills and talent in a more productive manner. Paraprofessionals in counseling are here to stay. Counselors who are flexible can help determine the paraprofessional's role, status and functions, so that their own professional skills can be maximized and clerical duties minimized.

In the future there will be much greater use of computers in counseling. This will relieve counselors of much clerical work that now occupies too much of their time. Time so released can be used effectively for professional activities. As computers become more and more commonplace in many work settings, including schools, we shall see less resistance to the computer by those counselors who view it as a threat rather than an aid.

Through use of a computer, a student can relate knowledge about himself to data. A body of information on which to base decisions can be created. This recognizes a growing belief in the guidance field that vocational decision-making is not a "choice-point," but a series of choices and a continuous process of development. Counselors have barely scratched the surface of the many ways in which computers can be used to facilitate maintenance of current information and decision making.

Various organizations, such as B'nai B'rith Career and Counseling Services, Kiwanis, Rotary, and other service groups, utilize resource adults who serve as "career advisors." They supplement and complement the work of well-trained counselors. They do not counsel. As successful people in a wide variety of jobs, occupations and professions, they may help youth and young adults by revealing the taste, sounds, feelings and other nuances of the life style related to a certain occupation or career. This technique has added an extra dimension to what youth may learn through films, books, pamphlets, TV and many other varieties of audio-visual aids.

Of even greater importance in counseling in the years ahead is the way in which parents are involved. There is tremendous demand by parents throughout the United States for parent-effectiveness programs. In our society one seems to need training for just about everything except how to be a "professional" parent.

More and more counseling services now see the need for bringing the parent into the counseling process, particularly if the counselee is a minor. This new thrust is in line with the all-over importance of the family in counseling. Many parents, and youths themselves, seem to accept this new facet of counseling as a most helpful device. In our B'nai B'rith Career and Counseling Services offices we find that, with minors, if we do not include the parents, we are working with youth in a vacuum. Parents, too, need assistance to cope with the rapid changes in child-rearing practices.

In the United States, films and filmstrips in the area of careers show an accelerated growth during the past five years. The National Vocational Guidance Association Film and Filmstrip Evaluation Guidelines are now being used to a greater extent by commercial film manufacturers. Business and industry are also using National Vocational Guidance Association members as consultants from the beginning of a script to completion of the film. There will probably be fewer public relations films, reciting only the advantages of a particular career or covering the subject superficially rather than in professional depth.

Establishing Future Goals for the Counseling Profession

Future Orientation

Counseling will possibly in the future be even more future-oriented than it is now. Faith is future-oriented. Having faith implies belief in the probability that something desired can occur and, on the basis of this belief, change is made. Counselors of the future will have more faith in their own capacity to become something more than they are now, in terms of specific skills, attitudes and information. The thrust is not merely in terms of a title but more in the area of effective life functioning. The creative counselor is more involved with a variety of roles, as well as specialized techniques and materials, rather than adding to any routinized format.

The new futurist counselors will help the future that they want, rather than letting events take place in a random manner. Futurist counselors working with students in the elementary school grades are already setting the stage for these young people to lessen future shock and to cope successfully with a world which will be far different than that we know in 1976. As a result, today's young people should be enabled to face a future of more intense and rapid change with less shock than have those people who experienced both horse-and-buggy travel and the Concorde plane's 2,000-miles-per-hour flights.

Where do we, as counselors, want to be in the year 2000? As a world futurist and charter member of the World Futurist Society, your speaker (perhaps unduly) is concerned when he sees colleagues in the physical

sciences moving so rapidly ahead in scientific developments and achievements. They have accomplished many goals earlier than predicted.

We counselors are nowhere near the new, creative discoveries that
physical scientists are projecting. Why? Is it that the helping professions
are not attracting the most qualified people or that the social sciences are
so much more complex? Counselors will have to be futurists if they are
to meet challenges of the future. Counselors can, as agents of change,
define their own roles, status and functions. Like physical scientists, we
must have goals for which our profession can strive.

Counseling will probably start much earlier than the elementary
grades, beginning with genetic counseling and continuing on to pre- and
post-retirement counseling.

At both ends of the continuum there will be the need for well-trained
specialized counselors. Our population continues to grow at both ends of
the continuum. Elementary and earlier school counseling will have a
renewed interest in spite of recent budgetary cuts. Retirement counseling
has not yet "made it" in spite of talks, meetings and conventions on the
subject over the past twenty-five years. Nevertheless, the future looks
bright for both.

There are also thousands of future opportunities for qualified persons
with a counseling background in work in day-care centers, recreation
centers, centers for the aging, centers for the handicapped, etc. Counseling as well as education will be viewed as a life-long concept. People
will see a counselor with the same degree of timeliness as they see their
physician or dentist. New divisions will be formed within the American
Personnel and Guidance Association (APGA) framework that will
represent these emerging interest and professional groups. This, at the
same time, will swell the membership lists of APGA, which have
already shown a phenomenal growth from some 10,000 members in
1952 to almost 45,000 in 1976. By the year 2000, there will probably be
over 100,000 counselors who will belong to APGA.

Goals

The approximately three million people in the United States born in
1976 will be twenty-four years old in the year 2000. The world of 2000
will differ much more from ours of 1976 than our world today differs
from the world of 25 years ago. Those of us who are future-oriented
must move rapidly ahead to create short- and long-term futuristic goals.

Counselors must act rather than react to our changing environment, changing world of work, and changing values.

We need a new kind of professional counselor with new alternative education and training for new helping and administrative roles. Work in such roles will include helping in complex decision-making as well as gathering and organizing up-to-date knowledge, observing trends in the changing world of work, and deciding how information about it can effectively be disseminated. The new counselor can be much more of an activist and agent for change. Counselors cannot merely predict trends in the world of work, but should try to do something about them NOW. I believe that counselors can and will help to change the occupational structure.

The future is now. Everyone everywhere is a VIP (Very Important Person). Everyone can make a contribution. For many people, what contribution they make will depend on their potential to recycle and renew their ideas and skills. People are more important than machines. Counselors can help avoid future shock by accentuating the positive and innovative changes of the future. Then we will not find that we were much too conservative in predicting our development. We may instead find, happily, that many more of our population will be able to cope with their tomorrows.

Though we are all on the spaceship EARTH, as a science fiction buff I expect that we as a people will ultimately move on to other planets. As I view this long, long, long future ahead, while looking back at the millions of years that have preceded our present, I believe our futurist dreams and visions may be too simplistic, and not nearly so dramatic and innovative as the reality that lies ahead.

Selected Bibliography

American Personnel and Guidance Association, Professional Information Services. (1975). *Career development and vocational education.* Washington, DC: American Personnel and Guidance Association.

American Personnel and Guidance Association, Professional Information Services. (1976). *An overview of American Personnel and Guidance Association involvement in career development.* Washington, DC: American Personnel and Guidance Association.

American Personnel and Guidance Association, Professional Information Services. (1976). *Some recent occupational literature related to careers in guidance and counseling.* Washington, DC: American Personnel and Guidance Association.

Belkin, G. S. (Ed.). (1974). *Foundations of counseling.* Dubuque, IA: Kendall/Hunt Publishing Company.

Bloom, B. L. (1975). *Psychological stress in the campus community.* New York: Behavioral Publications, Inc.

Bloomfield, M. (1915). *Readings in vocational guidance.* Boston: Ginn and Company.

Bloomfield, M. (1917). *Finding one's place in life.* Chicago: Howard Severance Company.

Bolles, R. N. (1976). *What color is your parachute? A practical manual for job hunters and career changers* (rev. ed.). Berkeley, CA: Ten Speed Press.

Borow, H. (Ed.). (1973). *Career guidance for a new age.* Boston: Houghton Mifflin Company.

Cochran, J. R., and Peters, H. J. (1972). *Guidance: An introduction— selected readings.* Columbus, OH: Charles E. Merrill Publishing Company.

Davis, H. V. (1969). *Frank Parsons: Prophet, innovator, counselor.* Carbondale, IL: Southern Illinois University Press.

Downing, L. N. (1975). Counseling theories and techniques summarized and critiqued. Chicago: Nelson-Hall.

Evers, D., and Feingold, S. N. (1972). *Your future in exotic occupations.* New York: Richards Rosen Press.

Feingold, S. N. (1964). *A career conference for your community.* Washington, DC: B'nai B'rith Career and Counseling Services.

Feingold, S. N. (1969). *The vocational expert in the social security disability program: A guide for the practitioner.* Springfield, IL: Charles C. Thomas, Publisher.

Feingold, S. N. (1972). *A counselor's handbook: Readings in counseling, student aid and rehabilitation.* Cranston, RI: The Carroll Press.

Feingold, S. N. (1972). *Scholarships, fellowships and loans.* Vol. 5. Arlington, MA: Bellman Publishing Company.

Feingold, S. N., and Swerdloff, S. (1969). *Occupations and careers.* New York: McGraw-Hill Book Company.

Fitzgerald, L. E., Johnson, W. F., & Norris, W. (Eds.). (1970). *College student personnel: Readings and bibliographies*. Boston: Houghton Mifflin Company.

Folger, J. K., Astin, H. S., & Bayer, A. E. (1970). *Human resources and higher education*. New York: Russell Sage Foundation.

Ginzberg, E. (1971). *Career guidance*. New York: McGraw-Hill Book Company.

Harkness, C. A. (1976). *Career counseling: Dreams and reality*. Springfield, IL: Charles C. Thomas, Publisher.

Harrington, T. F. (1974). *Student personnel work in urban colleges*. New York: Intext Educational Publishers.

Hoyt, K. B. (1975). *Career education: Contributions to an evolving concept*. Salt Lake City: Olympus Publishing Company.

Lynch, E. C. (1970). *Meyer Bloomfield and employment management*. Austin, TX: Bureau of Business Research, University of Texas at Austin.

Magisos, J. H. (Ed.). (1973). *Career education*. Washington, DC: American Vocational Association.

Marland, S. P., Jr. (1974). *Career education: A proposal for reform*. New York: McGraw-Hill Book Company.

Miller, C. H. (1964). Vocational guidance in the perspective of cultural change. In H. Borow (Ed.), *Man in a world at work*. Boston: Houghton Mifflin Company.

Parsons, F. (1909). *Choosing a vocation*. Boston: Houghton Mifflin Company.

Peterson, J. A. (1976). *Counseling and values: A philosophical examination*. Cranston, RI: The Carroll Press.

Slocum, W. L. (1974). Occupational careers: A sociological perspective (2nd ed.). Chicago: Aldine Publishing Company.

Smith, C. E., and Mink, O. G. (1969). *Foundations of guidance and counseling: Multidisciplinary readings*. Philadelphia: J. B. Lippincott Company.

Tollefson, A. L. (1975). *New approaches to college student development*. New York: Behavioral Publications, Inc.

Warnath, C. F. (1971). *New myths and old realities*. San Francisco: Jossey-Bass, Inc.

Wigglesworth, D. C. (Ed.). (1975). *Career education: A reader*. San Francisco: Canfield Press.

Chapter 2

Counselor Education Programs— The Preparation of the Secondary School Counselor

How does one become a school counselor? What competencies are necessary? What experience beyond a graduate degree should one have? Teaching experience? Licensure? Clinical training in a therapeutic setting? The American School Counselor Association (ASCA) and the Association for Counselor Education and Supervision (ACES) have devoted much attention to these and similar questions. Their publications suggest trends in counselor education which are reflected in the following readings.

First, Beale offers a series of novel activities that can be used to introduce prospective counselors in career counseling classes to standard career resources such as the *Dictionary of Occupational Titles* (DOT) and the *Occupational Outlook Handbook* (OOH). He suggests lively ways to approach these rather "dry" publications, thus enabling future counselors to become familiar and comfortable with their use.

Next, Paisley and Hubbard surveyed officials from State Departments of Education to learn their perceptions of certification and employment trends for school counselors. The study documents an important perceived increase in respect for counselors, and notes that the average age of school counselors is 55, indicating a crucial need for recruiting new counselors over the next decade.

In the third article, Lee and Pulvino explain how learning to use computers can parallel the learning of counseling principles. They compellingly make the case that many of the processes involved in learning to use computers and computer applications parallel the processes involved in working effectively with clients, and that many counseling skills can be enhanced and reinforced while learning to use computers.

The Standards and Procedures for School Counselor Training and Certification from the Association for Counselor Education and Supervision (ACES) conclude this chapter. ACES as an organiztion strongly promotes the establishment of consistency in the application of professional standards across school counselor preparation programs, the accreditation of school counselor preparation programs and the credentialing of school counselors by state education agencies.

Infusing Life and Vitality Into Career Counseling Classes

Andrew V. Beale

Familiarizing prospective counselors with basic career information resources is one of the primary goals of most career counseling classes. This article illustrates a series of novel activities that can be used to introduce students to standard career resources.

The world of work is becoming increasingly complex, and individuals must have accurate, reliable, and usable information about occupational demands, working conditions, monetary rewards, and resources for assistance if they are to make wise career decisions. The statement of counselor competencies by the Association for Counselor Education and Supervision emphasized the need for counselors to have knowledge of and competence in the use of occupational information resources (Hansen, 1978). Authors of career counseling textbooks, from Baer and Roeber (1951) to Zunker (1981), have repeatedly maintained that a counselor's thorough understanding of occupational information resources is a prerequisite to helping clients in the process of career development. If clients are to be well served, the counselor must know how to locate and how to help clients use occupational information (Isaacson, 1985).

Simple exposure to information about the marketplace is insufficient (Herr & Cramer, 1984). Rather, to increase the probability that occupational information resources will be investigated and understood, graduate counseling students, as well as students in undergraduate career exploration classes and groups (Bolles, 1986; Kennedy & Laramore, 1988; Shertzer, 1985), need to be motivated to understand and use existing career resources. Experience has shown that merely suggesting that preservice counselors explore the *Dictionary of Occupational Titles* (*DOT;* U. S. Department of Labor, 1977), the *Occupational Outlook Handbook* (*OOH;* U.S. Department of Labor, 1988), and other related resources on their own is hardly a guaranteed method for ensuring that students will learn to use and appreciate the value of these career resources. Perhaps, as Herr and Cramer (1984) suggested, these materials on their own are just too dry and uninspiring to motivate students to use them.

No matter how uninteresting the materials may seem initially, preservice counselors need to become familiar with basic occupational information resources if they are to meet the needs of their clients. Recognizing that occupational information is vital to sound career decision making, Bradley (1983) and Miller and Soper (1982) called for an integrated series of learning strategies that would serve to make career counseling classes informative as well as enjoyable. According to Fredrickson (1982), career information needs to be "communicated with a zeal and excitement that communicates its vitality and power" (p. xiii). In the same vein, Fuhrmann and Grasha (1983) reminded college professors that they stand a much better chance of holding the attention of their students if novelty is introduced into the classroom setting. The goal is to enable students to sense that "something's different today" (p. 55).

This article presents several "novel" activities that, when completed by preservice counselors, will enable participants to become more familiar with the local and national occupational scenes. Specifically, the activities involve use of the *DOT, Selected Characteristics of Occupations Defined in the Dictionary of Occupational Titles (SCOD-DOT;* U. S. Department of Labor, 1981), *OOH, The Guide for Occupational Exploration (GOE;* Harrington & O'Shea, 1984), *Yellow Pages,* and the completion of a community occupational survey.

Dictionary of Occupational Titles

The *DOT* is easily the single most comprehensive document of its kind available for learning about the world of work. With more than 20,000 titles within its pages, the *DOT* serves as a reservoir of job information. It provides information on: (a) the structure of work, particularly the data-people-things functions of occupations; (b) the relationships among occupations; and (c) a summary of what a particular worker does. It is no wonder, then, that Landrum and Strohmenger (1979) encouraged counselors to put the *DOT* to work for themselves and their clients.

A companion publication, *Selected Characteristics of Occupations Defined in the Dictionary of Occupational Titles,* provides more detailed supplementary information about jobs contained in the *DOT*. It describes a job's physical demands, the environmental working conditions, and the amount of training time required.

Unfortunately, many counselors find "the overwhelming amount of information contained in the *DOT* system insurmountable and too difficult to manage" (Zunker, 1981, p. 314). Perhaps it is the sheer size of the volume that discourages users. Whatever the reasons, it is accepted that many preservice counselors will not learn about the *DOT* on their own. To help prospective counselors discover and appreciate the value of the *DOT* in career counseling, the following activities are suggested as "fun" ways of introducing students to the *DOT* (Figure 1). It is hoped that once preservice counselors learn how easy it is to use the *DOT*, they will be more likely to use it with their *counselees*.

Activity 1
What is in a Name

Objective: To allow students to realize that they cannot always tell what workers do by knowing only their job titles

Directions: Read each of the occupational titles below and determine if you can correctly identify what the worker does on the job. Once you are finished, use the *DOT* numbers to check how well you did.

1. Impregnator (599.685-026)
   a. an animal husbandry worker
   b. an artificial insemination technician
   c. a dip painter

2. Band Tumbler (551.685-010)
   a. a person who performs with jazz groups
   b. a worker who removes water from rubber bands
   c. a member of a musical circus troupe

3. Cradle Placer (869.664-014)
   a. a worker who places furniture in children's stores
   b. a construction site worker
   c. a hospital nursery attendant

4. Bottom Presser (690.685-034)
   a. a shoe factory worker
   b. a worker who presses men's trousers
   c. A first floor laundry worker

Answers: 1-C, 2-B, 3-B, 4-A.

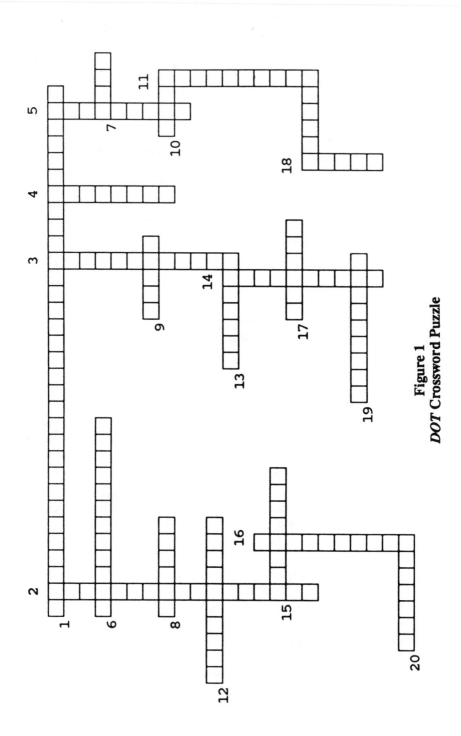

Figure 1
DOT Crossword Puzzle

Activity 2
Sedentary, Light, Medium, Heavy, and Very Heavy Work

Objective: To acquaint students with the *DOT* supplement, *Selected Characteristics of Occupations Defined in the Dictionary of Occupational Titles (SCOD-DOT;* 1982), specifically Appendix A: Physical Demands

Directions: Your client's physician has limited him or her to no more than light physical exertion. From the clusters of occupations below, see if you can identify the occupation that would be suitable for your client purely from an exertional standpoint. Once you have identified what you believe to be the correct choices, consult the *SCOD-DOT* to check your answers.

1. Which occupation qualifies?
   a. soap chipper 555.686-014
   b. glass beveler 673.685-018
   c. burr grinder 673.686-014

2. Which occupation qualifies?
   a. brick tester 579.384-010
   b. cobbler 788.381-010
   c. doughnut maker 526.684-010

3. Which occupation qualifies?
   a. hooker inspector 689.685-078
   b. fireworks maker 737.684-018
   c. rubber molder 556.684-026

4. Which occupation qualifies?
   a. stripper 749.687-030
   b. tumbler 599.685-106
   c. candy puller 520.685-046

Answers: 1-C, 2-A, 3-C, 4-B.

Activity 3
DOT Crossword Puzzle, Figure 1

Objective: To familiarize preservice counselors with *DOT* code numbers and the way occupations are divided into categories, divisions, and groups

Directions: Use your copy of the *DOT* to complete the crossword puzzle. Remember, the nine-digit *DOT* numbers are presented in numerical order beginning on Page 15. Category, divisions, and group titles begin on page xxxiv.

Across

1. What do the initials D.O.T. stand for?
6. The number 073.101-010 stands for which job title?
7. The number 313.131-014 stands for which job title?
8. 844.364-010 stands for _____ mason.

9. 241.267-018 stands for _____ examiner.
10. 007.167-018 stands for _____ programmer.
12. 160.167-010 indicates which job title?
13. 372.667-018 stands for Correction _____.
15. 013.061-010 is an Agricultural _____.
17. 142.081-010 is a _____ designer.
18. The group title for 110 is _____.
19. _____ is the job title for 024.061-018.
20. The group title for 072 is _____.

Down

2. The group title for 205 is _____.
3. What is the alternate title for 376.367-014?
4. The number 165.017-010 stands for which job title?
5. The division for 09 is Occupations in _____.
11. The alternate title for 408.161-010 is _____.
14. 050.067-010 stands for _____.
16. 041.061-026 indicates which job title?
18. 713.681-010 stands for _____ mounter.

Answers

Across
1. Dictionary of Occupational Titles
6. Veterinarian
7. Chef
8. Cement
9. Claim
10. Tool
12. Accountant
13. Officer
15. Engineer
17. Floral
18. Lawyer
19. Geologist
20. Dentist

Down
2. Interviewing Clerk
3. Investigator
4. Lobbyist
5. Education
11. Landscaper
14. Economist
16. Biochemist
18. Lens

Occupational Outlook Handbook

The *OOH,* originally prepared to provide occupational information to returning World War II veterans, continues to be an affordable standard reference on current and future job prospects. The 1988–89 edition of the *OOH* describes in detail approximately 225 occupations (comprising about four of every five jobs in the economy), plus summary information on 125 additional occupations.

Published biennially, the current edition of the *OOH* gives the most attention to those occupations that require lengthy training or education or which are projected to grow most rapidly through the year 2000. A description of the nature of the work; working conditions; employment, training, and advancement opportunities; job outlook; earnings; and sources of additional information are provided for each of the selected occupations.

As with the *DOT*, counselors must use the *OOH* if they are to begin to fully appreciate its value in career counseling. The activities that follow are designed to help preservice counselors find answers to frequently asked client questions such as "What is the job market like?" and "How much money will I make?"

Activity 1
Where is the Growth?

Objective: To help counselors better understand the expected changes in employment through the year 2000

Directions: For the clusters of occupations presented below, see if you can identify the occupation with the greatest anticipated employment growth. Use Appendix A and the "Job Outlook" section of the *OOH* to check your hunches.

1. The job outlook is better for:
   a. counselors
   b. psychologists
   c. college professors

2. The job outlook is better for:
   a. service station attendants
   b. credit authorizers
   c. parking lot attendants

3. The job outlook is better for:
   a. electrical engineers
   b. civil engineers
   c. chemical engineers

4. The job outlook is better for:
   a. painters
   b. roofers
   c. carpenters

Answers: 1-B, 2-C, 3-A, 4-B.

Activity 2
Who Makes the Most Money?

Objective: Realizing that clients are often interested in knowing how much money they may earn in a particular occupation, this activity introduces students to the "Earnings" section of the occupational descriptions for answers.

Directions: For each of the 10 groups of occupations listed below, see if you can "guess" which occupation generally has the highest earnings. When you have finished, use your copy of the *OOH* to check your answers. Please keep in mind that earnings depend on a number of factors, so do not read the salaries as absolute. Look upon the earnings as a clue to an occupation's attractiveness and its *potential* for long-term monetary reward.

1. Who earns the most?
   a. file clerk
   b. fire fighter
   c. licensed practical nurse

2. Who earns the most?
   a. urban planner
   b. architect
   c. lawyer

3. Who earns the most?
   a. aircraft pilot
   b. television announcer
   c. veterinarian

4. Who earns the most?
   a. bartender
   b. mail carrier
   c. secondary school teacher

Answers: 1-B, 2-C, 3-A, 4-C.

Guide for Occupational Exploration

Originally published in 1979 by the Department of Labor, the *Guide for Occupational Exploration (GOE)* is designed to assist job seekers enter occupations that are in accord with their interests, skills, values, and abilities. A second edition, edited by Harrington and O'Shea (1984), is published by the National Forum Foundation and distributed by American Guidance Service. The revised *GOE* groups occupations listed in the *DOT* by interests and by ability and traits required for successful performance. Descriptive information, such as physical demands, work settings, skills and abilities required, how to prepare for this kind of work, licenses and certificates needed, and sources of additional information, is provided to assist users in evaluating their own interests and potentials and relating them to selected work areas.

The *GOE* also helps the user move from military specialties to civilian jobs; relates work values, home and leisure activities, school subjects, and work settings to work groups; identifies physical strength and training requirements for each occupation; lists jobs that offer on-the-job training through apprenticeships; and includes a checklist and a worksheet to help users identify the type of work in which they may find satisfaction (O'Shea, Harrington, Padgett, & Dosch, 1985). It is easy to see that the *GOE* is indispensable in assisting clients to make comparisons between the characteristics of various occupational groups and the information they have about themselves.

The following activities are designed to assist preservice counselors in appreciating the value of the *GOE* in career counseling.

Activity 1
Returning to Civilian Life

Objective:	To familiarize users with how the *GOE* can be used to help a person who has acquired skills while serving in the military find jobs in the civilian work force in which such skills are important
Directions:	"But there's no such thing as a civilian boatswain's mate," laments your client who was recently discharged from the Navy. Are there civilian counterparts to the military occupations performed by your clients? Using the Military Occupational Specialties with Corresponding Subgroups section of the *GOE* (p. 69), identify civilian occupations that correspond to the occupations your clients performed in the Navy.

Navy Occupation	*Civilian Equivalent Occupation*
a. boatswain's mate	_____
b. yeoman	_____
c. combat swimmer	_____

Activity 2
Help! I Lost My Job

Objective: To familiarize users with how the *GOE* can assist a person who has lost a job in identifying jobs that involve similar work situations and require similar skills

Directions: Due to circumstances beyond their control, a number of workers in your area have lost their jobs. They come to you for help. Because they enjoyed and were good at their previous jobs, they are interested in securing employment in comparable occupations. Using Appendix E: Alphabetical Arrangement of Occupations (p. 619), see if you can identify two occupations that require training and skills similar to those required by your clients' previous occupations.

Client's Previous	GOE Subgroup Number	Similar Occupations
a. fly raiser	_____	_____ & _____
b. gut puller	_____	_____ & _____
c. arm maker	_____	_____ & _____

The Telephone Yellow Pages

Local career information, according to Tolbert (1980, p. 185), is often the most difficult and time-consuming occupational information for counselors to obtain. Tolbert noted that, in contrast to the abundance of reliable state and national level information, local occupational information is frequently spotty, fragmented, and time-consuming to obtain.

One way for preservice counselors to learn more about the configuration of the employment picture in their areas is to make use of the local *Yellow Pages* (Fredrickson, 1982). Using the same general classification system throughout the country, the *Yellow Pages* readily reveal employer names, addresses, and telephone numbers; the number of companies in various occupational categories; and mention of local products and services.

The following activity has proven useful in enlivening a discussion of local employment possibilities. Graduate students are often surprised at how little they actually know about the local employment scene.

Activity 1
Local Employment Scene

Objective: To familiarize counselors with career opportunities in their localities

Directions: Answer the following questions based upon your understanding of the employment picture in your community. When you have completed the 10 items, consult your *Yellow Pages* to check the accuracy of your answers. Count the number of listings for each occupation to determine the correct choice.

In your opinion, in your community are there more . . .   *Answers*
1. muffler shops or music stores?   _____
2. opticians or ophthalmologists?   _____
3. pest-control services or preschools?   _____
4. pediatricians or psychiatrists?   _____
5. janitorial services or jewelry stores?   _____
6. travel agents or transmission repairers?   _____
7. plumbers or plasterers?   _____
8. video stores or vacuum cleaner dealers?   _____
9. accountants or architects?   _____
10. lawyers or landscape contractors?   _____

Community Occupational Survey

While knowledge of occupational information resources is essential, career counselors also need a direct, firsthand familiarity with the local labor market. Counselors need to observe and, in many instances, interact with workers if they are to have a realistic view of the employment situation in their communities (Beale, 1983a).

The need for local occupational information is neither new nor difficult to understand. Textbook authors (Hoppock, 1976; Norris, Hatch, Engelkes, & Winborn, 1979; Shartle, 1959; Tolbert, 1980) have repeatedly emphasized the necessity of reliable information about the local labor force. To help meet the need of preservice counselors for up-to-date local employment information, career counseling students may be encouraged to carry out a community occupational survey.

Following the steps set forth by Tolbert (1980, pp. 192–194), class members may systematically survey area employers using a standard data collection instrument. Along with basic information such as company name and address, total number of employees, and the name and telephone number of the contact person, participants provide *DOT* numbers, the number of positions, and a brief description of the general duties and worker qualifications for each occupation observed. In this way, class members learn firsthand about the local job market, plus develop their own lists of employment contacts and learn appropriate job survey and interview skills. The completed interview guides may be reproduced and copies may be given to all class members. In this manner, class members benefit not only from their own surveys but also from the surveys completed by classmates. Similar surveys conducted by teachers (Beale, 1983b) and practicing school counselors (Beale, 1980) have proven successful in introducing participants to the employment conditions and opportunities in their local areas.

Conclusion

The author's counselor education experience over the past 5 years has shown that preservice counselors enjoy getting to know more about the world of work by participating in the activities presented herein. Realizing that for many students the *DOT, OOH,* and other occupational resource materials are not intrinsically mesmerizing reading, career counseling instructors are constantly challenged to infuse life and vitality into their career classes. By challenging students to be the first to complete a particular activity or to get the highest score, a bit of good natured competition and novelty is introduced into class sessions that have the potential for becoming deadly dull. Instructors and preservice counselors may very well enjoy and benefit from developing and using the suggested activities. After all, there is more than one way to "skim" the *DOT*.

References

Baer, M. F., & Roeber, E. C. (1951). *Occupational information*. Chicago: Science Research Associates.

Beale, A. V. (1980). Community survey: Combining inservice training with data collection. *The School Counselor, 28,* 50–53.

Beale, A. V. (1983a). Experiencing the business community enhances attitudes toward career guidance. *The Guidance Clinic, 15*(9), 7–9

Beale, A. V. (1983b). Developing local career information: Filling a void. *Journal of Career Education, 10*, 48–54.

Bolles, R. N. (1986). *What color is your parachute?* Berkeley, CA: Ten Speed Press.

Bradley, R. W. (1983). Teaching preservice career counseling classes. *The Vocational Guidance Quarterly, 32*, 119–121.

Fredrickson, R. H. (1982). *Career information.* Englewood Cliffs, NJ: Prentice-Hall.

Fuhrmann, B. S., & Grasha, A. F. (1983). *A practical handbook for college teachers.* Boston: Little, Brown.

Hansen, L. S. (1978). ACES position paper: Counselor preparation for career development/career education. *Counselor Education and Supervision, 17*, 168–179.

Harrington, T. F., & O'Shea, A. J. (Eds.). (1984). *Guide for occupational exploration* (2nd ed.). Minneapolis: National Forum Foundation.

Herr, E. L., & Cramer, S. H. (1984). *Career guidance and counseling through the life span* (2nd ed.). Boston: Little, Brown.

Hoppock, R. (1976). *Occupational information* (4th ed.). New York: McGraw-Hill.

Isaacson, L. E. (1985). *Basics of career counseling.* Boston: Allyn & Bacon.

Kennedy, J. L., & Laramore, D. (1988). *Career book.* Lincolnwood, IL: National Textbook.

Landrum, J. H., & Strohmenger, C. T. (1979). A basic in educational and agency career counseling: The new DOT. *The Vocational Guidance Quarterly, 27*, 291–300.

Miller, M. J., & Soper, B. (1982). The art of creating enjoyable career counseling classes. *The Vocational Guidance Quarterly, 31*, 144–148.

Norris, W., Hatch, R. N., Engelkes, J. R., & Winborn, B. B. (1979). *The career information service.* Chicago: Rand McNally.

O'Shea, A. J., Harrington, T. F., Padgett, A., & Dosch, A. (1985). The guide for occupational exploration, second edition. *The Vocational Guidance Quarterly, 34*, 69–76.

Shartle, C. L. (1959). *Occupational information.* Englewood Cliffs, NJ: Prentice-Hall.

Shertzer, B. (1985). *Career planning: Freedom to choose* (3rd ed.). Boston: Houghton Mifflin.

Tolbert, E. L. (1980). *Counseling for career development* (2nd ed.). Boston: Houghton Mifflin.

U.S. Department of Labor. (1977). *Dictionary of occupational titles* (4th ed.). Washington, DC: U.S. Government Printing Office.

U.S. Department of Labor. (1981). *Selected characteristics of occupations defined in the Dictionary of Occupational Titles.* Washington, DC: U.S. Government Printing Office.

U.S. Department of Labor. (1988). *The occupational outlook handbook, 1988-89 edition.* Washington, DC: U.S. Government Printing Office.

Zunker, V. G. (1981). *Career counseling: Applied concepts of life planning.* Monterey, CA: Brooks/Cole.

School Counseling: State Officials' Perceptions of Certification and Employment Trends

Pamela O. Paisley
Glenda T. Hubbard

The purpose of this research was to assess the perceptions of officials of state departments of education regarding school counseling.

Decreasing attention to the preparation, certification, and employment of school counselors during the past 25 years has been discussed in three recent American Association for Counseling and Development (AACD) projects. A "think-tank" supported by an AACD Foundation Grant began exploring these school counseling concerns in a workshop prior to the 1985 Southern Association for Counselor Education and Supervision Convention. This effort led to an open forum, a summary of which was published in a monograph titled *Development of Strategies for the Preservation of School Counselor Preparation Programs* (Cecil & Comas, 1987). This project was motivated by the perception that a crisis was imminent in school counseling as indicated by "declining enrollments along with little student interest in school settings, lack of administrative support for school counselors, mounting bureaucracy in state departments of education and institutions of higher education, and a siphoning off of faculty into nonschool counseling involvement" (Cecil & Comas, 1987, p. ii).

A second program, the 20/20 Conference on School Counseling Research, was held in Washington, D.C., during the fall of 1987 and attracted 150 counselors, counselor educators, and supervisors from 35 states. This program was jointly sponsored by AACD and the Educational Resources Information Center/Counseling and Personnel Services Clearinghouse (ERIC/CAPS). Looking toward the future, professionals addressed the problems presented in the Cecil and Comas monograph. At that conference, Sweeney (1987) reported a significant reduction in the number of journal articles dealing with school counseling certification in the previous 10 years. He also reported indications in some states that state boards of education did not seem to take counselors seriously and that some are requiring master's degrees in subject areas in addition to master's degrees in counseling.

The third effort, an outgrowth of the earlier programs, led to the establishment of the AACD School Counseling Task Force. This task force was "originally directed to study the supply and demand of school counselors and recruitment of qualified candidates for the future" (Hardy, 1988). They are currently investigating questions regarding the counselor's role, as well as possible national standards for and advocacy issues related to preparation, credentialing, supervision, and program development. They plan to issue a report containing specific recommendations.

As interested professionals attempt to maintain a focus on issues in school counseling and to understand and plan for the future, information from relevant sources will be required. The following survey of state department of education officers was undertaken to provide some of the needed information. This information, which focuses on state officials' perceptions of certification and employment trends, can be used to supplement data reported by counselor educators and by school counselors and can give insight into future needs.

Method

After a review of the relevant literature (Cecil & Comas, 1987; Sweeney, 1987; Walz & Bleuer, 1987), the following research questions were addressed in our survey. Which state departments of education report that they:

1. Require teaching experience before certification of school counselors?
2. Allow classroom teachers who hold master's degrees and certification in school counseling to receive a salary increase while waiting for a school counseling position?
3. Allow provisional employment for school counselors before they have full certification?
4. Perceive that a sufficient supply of qualified school counselors is available?

5. Have witnessed an increase in employment of school counselors in their states during the past 5 years?
6. Anticipate a change in the number of school counseling positions in the next 10 years?
7. Anticipate a change in the proportions of elementary, middle, and secondary school counseling positions during the next 10 years?
8. Have experienced a change in the status of school counselors with regard to public respect in the past 5 years?
9. Have observed an impact of the National Board for Certified Counselors (NBCC) and the Council for the Accreditation of Counseling and Related Educational Programs (CACREP) standards on employment decisions?

In addition, we were interested in identifying factors contributing to the perceived changes and issues that state department officials considered important to the future of school counseling.

We developed survey items to address the areas of research interest listed above. Questions with response alternatives were used for most of the items. These questions also included an "other" response or comment section to provide respondents with sufficient range of expression. Three open-ended questions were used to identify perceptions of factors contributing to any changes in employment patterns and to project important professional issues. The survey questions were reviewed and edited by two counselor educators and a nationally published researcher.

The questionnaires were sent to the state superintendent of public instruction or person with equivalent title in all 50 states and the District of Columbia, along with two cover letters and a stamped, self-addressed envelope. One cover letter, addressed to state superintendents, described the purpose of the study and requested that they forward the survey, the second cover letter, and the return envelope to the person in the state educational agency who directs and supervises counseling and guidance services in the public schools of that state. This method was chosen because school counseling programs in state agencies are administered by various officials with many different job titles, making it impossible to use a standard address to identify the correct person in each state.

The first mailing resulted in an 86% return within 1 month. A follow-up questionnaire was sent to those who did not respond using the same procedures described above. Of the states, 92% responded ($N=47$). Because officials in only four states failed to respond, the decision was made to telephone the appropriate officials in those states and ask the same questions that were on the questionnaire. This resulted in a 100% rate of response (*N*=51). Usable responses were obtained for all questionnaire items except one requesting information on the proportions of elementary, middle, and secondary school counselors. Responses to this question were presented in such varied ways that no discernable pattern could be observed. We summarized responses to all other questions.

Results

Certification

Respondents were asked three questions specific to certification issues. These responses are provided in Table 1. Of the respondents, 29 (56.9%) indicated that teaching experience was required before certification and employment as a school counselor; 21 respondents (41.2%) indicated that teaching experience was not required. Four (7.8%) of the respondents who indicated that teaching experience was required also noted

Table 1
Certification Requirements Reported by Officials in State
Departments of Education

State	Teaching Experience Required	Master's Pay in Classroom	Provisional Employment
Alabama	yes	no	no
Alaska	no	local	no
Arizona	yes	yes	no
Arkansas	yes	local	yes
California	no	local	no
Colorado	yes	local	yes
Connecticut	no	yes	yes
Delaware	yes*	yes	yes
Florida	no	local	yes
Georgia	yes*	no	yes
Hawaii	no	yes	yes

Table 1 (Continued)

State	Teaching Experience Required	Master's Pay in Classroom	Provisional Employment
Idaho	yes	local	no
Illinois	yes	local	no
Indiana	yes	yes	no
Iowa	yes	yes	yes
Kansas	yes	yes	yes
Kentucky	yes	yes	no
Louisiana	yes	yes	yes
Maine	no	local	no
Maryland	no	local	yes
Massachusetts	yes	yes	no
Michigan	yes	yes	
Minnesota	no	local	no
Mississippi	yes*	no	yes
Missouri	yes	yes	yes
Montana	yes	yes	yes
Nebraska	yes	local	yes
Nevada	no	yes	yes
New Hampshire	no	yes	yes
New Jersey	yes	yes	no
New Mexico	no	yes	yes
New York	no	yes	yes
North Carolina	no	no	yes
North Dakota	yes**	yes	no
Ohio	yes	no	yes
Oklahoma	yes	yes	yes
Oregon	yes	yes	yes
Pennsylvania	no	yes	no
Rhode Island	yes	local	no
South Carolina	no	yes	yes
South Dakota	no	yes	yes
Tennessee	yes	yes	no
Texas	yes	yes	yes
Utah	no	yes	yes
Vermont	no		no
Virginia	yes		no
Washington	no	local	no
West Virginia	no	yes	no
Wisconsin	yes*	local	yes
Wyoming	yes	yes	yes
Washington, D.C.	no	yes	yes

*An internship may be substituted.
**Two years of related human services experience may be substituted.

that an internship could be substituted, and in one state, 2 years of related human services employment could be substituted. Therefore, in 5 states (9.8%) that require teaching experience, an alternative can be substituted.

Thirty (58.8%) respondents indicated that teachers with a master's degree and certification in school counseling could be paid on a master's degree scale if that individual remained in the classroom. Five respondents (9.8%) indicated that these individuals could not be paid on the master's scale; 14 respondents (27.5%) indicated that it depended on local district; and 2 respondents (3.9%) gave no answer.

Thirty respondents (58.8%) indicated that an individual could be provisionally employed before completing all requirements for school counselor certification. Twenty (39.2%) indicated that such provisional employment would not be possible, and one (2%) provided no response.

Employment Patterns

Respondents were asked to address several questions related to current and predicted employment patterns. These responses are given in Table 2. Thirty-two (62.7%) respondents indicated that there were currently sufficient numbers of certified people in their states to fill

Table 2
School Counseling Employment Patterns Reported by Officials in State Departments of Education

State	Sufficient Numbers	Changes in Past 5 Years	Anticipated Change
Alabama	varies	none	increase
Alaska	varies	none	increase
Arizona	no	decrease	increase
Arkansas	yes	increase	increase
California	yes	increase	increase
Colorado			
Connecticut	yes	increase	increase
Delaware	yes	increase	increase
Florida	yes	increase	increase

Table 2 (Continued)

State	Sufficient Numbers	Changes in Past 5 Years	Anticipated Change
Georgia	varies	increase	increase
Hawaii	no	increase	increase
Idaho	yes	increase	increase
Illinois	yes	decrease	decrease
Indiana	no	increase (elementary) decrease (secondary)	none (secondary) increase (elementary)
Iowa	yes	none	increase
Kansas	yes	increase	increase
Kentucky	yes	increase	increase
Louisiana	no	increase	increase
Maine	no	increase	increase
Maryland	varies	increase	
Massachusetts	yes	decrease	increase
Michigan	yes	increase	increase
Minnesota	yes	decrease	increase
Mississippi	yes	none	none
Missouri	yes	increase	increase
Montana	yes	decrease	decrease
Nebraska	yes	none	none
Nevada	no	increase	increase
New Hampshire	no	increase	increase
New Jersey	yes	none	
New Mexico	yes	decrease	none
New York	varies	increase	increase
North Carolina	no	increase	increase
North Dakota	no	none	increase
Ohio	yes	none	decrease
Oklahoma	yes	decrease	
Oregon	yes	decrease	none
Pennsylvania	yes	none	none
Rhode Island			
South Carolina	yes	increase	increase
South Dakota	no	increase	none
Tennessee	yes	increase	increase
Texas	no	increase	increase
Utah	yes	decrease	decrease
Vermont	no	increase	increase
Virginia	yes	increase	increase
Washington	yes		
West Virginia	no	increase	decrease
Wisconsin	no	increase	increase
Wyoming	yes	decrease	increase
Washington, D.C.	yes	increase	none

school counseling positions as they became available. Fourteen (27.5%) respondents indicated that there were insufficient certified counselors available, 2 respondents (3.9%) reported that they did not know or did not have the data available, and 5 respondents (9.8%) indicated that this depended on the local school district. In unsolicited comments, 15 respondents (29.4%) (including some who had indicated sufficient numbers) identified a concern related to recruiting certified school counselors in rural areas of these states.

In reference to the current number of school counseling positions in their states, 9 respondents (17.6%) indicated that no changes in numbers had occurred in the past 5 years. Twenty-eight (54.9%) indicated that they had experienced an increase; 10 respondents (19.6%) had experienced a decrease; 3 indicated that they did not have data (5.9%), and 1 respondent (2%) stated that the numbers were increasing in elementary schools but decreasing in secondary schools.

When asked to anticipate changes in the number of positions during the next 10 years, 7 respondents (13.7%) indicated that they expected no changes. Thirty-two (62.7%) respondents anticipated an increase; 5 respondents anticipated a decrease (9.8%); 6 did not have data (11.8%); and 1 respondent (2%) expected an increase in elementary school positions and no change at the secondary school level.

If respondents observed an increase or decrease in numbers of school counseling positions, they were asked to identify the factors contributing to the change. For decreases, respondents identified the following factors: funding problems (5 responses), decrease in population (5), low birthrate (1), and retirements (1).

Reasons given to explain increases included the following factors: increase in the number of elementary and middle school positions (13 responses), increased student populations (8), recognition of benefits of school counseling for high-risk students (7), state mandates (6), use of a developmental model (4), Southern Association of Colleges and Schools standards (4), increased funding (3), improved public support (2), local priorities (2), attempts to reduce student-to-counselor ratios (2), quality of programs (1), career-placement positions in high schools (1), broadening roles (1), actual student needs (1), increasing graduation rate (1), expanding school curriculum (1), and the increased need for alcohol and drug counselors (1).

When asked about changes in proportions of positions in elementary, middle, and high school counselors, 9 respondents (17.6%) indicated that no change had occurred. Twenty-six (50.1%) respondents indicated an increase in elementary positions; 2 indicated a decrease in elementary positions (3.9%); and 14 either gave no answer or their answers were unclear (27.5%).

Respect for School Counseling

Respondents were asked to consider the status accorded school counseling in their states by the public. Twelve (23.5%) respondents indicated that no change had occurred during the past 5 years. Thirty-two (62.7%) indicated an improvement during the past 5 years; 1 respondent (2%) indicated a decline; and 6 either failed to respond or did not report a pattern (11.7%).

Respondents were given an opportunity to provide explanations for either an improvement or decline in the status accorded school counseling by the public. The explanations cited for improvements included the following: public relation efforts (3 responses), visibility (2), accountability (1), extensive competencies of counselors (1), parent involvement (1), less paperwork (1), more emphasis on individual and group work (1), better communication and awareness (1), focus on at-risk youth (1), developmental model (1), better understanding (1), and more counselors serving all students (1).

The only respondent reporting that respect for school counseling had declined cited as an explanation that secondary counselors were perceived as working only with college-bound students and with schedules.

Effects of NBCC and CACREP Standards

Respondents were asked to consider the impact of the NBCC and CACREP standards on the preparation and employment of school counselors. The respondent from Maine reported that nationally certified counselors in that state were considered more qualified and received preferential treatment in employment or certification. Nine (17.6%) respondents indicated that graduates of CACREP programs were considered more qualified or were in some way given preferential treatment in employment or certification in their states (Alaska, Arizona, Idaho, Maine, Maryland, Mississippi, Ohio, South Carolina, and Texas). Respondents from Illinois and North Carolina indicated that the CACREP standards had been used as a guideline for state-approved program standards. Four respondents (7.8%) did not answer the questions related to NBCC and CACREP standards. Remaining respondents indicated that NBCC ($n=46$, 90.2%) and CACREP ($n=36$, 70.6%) made little or no difference in employment decisions.

Important Issues in School Counseling

The respondents were asked to identify the most important issues facing school counselors during the next 20 years. The most frequently mentioned issues included accountability (14 responses), recruiting and employing well-prepared school counselors (14), maintaining a developmental focus (13), working with special populations (11), and role definition (10). Other respondents cited pre-service and in-service training (6), funding (6), public relations (5), and career education (5). Other issues identified were competency-based programs (1), consultation (1), coordination of services (1), licensure (1), individualized guidance plans (1), expectations (1), state-level support (1), ethical issues (1), computer technology (1), proliferation of mental health workers and the need to coordinate programs with these professionals (1), and new training needs in specific content areas (e.g., drugs-alcohol, pregnancy prevention, contagious sexual diseases) (1).

Discussion

The majority of respondents to the survey indicated an increase in the number of school counseling positions. Twenty-seven percent ($n=14$) indicated that insufficient numbers of certified counselors are available to fill existing positions. Difficulty in recruitment seems to be particularly prevalent in rural areas. In addition to the needs identified in this survey, it has been reported that the mean age of practicing school counselors nationally is 55 (Whitledge, 1988). Retirements, coupled with the observed shortages, may make the recruitment of school counselors crucial during the next decade.

Several certification issues were highlighted in the responses. A slight majority of respondents indicated that teaching experience is required for certification as a school counselor. This requirement may discourage or delay entry into school counseling. In a few states, classroom teachers who receive a master's degree in counseling are not paid on the master's degree pay scale while waiting for a school counseling job to become vacant. In these states, teachers who wish to become a school counselor may seek master's degrees in other fields, resulting in a smaller applicant pool when school counseling vacancies occur. Sweeney (1987) reported that some states require a master's degree in teaching in addition to counseling certification and that this is another discouraging or delaying factor in some states.

Of perhaps greater concern nationally is the fact that most of the states reported policies allowing employment in school counseling before the person obtains full certification. Although these policies may be necessary to maintain some semblance of counseling services in the schools, problems related to quality control will be created. Moreover, ethical problems may arise when provisionally employed persons are presented with decisions for which they are not prepared. In addition, these unqualified personnel may not receive adequate supervision or in-service educational programs, resulting in substandard services.

An encouraging finding from this study was the perceived increase in respect for school counseling. Efforts made in the areas of counselor accountability, public relations, and provision of K–12 developmental counseling services are perceived as having a particularly positive impact on the status of school counselors.

Based on the perceptions of respondents, NBCC and CACREP standards are beginning to have some impact on the employment of school counselors. In fact, CACREP seems to have been influential in 11 states (21.6%). It is unclear whether the lack of perceived impact in other states results from the recent implementation of these programs, from lack of familiarity with them, from dissatisfaction with the standards, or from unknown causes.

Implications

In considering implications, it is important to remember that this study reflects only the perspective of officials in the state departments of education. Several certification and employment patterns identified in this study indicate areas that need advocacy with both agencies and legislatures by the American School Counselor Association (ASCA) and the Association for Counselor Education and Supervision (ACES).

If the anticipated increases in school counseling positions are actually realized, the need for recruitment efforts is apparent. This effort should include recruitment of both qualified candidates for school counselor preparation programs and qualified counselors for school districts. In states with small applicant pools for school counseling positions, advocacy may also be needed with local school boards, state departments of education, and legislatures to remove unnecessary "roadblocks" to recruitment (e.g., re-evaluating the teaching experience requirement; making master's degree salaries available to classroom teachers holding certification in school counseling) and to maintain quality in the provisional employment process. Clarification of related supervisory and credentialing responsibilities by state departments of education, counselor preparation programs, and local school districts will be needed.

The impact of NBCC and CACREP standards on school counseling may need to be evaluated after the programs have been in existence for a longer time period. If the lack of perceived impact in several states reflects a lack of familiarity with the standards, then educational information concerning these agencies may need to be incorporated in public relations efforts. If state officers are unfamiliar with these standards, it is even more unlikely that individual principals and personnel officers will recognize the potential significance of the certification or accreditation. If NBCC and CACREP are to prove helpful, the professional organizations must refine these programs and educate decision makers about their use in the preparation and employment of school counselors.

The current support for school counseling indicated by officials is apparent through both the increase in allocations of positions and by the general increase in respect by the public for school counseling. To maintain these gains, several factors will need attention. Quality preparation programs and continued concentration on public relations and counselor accountability will be essential. In addition, professional organizations must continue to influence decision making at the local, state, and national levels through cultivation of positive relationships with legislators, lobbying efforts, and public relations campaigns.

Finally, although definition of the school counselor's role has been addressed in numerous publications, continued articulation of both overlapping and divergent responsibilities and competencies that are required at secondary, middle, and elementary levels will determine the direction for and quality of school counseling. Specialized pre-service training to meet the needs of children and adolescents at various developmental levels will also be necessary as attempts are made to fill the anticipated increase in elementary and middle grades positions.

References

Cecil, J. H., & Comas, R. E. (1987). *Development of strategies for the preservation of school counselor preparation programs* [Monograph]. Alexandria, VA: American Association for Counseling and Development Foundation. (ERIC Document Reproduction Service No. ED 288 111)

Hardy, N. (1988, Fall). AACD school counseling task force: Getting it all together. *The ASCA Counselor, 26,* p. 16.

Sweeney, T. J. (1987). Building strong school counseling programs: Implications for counselor preparation. In G. R. Walz and J. Bleuer (Eds.), *Papers of the 20/20 conference: Building strong school counseling programs* (pp. 287–309). Ann Arbor, MI: ERIC/CAPS.

Walz, G. R., & Bleuer, J. (Eds.). (1987). *Papers of the 20/20 conference: Building strong school counseling programs.* Ann Arbor, MI: ERIC/CAPS.

Whitledge, J. (1988, November). *ASCA greetings.* Remarks presented at the fall conference of the North Carolina School Counselors Association, Raleigh, NC.

Computer Competency: A Means for Learning to Be a Better Counselor

James L. Lee
Charles J. Pulvino

Computers are gaining acceptance in counselor training programs. In most programs computers are used for manipulating data, word processing, or, in some cases, for providing students simulation of the counseling process. The purpose of this article is to point out parallels in learning processes between some of the principles involved in learning to be a counselor and in learning to use computers. A rationale is presented for pointing out to counseling students how learning to use computers is not entirely different from learning to counsel. Seven counseling process principles are presented. Each is discussed from the perspective of counseling and computer usage.

Computers are becoming more widely used for many counseling related functions, such as record keeping (Katz & Shatkin, 1983), data analysis (Harris-Bowlsbey, 1983), information processing (Gerardi & Benedict, 1986), and direct client service (Jason, Pillen, & Olson, 1986). In addition, counselor educators are beginning to see applications of computers in the training of counselors (Cairo, 1984). Lichtenberg, Hummel, and Shaffer (1984) proposed that computer simulation can provide trainees opportunities for practicing meaningful facilitation skills. Froehle (1984) discussed how computers can be used to provide counselor trainees process feedback. Using microcomputers in any of the ways suggested by these authors requires that counseling students learn how to use microcomputers and various software applications.

We have spent considerable time and effort in the last several years learning to program and apply microcomputers in counseling and counselor training. Student counselors respond to learning how to use computers with varying degrees of openness. Some readily see the potential application of computers to help them both as students and as future professionals, especially with word processing and database management systems. Others, however, approach the computer with a great deal of fear and resistance; they view the computer as a technology having little relationship to humanistic qualities that are normally associated with their field. Teaching student counselors how to use microcomputers has led us to believe that learning how to use computers need not be antithetical to learning about the counseling process. Many of the processes involved in learning to use computers and computer applications parallel the process involved in working effectively with clients. When students understand these potential parallels, their motivation for learning to use computers can be enhanced. At the same time, some counseling skills and processes can be enhanced and reinforced while learning to use computers. Outlined below are a number of principles that have emerged from our practice and are offered to show some of the parallels between learning to use computers and learning to effectively work with clients.

Principles

The following counseling principles are important in counselor education programs and are discussed to show how learning to use computers may parallel the learning of counseling principles.

Establishing a relationship. Beginning counselors must learn to overcome inherent fears of interaction and learn how to relate to their clients. These fears often stem from doubts about their own counseling competencies and concern that they might not be able to understand their clients. In a similar manner, when counselors learn how to use computers, they must overcome initial fears: fear of technology, fear of incompetence, or fear of failure. Just as a counselor must begin a counseling relationship by attempting to understand clients and their nuances, the computer student must begin by learning about the computer's makeup; that is, the basic processes that the computer uses to input and output information, and the function of various programs the computer uses to process information.

Learn the client's language. An important principle in counseling is that an empathic relationship is established when counselors enter clients' worlds, when they understand how clients' think about issues central to their life, and when they communicate that understanding. In effect, counselors need to learn the client's language. Counselors cannot expect clients to learn their language.

Similarly, students cannot expect computers to use their "language" (i.e., to respond in direct English). Parallel with counseling, interaction with a computer entails learning how the computer represents information. Understanding computer terminology, software conventions, and programming languages is similar to learning to understand how clients communicate.

Learn to model clients' thinking processes. To learn to use computers effectively, it is necessary to learn how information is processed in specific software applications (e.g., word processing, spreadsheets, database systems, or user-created personal software applications). All software applications are based upon certain assumptions about the nature, form, and function of the information to be processed. Once users become familiar with this structure, they can more creatively use application programs. For example, spreadsheet applications were originally designed for accounting and financial modeling. Individuals who have learned the underlying structure, however, have been able to use spreadsheet programs to develop grade books, to teach mathematical principles, to teach concepts in decision making, and even to maintain client records.

The process of attending to structures that underlie information processing with software or programming languages models the process necessary for being a creative, effective counselor. Regardless of theoretical orientations, those counselors who are able to understand how their clients think about personally relevant issues can have greater flexibility in addressing clients' needs. When counselors know the structure underlying their clients' "programs," they have increased flexibility to try relevant counseling interventions that have a high likelihood of being meaningful in their clients' lives.

Establishing goals and designing specific steps to achieve goals. Once counselors have identified client concerns, counseling goals are established. This can be done a number of ways depending upon the counselor's theoretical orientation and institutional constraints. The general approach for establishing goals used by most counselors is to redefine general goals into progressively smaller units, which are more readily defined and easier to achieve. Successful counseling is frequently defined as the degree to which counselors help clients to define goals and to take steps necessary to achieve those goals. For example, helping a client learn good study habits is usually broken down into smaller objectives like planning, time utilization, note taking, and so on.

Specific goal setting is as central to effective computing as it is to effective counseling. For instance, in using software programs, users must have specific goals in mind. This is true because specific application programs, due to their inherent nature, will limit which goals can be achieved. Some application programs allow for broadly conceived goals, whereas others are much more specific in nature. For example, word processing is an application program that allows for specification and achievement of a broad array of goals. The user can use a word processing application to write many different documents. By contrast, spreadsheets or database applications require that the user have the ultimate goal in mind—what is the information generated by the application going to be used for and what form is it going to take? To accomplish these goals, the user must define specific small units of information that will be used and assess what tasks must be accomplished to achieve the overall outcome.

When one learns to program, one is confronted with the need to reduce large goals into smaller units. To do this, programmers must define the types of outputs desired from the program—the general goal. Once these outputs have been defined, programmers must define specific steps necessary for accomplishing the specified goal(s). Although clients, unlike computers, are creative as well as responsive, they often need help in defining specific steps necessary to accomplish their goals. It is apparent that the structuring of thought and action necessary to accomplish a task on the computer parallels what is needed to help clients resolve complex personal issues.

Obtain feedback about task completion and goal achievement and modify the intervention as needed. One aspect of the counseling process is to obtain feedback from clients about goal achievement. In most situations it is unusual for the initial counseling intervention to be totally satisfactory in reaching desired outcomes. Consequently, counselors must use feedback continuously to adjust counseling interventions to meet the needs and circumstances of clients (Pulvino & Sanborn, 1972).

This process of continual adaptation to dynamic changes also exists when one works with computer applications. Using or programming computer applications usually requires many changes and adjustments before one can meet goals that have been established. For example, as a database is being built, the user frequently discovers other things that would enhance the final product. The art of building a good comprehensive database is related to the user's ability to make *a priori* decisions about what is needed and to make adjustments as needs arise. Users of computers soon learn, as counselors do, that there is a constant adaptation and redesigning that is necessary for achieving effective outcomes.

If what you are doing does not produce the response you want, then try something different. This principle is important in communication and counseling. In a communicative interaction, if you do or repeat the same thing, you probably will continue to receive a similar response from the other person. The key is to *do something different* that will produce the desired response. The caveat in this principle is two-fold. First, you must know what kind of response you want. Second, you must be flexible enough to recognize that you should try something different and have a repertoire of different things to try. This need provides the rationale for teaching counselors a variety of techniques and intervention strategies that can be used with different clients in varying situations. A corollary to this principle suggests that counselors with the greatest flexibility will be the most effective.

Computer students either learn to apply this principle or quickly become frustrated. Whether learning to use a specific application program or learning to program, students soon realize that the computer will respond only to the inputs they make. If the user continues to repeat the same input, the computer will continue to make outputs in an identical manner. The behavior exhibited by these students of exact repetition and consequent frustration with the computer is akin to blaming clients for being resistant. Although clients may be resistant, effective counselors develop flexible ways of responding that either circumvent or utilize the resistance. Learning to use the computer in a flexible manner parallels the flexibility necessary for working effectively with different clients in varying situations.

Creative adaptation and development of intervention strategies. No two clients or client problems are exactly the same. Thus, counselors must continuously and creatively adapt, change, and develop strategies to meet client needs and to help clients achieve goals. There is a similar process using computers to accomplish tasks. A program solution can be solved in a variety of ways. Various programmers will use a different code to produce identical results. Programs that accomplish the same outcomes may vary in length, design, and structure. The same is true in building database systems or spreadsheet applications. One can rightfully conclude that there is more than one right way to write a program or to build a computer application. It is also true in counseling, within certain parameters, that there is more than one right way to counsel, as evidenced by a number of differing theoretical orientations and their resulting intervention techniques.

Summary

Should counselor educators, then, discontinue their extensive counseling skills training efforts and turn to helping new counselors in developing relationships with microcomputers? Of course not! Neither is it suggested that counselors-in-training become computer experts or programmers. Nonetheless, it is truly remarkable how many parallels exist between counseling processes and learning how to use a computer. In many ways the total predictability of a computer, once you have gained knowledge about its operation, is at the opposite end of the spectrum from the inevitable unpredictability of human clients. For the beginning computer user, however, the experience of a computer's unpredictability is likely to be similar to that of dealing with a new client. Eventually, an experienced computer user does begin to approach a predictable understanding of the computer that is never approximated by the counselor in understanding a "real, live" client.

Although learning to use a computer and helping clients are not identical and can never approach such a oneness, it is hoped that this discussion has provided a basis for identifying computer learning as a process not totally antithetical to the learning inherent in becoming an effective counselor.

References

Cairo, P. C. (1984). Investigating the effects of computerized approaches to counselor training. *Counselor Education and Supervision, 24,* 212–221.

Froehle, T. C. (1984). Computer-assisted feedback in counseling supervision. *Counselor Education and Supervision, 24,* 168–175.

Gerardi, R. J., & Benedict, G. C. (1986). Computerized information systems. *The School Counselor, 34,* 105–109.

Harris-Bowlsbey, J. (1983). The computer and the decider. *The Counseling Psychologist, 11,* 9–14.

Jason, L. A., Pillen, B., & Olson, T. (1986). Comp-tutor: A computer based prevention program. *The School Counselor, 34,* 116–122.

Katz, M. R., & Shatkin, L. (1983). Characteristics of computer-assisted guidance. *The Counseling Psychologist, 11,* 15–31.

Lichtenberg, J. W., Hummel, T. J., & Shaffer, W. F. (1984). CLIENT 1: A computer simulation for use in counselor education and research. *Counselor Education and Supervision, 24,* 155–167.

Pulvino, C. J., & Sanborn, M. (1972). Feedback and accountability. *Personnel and Guidance Journal, 51,* 15–20.

Tiedeman, D. V. (1983). Flexible filing, computers, and growing. *The Counseling Psychologist, 11,* 33–47.

Wagman, M., & Kerber, K. W. (1984). Computer-assisted counseling: Problems and prospects. *Counselor Education and Supervision, 24,* 142–154.

Standards and Procedures for School Counselor Training and Certification

Association for Counselor Education and Supervision

Over a period of several years, ACES has had involvement in a number of activities directed toward the enhancement of school counseling, including representation on the AACD School Counseling Task Force, and a series of ACES-ASCA Collaborative Workshops, as well as a SACES working conference, supported by the AACD Foundation. Each of these activities has resulted in specific recommendations for action by ACES; none has been formally implemented.

Careful review of all of the recommendations resulted in the identification of two dominant themes that are especially relevant for the work of the Association. The first is the urgent need to establish consistency in the application of professional standards across school counselor preparation programs, accreditation of school counselor preparation programs, and credentialing of school counselors by state education agencies. The second is the necessity to engage in review and possible revision of school counselor curriculum, with emphasis given to curricular areas identified as weaknesses.

Recommendation I

That ACES initiate, immediately, strong efforts to bring about greater standardization of the counselor preparation programs, the accreditation of school counselor preparation programs, and the credentialing of counselors to work in school settings.

Implementation

Suggestions for implementation of this recommendation are included, but are not limited to, the following:

1. ACES reaffirms its support for two-year, graduate level programs of preparation for school counselors, including supervised internship in a

school setting as described by the Council for Accreditation of Counseling and Related Programs (CACREP) standards.

2. ACES promotes and endorses the use of the CACREP Standards as minimum requirements for certification of school counselors in all states in the United States, and, further, endorses the full term of supervised internship as described by CACREP standards.

3. ACES will involve itself in the CACREP Standards review process by establishing a representative group (i.e., committee; task force) for the purposes of: (a) receiving, reviewing, and evaluating proposals for changes in CACREP Standards, as they relate to school counseling; (b) formulating proposals for change and allowing ample time and opportunity for the membership to react to those proposals; (c) inviting participation of ASCA in the review process; and (d) monitoring closely, through report from the ACES representative to the CACREP Council, the proposals being considered by the CACREP "Standards Revision Committee" for changes in the 1993 Standards for preparation of school counselors.

4. ACES will develop and implement methods of networking that involve ACES members at the regional and state levels in the promotion of uniformity of certification/licensure standards for school counselors across states. A lobbying package, prepared by a national committee, will be distributed to regional and state leaders. That package will clearly outline the association's goals for school counseling, provide strategies and activities for implementation of the goals, and encourage strong and sustained participation at the state level. Contacts will be encouraged with ASCA counterparts, state education agency certification officers, state guidance coordinators/consultants/supervisors, school administrators, and school boards to bring about changes in certification standards that are reflective of professional preparation standards, allow for reciprocity across states, and empower school counselors to design and implement comprehensive, developmental programs of guidance and counseling.

Recommendation II

That ACES assume leadership for encouraging increased focus on the review and revision of school counselor curriculum. In each of the various school counseling reports, existing curricular weaknesses have been clearly targeted. Chief among these are the areas of: (a) needs-based program development, (b) multicultural concerns and issues, (c) developmentally-based intervention strategies, (d) research, (e) counselor supervision and (f) development of school-based internships.

Implementation

1. ACES will extend to ASCA an invitation to provide representative participation in any formal efforts directed toward school counseling curriculum review and revision.

2. The ACES Executive Council will include as an annual and long-term goal for the association a clear focus on the enhancement of school counselor preparation. This goal will be accomplished through use of the ACES regional meetings and the AACD convention as vehicles to provide a forum for: (a) discussion of position papers dealing with school counseling curriculum; (b) sharing course syllabi that reflect innovative method, content, and/or activities; (c) describing attempts to transform school counseling programs, especially when the transformation has been adjudged effective; and, (d) development of school counselor oriented pre-convention workshops that provide continuing education units for NBCC or other related certification.

3. Through the Executive Council, the Editor and Editorial Board of *Counselor Education and Supervision* will be informed of the association's goals for school counseling, will be sensitized to the issues involved, and will be requested to give strong consideration to filling the current Editorial Board vacancy with an individual with recognized expertise in school counseling.

4. Through the Executive Council, the ACES Resources and Research Interest Network (along with regional counterparts) will be requested to give strong consideration to funding at least one proposal that encourages school counseling innovation and evaluates the effectiveness of that innovative practice.

5. Should it be funded, ACES will actively support the proposed ASCA-ACES-AACD collaborative project submitted in December to the AACD Foundation. The proposed project addresses many of the recommendations made in the reports of the AACD School Counseling Task Force and the ACES/ASCA Collaborative Workshops.

6. The ACES Secretary will be charged with disseminating press releases describing efforts to implement any of the foregoing recommendations and any outcomes resulting from implementation to the *Spectrum, Guidepost,* and ASCA *Counselor.*

Chapter 3

Developing a Comprehensive, Developmental School Counseling Program

Counseling in high schools must change if it intends to make a significant difference in the lives of students. For the last decade, writers and researchers have criticized high school counseling. Aubrey (1982) maintained school counseling lacked a sense of its mission. Day and Sparacio (1980) argued that both public criticism of school counselors and deviations from their intended roles might seriously weaken their professional image while Peer (1985) proposed that secondary school guidance is in serious trouble unless and until secondary counselors assume the initiative in stimulating their communities and states to assist in revitalizing their guidance programs. Perhaps one of the reasons high school counseling is not perceived as more successful is that counseling programs are not guided by statewide or districtwide plans. School counseling program planning has been considered an exciting and viable idea for many years, but surveys reveal an absence of meaningful planning at both the state and district levels. The articles in this chapter focus on issues related to school counseling programming, ranging from a descriptive portrait of existing programs, to a case study of how one district changed its counseling program.

In the first article, Oliver C. Moles examines the results of a survey of directors of secondary school guidance programs in a nationally representative sample of public high schools. The author discusses the survey results as they relate to the College Entrance Examination Board's recommendations for changes in school counseling which include: broad-based planning for determining the needs of students; counselor leadership in monitoring and promoting student potential; more parent involvement in the choices, plans, decisions, and learning activities of students; and greater collaboration with the community. Moles' findings can serve as a springboard for serious discussion about the current status and future directions of counseling in today's schools.

While the school reform movement has largely ignored school counseling, counselors must not make the mistake of ignoring the school reform movement when trying to improve counseling programs. Counselors have always been encouraged to understand the context in which they work. That context, the school, is undergoing enormous change. The author of the second article, M. Donald Thomas, a former superintendent, describes the Effective School Movement and suggests ways counselors can promote positive, supportive, people-oriented school climates.

Developmental guidance is not a new idea, but it is one that needs reaffirmation at least once every decade. John C. Dagley's article describes a model for developmental guidance programs that provides specific direction and substance for the school counselor's goals and activities. He suggests a framework for addressing student needs and includes goals and activities in three distinct areas of competency: lifelong learning, personal effectiveness, and life roles.

Barriers to change are legion. Change takes time—something few counselors believe they have. Change implies that counselors know what student outcomes they want to achieve. Too many times, counselors have not established student-oriented goals and objectives. In today's school, change may even mean getting the approval of the teacher's union for a new job description. All in all, change ain't easy. However, Northside Independent School District has changed its guidance program as well as the role of the school counselors in their program. In the last article in this chapter, Patricia Henderson describes "eleven steps to change" that worked in her district. Henderson says that successful program improvement must include a vision, a willingness to make the commitment to change, and a cautious and careful approach to ensure quality changes.

References

Aubrey, R. F. (1982). A house divided: Guidance and counseling in 20th century America. *The Personnel and Guidance Journal, 61,* 198–204.

Day, R. W., & Sparacio, R. T. (1980). Impediments to the role and function of school counselors. *The School Counselor, 27,* 270–275.

Peer, G. G. (1985). The status of secondary school guidance: A national survey. *The School Counselor, 32,* 181–187.

Guidance Programs in American High Schools: A Descriptive Portrait

Oliver C. Moles

The field of secondary school guidance is undergoing intensive reappraisal. Counselors and educators agree that such programs are in need of ongoing examination. They have noted public criticism of school counselors and role changes that may seriously weaken their professional image (e.g., Day & Sparacio, 1980; Peer, 1985). Critics have observed the brief and occasional nature of pupil contacts, the emphasis on a therapeutic counseling role that disregards how the school environment may affect students, and the general lack of coherent theory and practice in guidance and counseling (Sprinthall, 1980).

In the same vein, the College Entrance Examination Board established a commission in 1984 to study precollege guidance and counseling. The commission held dialogues across the country with counselors, high school students, school administrators, parents, staff of local youth-serving agencies, and many others. They also visited special programs, reviewed recent writings, consulted with the major professional associations, and commissioned special analyses.

The commission's report (College Board, 1986) concluded that although the school reform movement has largely ignored guidance and counseling, the guidance services offered by most high schools are important to school success, especially for at-risk youths. It also asserts that school counseling as a profession is in trouble because of structural changes in the profession—required administrative tasks that are irrelevant to counseling, high student:counselor ratios, and cutbacks in funding for counseling programs. Among a number of recommendations, the commission urged individual secondary schools to take the following actions:

- Establish a broad-based process for determining the guidance and counseling needs of students and how to meet them.

- Develop school programs under the principal's leadership that emphasize the guidance counselor as a "monitor and promoter of student potential, as well as a coordinator of the school's guidance plan." (College Board, 1986, p. 11)
- Inform and involve parents in the choices, plans, decisions, and learning activities of students.
- Strengthen collaboration of schools with community agencies, colleges, businesses, and other community resources to enhance available student services.

The commission tapped a wide range of involved persons and sources of information and made a number of important recommendations. Even those close to individual programs, however, were not selected in a way that would allow for scientific generalization from their experience to programs across the country. Thus, one may ask how well the findings and conclusions of even astute and diverse observers coincide with the actual experience of guidance programs nationwide if each program reported for itself.

There is little data from broadly representative samples of the key actors in secondary guidance and counseling. One exception is Peer's (1985) study of state guidance directors. He found considerable support for the concerns of earlier analysts. State directors expressed strong concern about the use of counselors in nonprofessional tasks, the programs that serve primarily the college bound, the "underdelivery" of established services such as career guidance and group counseling, and the vulnerability of programs to cutbacks.

The notion that career planning guidance may not reach all students is amplified in another study. Using national sample survey data from High School and Beyond (HS&B), a longitudinal study of sophomores and seniors beginning in 1980, Lee and Ekstrom (1987) found that students from lower socio-economic status families, those of minority status, and those from small schools in rural areas were less likely to have access to guidance counseling for planning their high school course of study. These same students were then more likely to be placed in nonacademic tracks and to take fewer math courses.

A second study using HS&B data noted that youths in schools emphasizing counseling and in which counselors expressed positive attitudes about the program tended to have higher career goals and college attendance. Where school guidance programs emphasized occupational information, students demonstrated less improvement on test scores (Hotchkiss & Vetter, 1987). These findings suggest that the nature of guidance programs may make a difference in student careers, although the authors cautioned that the relationships are not strong and that the study needs replication.

With both the potential strengths and weaknesses of guidance programs in mind, directors of secondary school guidance programs in a nationally representative sample of public high schools were surveyed about the priorities and activities of their programs. Examination of their responses may help to assess both the vulnerability of programs to the criticisms levied and their strengths.

Study Design

This study is based on questionnaire responses from the heads of guidance programs in a national sample of high schools. Only public schools were included in this analysis, because the activities and role of guidance counselors in private high schools are considerably different (Bryk, Holland, Lee, & Carriedo, 1984). These public schools constitute a subsample of the HS&B study, a major data source on secondary student achievement and development sponsored by the U.S. Department of Education. HS&B is a national longitudinal study of sophomores and seniors in 1980 who were queried thereafter at 2-year intervals to 1986 regarding their further education and careers.

In the spring of 1984 a consortium of research centers supported by the U.S. Department of Education collected data from teachers and administrators on school programs, practices, and improvements in almost half of the original 1,015 HS&B schools. This study is known as the Administrator and Teacher Survey (Moles, 1988). The heads of public school guidance programs in this survey (n=333) came from a subsample of 505 public and private schools. The overall response rate for guidance program heads was 80%.

The current study describes salient features of high school guidance programs as reported by these heads of guidance programs. The results are organized by the broad categories of guidance activities in the typical high school: staffing and staff development, program development, program goals and priorities, broad activities, specific guidance activities, and the director's assessment of guidance programs. The data have been weighted to represent the public high schools of the nation, and cases with missing data (usually less than 5%) have been removed so that percentages and other statistics refer only to those responding. The findings are stated in words identical or very similar to those used in the 62-item questionnaire of the Administrator and Teacher Survey (Moles, 1988), and all appropriate questions from it were used.

Staffing and Staff Development

Most of the directors of the high school guidance programs surveyed are white men, have over 10 years experience in guidance counseling, and have five or more years experience in their current position as director. Seven percent are Black and 3% report a Hispanic or Spanish origin. Nearly all of the directors (86%) have a master's degree in guidance and counseling.

School guidance heads may have various titles such as director of guidance, director of student services, or lead counselor. Respondents could choose as many titles as applied to their position. Almost half (48%) also described themselves as "counselors," suggesting more than administrative responsibilities. In some places an administrator (8% of the schools) or teacher (3%) is the head of the guidance program. This kind of dual responsibility would seem to restrict the professionalization of guidance personnel and prevent guidance counselors from playing the prominent role in school guidance plans envisioned by the College Board (1986) report. On the other hand, the majority of public high schools do seem to have a separate, specialized guidance staff.

The program heads, or directors as they will also be called, spent an average of 45% of their time administering the guidance program. The average guidance program at a high school had 2.4 full-time professional staff members, although the number of staff will obviously vary with the size of the school. Fewer than 1% of the directors worked half-time or less.

Guidance counselors are reasonably active in professional development activities. Directors reported that the typical counselor attends three in-service programs each year. The typical staff member also attended an average of 5.5 meetings of professional organizations, 3.8 meetings with employers, 2.5 meetings with community groups such as the Rotary or Chamber of Commerce, and 4.1 topical conferences during "the past school year."

Program Development

The College Board Commission on Precollege Guidance and Counseling recommended use of a broadbased process for determining the guidance and counseling needs of students and how to meet those needs. Several items on program development in the questionnaire apply to this recommendation. A third (33%) of the schools had a committee for planning, implementing, evaluating, and reviewing the guidance program. Among these schools, the committees typically included the principal (78%), teachers (66%), and guidance counselors (94%). Committees less often included students (45%), parents (51%), local employers (24%), or community representatives (27%)—groups that the College Board Commission advocated including to increase the credibility and effectiveness of school plans. Lack of community and business representation is particularly unfortunate given the need to prepare many students for immediate job entry.

A written plan for the career guidance program had been prepared in over half of the schools (56%), and one-third (31%) of these schools had "developed or thoroughly revised" their plan within the current (1983–1984) school year. The benefits of developing and using the plan were judged to outweigh the time and resources required to develop it in only a little over one-third (36%) of the schools and were judged about equal to the costs in another 41% of schools with written plans.

Considering that half (49%) of these schools spent less than 20 hours of time in reviewing, revising, and rewriting the plan, and that another 29% spent only 20–59 hours, the expenditure of time by staff and nonschool personnel was not large for most endeavors. Why more directors did not see greater benefits in the plan's development and use than costs of preparation cannot be determined from available data. If guidance staff, however, are required to perform many nonguidance tasks or find their ranks cut or caseload increased, guidance directors could feel that significant aspects of guidance work are beyond their control and planning. This could also make the creation of program plans less meaningful. More understanding of plan development is important if the planning process, and particularly the use of written plans, is to gain greater acceptance.

Program Goals and Priorities

The directors ranked the emphasis placed by their guidance programs on promoting academic achievement, personal development, postsecondary education, and future work plans of students. As shown in Table 1, they reported the greatest emphasis on helping students plan and prepare for postsecondary schooling and on helping students with academic achievement (means of 2.7 for each goal, or slightly above the midpoint on a scale in which 1 is *lowest emphasis* and 4 is *highest emphasis*). These goals were closely followed by helping students with personal growth and development (mean of 2.5). Least emphasized was helping students prepare for their work roles after high school (mean of 2.0). None of these means, however, is different from any other by statistical significance standards (.05 level of probability).

Table 1
Goals for Guidance Programs: Means of Rankings

Goal	Currently emphasized	Desired by guidance staff	Desired by school administrators	Desired by teachers	Desired by parents
Help students with their academic achievement in high school[a]	2.7	2.6	3.2	3.6	2.9
Help students plan and prepare for postsecondary schooling	2.7	2.3	2.4	2.1	2.2
Help students with personal growth and development	2.5	3.1	2.4	2.6	2.6
Help students plan and prepare for their work roles after high school	2.0	2.0	2.0	1.7	2.3

Note. 1 is lowest, and 4 is highest emphasis.
[a]Phrased as "Help students improve their achievement in high school courses" in the question for columns 2–5.

When the same four goals were ranked in terms of what the guidance staff, including the head, would like to see emphasized, the pattern shifted (see Table 1). The most *desired* goal was helping students with personal growth and development (mean of 3.1), followed by helping with academics (2.6) and helping with postsecondary educational plans (2.3). Helping students prepare for future work roles again came last with the same average ranking (2.0) as was given for current program emphasis. (Only this lowest rank and the highest are significantly different from each other.) This suggests that if guidance staff had their say, programs would not be strongly oriented toward students with immediate occupational plans.

Program heads were also asked their perception of the goals of other key actors for guidance programs. As shown in Table 1, the most favored goal perceived among school administrators, teachers, and parents was clearly helping students improve their academic achievement in high school courses (means of 3.2, 3.6, and 2.9). The gap between this and the next most-favored goal was large for administrators and teachers, although not statistically significant for any group. Nevertheless, the relative rankings suggest a tension with the guidance staff whose clear first preference is to help students with personal growth and development. Other staff and parents were believed to see helping students with personal growth and development as the second most important goal. For administrators this second place was tied with helping students plan and prepare for postsecondary schooling, which was ranked third by teachers and fourth by parents.

The school administrators and teachers were perceived to support current program emphases and the desires of guidance staff in giving lowest priority to helping students plan and prepare for work roles after high school (means of 2.0 and 1.7). The parents were seen to favor this goal only slightly more than their least favored one, which was helping students prepare for postsecondary schooling (means of 2.3 and 2.2). Thus, the low emphasis of guidance programs on helping students prepare for work roles is reinforced by administrators, teachers, and parents, at least as viewed by guidance directors. For parental desires, however, the goal rankings cannot be distinguished by statistical significance standards, and for administrators and teachers only the highest and lowest rankings are significantly different.

Finally, one may ask whose priorities most closely match the guidance program's current emphases. Table 1 shows that school administrators, teachers, and parents, but not the guidance staff, were perceived to prefer helping students with academic achievement in high school most, which was one of the two most-emphasized goals of the current guidance programs. The second highly emphasized current program goal, helping students prepare for postsecondary schooling, was rated second along with personal growth and development by administrators and was given a lower rank by all other groups. Personal development was a close third in current program emphasis (see Table 1). From such ratings, the school administrators seem to have the most influence over the goals of guidance programs, as one might expect from their position of leadership in the school, although the lack of statistically significant differences among these rankings tends to blur distinctions among the goals.

In summary, three of the desired goals were ranked very similarly by staff and parents, as reported by the directors: helping students with academics, personal growth, and preparation for postsecondary schooling. Helping students prepare for work roles after high school was ranked last by all but parents.

Broad Activities

The differences in current emphasis among the four goals are generally compatible with the directors' reports of time spent by guidance staff in various broad areas. Only 28% of the staffs spent 15% or more of their time on job placement and employability skill development with 11th and 12th graders, in keeping with the low goal emphasis on helping students prepare for work roles. In contrast, 87% of the staffs spent 15% or more of their time on students' postsecondary education plans, and 71% spent the same time on choice and scheduling of upper-level courses in high school, activities related to the goals of helping students with academics. Somewhat more ambiguously, 15% or more of their time was spent on occupational choice and career planning by 77% of the staffs, an activity relevant both to future work roles and to post-secondary education. Finally, the goal of helping students with personal growth and development is closely related to work on attendance, discipline, and other school and personal problems. These activities consumed 15% or more of time for 63% of the staffs. But, they may also have included some of the paperwork that counselors dislike.

Directors estimated that the typical counselor spent an average of five hours per week outside of school hours on guidance activities, and another four hours on other school activities such as monitoring athletic events and making up class schedules. This suggests both a strong commitment to counseling and also a good deal of use of counselors for the kind of nonprofessional tasks that have worried critics.

Specific Guidance Activities

A number of possible staff activities were also presented to guidance directors. Their responses regarding time spent in each are grouped by goal and summarized in Table 2. On activities related to academic achievement, the most emphasized and widely preferred goal, guidance staff spent an estimated 20% of their time. Included in these activities were conferring with teachers about individual students; planning, administering, and interpreting tests; and preparing and monitoring individual education plans (IEPs) for handicapped students. A large proportion of the staffs (42%), however, spent no time on IEPs, which is somewhat surprising since IEPs are required nationally for all handicapped children.

On preparing students for postsecondary schooling, only one question regarding staff time was uniquely relevant. Guidance staff spent about 6% of their time meeting with recruiters from postsecondary institutions. They also spent 7% of their time directing planned career guidance activities, which could also apply to future work roles. Data not shown indicate that most schools do provide a range of activities relevant to postsecondary activities for their juniors and seniors, such as courses on career decision making, tests for career planning purposes, career information resources, and tours of postsecondary institutions.

In the third goal category, student growth and development, the staff devoted a quarter of their time to individual counseling, and another 8% to group guidance or counseling. Everyone spent some time providing individual counseling, and only 8% provided no group guidance or counseling. Here again, the categories are not entirely discrete since counseling may also concern academic performance and postsecondary plans. But, it is noteworthy that this large expenditure of time coincided with the desire of guidance staff to make this area a first priority. In fact, four of five students (79%) had at least one individual counseling session sometime during their junior or senior year, and 57% had at least one group guidance counseling session, as reported by the guidance directors.

Table 2
Time Spent by Professional Guidance and Counseling
Staff in Various Activities

Activity	Percentage of staffs with no time spent	Average percentage of staff time[a]
Student achievement in high school		
Conferring with teachers about individual students	3	9
Planning, administering, and interpreting tests[b]	1	9
Preparing and monitoring IEPs	42	3
Postsecondary schooling		
Meeting with recruiters from post-secondary institutions	4	6
Directing planned career guidance activities[c]	7	7
Student growth and development		
Individual counseling (not test related)	0	25
Providing group guidance or counseling (not test related)	8	8
Future student work roles		
Developing contacts with business and industry	41	2
Meeting with military recruiters	3	4
Various guidance activities		
Teaching guidance-related courses or units	41	4
Conferring with teachers about the guidance program	10	5
Committee work (except committees preparing IEPs)	16	4
Nonguidance activities		
Administrative duties	20	8
Teaching classes	76	3
Hall duty, study hall, homeroom, lunchroom duty, bus duty, or disciplining students	48	3
Directing extracurricular activities	44	3

Note: 1% to 5% missing data on all activities (7% on activities concerning individual education plans) were excluded from this analysis.
[a]Fractions of 100% column total.
[b]Also relevant to Various guidance activities.
[c]Also relevant to Future student work roles.

For those students who participated in counseling sessions as juniors or seniors, the typical student had four or more individual sessions in almost two-thirds of the schools (65%) and four or more group sessions in half of the schools (52%). If spread evenly over time, this amounts to about one individual session per semester in two-thirds of the schools, and fewer in the other schools. Nevertheless, only about half of the seniors in the student surveys of HS&B reported that a guidance counselor had influenced their plans for after high school (Lee & Ekstrom, 1987). So use of counseling services, at least for career planning, may be much more restricted than the data from the directors alone would lead one to assume.

The final and least emphasized goal, helping students prepare for future work roles, is represented by three questions in Table 2. Directing planned career-guidance activities, also applicable to postsecondary education, took an average 7% of counselor's time; developing contacts with business and industry, 2%; and meeting with military recruiters a bit more of their time, 4%. Perhaps most striking is the report that 41% of the staffs spent no time at all developing contacts with business and industry, an area of collaboration recommended by the College Board Commission and an important source of job leads for students not going on to college. Vocational education staff probably develop some of these contacts, however, so many schools are not necessarily without these connections.

Some kind of job-oriented activities offered in most high schools (88% or more) would not take much staff time, and questions regarding these activities were asked in another context. These include career days and vocation-oriented speakers, job site tours, student use of career information resources, and exploratory work experience programs.

A few other activities described in Table 2 could apply to various guidance goals: teaching guidance-related courses or units; conferring with teachers about the guidance program; committee work other than on IEPs; and planning, administering, and interpreting tests. Combined, these took up an estimated 21% of staff time.

A set of nonguidance activities took one-sixth of the guidance and counseling staff time as well (see Table 2). These are nonguidance administrative duties and, less commonly, teaching classes unrelated to guidance, supervising school areas and buses or disciplining students, and directing extracurricular activities. Although the direction of extracurricular activities and bus duty are likely to occur outside normal school hours, these nonguidance activities in total still take a substantial amount of the professional's time. These nonguidance activities, however, seem to be clustered in certain schools, perhaps the smaller ones that have more limited staff resources. Table 2 shows that in three-quarters of public high schools professional guidance staffs do *not* teach unrelated courses, and in about half of the schools, staffs have no general supervisory or disciplinary responsibilities, nor do they direct extra-curricular activities. The criticism of using guidance staff for nonprofessional school duties would seem most applicable to perhaps half of all American public high schools.

If students want to see counselors, directors in three-quarters of the schools (75%) said they can be seen within a few minutes, and in another 11% within a few hours. (Two-thirds of the directors [66%] said that students can take time from math, English, or other subjects to take part in guidance activities.) So as reported, almost all students have ready access to counselors. But the generally large number of students per counselor suggests that some might have to wait. Moreover, only about half of the sophomores in the HS&B student survey said they had talked to a guidance counselor about planning their school program (Lee & Ekstrom, 1987). Thus, the reality of counselor contacts and influence on the entire student body may be considerably less than these indicators of access would imply.

A different sort of activity is the staff linkage with parents. The College Board Commission urged that parents be informed and involved in the choices, plans, and learning activities of students. Program directors were asked how many parents met with counselors to confer about career decisions of their children. For a typical school year, only 10% of the school counselors conferred with 33% or more of the parents, and another 32% conferred with 11%-30% of the parents. On this important point of career decisions, clearly most parents in most schools are not in contact with the counseling staff. This stands in stark contrast to the 93% of directors who reported that success in working with parents was of moderate or major importance to the director's supervisors in judging the quality of the guidance program. The need to mount better programs to inform and involve parents, as the College Board Commission recommends, would seem to be recognized by most program directors.

The College Board Commission also encouraged the use of computer programs both to reduce administrative and clerical duties and also to assist students in making choices, plans, and decisions on careers and colleges. The use of computers to schedule students into classes was reported by 43% of the program directors, and use of online administration of tests and inventories by 11%. Regarding student career planning, 78% of the programs used computers for career information, 27% used computers for teaching career decision-making skills, 37% for simulated occupational exploration experience, and 8% for teaching resume and job application writing skills.

The use of computers for "career information" probably refers to one of the computerized proprietary state or local career information systems available in many schools. Except for this, computers are used by well under half of schools in their guidance programs. The potential of computers to help guidance counselors promote student progress, as envisioned by the College Board Commission, remains untapped by many schools.

Director's Assessment of Guidance Programs

A majority of the directors seemed satisfied with their school's guidance services. Unfortunately, these data do not indicate how satisfied the students and teachers, who are the consumers of guidance services, are. Eighty-three percent of the directors agreed with the questionnaire statement that "the guidance services at this school are unusually successful in meeting student needs." Specific aspects of their work were also rated by the directors.

They felt that the goals and priorities of the guidance program are clear (mean of 4.4 on a scale in which *strongly agree* is 6 and *strongly disagree* is 1) and that the school administration had a clear philosophy regarding the guidance program (mean of 4.2). They also believed that there was a great deal of cooperative effort among staff members (mean of 4.4) and that most of the guidance staff share their own beliefs and values on the central mission of the school (mean of 4.7).

On the other hand, the directors were more likely to feel that the school does not reward counselors for performing their jobs well (mean of 3.0) and that routine duties and paperwork interfere with the job of counseling (mean of 4.2). Taken together they neither agreed nor disagreed that guidance staff members are recognized for a job well done (mean of 3.4) or that financial support for the guidance program in their school was adequate compared with support for other departments in the school (mean of 3.7). They gave somewhat higher marks to community support (mean of 4.0) and parent support (mean of 4.2) of their school's school's guidance program. In these cases, the question asked if they were "very supportive," so this mild agreement really represents a somewhat stronger endorsement.

Discussion

The results of this national sample of public high school guidance program directors paint a rich and varied picture. Although these findings only present the guidance directors' perspective and may not adequately represent the views of others on whom they report, these directors are still key actors in ongoing programs and any plans for improvements. What they report must be taken seriously, even when it is their perception of what others think and do.

It is instructive to reexamine the criticisms of guidance services in light of the findings just presented. In response to several questions, the guidance directors reported a diversion to nonguidance activities. The one-sixth of staff time spent on various nonguidance activities in and out of school hours, including the approximately 4 hours per week after school, suggests that a substantial amount of staff time is not being used for guidance purposes (see Table 2). The largest part of this seems to be nonguidance administrative tasks. The directors also tended to agree that routine duties and paperwork interfere with their main job. Nevertheless, many directors reported no staff time spent on four key nonguidance activities: hall or lunchroom duty, administrative duty, teaching nonguidance classes, and extracurricular activities (see Table 2). Guidance staff working in these nonguidance activities seems to be concentrated in about half or fewer of the high schools of the nation.

Regarding another criticism, the student:counselor ratio stands at approximately 350:1 based on student data from HS&B, somewhat greater than the 250:1 ratio urged by the counseling profession (College Board, 1986). With this high ratio, it would seem that few students can get personal attention. The directors' claim that few students wait long to be seen does not necessarily mean that counseling services are adequate to students' needs, although they may be adequate to student demand. The lack of any counselor influence on their school program or post-high school plans, reported by half of the sophomores and seniors (Lee & Ekstrom, 1987), also indicates that for whatever reason many have no counselor assistance with major decisions.

The concern with program cutbacks expressed by the College Board Commission and others is no doubt a real problem for some schools. Directors as a whole, however, do not believe that financial support for the guidance program in their school is inadequate compared with support for other departments in the school.

A few schools did not offer some basic guidance activities: testing and test interpretation for career planning (8%), group counseling (6%), training in job seeking skills (8%), and use of computerized career information resources (10%). In contrast, large numbers of staffs spent no time teaching guidance-related courses or units (41% of schools); a few spent no staff time providing group counseling (8%) or directing planned career guidance activities (7%), as shown in Table 2. All of these services might have been victims of program cutbacks or perhaps never were available in some places. Either way, some basic guidance services are lacking in 6%–8% of public high schools, and guidance-related courses are lacking in many more.

The four College Board Commission recommendations for action at the individual-school level can now be reviewed in light of the information from this national survey. The first recommendation, to establish a broad-based process for determining the guidance and counseling needs of students and how to meet those needs, is clearly needed in many schools. Only a third of the schools had a committee to plan and review their guidance programs. Approximately half of these committees included students and parents, and one-fourth included local employers or community representatives. Thus, a consultative planning process is not in place in two-thirds of the nation's public high schools. Where one exists, it frequently excludes persons who should be key participants in the guidance process. It could be that the lack of enthusiasm for written program plans expressed by many directors would be improved if a broader range of persons provided input. The inevitable complexity of considering more viewpoints might be outweighed by more realistic advice and practical suggestions from those receiving the services and others providing local employment and career opportunities.

The College Board Commission also recommended strengthening collaboration with community resources including businesses. This seems to be a very real need in many places, judging from the 41% of schools that spend no time at all contacting businesses and industries and the miniscule percentage of time spent on this (see Table 2). We have already seen that businesses or community representatives are not often involved in program planning. The chances for business and school collaboration are dimmed by not bringing them into the planning process.

The commission also recommended informing and involving parents in the choices, plans, decisions, and learning activities of students. The evidence presented here suggests that most parents in most public high schools are not in contact with the counseling staff about their children's career decisions. Only 10% of the counselor staffs conferred with 33% or more of parents, and other staffs conferred with fewer parents. The commission suggested that active encouragement and outreach to parents might be necessary to involve them in the full range of guidance activities, including curricular choices of students. The commission also recommended phone calls, discussion groups, conferences during later hours to accommodate working parents, and the use of paraprofessionals.

The commission's central recommendation to develop school guidance programs with the counselor as coordinator, and also as monitor and promoter of student potential, gains support from several sets of findings. First, the heads of guidance programs seem ready for such a task. Almost all have training beyond the bachelor's level, and 86% hold an advanced degree in guidance and counseling. Most have 10 or more years of experience and have held their current position for at least 5 years. Thus, in most places the directors are well versed in their field. Second, the directors sensed a strong common purpose among the guidance staffs. They rated cooperative effort and shared belief in the central mission of the school highly. They seem to believe that they have a dedicated staff to rely on.

Several factors may limit the ability of guidance counselors to assume such a central role. One is the substantial amount of time devoted to nonguidance tasks. A second is the total absence of conferring with teachers about the guidance program or individual students in a few schools and the low proportion of time (13%) spent on these combined activities elsewhere (see Table 2). Creating opportunities for more such contacts with teachers and other school staff would seem important if guidance staff are to play the coordinating role envisioned by the College Board Commission. Third is the lack of recognition, reflected in the directors' feelings that counselors are not rewarded for performing their job well and in the directors' neutral stance on whether counselors are recognized for a job well done. Such views could undermine the motivation to assume a more prominent role and may reflect actions by others that minimize the guidance staff's role in student development.

In seeking to monitor and promote student potential, guidance staffs are likewise handicapped by the three points discussed previously. In addition, the infrequent counseling sessions with students, estimated at only once a semester for juniors and seniors in two-thirds of the schools and less in others, limit opportunities to influence students. Counseling sessions are likely to be even less common if the student reports of infrequent contact with guidance counselors are taken into account. The high proportion of White and the few Black and Hispanic directors suggest the need for more minorities who know intimately the students' cultural backgrounds to head guidance programs in areas with large minority populations, and in more places in the future as well, because increasing proportions of students will be minorities (Hodgkinson, 1985).

Guidance programs currently give lowest priority to the preparation of students for work roles after high school, and all groups would place this goal last according to the directors' rankings (see Table 1). This suggests that the nation's guidance programs are not serving well, nor do they want to serve, those students who will drop out or end their formal education with high school graduation. For example, only 28% of the staffs spent a significant amount of time on job placement and employ-ability skill development with juniors and seniors. Also, many schools do not offer a course on career decision making (31%), job shadowing (25%), or exploratory work experience programs (12%) to juniors or seniors. The absence of contacts with business and industry in many schools further suggests a slighting of preparation for employment immediately after high school. How well this goal can be addressed by counselors while also performing their other duties with limited resources is, of course, a serious problem; nevertheless, some students seem to receive much less attention than others. Their numbers are not small; half of all high school graduates do not go on to college.

The overall picture from this study of public high schools reveals an experienced and dedicated guidance staff working to provide important guidance services on top of substantial nonguidance demands in many schools. Some schools do lack basic guidance services, and most could probably do more to help students who will end their formal education with high school. The current program priority of helping students with academic achievement in high school may help job-oriented students to some extent, and the preference of guidance staff for helping students with personal growth and development could also benefit the many who will end their formal education with high school. Because many students report no contact or influence by guidance counselors, a more aggressive stance toward seeking out students, particularly minorities and the disadvantaged, seems necessary to bring guidance services to those most in need.

The College Board Commission (1986) recommendations for broad-based planning, more parent involvement, and collaboration with the community are yet to be realized in many, if not most, high schools. The commission's recommendation to make the guidance counselor the central figure in the school's guidance plan, although supported in some ways, is limited by factors such as infrequent contact with most students, little time spent on coordination with the teaching staff, and various nonguidance responsibilities. Educators and counselors should welcome the College Board report and the findings of this study as an opportunity to think critically about the current status and future directions for guidance and counseling programs in the nation's public schools.

References

Bryk, A. S., Holland, P. B., Lee, V. E., & Carriedo, R. A. (1984). *Effective Catholic schools: An exploration.* Washington, DC: National Catholic Education Association.

College Board. (1986). *Keeping the options open—Recommendations: Final report of the Commission on Precollege Guidance and Counseling.* New York: College Entrance Examination Board.

Day, R. W., & Sparacio, R. T. (1980). Impediments to the role and function of school counselors. *The School Counselor, 27,* 270–275.

Hodgkinson, H. L. (1985). *All one system: Demographics of education, kindergarten through graduate school.* Washington, DC: Institute for Educational Leadership.

Hotchkiss, L., & Vetter, L. (1987). *Outcomes of career guidance and counseling.* Columbus, OH: National Center for Research in Vocational Education, The Ohio State University.

Lee, V. E., & Ekstrom, R. B. (1987). Student access to guidance counseling in high school. *American Educational Research Journal, 24,* 287–310.

Moles, O. (1988). *High school and beyond administrator and teacher survey (1984): Data file user's manual.* Washington, DC: Office of Educational Research and Improvement, U.S. Department of Education.

Peer, G. G. (1985). The status of secondary school guidance: A national survey. *The School Counselor, 32,* 181–189.

Sprinthall, N. A. (1980). Guidance and new education for schools. *The Personnel and Guidance Journal, 58,* 485–489.

The Counselor in Effective Schools

M. Donald Thomas

The Effective School Movement, initiated by Ron Edmonds, is rapidly becoming the most powerful reform effort to implement the recommendations made by the various school reform reports. The common-sense approach of *effective* school practices is appealing to both educators and the general public. It is an effort in which counselors can play an important part to restore the credibility of what they have been saying for a long time—schools are for people and not for objects.

The effective school research states clearly that a positive, supportive, people-oriented school climate is basic to effective schools. It is in this area that counselors can make their contribution establishing a school climate from which the other correlates of effectiveness can be implemented.

The culture of a school is made up of several elements. The major elements are purpose, quality, affection, collegiality, teamwork, recognition, and character. It is these qualities that counselors can promote best.

They are the "soft data" of schools to balance the "hard data" of effectiveness: achievement, test scores, attendance, dropout ratios, and expenditure per pupil. Although both are needed to establish effectiveness, the "soft" items are a precondition to the "hard" ones.

Here is what counselors can do to promote a positive, supportive, people-oriented school climate—a culture that values both students and teachers:

1. Support the position that success for every student is the basic purpose of schools. Make success the measure by which everything the school does is measured. (Establish the position that educating every student well is a basic purpose: that it is the moral equivalent to war.) It is important to succeed because society depends on students' being well educated. It is important to the nation socially, economically, and aesthetically. To counselors, seeing that every student is a winner must be similar to the War on Poverty or the Save the Whales Campaign. It is immensely important—and attainable.

2. Expect the best from everyone. Establish quality as the minimum performance. Promote a school environment that expresses quality, attractive surroundings, art pieces on display, comfortable offices, neat dress, plants inside and outside of the building, classical music, and so on. Let everyone know that each has a special obligation to be a model for others. Providing a model for excellence is as important as the curriculum—and counselors must articulate that as often as they can.

3. Express affection for the students and help others to do the same. Point out to staff members that frequent contacts with students support learning and enhance the worth of individuals, especially if the contacts show interest in the person's welfare. Many individuals are extremely lonely in school. Counselors can appreciate the need for human affection, for support systems, and for assisting students through difficult emotional experiences. Stress the position that it is still appropriate to like students—that liking them is a prerequisite to effective teaching.

4. Promote collegiality and teamwork in the school. Develop the idea that whatever is done is best done as a group effort. Stress that teamwork is built on that belief that everyone can make a contribution, that all individuals are worthy, that working together brings satisfaction and establishes pride. Teachers and other staff members need to feel that they are part of a winning team—that each person is important.

5. Initiate a comprehensive recognition program for staff members and students. All people are motivated by recognition, status, identification with success, and personal attainment. Recognition programs should be broad so that there are many winners—not just a few. Counselors can identify large numbers of students who have small and large successes in their school lives. Counselors can also help staff members to look for improvements in what students do—to recognize that some students overcome tremendous odds to succeed in school.

6. Promote ethical practices, or as Edward Wynne said, "Establish schools of character." These are schools in which staff members and students learn and practice character traits that support trust, honesty, loyalty, fairness, justice, and equal opportunity. Such schools also protect the rights of individuals, promote historical principles associated with an open democratic society, and hold each individual accountable for his or her own actions. In such schools, all members practice good citizenship behaviors, use peer influence to correct inappropriate acts, and protect the "commonweal" of the school above personal interests. Character is expressed in the individual acts of people and in the operation of the school.

Some counselors may say that they are already too busy doing their jobs without trying to establish a positive school climate. Others may say that establishing an appropriate climate is the responsibility of the principal. Some may even claim that climate is the primary responsibility of the athletic department. What should be appreciated is that in many schools, counselors—the people who know best how to create a good climate—are rarely asked to do so. In such cases, counselors should take the initiative to do what they know how to do—make schools satisfying places for students and staff members. In doing so, counselors will have greater self-esteem and be valued more by all members of the school.

Counselors may need help with the political processes that are required to convince others that climate is a necessary precondition to effectiveness. Here are a few suggestions:

1. Collect information about items that indicate the status of school climate: attendance levels for staff members and students, drop-out ratio, attitudes toward school, school pride, vandalism expenditures, discipline problems, suspensions, social problems, and so on.

2. Compare these data to the corresponding data for effective schools—not any group of schools, but to a subgroup of effective schools. Such schools have usually been identified by the U.S. Office of Education, the state departments of education, or the Network of Effective Schools.

3. Discuss the school data with the principal and demonstrate to the principal where improvements can be made. Be sure to indicate what counselors can do to make those improvements. Impress on the principal that improving the climate is the "meat and potatoes" of any school improvement effort. Present possible strategies for staff involvement, so that the principal feels secure in knowing that staff support can be developed.

4. Discuss the data with selected teachers to indicate the counselors' interest in improving school climate. Indicate to teachers the benefits that come with school climate improvement. Encourage teachers to become active in the activities of school climate improvement groups: The National Council for Self-Esteem and CADRE (The Collegial Association for the Development and Renewal of Education). Both groups can provide extensive assistance in school climate improvement cfforts.

5. Develop some ideas related to school climate and present them to the staff for their consideration. Show them the typical data for effective

schools that have a positive climate. Express the desire of counselors to work on school climate, indicating that you have the support of the principal and other faculty members.

6. Establish task forces to develop plans to improve specific parts of the school climate. Each task force should be under the supervision of a staff member who has some knowledge of school climate improvement efforts. Task forces should make periodic reports to the entire staff.

7. Reward school members for improvements made and objectives achieved. Rewards need not be monetary. Recognition and status rewards are just as effective. Provide certificates, recognition luncheons, small, low cost products (date book, pen-and-pencil set, briefcase, etc.), all of which give recognition for results.

Counselors are the key to school climate improvement efforts. They have the training, the experience, and the expertise to make it happen. They are dedicated to improving the quality of life in our school. In becoming more aggressive in this area, counselors reaffirm their beliefs in the dignity of all individuals and in the ability of all to contribute to improvement efforts.

After all, it was on the basis of those beliefs that most of us became counselors. In schools in which such beliefs are practiced, effectiveness seems to occur more often than in schools in which they are not in operation. A vital part of that effectiveness is determined by school counselors. It is an appropriate responsibility for counselors to assume.

As I said in the beginning, the effective school reform efforts are rapidly becoming the major strategies for improving schools. For counselors, this is a most fortunate occurrence. It is an opportunity for them to demonstrate their importance to the school and to the success of the school. It is an opportunity that many counselors have waited a long time to develop.

A New Look At Developmental Guidance: The Hearthstone of School Counseling

John C. Dagley

> Developmental guidance is a reaffirmation and actualization of the belief that guidance is for all students and that its purpose is to maximally facilitate personal development. (American School Counselor Association, 1979)

The work of the school counselor has long been characterized by a strong belief that guidance is for all students and that the purpose of guidance is to promote maximum personal development in all spheres of life. Counselors have experienced some difficulty in the past, however, when they have attempted to translate personal development goals into action. In this article I describe a model for developmental guidance programs that provides specific direction and substance to the school counselor's goals and activities. The model adds substance and a framework for integration to the general principles of development previously targeted as essential to comprehensive programs of guidance and counseling in the schools (Allport, 1965; Mosher & Sprinthall, 1970, 1971; Sprinthall, 1973; Zaccaria, 1965).

Goals of a Guidance Program

A guidance program can be most effectively implemented when its goals and activities are well defined. The comprehensive guidance model presented in this article provides a framework for addressing student needs, but allows the specific nature of a program to vary according to local needs and resources. The program includes goals and activities in three distinct yet overlapping areas of competency: lifelong learning, personal effectiveness, and life roles. As shown in Table 1, these inter-related competency areas (described below) further define and give substance to the meaning of maximal personal development.

Table 1
A Developmental Guidance Model—Outcomes

Personal Effectiveness Competencies

Self-understanding
Identity
Autonomy
Acceptance and validation

Human relations
Respect and empathy
Social interest
Conflict resolution

Health development
Intimacy
Leisure
Growth stages

Lifelong Learning Competencies

Communication
Reading and writing
Listening
Expressiveness and assertiveness

Information processing
Study and analysis
Evaluation
Problem solving

Personal enrichment
Time management
Renewal
Change

Life Roles Competencies

Daily living
Child rearing
Consumer
Community involvement

Career planning
Values clarification
Decision making
Planfulness and goal setting

Employability
Self-placement
Work habits
Educational and occupational preparation

Lifelong Learning Competencies

Change is so much a part of modern life that a person is no longer able to "learn something, once and for all." Because of the current knowledge explosion, in which the quantity of new information increases exponentially, learning is not merely a worthy leisure time pursuit; instead, it is a requirement for effective living. To become lifelong learners, students need to master the basics in the following three areas:

1. *Communication skills.* To participate effectively in the learning process, an individual must be confident of his or her ability to learn. Because confidence in learning largely depends on the development of communication skills, a lifelong learner needs to be competent in listening, speaking, reading, and writing. Among the outcomes for an individual who has developed these skills well are expressiveness and assertiveness.

2. *Information processing skills.* Faced with unprecedented amounts and varied sources of information, learners need help in analyzing, evaluating, and making constructive use of information. To process information as it relates to daily life, learners must possess study and problem-solving skills.

3. *Personal enrichment skills.* The increasing complexity of life requires a commitment to personal growth and change and professional renewal. Faced with unrelenting time pressures, individuals can easily fall into a quagmire of daily routines. To do so is to stagnate. Personal growth, career advancement, and career change require time management as well as continuous learning skills. More specifically, individuals need to assume a personal responsibility for growth.

Personal Effectiveness Competencies

Human development occurs as a continuous process, with or without intervention. Individuals learn to interact with others, effectively or ineffectively. The challenge for guidance personnel is to intervene systematically in such a way that young people develop healthy self-concepts and effective interpersonal skills.

1. *Self-understanding.* Feelings of competence, confidence, and self-acceptance are difficult to achieve in a mistake-conscious society. The task of developing positive feelings about oneself is complex and elusive. Building a firm sense of personal identity and autonomy requires self-appraisal skills and opportunities for students to test their

mettle. Otherwise, they may see more than they understand, observe more than they participate, and respond more to peer pressure than they act according to their own volition.

Through development of the ability to validate their own sense of worth, students can be stimulated to shift from an external locus of control (one's sense of personal value depends on evaluations of peers) to an internal locus of control (personal valuing is natural and nonjudgmental). Encouragement needs to become a more noticeable part of every child's school experience because effort deserves recognition, regardless of the comparative quality of that effort. Students need to build the courage to be imperfect, to catch themselves feeling good and doing well, and to appreciate and accept their own unique characteristics (Dreikurs, 1967).

2. *Human relations skills.* Mutual respect and empathic understanding are key contributors to successful human relationships. These qualities, conflict resolution competencies, and other important interpersonal relationship skills can promote effective classroom learning, improve interpersonal relationships among employees and marital satisfaction, and increase general interpersonal involvement. The need for such skills is demonstrated by:

- The increasing number of employees dismissed because of interpersonal conflicts rather than job skills.
- A growing sense of alienation from society fostered by depersonalized interactions with transient neighbors and anonymous bureaucracies.
- The high percentages of marriages ending in divorce.
- Rising rates of crime, violence, and vandalism.
- The struggle of various groups in developing new relations (i.e., men and women, majorities and minorities, subcultures, and nations).

Social interest, a term defined by Alfred Adler (1931), refers to the feelings of genuine concern for others within us all that need to be evoked and nurtured to maturity. Social interest can enrich our relationships with significant others, because, in the area of human relationships, there is no substitute for a genuine interest in others.

3. *Health development skills.* Traditionally, the focus on health in American society has been remedial and rehabilitative rather than preventive or habilitative. Attention is now shifting toward the development of attitudes and skills that enhance physical and mental health. To promote better physical health, medical professionals can encourage

people to increase their exercise or other physical activity to balance the sedentary activities often engaged in during educational and occupational pursuits. To promote better mental health, professionals in this area can encourage people to develop varied and lasting avocational and leisure-time interests that will help balance the heavy emphasis usually placed on vocational pursuits when those individuals reach young adulthood. In addition, by understanding the issues and concerns of various growth stages of adulthood, individuals may be able to reduce stress and enhance the quality of their lives.

Intimacy is not typically described as a skill, but in this model it is defined as a developmental task comprised of specific human relations skills and personal characteristics that combine to enable a person to achieve self-enhancing intimate relationships with others. Unfortunately, many people have assumed that they automatically learn how to achieve intimacy, particularly with those of the opposite sex; reality, though, as indicated by the inequality and shallowness of some intimate relationships, would suggest that this developmental task remains an elusive goal.

Life Roles Competencies

Throughout an individual's life span, he or she encounters many roles, settings, and events. The roles a person may experience include friend, sibling, producer, spouse, parent, student, consumer, and citizen. The roles are experienced in and are related to various settings—school, home, workplace, community—and to several important events—formal education, entry-level work, career advancement and change, marriage, retirement, birth of children, death of loved ones, and possibly economic and social crises. The degree of happiness and success experienced in these encounters and events can be enhanced by developing specific skill areas.

1. *Daily living skills.* Northcutt's studies of adult performance levels (U.S. Office of Education, 1975) showed that almost one-fourth of American adults can be considered functionally incompetent as consumers. Moreover, most of today's consumers lack the knowledge and skills needed to function without difficulty in everyday life. Too few adults have mastered the basic organizational and computational skills involved in such daily tasks as balancing a checkbook or making the most economical purchase of variously priced foods. In addition, society can no longer afford to assume that child-rearing skills will develop

automatically. The need for these skills is particularly urgent and important for new teenage parents, who now account for approximately 20% of annual births (Jaslow, 1982). Other daily living skills requiring added attention are citizenship and community involvement.

2. *Career planning skills*. An uninformed choice is no choice at all. Informed and reasonable choices are based not on error or accident but on planning. A sense of personal freedom and control over one's destiny requires motivation, a commitment to planning and preparation, and the abilities to defer short-term gratification for long-term goals and to choose among a multiplicity of educational and occupational options. In addition, maturity in career decision making requires a knowledge of personal interests and abilities resulting from experience. When young people are supported in efforts to clarify and to build personal value standards and priorities, they can master the developmental tasks of career planning and goal setting. Special assistance should be provided to minorities, women, and other groups as they encounter special needs related to shifting career patterns and opportunities.

3. *Employability skills*. Because work is such an integral part of life, students deserve opportunities to acquire marketable skills and to build an understanding of the world of work based on experience. Employability skills include effective work habits, job-seeking skills, self-placement competencies, and a knowledge of the occupational and educational requirements and needs of the working world. Students need to understand what it is like to work, not only in their roles as students or as part-time workers, but also as part of the full-time labor force.

The goals described above constitute a new outlook for developmental guidance and provide added substance to the traditional work of school counselors.

The content of a comprehensive guidance program is shaped by the needs of both youths and adults. Although the nature of local program goals may vary according to priorities, a high quality guidance program possesses the following key characteristics:

- Goals are based on identified student needs.
- Goals are sequentially organized, K–12, according to the continuous process of human development.
- Goals are sufficiently comprehensive and specific to encourage the personal development of all students in all guidance-related areas (lifelong learning, personal effectiveness, and life role competencies).

Guidance Activities and Processes

Comprehensive guidance programs consist of a great variety of activities. In the list below, I present a summary of the kinds of guidance-related activities that school counselors, teachers, administrators, and various support personnel can provide. The categories of activities—curriculum based, individual development, on call or responsive, and system support—are offered as an organizational framework for understanding the work of a guidance team.

These categories should be conceptualized as flexible rather than rigid because many of the topics can be addressed in varied formats depending on the unique needs of students and schools. Implementation of a comprehensive program requires a balance of activities in each of these interactive categories.

A Developmental Guidance Model: Processes

Curriculum-Based Activities

1. Courses: career development, psychological education
2. Mini-Courses or Units: reading and study skills, human relations training and communication skills, health development and leisure skills, human sexuality, marriage and family living, consumer and daily living, moral development, decision-making skills, goal-setting skills, time-management skills, stress reduction skills

On-Call and Responsive Activities

1. Developmental Guidance Groups: motivation for achievement, reduction of test anxiety and relaxation training, drug awareness and education, assertiveness and expressiveness training, orientation for incoming and outgoing students
2. Group Counseling: divorce adjustment, death education, conflict resolution, personal growth, adjustment to a stepfamily
3. Individual Counseling: crisis intervention, personal development
4. Consultation: staffing and referral
5. Peer Counseling

Individual Developmental Activities

1. Advisory System: educational and career planning, parent involvement program, decision-making skills, values clarification
2. Self-Placement Program: employability and job-seeking skills, development of personal credentials, work exploration experiences (either home based, community based, or school based), independent learning projects, career guidance centers, computer interaction system, multimedia kits and materials

System Support Activities

1. Staff Development Program
2. Standardized Testing Program
3. Program Planning and Management
4. Groups for Parent Education, Student Government, and Orientation
5. Supervision and Training of Paraprofessionals and Peer Helpers
6. Community Relations
7. Development of Materials
8. Process and Outcome Evaluation
9. Alternative Funding Sources

Curriculum-Based Activities

The curriculum-based category brings together those guidance activities that take place primarily within the regularly scheduled curriculum. These activities may be part of regular school subjects or they may be organized around special topics in the form of units, short courses, or modules. They are based on need statements, instructional goals, and performance objectives necessary for the growth and development of all individuals. Typical topics may include self-understanding, interpersonal relationships, decision making, value clarification, and career development. School counselors may be involved directly with students through class instruction (commonly referred to as classroom guidance), group processes, or individual discussion. In other instances, the guidance staff may work directly with teachers to provide resources and consultation.

Individual Development Activities

Individual development activities include systematic intervention strategies designed to assist all individuals in continuously monitoring and understanding their growth and development in terms of their own personal goals, values, abilities, aptitudes, and interests. The goal is to help students assume more personal responsibility for tracking their progress in learning. In this context, traditional placement programs are replaced by programs in which the emphasis changes from doing something for students to helping them perform some placement activities themselves. The counselor or teacher can accomplish this by helping them to acquire employability and job-hunting skills. Thus, school counselors and teachers serve in the capacity of "advisers," "learning managers," or "development specialists." Personalized, continuous involvement is stressed rather than superficial contact with each student once a year to fill out a schedule. The activities in this category provide the individual accountability needed in a school to ensure that the uniqueness of each student is not lost and that educational resources are being used to promote optimal personal development. In performing these activities, counselors may become involved in cooperative planning with several significant persons; such guidance programs may also focus on concerns outside of the school as well as those within it.

On-Call and Responsive Activities

On-call activities are considered immediate and direct responses to meet specific individual needs. Activities in this category include direct service provided for students by the counselor. Individual counseling and developmental group counseling are important programs of this type. These counseling services support the curriculum-based and individual development activities, but differ in that they are more restrictive in responding only to students who need such support and intervention. Peers, paraprofessionals, volunteers, and support staff members may aid school counselors and teachers in carrying out on-call or responsive activities. Peers can be involved in tutorial programs, orientation activities, and leadership in formal dialogue centers. Paraprofessionals and volunteers provide meaningful service in career guidance centers, community liaison, and club leadership.

System Support

Varied support activities are required if other intervention strategies are to be effective. A comprehensive guidance program includes staff development and administrative activities, orientation and testing programs, materials acquisition and development efforts, and activities to improve school learning environments. The focus in this category of activities is more indirect and is often group oriented. Effective counselors have for many years developed curriculum materials and have disseminated these to teachers to help enhance students' self-understanding and related affective areas.

Many methods and techniques are available for developmental guidance and intervention in a comprehensive program. The selection of particular strategies and activities will vary according to annual priorities, locally identified needs of students, and the competencies and resources of the guidance team; however, the following characteristics should be evident:

- The program reflects a balance of activities in each of the major process areas (curriculum based, individual development, on-call or responsive, and system support).
- Program activities are implemented by a guidance team, not just by the counselor.
- Program activities are selected on the basis of evidence of effectiveness and efficiency in meeting the identified needs of students.

In the process and outcome models described above, I have presented a comprehensive perspective on the work of a school counselor. This substantial program of developmental guidance activities offers the school counselor the opportunity to contribute significantly to educational excellence. Developmental guidance can, in fact, become the hearthstone of school counseling.

References

Adler, A. (1931). *What life should mean to you.* New York: Putnam.

Allport, G. (1965). Psychological models for guidance. In R. L. Mosher, R. F. Carle, & C. D. Kehas (Eds.), *Guidance: An examination* (pp. 13–23). New York: Harcourt, Brace & World.

American School Counselor Association. (1979, April 1). Developmental guidance. *ASCA Counselor, 16,* 2–3, 11–12.

Dreikurs, R. (1967). *Psychodynamics, psychotherapy, and counseling.* Chicago: Alfred Adler Institute.

Jaslow, C. K. (1982). *Teenage pregnancy* (Highlights: An ERIC/CAPS fact sheet). Ann Arbor: University of Michigan, Counseling and Personnel Services Clearinghouse.

Mosher, R. L., & Sprinthall, N. A. (1970). Psychological education in secondary schools: A program to promote individual and human development. *American Psychologist, 25,* 911–924.

Mosher, R. L., & Sprinthall, N. A. (1971). Psychological education: A means to promote personal development during adolescence. *The Counseling Psychologist, 2*(4), 3–84.

Sprinthall, N. A. (1973). A curriculum for secondary schools: Counselors as teachers for psychological growth. *School Counselor, 20,* 361–369.

U.S. Office of Education. (1975, November 5). Adult performance level study. *Manpower and Vocational Education Weekly.*

Zaccaria, J. S. (1965). Developmental tasks: Implications for the goals of guidance. *Personnel and Guidance Journal, 44,* 372–375.

How One District Changed its Guidance Program

Patricia Henderson

Northside Independent School District has changed its guidance program and the roles of the school counselors in that program. This article is about how the changes were made. It is not an article about the entire program development process; that is rather fully described in *Developing and Managing Your School Guidance Program* (Gysbers & Henderson, 1988). Nor is it an article elucidating a theory of change; instead I have provided highlights of Northside district's experiences, which seem to have worked. I hope that by reading about these experiences, counselors in other schools will feel emboldened to work to change their programs and working conditions. (Northside is a medium-sized school district with more than 48,000 students. There are 31 elementary schools, nine middle schools (Grades 6–8), five comprehensive high schools, and several special schools. There are currently 107 counselors.)

The premises underlying the change efforts in the Northside district are: (a) Changes are made by people and (b) for people to make changes, they must feel dissatisfied with "what is," believe in a vision of "what could be," feel that making the changes that are called for would be valuable, and believe that change is possible.

The 11 steps taken first by counseling and administrative leaders and subsequently by all of the counselors and their principals are as follows:

1. Commit to change.
2. Establish leadership to steer the change process.
3. Adopt a program model that provides the vision of what could be.
4. Identify the discrepancies between what is and what could be.
5. Define the vision operationally.
6. Set goals for the changes.
7. Enlist the support of those who can help you reach your goals.
8. Help all school counselors feel competent to make the needed changes.

9. Collaborate with others who will be affected by changes.
10. Make effective changes in program strategies.
11. Evaluate the changes made.

Commit to Change

Making a commitment to change is no small task. Change requires that some hard decisions be made, involves work, and takes time. Change leaders need to be identified and be committed to making the decisions, doing the work, and spending the time.

In Northside district, the school-district-level administrators (superintendent, deputy superintendent, associate superintendent, and director of guidance) echoing the dissatisfaction of some campus administrators and counselors, clearly stated that they wanted changes in the guidance program. They asked formal and informal leaders of the school counselors to tell them what changes to make. They also wanted to or did participate in the determination of the nature of change—the definition of the vision of what could be.

The director of guidance developed an outline of the steps that would be required to effect real and permanent changes in the program and proposed a time frame of three years. This seemed to be too long, especially to the administrators who wanted change now, but it took three years to arrive at full-scale implementation of the program changes. It has now been five years, and changes are still occurring at the program strategy level.

Establish Leadership to Steer the Change Process

As a school counselor, you cannot overhaul your program by yourself. You must have administrative support. In planning changes, you need to involve the people (or their representatives) who will be affected by the changes. Key people include your district or building decision makers and policy setters, the counselors who staff the program, and the consumers of your program.

In Northside district, a steering committee was established by the director of guidance and the associate superintendent for instruction. The charges to this committee were to define a basic structure for the program and to guide the change process. The members of the committee included the deputy superintendent, the associate superintendent for instruction, and other central office directors who represented the consumers of the program, specifically, the directors of elementary, secondary, vocational, and special education. Also serving on the committee were principals and counselors from each of the school levels (i.e., elementary, middle, and high). For change efforts at the building level, teacher and student representatives would also be included. A decision about whether to involve parents and community representatives on such a steering committee depends on the local situation, but advisory committees made up of lay people are useful.

Having cross representation on the committee establishes, from the outset, a team approach to decision making by administrators, counselors, the central office, and representatives of the building-level staff. Not only does this approach bring counselors and administrators together on the same team, it provides a model of teamwork as desirable for the rest of the district and the process. The team approach also better ensures that when changes are made they will be the *right* changes. In Northside district, right was defined as follows: When agreement is reached, you will have made decisions that reflect what the system wants, what the consumers want, and what the counselors want. Also, as these decisions are made, the members become the educators of those who have to change: The counselors communicate with the other counselors, the principals with principals, and the other program administrators with their department staff members.

Adopt a Program Model That Provides the Vision of What Could Be

The Northside Guidance Steering Committee's first task was to adopt a program model that represented the goal of the change efforts, the vision of what could be. The committee learned about varied ways guidance programs could be organized. The program in Northside district had been organized by the list of duties that school counselors perform, such as counseling individuals, interpreting test results, consulting with parents, and so on.

The committee chose the comprehensive guidance program concept. The leadership decided on the following criteria for a program, that it should:

- Serve all students in a developmental mode and some students who present problems that threaten their success in school.
- Assist all students in developing and applying skills needed to enhance their personal, social, career, and educational development.
- Make optimum use of the professional skills of the school counselors: teaching, guiding, counseling, consulting, and referral.
- Apply the program resources equitably across all three school levels.
- Define the guidance program as an independent program within the overall educational program, as well as a support system to other programs.
- Further define the guidance program as having four components through which it serves its clients: the guidance curriculum, the individual planning system, responsive services, and system support (Gysbers & Moore, 1981).

Northside district chose to change the basic concept of the program and then to change the strategies used within the program. It is also possible to go the other way around: to decide to change the program strategies and aggregate these changes into an overall design change.

Identify the Discrepancies Between What Is and What Could Be

Before you can change your existing program, you must know what that existing program is. This allows you to identify discrepancies between what you are currently doing and what you want to be doing. This step results in the concrete specification of your dissatisfaction with what is.

Assessing the current program entails a lot of work not only by the change leaders but also by the counselors. In Northside district, defining the current program in terms of the new program model meant gathering and analyzing an enormous amount of data, such as who the clients were, what skills and outcomes they were being helped to attain, how and in what proportion the counselors' professional skills were being used, and how their time was being spent.

Northside district's school counselors defined the various roles that they played, kept logs of their time, and identified student outcomes from the program activities as well as the people they worked with and the various nonguidance programs they supported. The compiled data were analyzed and aligned according to the four program components of the new model. It took a year to gather and study the information.

Much was learned about the existing program and in many ways quantified what district staff members already knew. Counselors and their special skills are the basic resource of the guidance program. How they spend their time is of the utmost importance in determining the shape of the guidance program. From the time studies, staff members learned that different counselors conducted their jobs differently by making individual choices about what they did each day. For example, some spent lots of time in individual counseling; some spent lots of time doing paperwork. All of them spent relatively small amounts of time doing some of the 23 duties that were defined. The counselors learned that some activities took a lot of time to achieve modest student outcomes; that elementary counselors did more group developmental guidance than did counselors at other levels, but that high school counselors spent the same proportion of time in *individual* developmental guidance. The staff also learned that parents did not get much of the school counselors' time, and that teachers did—in some instances more time than the students.

The Steering Committee led the data analysis process and presented it in detail. The counselors were assisted in their efforts to compare and contrast the current program with the desired program by the counselors from the Steering Committee. The principals were also provided information about the discrepancies that had been identified. It was clear that there were discrepancies between the priorities of the current program and those desired for the program, as shown in Table 1.

Assessment of the program helped counselors to better understand the program model, to be clearer about why they and others were dissatisfied with the current program, and to be extremely aware that change was coming. It also helped them to feel comfortable that change decisions would be based on data-documented problems rather than on some individuals' impressions or perceptions of the program.

Define the Vision Operationally

This step results in the specification of what could be. It entails defining the model in concrete terms, a realistic ideal to try to achieve. The definition states the design for the program. Making the definition

Table 1
Guidance Program Priorities by Component

Component	Current program priorities			Desired program priorities		
	Elementary	Middle	High	Elementary	Middle	High
Guidance curriculum	4	4	4	1	1	2
Individual planning	1	3	3	2	1	1
Responsive services	3	2	2	2	3	1
System support	2	1	1	4	4	4

Note. 1 = highest priority; 4 = lowest priority.

operational includes identifying what elements of the current program fit into the new program, identifying what new elements are needed and what needs to be dropped.

Whatever your model, the portrayal of the realistic ideal needs to relate to the program model you have set out to achieve. Thus, the Northside Guidance Steering Committee defined the proper balance between the program components. Because the district's priority was developmental guidance, the committee established percentages of time that counselors at different levels should spend on such activities: elementary, 40%; middle school, 30%; and high school, 25%. The committee also recommended that elementary counselors spend 10% of their time in system support activities; middle and high school counselors, 15%. These represented major shifts in use of counselor time.

One challenge in improving a guidance program is to maintain what is good and to change what needs to be changed. Applying elements of the current program that fit into the new program concept has provided a foundation for building the new program. The major activities that make up the Individual Planning System component, such as educational and career planning, test results interpretation, and orientation to new school settings are basic stock in any guidance program. Northside district's counselors had been spending approximately the right amount of time on these activities, but the Steering Committee established new priorities for how they were to spend this time. The committee stated that, for example, helping ninth graders get off to a good start in high school is an important priority, as is helping sixth graders make a successful transition to middle school. These priorities caused the design of new activities.

The counselors were spending an appropriate amount of time in Responsive Services, but were serving too few students and parents. Thus, group work has become the basic mode of counselor functioning. Counselors are expected to respond rather than react (e.g., to do planned, small-group counseling, at all levels, with students on topics that are known to recur, rather than to react to those students who present themselves at their doors).

Some traditional activities have been dropped. School counselors in Northside district are appreciated for their contributions to the education of students; problems associated with mental illness need to be attended to in the community. Time consuming quasi-administrative and clerical tasks, which accounted for much of the time spent in the System Support component, have been delegated to clerks or to other department staff. At the elementary level, counselors spend less time on activities related to special education; at the secondary level, they spend less time on maintaining student records.

The counselors and principals who were not on the Steering Committee needed continuous education about the program, the priorities, and the directions for change. All of the leaders for guidance program change helped others to grow in their understanding of the new design. Many hours of discussions were held, workshops done, and exercises conducted that helped to make the program components meaningful. But the most important educational tool has been the written program description; it is called the *Northside Comprehensive Guidance Program Framework* (Northside Independent School District, 1986). The power of the written word for promoting change is astounding.

Set Goals for the Changes

The Steering Committee stated the goals and priorities for change. The goals were broadly stated: For example, counselors should spend more time in developmental guidance and less time in system support. They should strive for more effective involvement of parents in their children's schooling and problem solving. They should provide more group counseling for students with school-related problems.

Because of the interrelatedness of the guidance program with other programs, it was evident that changes could not just happen. A list of wants-needed-for-change-to-occur, the order in which they were needed, and a time frame for accomplishing them was developed. The development of the Master Plan (the 1–100 year plan) made it clear to others what was needed.

The "want list" is one way to help the counselors feel that the changes that are to be made are valuable to them. They should see in that list some items that they strongly want. In addition, with the clarification of the realistic ideal and the specification of the change goal areas, the counselors who have not been part of the leadership should begin to feel good about improved opportunities for using their unique skills. Administrators should by now have renewed understanding of the valuable contributions counselors can make if they are provided the opportunities to apply their skills.

A useful exercise was to have groups of counselors and administrators brainstorm about ways to accomplish the change goals. It educated them about the desired changes and helped them to see new ways to change. The ideas were shared with relevant others in the district.

Enlist the Support of Those Who Can Help You Reach Your Goals

Although written guides and plans are available, the change goals are clear and the guidance leadership team is feeling optimistic, the change leaders are not operating in a vacuum nor have they the power to respond to all the change needs. Even to attain the goals that counselors can achieve for themselves, others must be involved who will be affected by the operational changes that are about to occur. Support must be sought from other school counselors, other district and campus administrators, faculty, parents, and students.

To reach the goals set, Northside's counselors learned to be assertive in communicating what they wanted from supporters. At this point in the change process, counselors needed to empower themselves to express their needs. Most of the big, costly changes were beyond their power to obtain directly, such as lower ratios, improved job descriptions, larger materials budgets, and appropriate facilities. It was the counselors' responsibility, however, to make their wants known and to express the rationale for them. An understanding of the larger system was also required.

Help All School Counselors Feel Competent to Make the Needed Changes

As stated at the beginning, for people to change, they have to believe that the outcomes are worth the risks and effort and they need to believe that making change is feasible. Counselors' needs for enhanced skill development and professional self-confidence have to be met if the changes are to occur.

Counselors in Northside district were motivated to change by varied means: (a) by encouraging their professionalism, (b) by nurturing professional growth and development, and (c) by empowering them through skill and knowledge development.

Encouraging their professionalism meant helping them with their professional identity and reminding them of the value of *school* guidance and counseling. Northside district's counselors have been encouraged to and have joined their professional associations. In defining the realistic ideal for the program, a great deal of time and energy was spent discussing the professional contributions counselors make—to students, their teachers, parents, and the school system.

A corollary to this is nurturing counselors' professional growth and development. Making professional growth the "norm" was partially accomplished by reading and discussing articles from professional journals, by supporting attendance and presentations at professional conferences and workshops, and through in-service education and training activities in the district. For example, the district staff expressed expectations that counselors conduct effective small-group counseling; thus, it was incumbent on them to provide the renewal training needed.

In Northside district, the roles of the Head Counselors were reclarified and a supervision and performance-evaluation system was developed, based on the new counselor job descriptions. The focus of these efforts are performance improvement in the skills demanded by the new program. Counselors develop and implement Professional Growth Plans each year.

Collaborate With Others Who Will Be Affected by Changes

The "others" who will be effected by guidance program changes include principals, teachers, parents, other counselors, other school-related specialists, and community representatives. Some of these "significant others" will have been involved already in providing input to the ideas for change. Now it is necessary to collaborate with them to implement the changes.

Collaborate means to work with. To effect guidance program improvement there is a continuum of collaboration, which ranges from informing others to teaming with them to delegating responsibilities to them. Others need information about the changes and what the changes mean to them. Teamwork is essential in the implementation of new strategies (e.g., counselors need to team with teachers to teach the guidance curriculum). Delegating may be "up," "down," or "out," depending on what responsibilities are being shifted away from the counselors. For example, in shifting the responsibility for the testing program, responsibilities for setting policies and getting the staff's attention for taking testing seriously are delegated "up" to the principal. Tasks that may be delegated "out" to the teachers include helping in the logistics of test administration, preparing the students, and following standardized procedures. Delegation "down" might mean letting students do tasks that they can do. For example, office aides can count the returned test booklets.

A brief word about delegating activities to someone else: As counselors add new activities to their program, old tasks that were done by counselors but can be done by others will be delegated to others. It is important in this transition for counselors to work with the people who pick up these responsibilities—and who are probably not happy about getting them. If counselors have historically coordinated the admission, review, and dismissal meetings for special education students and that task is to be assigned to a clerk, it is important for the counselor to work with that clerk so that he or she understands the job and knows how to do it comfortably. If counselors have historically administered the standardized testing program and that job is to be carried out by administrators and teachers, it is important that the counselor again help those newly responsible to understand the tasks involved and any "secrets" learned by experience.

Collaboration involves compromise, negotiation, mutual goal setting, and enlisting and maintaining support. Some examples from Northside district's experiences include the compromise that was struck with the special education department: They coordinate the reevaluation process, and the counselors handle initial referrals. After negotiation with middle school administrators, new student registrations occur in the administrative offices, because more of the required information is for their use than for ours. Mutual goal setting finds counselors participating in campus problem solving. Counselors have had to learn to do this without always being a part of the solution strategy.

One way to gain and maintain support is to listen and respond to others' priorities and, at the same time, seize opportunities to help them in ways that will help you to achieve what you want. With the renewed interest in testing, counselors have expanded their role as consultants regarding appropriate use of test results. Failure rates are a concern of the high school principals: High school counselors conduct small-group counseling activities with at-risk students. The Parent-Teacher Association is concerned about adolescent suicide and depression: Counselors have been collaborating with the leaders by writing articles for newsletters and presenting programs. This school district prides itself on the stringency of its discipline management plan: School counselors provide the mandatory parent effectiveness workshops.

Make Effective Changes in Program Strategies

Implementation of the new program dictates changing the strategies used to deliver the program. Changes need to be consistent with identified priorities, planned thoroughly, and carried out to the best of the counselors' abilities.

Choices about which program strategies to add or modify must relate to the priorities expressed in the overall program-change process, must be based on the students' and the school's needs, should be feasible, and should indicate a high probability of success. For example, the middle school counselors had a change goal of conducting more classroom guidance. To effectively implement new classroom guidance offerings, counselors assessed the needs of students and teachers. On most campuses, the initial year of providing developmental guidance systematically saw the middle school counselors in classes no more than six times. Thus, selecting topics that had high priority in the local community was imperative.

These needs also had to be balanced with the counselors' assessment of the feasibility of implementing the planned agenda successfully. Feasibility considerations included political support (e.g., sexuality may be an important topic for seventh graders, but it may not be the favorite of the principal or the parents) availability of support materials, the time allotted for the lesson(s), and so forth. Assessment of the probability of success is related to considerations of the counselor's knowledge of and skill in presenting the topic.

Thorough planning is also a key to successful implementation. Planning when an activity will occur better assures that it will get done, and thoroughly planning the activity enhances its quality. This seems like an obvious truth, but counselors in traditional programs are used to reacting to immediate concerns and situations and may not have had a lot of experience with planning. In August when they return to duty, Northside district's counselors are asked to outline their plans for the year on a calendar. Particular attention is given to the start-up time for new activities. Yearly program improvement goals are developed and written as Action Plans, which delineate which tasks are to be done, who is to do them, by when, and how the activity will be evaluated.

Counselors are encouraged to be creative in developing new activities, but to strive for effectiveness and efficiency. If students can achieve the same outcomes through an activity that takes less time, allows for more participation, or both, then do that activity. Planning new activities entails clarifying the expected student outcomes, identifying and becoming familiar with the support materials to be used, attending to logistics such as time schedules, audiovisual equipment, facilities, and ensuring the competence of the staff members who will be implementing the strategies. High quality is stressed, because any new activity will be observed and judged by both supporters and detractors. This whole effort has been about program improvement, and new activities should be just that, improvements.

Evaluate the Changes Made

Evaluation is critical to the ongoing program improvement process. Successes, failures, and areas for further improvement need to be clearly identified. Through program evaluation in Northside district, staff members know whether they are meeting the standards established by the Guidance Steering Committee for the comprehensive program. Through evaluation of program strategies, counselors know whether or not they are providing effective and efficient methods for helping students grow. Through counselor performance evaluation, counselors know whether they are performing at their optimum or, if not, what in-service training is needed.

Evaluation was not a skill area that the counselors felt comfortable with; thus, knowledge and skill-development sessions on the topic had to be conducted before expectations for evaluation could be met. Some mechanisms were also developed to assist counselors in conducting evaluations. To evaluate the comprehensiveness and balance of their campus program, for example, counselors complete a self-study that is based on the established program standards. Program strategy evaluations are based on the objectives established for the activities.

The counselors have learned that data are important to them and impressive to others. It helps them feel good to know that their change efforts have been successful, and the data provide them with good information to support their ongoing improvement requests from their administrators and the faculty. It is easier to convince teachers to allow counselors to take more of their instructional time for classroom guidance if they know how effective the previous activities have been.

Conclusion

The Northside district's guidance program has changed. The counselors are pleased with the results, as are their principals. As teachers become more aware of the improved program, they too are better satisfied with the services the program provides. Some tangible results include extended contracts for counselors and higher annual salaries; focused professional supervision, evaluation, and professional growth opportunities; and more money budgeted for program materials and for special projects. Role clarification and better ratios are still needed at the middle school level.

In summary, some critical skills that are needed by counselors to improve their programs are those attendant to making commitments and decisions, setting priorities and goals, communicating and collaborating, risk taking, and problem solving. All of these skills are used in counseling roles. Counselors need to be and to feel empowered to apply them in this different arena. Other keys to successful program improvement include having vision, being willing to make the commitment needed to change, and being cautious and careful to ensure making quality changes.

References

Gysbers, N. C., & Henderson. P. (1988). *Developing and managing your school guidance program.* Alexandria, VA: American Association for Counseling and Development.

Gysbers, N. C., & Moore, E. J. (1981). *Improving guidance programs.* Englewood Cliffs, NJ: Prentice-Hall.

Northside Independent School District. (1986). *Comprehensive guidance program framework.* San Antonio, TX: Author.

Chapter 4

The Role of the Secondary School Counselor

Increasingly, it seems that the role of secondary school counselors is being scrutinized and criticized. This is not, however, a recent development. From the shaky beginnings of our profession in the formative years, school counselor role has been discussed, deliberated and debated, seemingly to come to the same conclusion—role confusion! Those traditionally involved, such as counselor educators, administrators, professional associations, and counselors have not been joined by legislators, certification boards, school boards, parents, teachers and students. All groups with any vested interest are concerned about the role of secondary school counselors and the basic underlying question is: "What is the job of a secondary school counselor?"

Many studies have attempted to examine the secondary counselor's role by surveying the perceptions of teachers, students, parents, administrators and counselors. The articles in this chapter by Tennyson, Miller, Skovholt and Williams (1989); Gibson (1990); and Hutchinson and Reagan (1989) fit into this category.

The article by Tennyson et al. compares secondary school counselor role perceptions with expectations set forth in professional guidelines. Reasons are discussed regarding the discrepancies between actual functions and a developmental approach.

Gibson surveys secondary school teachers about high school guidance programs and concludes that teachers continue to believe that counseling programs make a positive contribution to schools. However, the continued failure of school counselors to adequately communicate their role to teachers is stressed. The author proposes one approach to a counseling program communication plan.

The failure of counselors to adequately and accurately communicate their role to students is highlighted in the article by Hutchinson and Reagan. The authors point out that students' perceptions of counselors have not changed much over the last two decades and suggest that this is due in part to counselors' uncertainty and confusion about their own professional identity.

Research on effective schools provides a new opportunity for an expanded counselor role. The article by Kaplan and Geoffroy (1990) stresses the importance of a positive school climate in creating an effective school environment. Kaplan and Geoffroy propose eight roles for counselors in creating a positive school climate and emphasize the preparation that school counselors have as change agents.

In 1990, the American School Counselor Association (ASCA) adopted a new role statement for school counselors. It updated the 1981 role and function statement which, in turn, had replaced previous documents. The focus is on the implementation of comprehensive developmental counseling programs which address the educational, career, personal and social needs of students. Counselors assist those with whom they work through the three processes of counseling, consulting and coordinating. Furthermore, counselors organize their work around fundamental interventions which are also sometimes referred to as functions, services, approaches, tasks, activities or jobs. The basic counselor interventions are individual counseling, small group counseling, large group guidance, consultation and coordination.

This chapter on secondary school counselor role is but a beginning point for further study. For additional information, readers are referred to the March, 1989 issue of *The School Counselor* which contains a special theme section on this topic. The current ASCA statement on counselor role is not the final word! Counselor role must constantly undergo examination to determine if it meets the needs of those served. This can be best accomplished through a comprehensive developmental counseling program, however, many counselors are not familiar with this approach and will need to be retrained in the developmental model. The profession is making headway and the developmental perspective is being adopted but it will never be fully implemented unless counselors are enabled to function in the defined areas.

The secondary school counselor's role has been, and will continue to be, defined by what counselors *do,* not by what they would *like* to do or by what the counseling profession thinks they *should* do. Counselors have too often been guilty of accepting conditions over which they could exercise some control, that is, they exhibit a lack of assertiveness to change their image. If counselors desire others to see them as fulfilling certain roles, they must take the responsibility to actively establish those roles. Only then will the gap between perceived and ideal roles be narrowed. When counselors know who they are and what they do, they will be able to adhere to ASCA Ethical Standard D.3, "The school counselor delineates and promotes the counselor's role and function in meeting the needs of those served."

Secondary School Counselors: What Do They Do? What is Important?

W. Wesley Tennyson
G. Dean Miller
Thomas G. Skovholt
R. Craig Williams

One aim of guidance is to promote healthy self-concepts and psychological growth through the curriculum. This point of view, summarized by Miller (1981), corresponds closely to the American School Counselor Association's role statement (ASCA Governing Board, 1981), which is an incorporation and revision of four role statements prepared separately for the association in the 1970s. The developmental conception of guidance set forth in these statements figured prominently in the writing of a new Minnesota licensure rule for school counseling adopted in 1982. This rule set forth competencies previously not required of counselors, in areas such as psychological education, staff and parent consultation, and guidance program management and evaluation.

Given these new expectations for school counseling, there was a need to determine whether or not counselors currently function in accordance with the intent of the license. A series of studies, conducted in cooperation with the Minnesota Department of Education, was initiated in 1985 to investigate aspects of the role and function of Minnesota school counselors. This article provides a descriptive summary of survey findings obtained from a 20% ($N=165$) random sample of the state's secondary school counselors.

We received responses from 163 counselors, giving a 98.8% return. Eight questionnaires were found to be unuseable; therefore, data are reported for 155 counselors, or 93.9% of those surveyed. Included in this sample were 77 senior high, 33 junior high, and 45 junior-senior high school counselors. The data presented in this report are for the total group of counselors only, without consideration of the level at which they were employed.

In keeping with what is generally known about the ratios for secondary school counselors in Minnesota, the sample was made up predominantly of men (68%). Only 22% of the respondents were under age 40. The majority (41%) were between 41 and 50 years; 32% were over 50. Eight counselors did not report their age. It is important to note that 28% of the counselors had been in their present position less than 5 years; 45% less than 10 years. For those employed in their present position 15 years or more, the figure was 35%.

Survey Instrument

A questionnaire listing 58 functions was developed by a committee composed of the research team and counseling practitioners. The functions were classified under six broad categories of guidance services distributed as follows: Counseling—10 items; Consulting—11 items; Developmental and Career Guidance—8 items; Evaluation and Assessment—7 items; Guidance Program Development, Management, and Coordination—8 items; and Administrative Support Services—14 items. The first five categories were taken directly from the licensure rule, and items were formulated by translating specified competencies into identifiable functions. Items for the sixth category, Administrative Support Services, were obtained from previous studies of counselor role and function. A pretesting of the survey instrument* with 10 secondary school counselors resulted in the addition of several items and a rewording of others.

Those surveyed were asked to respond to two questions in rating the function categories. First, counselors were asked, "How often do you perform each function?" Response categories were as follows: *Never* (1), *Rarely* (2), *Occasionally* (3), *Fairly Often* (4), and *Frequently* (5). Second, they responded to the question, "How important is each function for school counselors?" by checking: *Unimportant* (1), *Slightly Important* (2), *Important* (3), *Very Important* (4), or *Crucially Important* (5).

---

*Author's Note. A copy of the survey instrument may be obtained from the senior author at 137 Burton Hall, College of Education, University of Minnesota, Minneapolis, MN 55455.

Analysis

Means and standard deviations for both the categories and the individual items were computed. Means for categories were obtained by averaging across all items within each respective group. A Cronbach alpha reliability analysis revealed high internal consistency of the items within each category. To analyze individual items, means of 4.0 and above and those under 3.0 were assumed to have functional significance and are reported. For selected items showing a bimodal distribution, percentages are given to aid interpretation. Data are examined to determine whether or not the functions counselors see themselves performing, and the importance they attach to those functions, are related to competency requirements of the new Minnesota license and changes in counselor role expectation.

Findings

A review of the means for each category, shown in Table 1, suggests that the perceived Frequency of guidance services performed was generally less congruent with counselor licensure than were the data on the Importance counselors assign to these broad services. Looking first at the Frequency column, counseling is the only guidance service for which the category mean was greater than 3.5, the midpoint between *Occasionally* and *Fairly Often* performed. Developmental and Career Guidance, with a mean of 2.9, was perceived to be the least frequently performed service. All other category means fell between 3.0 and 3.5. A comparison of the Frequency data with that for Importance shows that the means of the latter parallel the former and are slightly higher for all services except Administrative Support. It seems, therefore, that perceived Importance of functions had slightly greater congruence with the counselor licensure requirements than did performance Frequency of functions. But the overall picture for both Frequency and Importance falls far short of what is necessary in implementing the new counselor model set forth in the Minnesota licensure rule, as well as what is recommended by ASCA.

Although averaging across items is useful in showing the relative attention given to the various categories of guidance services, a clear picture of whether or not counselors see themselves performing in accordance with the new expectations can be obtained only by examining

Table 1
Means and Standard Deviations by Category for Counselors'
Perceptions of Functions Performed

Category	Frequency[a]			Importance[b]	
	N	*M*	*SD*	*M*	*SD*
1. Counseling	155	3.77	.483	4.00	.470
2. Consulting	155/154	3.35	.497	3.61	.493
3. Developmental and Career Guidance	155	2.85	.639	3.42	.534
4. Evaluation and Assessment	152	2.98	.582	3.30	.512
5. Guidance Program Development, Management, and Coordination	155/154	3.06	.669	3.51	.588
6. Administrative Support Services	154/155	3.28	.530	2.88	.506

[a]How often do you do these things? *Never* (1); *Rarely* (2); *Occasionally* (3); *Fairly Often* (4); or *Frequently* (5).
[b]How important is the function for school counselors? *Unimportant* (1); *Slightly Important* (2); *Important* (3); *Very Important* (4); or *Crucially Important* (5).

responses to specific functions. The variation between 1.4 and 4.6 for item means indicates that respondents did, indeed, perceive the functions differentially. Applying criteria established by the research team (means of 4.0 and over; 2.9 and under), 37 items were perceived to be performed with either high or low Frequency, whereas 22 items were considered to be of high or low Importance. Two-thirds of the Frequency items meeting the criterion were found to be low, whereas the Importance items were more nearly balanced between high and low.

Counseling. Guidance programs in the schools, following traditional certification patterns, have stressed individual counseling. That tradition is reflected in this study, with more than twice as many high-item means for combined Frequency and Importance appearing in the counseling section than in any other category. All functions having to do with individual counseling of students were found to meet or closely approximate the criterion (4.0) for high Frequency and high Importance. Listed below are items perceived to be done *Fairly Often* and perceived as *Very Important:*

1. Meeting with a student to address a developmental need (e.g., decision making).

2. Meeting with a student to resolve or remediate a problem (e.g., interpersonal conflict).
3. Interpreting a test or student record in counseling.

In contrast with individual counseling, the respondents only *Occasionally* perceived themselves as counseling a small group to resolve or remediate personal problems (3.0), although they did assign a degree of importance to this function (3.6). More than two-thirds of the counselors viewed working with families to meet developmental needs or resolve problems of students to be *Very Important* or *Crucially Important*, but only half of those surveyed indicated that they counsel *Fairly Often* with families.

Consulting. The consultative activities that respondents said they engage in *Fairly Often* to *Frequently* have the primary purpose of solving student problems—for example, conferring with a teacher (4.5), participating in a case conference (4.3), and making a referral (4.1). More than two-thirds of the counselors rated these three functions from *Very Important* to *Crucially Important*. The counselors were, however, less inclined to do consulting to meet student developmental needs through the curriculum. Thus, most respondents said they *Rarely* to *Occasionally* help teachers individualize instruction to meet student needs (2.5) or serve as a staff resource in the design of curriculum (2.6). Nor are they very involved in designing and conducting in-service training (2.2).

Developmental and Career Guidance. Although the school counselors in this survey consider the promotion of psychological growth through small groups and the classroom to be *Important* to *Very Important*, they engage infrequently in activities designed to accomplish this. Approximately half of the counselors perceive themselves as *Rarely* or *Never* conducting small group or classroom activities to develop interpersonal skills (2.6), facilitating decision making and values development (2.7), or promoting social development (2.3). One-third of the counselors perceive themselves as *Rarely* or *Never* working with groups to facilitate self-awareness (2.9). We concluded that psychological education, as practiced by these counselors, falls short of the importance they attach to it or the importance attached to this activity by others (Miller, 1981).

Several questions are pertinent to the continuing criticism that counselors are not doing enough career planning. Three-fourths of the respondents said they perform the following functions *Fairly Often* to *Frequently*: (a) helping students to explore educational and occupational information (4.4), (b) assisting students with career planning (4.1), and (c) helping students select post-high school education or training (4.1). This finding is tempered somewhat when one looks at other functions crucial to career guidance. For example, only half of the counselors use career and vocational assessment information (3.5) with students *Fairly Often* to *Frequently*. One-third of the respondents *Occasionally* to *Rarely* use groups to provide educational and occupational information (3.7). More than 40% *Rarely* or *Never* assist students in using the computer for career information (2.8). Although the counselors seem to give high priority to career counseling, the data raise questions about both the efficiency and effectiveness of their methods.

Evaluation and Assessment. Academic testing is one area in which respondents consistently saw themselves functioning with high frequency. They said they perform *Fairly Often* to *Frequently* such functions as the following: (a) administering the school's testing program (4.2) and (b) helping students or parents to use academic test information (4.2). But the majority *Rarely* or *Never* use inventories to assess students' developmental needs and characteristics (2.3), nor do they believe this function to be of great importance (2.9). The respondents also indicated that they conduct intervention and program evaluations (2.5) *Rarely* to *Occasionally*, although they do attach a degree of importance to this activity (3.1). These findings suggest that the counselors, for the most part, are functioning in the traditional way when it comes to testing.

Administrative Support Services. Counselors reported considerable involvement with functions related to administrative support. The one function, among all others, they viewed themselves as performing with greatest frequency is assisting students with scheduling, counting credits, or both (4.6), and this is an activity that close to three-fourths (4.0) considered to be *Very Important* to *Crucially Important*. Other administrative support functions perceived to engage substantial numbers of counselors *Occasionally* to *Fairly Often* include: (a) writing recommendations (3.7), (b) circulating information and arranging meetings (3.7), (c) preparing bulletins and announcements (3.5), (d) serving on school committees (3.5), (e) working on community or professional activities (3.2), and (f) performing clerical functions (3.2).

Discussion

A conclusion one may draw from this study is that only a limited parallel exists between the perceptions Minnesota school counselors hold of their roles and functions and the expectations set forth in current professional guidelines. Although there is agreement that functions associated with individual counseling have high priority, less fully realized is the expectation that school counselors will integrate developmental principles of human growth into the mainstream of education.

Why did the respondents not see themselves to be more involved with guidance services and functions that reflect the position of the profession and are implied in current Minnesota credentialing? First, it is possible that a heavy one-to-one counseling load may preempt whatever time might be given to developmental guidance activities. Though one often hears complaints that are critical of school counselors for not doing more individual counseling, the findings of this study warrant no such criticism. But one has to look carefully at the ends served by this counseling to evaluate both its effectiveness and efficiency. Assuming that what the counselors report is valid, they are spending enormous amounts of time working with individual students to accomplish three aims: (a) resolve personal problems, (b) formulate educational and career plans, and (c) schedule students' courses. Although it is recognized that some students experience unique problems that require personal attention, we believe that the individual approach must be examined critically against the promise of reaching larger numbers of students and perhaps doing a better job of developmental education through small-group and classroom guidance activities.

Most certainly questions might be raised about the way career guidance is currently delivered to students. The matching model of vocational guidance inherent in much of traditional career counseling fails to take into account that career decision making is a lifelong developmental process. It is a process whereby gradual insights and many small choices are made easier by appropriate and meaningful experiences. What is needed are educational experiences that enable students to search, design, and try out aspects of their evolving careers. The profession's role statements advocate increased use of various group approaches, the curriculum, and the resources of the community in providing students opportunities for self-exploration, exploratory work experience, and decision-making skills development.

A more likely deterrent to mainstreaming developmental goals is the extensive counseling associated with the scheduling of students. Not only is this function generally recognized to be time consuming, but the counselors themselves say they engage in it more frequently than any other single activity. Technology designed to support administrative functions that are attendant to the program is a resource not fully explored. The scheduling function, for example, could be conducted in a structured way by using new microcomputer software such as the High School Planner (McKinlay, 1986) or DISCOVER's junior high and middle school program (1986). These individualized approaches can become the culminating activity in a junior high school career guidance curriculum. Students develop a 4-year course plan based on local graduation requirements, career considerations, and postsecondary educational plans. This approach, and others like it, can then become the focal point of annual reviews of career thinking and planning. As a result, students will benefit from more systematic involvement in their career planning.

Second, when one looks at the extent of counselor involvement in scheduling and considers this function in conjunction with other administrative activities the counselors report doing, the conclusion may be drawn that such support services account for a high proportion of the counselors' time. These administrative functions seem to be performed to the neglect of other functions that are central in both the Minnesota counselor licensure rule and the curricula of the state's counselor education programs.

Other reasons for the discordance between perceived performance and current expectations may be suggested. It is quite possible that the schools are structured and administered in a manner incompatible with the developmental perspective held by the profession. Counselors often report, for example, that the system does not allow easy access to small-group or classroom guidance activities. In addition, counselors in the field who have been prepared in traditional ways may not feel secure in implementing the developmental philosophy; also, they may lack the skills to do group counseling, consultation, and developmental assessment. There are, however, examples of guidance programs in which counselors do manage to provide a developmental focus. In 1980, ASCA recognized Newton North High School in Newton, Massachusetts as an exemplary program (DeInlio & Mackie, 1982). Finally, schools today face multitudinous pressures created by community expectations, special interest groups, the "at risk" problems of many students, demands on the curriculum, and the continued cutbacks that result in an overloaded work life for all, including counselors.

Summary

The position taken by the profession—that school counselors must integrate developmental principles of human growth into the schools—is increasingly being mandated through state licensure and certification laws. If the situation in other states is similar to that of Minnesota, the findings of this study have implications for large-scale in-service education. First, there is a need for state departments of education, school counselor associations, and associations for counselor education and supervision to provide school counselors and principals with information about the changed expectations related to the counselor's role. Second, in-service activities should be targeted at enabling school counselors to function comfortably in areas of consultation, group counseling, developmental guidance and assessment, and program evaluation. These steps are necessary to bring counselor practice into accord with the most recent philosophy of the profession.

References

American School Counselor Association Governing Board. (1981). ASCA role statement: The practice of guidance and counseling by school counselors. *School Counselor, 29,* 7–12.

DeInlio, R. S., & Mackie, P. A. (1982). Secondary school guidance and counseling: A differentiated programmatic approach. In G. Dean Miller (Ed.), *Differentiated levels of student support services* (pp. 63–97). St. Paul: Minnesota Department of Education.

DISCOVER for junior high and middle schools. (1986). Iowa City: American College Testing Program.

McKinlay, B. (1986). *High school planner: Computer software for career planning.* Eugene: University of Oregon, National Career Information Systems.

Miller, G. D. (1981). Psychological maturity: A new aim of school guidance. *Counseling and Human Development, 13,* 1–17.

Teachers' Opinions of High School Counseling and Guidance Programs: Then and Now

Robert L. Gibson

In 1965 secondary school guidance programs were experiencing a "golden era." Subsidized from training to implementation by federal funding provided under the National Defense Education Act of 1958, 15,700 secondary school educators attended counselor training institutes, and the number of full-time high school counselors increased from 12,000 in 1958 to more than 30,000 in 1964 (Gibson & Mitchell, 1986). Secondary school counseling was clearly "on a roll."

Although external support was responsible for counseling and guidance programs "getting a foot in the door" of the secondary school, the "staying power" and eventual success would be largely determined by the internal support accorded these programs. From this perspective, no group was more critical, then or now, than the classroom teacher. Accordingly, a study was conducted in 1965 titled "Teacher Opinion of High School Guidance Programs" (Gibson, 1965).

The results of this study raised questions about excessive standardized testing, failure to understand theoretical foundations for career decision making, and inadequate communications with teachers and other critical audiences.

In the intervening 22-year period, the federal "goose" not only ceased laying "golden eggs" for school counseling; also (and equally disconcerting to many) school counselors were asked to become accountable and to prove that what they were doing was needed, that it was being done well, and it was being done efficiently. Often lacking both this evidence and the external support necessary, secondary school counseling programs frequently became prime candidates for cutbacks, even cutoffs, in the years of educational budget trimming and reform. Significant reform proposals such as *A Nation at Risk* (National Commission on Excellence in Education, 1983) and *Time for Results* (National Governors Association, 1986) completely ignored school programs of counseling and guidance.

Therefore, it seemed appropriate to once again assess the opinion of the classroom teacher regarding counseling and guidance programs in the secondary school. Although it seemed that the current opinions of this group would be of prime importance, the opportunity for comparison with the earlier study could also provide indications of possible changes in such viewpoints over the past 20-year period.

Methodology

This is a descriptive study. Descriptive research is concerned with depicting the present. The most popular descriptive method of determining conditions as they currently exist is labeled as survey research (Galfo, 1975). Survey research is especially useful when there is interest in the opinions of a specific group (in this study, secondary school teachers) regarding a specific activity (in this study, secondary school programs of counseling and guidance).

For this study, the same opinion-type questionnaire was used as for the 1965 study, with appropriate terminology and other revisions. The questionnaire consisted of 30 common items covering the areas of general information, individual assessment, individual counseling, career guidance, group counseling and guidance, placement, and follow-up (see Tables 1, 2, and 3). A sample of convenience (one readily available to the investigator) was used in both studies, with 180 secondary school teachers completing the questionnaire in the current study compared to 205 participants in the original study. The 180 teachers were employed in the 19 midwestern high schools in which organized programs under the direction of trained counselors had been functioning for a minimum of 5 years. (Eighteen high schools from a 5-state midwestern and southeastern area had participated in the 1965 study.) Information for supplementing the questionnaire data was obtained through follow-up interviews with approximately 10% of each group. The schools in both samples represented institutions with small, medium, and large enrollments from both rural and urban settings.

Results

In general, secondary school teachers continue to believe that the school counseling and guidance program does make a positive contribution to

Table 1
Teachers' Opinions (1986 and 1965) of School Counseling and Guidance Programs

Question	Percent Responding					
	Yes		No		Not Sure	
	1986	1965	1986	1965	1986	1965
1. In your opinion, does the counseling and guidance program make positive contributions to the school's instructional program?	71.8	84.1	14.5	5.7	12.7	10.2
2. Has the counseling and guidance program of your school ever been explained, described, or outlined to you for your information?	54.0	75.9	46.0	21.1	0.0	3.0
3. Could you tell a new student entering your school what most of the counseling and guidance services are that are available to the students in this school?	72.7	72.5	22.7	13.9	4.5	13.6
4. Do you feel that the counseling and guidance staff in the school is identified with the school administration?	50.9	36.5	38.8	45.1	10.3	18.4
5. Should the counseling and guidance staff in the school be identified with the teaching faculty?	81.4	37.5	3.8	46.1	14.8	16.4
6. Do you feel that the school counselors should have the responsibility of interpreting the counseling and guidance program to the community?	90.9	82.8	5.4	9.6	3.7	7.6
7. Should teachers have responsibilities in the school counseling and guidance program other than those that are performed within the classroom?	43.6	62.5	43.6	29.8	12.8	7.7
8. Do you feel that an in-service training program in counseling for the teaching staff would be worthwhile?	42.7	86.5	45.3	3.0	14.0	12.0
9. See Table 3						

Table 1 (Continued)

Question	Yes		No		Not Sure	
	1986	1965	1986	1965	1986	1965
10. Should the counseling office keep its records separate from regular school records?	42.9	57.6	30.0	18.2	27.1	24.2
11. In your opinion, should the school use standardized test results in pupil assessment?	81.2	88.5	11.1	4.8	7.7	6.7
12. Are you usually informed of those standardized test results that would be appropriate and useful to you?	44.4	48.0	51.9	33.6	3.7	18.4
13. Do you feel these test results are usually interpreted adequately?	30.0	44.8	25.7	28.8	44.3	26.4
14. See Table 2						
15. Do you feel that teachers in your school are likely to confer with the counselor regarding the problems of students?	71.4	98.0	17.8	2.0	9.8	0.0
16. Do you use the counselor as a referral agent when the student's problem is beyond your training or scope?	70.3	91.3	29.7	5.0	0.0	3.7
17. Is it desirable for the counselor to furnish a review of a student interview to the teacher who made the referral?	62.9	74.0	25.9	13.4	11.2	12.6
18. Should counseling records be available to all teachers?	29.6	91.3	32.0	4.8	33.4	3.9
19. Should counselors reveal to the teacher information that they receive concerning the student's attitude toward the teacher?	44.4	36.5	27.8	35.5	27.8	28.0
20. Should the teacher share her or his knowledge with the counselor that she or he may receive from the parents of a student?	88.8	95.2	0.0	2.4	11.2	2.4
21. Do you feel that the counseling staff should assist the classroom teacher in handling problems of classroom discipline?	59.2	38.4	27.8	30.8	13.0	30.8

Table 1 (Continued)

Question	Percent Responding					
	Yes		No		Not Sure	
	1986	1965	1986	1965	1986	1965
22. Should the counselor be the one to administer punishment to the student if it is necessary?	1.9	3.8	96.2	83.6	1.9	12.6
23. Do you feel that the teacher should acquaint students with the "world of work" through his or her classes?	85.1	88.4	1.9	2.4	13.0	9.2
24. Do you feel that the teacher should help students make educational plans?	88.8	85.0	7.4	6.7	3.8	8.3
25. Should the securing, organizing, and disseminating of career and educational planning information be the primary responsibility of the counseling staff as opposed to the instructional staff?	74.0	89.4	22.2	8.3	3.8	2.3
26. Are special activities such as "Career Days" and "College Days" of value to the students?	74.0	79.6	0.0	4.1	18.5	16.3
27. Should the teacher follow-up on "Career Days" and "College Days" and other special days in the classroom?	62.9	75.0	11.1	13.4	16.0	11.0
28. Do you think that special days and their planning disrupt the school too much?	11.2	17.3	7.7	67.3	11.1	15.0
29. In your opinion, should the school counseling and guidance department identify pupil interests and assist or direct the organization of group activities appropriate to these interests?	60.1	39.0	20.4	31.2	19.5	29.0
30. Should the guidance department conduct periodic follow-up studies of the school's former pupils (graduates and dropouts)?	82.2	77.4	1.0	4.9	16.8	12.7

Table 2
Ranking of Teacher Opinions on Standardized Testing

	Rank order of choice	
Testing area	1986	1965
Achievement	1	2
Aptitude	2	1
Intelligence or academic readiness	3	5
Interest	4	3
Personality	5	4

Note. Question No. 14: Of the following areas of standardized testing, please number the three (3) that you believe are the most valuable in order of their importance.

Table 3
Ranking of Teacher Opinions on the Responsibilities of School Guidance Personnel

	Rank order of choice	
Activity	1986	1965
Career information	2.0	2.0
Attendance checking and recording	9.2	7.0
Discipline	8.0	6.0
Test administration and interpretation	3.0	3.0
Administrative duties other than those of the guidance program	9.5	9.5
Individual counseling services	1.0	1.0
Coordination of the school activities program	6.0	8.0
Group counseling, guidance, and orientation programs	5.0	4.0
College placement	4.0	9.5
Job placement, part-time and full-time	7.0	5.0

Note. Question No. 9: Of the following activities, check those you think should be the responsibility of the school guidance personnel. Designate the three (by number) that you think are most important.

the instructional program of the school. They were most affirmative in their opinions that school counselors should be identified with the teaching faculty (81.4%); that their counselors should interpret their programs to their communities (90.9%); that standardized tests should be used in pupil assessment (81.2%); that teachers should share pupil information with counselors (88.8%); that they, the classroom teachers, should provide career information (85.1%) and assist pupils in educational planning (88.8%); and that school counseling and guidance departments should conduct follow-up studies of former students (82.2%). Teachers felt very strongly (96.2%) that counselors *should not* administer punishment to students. Teachers were most uncertain (44.3%) about the adequacy of test interpretation, and slightly more than half (51.9%) indicated that they were not always informed of the test results themselves. Table 2 provides data on specific areas of testing.

The biggest change in teacher opinions between the 1965 and current studies (1986) were in changes in affirmative responses to items regarding the receipt of counseling-program information, 75.9% in 1965 versus 54.0% in 1986; identification of counseling staff with teaching faculty, 37.5% versus 81.4%; in-service training for teachers, 86.5% versus 42.7%; use of counselors as referral agents, 91.3% versus 70.3%; availability of counseling records to all teachers, 91.3% versus 29.6% and organization of group activities based on pupil interests, 39.0% versus 60.1%. Teachers currently continue to recognize that individual counseling is the most important and primary responsibility of the school counselor (see Table 3). Other important activities, consecutively, were the provision of career and educational information, test administration and interpretation, college placement, and group counseling and guidance. These rankings may be compared to a recent survey by Gibson (1988) of secondary school principals who ranked the importance of counselor functions as: (a) individual counseling; (b) the detection, prevention, and early intervention of substance, child, and sexual abuse; (c) group counseling and guidance activities; (d) career development and planning; and (e) behavior modification and management.

Conclusion

In comparing the 1965 and 1985–1986 studies, one must keep in mind changes in the counselor's role and function over the past 20 years. For example, in three of the guidance texts that were popular during the

1960s (Crow & Crow, 1951; Downing, 1968; Haverin, 1953), no mention is made of consultation. Also, with the exception of several pages in Downing, group counseling is not presented, and cumulative record keeping is covered rather extensively with no discussions of computers. School counselors must also look to current recommendations for the future, such as those of the College Board's Commission on Pre-College Guidance and Counseling contained in their *Keeping the Options Open: Recommendations* (Commission on Pre-College Guidance and Counseling, 1986).

Notwithstanding changing roles and calls for new directions, it can be concluded that secondary school teachers continue to believe that counseling and guidance programs make a positive contribution to the total program of their schools. Interviews further confirmed that teachers have high respect for the skills and dedication of the counselors in their schools. This was especially noted in those schools in which counselors interacted with every teacher on a one-to-one basis at least once per semester.

In reviewing the comparative data of the two studies, however, school counselors and counselor educators must not become complacent about significant past accomplishments and a current, generally positive image. While recognizing the limits of this study, it is possible to heed warnings by noting the decline, even though slight in some instances, in positive responses to questions regarding program value, program information, and use of the counselor as a consultant or resource professional (see Table 1, Items 1, 2, 15, and 16). Also, the movement toward counselor identification with the school administration may not improve the counselor's image with the instructional faculty. A recent school counselor survey by the Indiana Task Force on Student Services (Reynolds, 1988) suggested that counselors may be reinforcing this perception of the counselor as administrator by the ways they spend their time. This study noted that even though counselors reported spending an average of 29% of their time doing individual counseling, the next two time-consuming activities were administrative tasks (19%) and clerical tasks (19%). These data reinforce the view of Hartmen (1988), who suggested that counselors must learn strategies for handling groups and managing programs if they are to contribute to their full professional potential.

Perhaps the biggest concern highlighted by this study should be the continued failure of school counselors to adequately communicate "what we are about." This is not only inconsistent with the claim counselors make to be skilled communicators but also is threatening to the base of teacher support and general support base that they must have.

In a broader sense, accountable organizations must, by their very nature, collect, organize, maintain, and use a large amount and variety of information. Information management, however, goes beyond internal manipulation; it forms the basis for external communications as well. School counselors must recognize that public communications skills are as critical to counseling program success as personal communications skills are to client counseling success. As one school counselor noted, "we not only want to inform our public, we want to persuade and influence them as well!" Another counselor noted that "the general public needs to know that counseling programs do make a positive difference."

Of the secondary school counselors interviewed, those who had planned communications programs shared in common the belief that it was important to identify the appropriate communications networks in the school as well as their external supporting community and develop a plan to use both of these. A recommended approach was the development of a counseling-program communication plan that identified: (a) the audiences to be addressed; (b) the information to share with each of these audiences; (c) the purpose (i.e., informing, involving, convincing, etc.); (d) the methods (i.e., letters, memos, news releases, personal and group discussions, etc.); (e) by whom; and (f) when.

Secondary school counseling and guidance programs are included in the critical and often microscopic examination of today's secondary schools. Such examinations can be either a threat or an opportunity. If the latter is to be realized, school counselors and counselor educators, including those involved in the preparation of school counselors, must give continued attention to how others perceive them. They must work closely with and respect the viewpoints of all their natural allies, especially the classroom teacher, if they are to continue to progress in their mission of developing optimal programs of counseling and guidance for all school youth.

References

Commission on Pre-College Guidance and Counseling. (1986). *Keeping the options open: Recommendations*. Evanston, IL: College Entrance Examination Board.

Crow, R. D., & Crow, A. (1951). *An introduction to guidance.* New York: American Book Co.

Downing, L. N. (1968). *Guidance and counseling services: An introduction.* New York: McGraw-Hill.

Galfo, A. J. (1975). *Interpreting educational research.* Dubuque, IA: (William C) Brown.

Gibson, R. L. (1965). *Teacher opinion of high school guidance programs.* Unpublished manuscript.

Gibson, R. L. (1988). *High school principals' opinions of role, function and training of school counselors.* Unpublished manuscript, Indiana University, Bloomington, IN.

Gibson, R. L., & Mitchell, M. H. (1986). *Introduction to counseling and guidance* (2nd ed.). New York: MacMillan.

Hartmen, K. E. (1988, June 1). Clarifying the role of school counselors. *Education Week,* p. 32.

Haverin, S. A. (1953). *Guidance services.* Bloomington, IL: McKnight & McKnight.

National Commission on Excellence in Education. (1983). *A nation at risk: The imperative for educational reform.* Washington, DC: U.S. Government Printing Office.

National Governors Association. (1986). *Time for results: The governor's 1986 report on education.* Washington, DC: Author.

Reynolds, S. (1988). School counselor survey for department of education task force on student services. (Indiana Association of Counseling and Development) *Hoosier Guidelines, 28*(1).

Problems for Which Seniors Would Seek Help from School Counselors

Roger L. Hutchinson
Cheryl A. Reagan

In the past decade, counselors have come under close scrutiny because school systems have been forced to work within strict financial limitations. Cutbacks have threatened to make the counselor an "endangered species"; yet, many of today's guidance services continue to be directed at routine maintenance activities (Wells & Ritter, 1979). A review of literature covering the past two decades reveals minimal change in students' perceptions of school counselors during that time (Hutchinson & Bottorff, 1986) despite increased emphases on credentialing of counselor education programs, supervised practicums, length of programs, and required internship experiences (Gladding, 1988; Hollis & Wantz, 1986). The need for accountability has demanded clarification of the counselor's role (Hutchinson, Barrick, & Groves, 1986; Hutchinson & Bottorff, 1986; Ibrahim, Helms, & Thompson, 1983).

In a letter From the Editor's Desk, Cole (1986) noted that conditions beyond the control of most counselors account for much of the mediocrity in the profession. But she observed that counselors often accept conditions over which they could exercise control. Such conditions include: "(1) lack of a written developmental guidance program or no program at all; (2) persistence in behaving like quasi-therapists, when time and again students and their parents tell us they want career and educational counseling; (3) acceptance of inappropriate tasks in their schools without protest; (4) failure to evaluate their effectiveness as professionals; and (5) professional isolation" (pp. 85–86).

Administrators, faculty members, and students, as well as counselors themselves, are often unsure of the counselor's functions (Ibrahim et al., 1983; Wells & Ritter, 1979). "Counselor training programs must become more relevant and field-based, as well as conscious of the needs and new directions of schools" (Gibson & Mitchell, 1986, p. 75). Departments of education historically have done a poor job of communicating a feeling of professional identity (Arbuckle, 1972). In turn, counselors fail to communicate clearly their role identity to superiors. Confusion over identity has resulted in many counselors feeling helpless and defeated. This discouragement is manifested by lack of assertiveness on the part of counselors to change their image from one of clerical paper pushing to one of being people oriented. It is likely that consumers of counseling services and other interested observers consider counselors just another administrator and consider administrators expendable commodities. Counselors need to clarify their goals, unite, and take an active part in communicating to the masses their expertise in carrying out these goals. Because students are the primary recipients of high school counselors' assistance, feedback as to how they perceive counselors is necessary in developing objectives to respond to students' needs.

Perceived Counselor Role

Students often view counselors in extremely general terms. The term "counselor" seems to be a catchall for varied specialists whose knowledge and training vary greatly in degrees of expertise. Students who have not experienced counseling tend to perceive the counselor in a less-flattering light (less knowledgeable, analytic, etc.) than do those who have been clients (Gelso, Brooks, & Carl, 1975). In addition, Peterson and DeGracie (1983) found that students who had experienced personal contact with a counselor at least once during the year were more positive toward the counselor regarding personal counseling, academic and vocational counseling, and distribution of information than were students who had not discussed their problems with a counselor. Students in this same study perceived counselors as spending most of their time on registration of students, academic and vocational counseling, and individual personal counseling in that order. They believed that, ideally, the counselor should spend the largest amount of time on individual personal counseling.

In a survey of 250 college freshmen about their perceptions of their high school counselors (Hutchinson & Bottorff, 1986), the researchers found that 89% of the students had needed career counseling, but only 40% received it while in high school. Seventy-nine percent (79%) had needed college information; 50% received it. Sixty percent (60%) said they had needed personal problem counseling while in high school; only 21% received it. In contrast, only 56% had needed help with scheduling, but 78% received that unsolicited help.

Historically, counselors have been identified by parents, students, teachers, and administrators as persons who know something about educational and vocational opportunities and who can be helpful with these concerns (Van Riper, 1971). Although students often perceive a counselor's role as one of providing personal help to them as opposed to disciplining or supervising, they do not clearly identify the counselor as one who helps with personal or academic problems (Crampton, 1981; Hutchinson & Bottorff, 1986; Lundt, 1981).

Van Riper (1971) found that students do not perceive clear distinctions between the roles of counselors, principals, and teachers and that counselors are closely identified by the functions they perform. It also has been known for some time (Van Riper, 1971; Wells & Ritter, 1979) that whatever functions are emphasized by the counselor are perceived as important by students, and the kinds of experiences they have actually had with counselors also influence their perceptions. For instance, if students' primary assistance from the counselor has been related to scheduling classes or monitoring truancies, they will perceive the counselor's role in a similar way. Because of the heightened demand for counselor accountability and the increasing awareness of the discrepancy between students' perceived needs and the services actually provided by counselors, it seems imperative that counselors not leave the perception of what they do, and what they are, to chance. If counselors desire to have students perceive them as fulfilling certain roles or functions, they must take an active part in carefully establishing those roles (Wells & Ritter, 1979). Unfortunately, neither students' perceptions of counselors (Hutchinson & Bottorff, 1986) nor counselors' perceptions of the functions they perform (Hutchinson et al., 1986) have changed drastically over the past two decades.

Where Students Go for Help

Most students apparently do not perceive the counselor as an appropriate person with whom to discuss personal problems. But a review of literature covering the past two decades indicates that a sizable proportion of both high school and post-high school students have reported being distressed by personal and vocational concerns. Thirty-nine percent (39%) of the students at Boston University reported needing help with academic problems; 35% needed assistance with vocational problems; 29% needed help with personal problems (Benedict, Apsler,

& Morrison, 1977). Similar concerns with which students need help from their counselors have also been revealed by other researchers (Fullerton & Potkay, 1973; Hutchinson & Bottorff, 1986; Kramer, Berger, & Miller, 1974).

Based on their experiences with high school counselors, college students often have modest expectations for beneficial counseling experiences (Tinsley & Harris, 1976). But one survey of university students and personnel (Tryon, 1980) disclosed an accepting attitude toward personal counseling in campus counseling centers. Although counselors as well as faculty and staff members perceived vocational and educational counseling as an appropriate function of counseling centers, counselors perceived social problems as a significantly more important topic for discussion by counselors and students than did other campus groups.

College students are more inclined than high school students to discuss uncomfortable feelings and emotions with their counselors (Gelso et al., 1975). When high school students were asked who they would talk to about almost anything, they rated their peers higher than teachers or principals (Van Riper, 1971). Leviton (1977) found that 67% of students surveyed had not had contact with their counselor about personal problems.

Van Riper's and Leviton's findings were confirmed by Wells and Ritter (1979) and again by Haughey and Bowman (1980). Haughey and Bowman also found that students most often contacted their counselor for help with school grades, planning their high school programs, and after-graduation job planning. Up to 80% of the students sampled in Wells' and Ritter's research reported that they would go to their counselor to change a class or ask about graduation requirements. The next highest counselor demand (51%) was in planning students' school programs. Forty percent (40%) of the students declared that they would ask a counselor for help with a teacher conflict. Leviton (1977) found exactly the same percentage of students who would see a counselor about deciding on a college major or examining career possibilities (25%) and assistance with a personal problem (4%) as did Wells and Ritter (1979).

When students in three school districts were asked to set priorities for how they would use counseling services (Haughey & Bowman, 1980), the need for counseling services for family problems was ranked 9, 12, and 7 by students in the various districts. Sex education was ranked 2, 9, and 11. Forty-five percent (45%) of the students said they would go to their parents for help with career decisions; only 26% would seek help from the counselor. A relative or friend would be the third most likely source sought out (16%). Yet, when students had concerns related to truancy, the counselor was most often the person consulted (54%).

In summary, even though the percentages reported vary and methods of study differ among researchers, students seem to consistently state that they do not perceive counselors as useful when they have a problem with a friend, a question about sex, a personal problem, or when they are in serious trouble (Wells & Ritter, 1979).

Why Students Seek Certain Persons

There are several possibilities to explain why students seek persons other than the counselor for assistance with personal problems. A study done by Leaverton (1976) revealed that one-third of the students were not adequately informed about the role of the counselor in their school. Students perceived the counselor as a disciplinarian; counselors did not perceive themselves in that role. Perhaps what the counselor believed to be personal counseling with the student was perceived by the student as a disciplinary action.

In studies analyzing rural vs. urban guidance programs, urban students were more often aware than were rural students that there was a counselor in their school. In both the Haughey and Bowman (1980) study and the Tryon (1980) study, only half of the student population was even aware that counseling services existed in their schools. Leaverton (1976) charged that if counselors perceive personal-problem counseling as a primary function, they need to clearly communicate this to their students. If students understand that this is a part of the counselor's role but still reject the service, counselors need to confirm their interest in working with students who have personal problems.

Additional reasons for why students have not taken their personal problems to counselors include observations that students perceive a lack of interest and understanding on the part of counselors, unavailability of counselors, and counselors not listening to or not really hearing student's concerns (Wells & Ritter, 1979). Other students have suggested that counselors need to be less dictatorial, provide more career counseling, show more personal interest in the student, and become more involved with the student (Leaverton, 1976).

Most counselors have entered the profession with the main objective of serving people and having the expertise to deal with personal problems. Research covering two decades seems to indicate that because counselors are still confused about their own professional identity, they may fail to communicate to their superiors what they perceive their role to be. As administrators have demanded that more and more administrative tasks be performed by the counselor, the counselor has been reduced to serving the system.

Concentration on clerical-type duties has also contributed to a narrow perception of the counselor's role. Record-keeping tasks keep counselors busy at their desks. This low profile creates an image to students that the counselor is inaccessible, lacking in interest, and lacking in involvement with students. A thorough and revealing study of clients' expectations of counselors (Tinsley, Workman, & Kass, 1980) revealed trends similar to those cited in other studies regarding the attitudes and behaviors of counselors and clients.

The possibility of abandoning personal counseling in the schools has been suggested (Bradley, 1978). She referred to the findings of Cox (1969) which concluded that counselors should either no longer concern themselves with personal problems or "rigorously campaign to convince others they can effectively deal with them" (p. 45).

Counselors are what they do. Their identity and the way they are perceived is likely to depend on the extent to which they emphasize certain distinctively serviceable functions (Van Riper, 1971). To be useful to students, counselors must be sensitive to the attitudinal responses of students and meet their needs. Students in the schools obviously have problems. To whom are students willing to talk about their concerns? If, indeed, students are unwilling to talk to their school counselors about personal problems, perhaps restructuring of school guidance programs is warranted. Our purpose in this study was to determine the problems for which selected high school seniors would seek help from their school counselors.

Method

Participants

This study was conducted during the 1987–1988 academic year and consisted of all Indiana senior high schools with enrollments of 900 to

1200 students in Grades 9–12. There are 48 such schools in Indiana. This enrollment size was chosen in an effort to make the results more easily generalized. Students in either smaller or larger schools might perceive counselors differently. Future research could compare schools of varying sizes to determine whether or not size is a factor. Ten schools, selected by random sampling, agreed to participate. High school seniors were surveyed because it was expected that they would have had the best opportunity for extensive experience with their counselors. A total of 1,734 students (885 boys, 849 girls) completed the questionnaires, for a 77% return rate.

Procedure

A letter was sent to principals of the schools selected by random sampling, requesting their participation in the study. All agreed to participate. Instructions for dissemination of materials, administration of the questionnaire, and a time schedule were then sent to the 10 principals. Students were given an introductory statement to read, which assured anonymity and informed participants that they could withdraw from the study at any time; they were asked to sign a form giving consent to participate. We had no direct control over administration of the questionnaires; however, principals were instructed not to allow counselors to administer them directly nor to be involved in collecting materials. Questionnaires were returned in prepaid mailing envelopes. Students' responses to the questionnaire were then tallied and converted to percentages.

Instrument

Literature covering the past two decades was reviewed to identify students' perceptions of counselors' roles. In a related study following this same line of research, one of the researchers had led 6 hours (three 2-hour sessions) of open forum discussion with 70 undergraduate students in groups of 17 or 18 students each. Discussion focused on their satisfaction with the services provided through their high school counseling programs. Based on the review of literature and the students' input, we developed a 24-item Likert-type questionnaire listing activities for which a counselor might be responsible. The instrument was designed to determine problems for which high school seniors would request help from their school counselors (see Appendix A).

Results

Student's responses clustered around two basic areas: school-related administrative type services and personal problems. Students were clearly most comfortable talking to their counselors about school-related administrative types of concerns and least comfortable discussing personal problems. Boys and girls alike strongly agreed that it was appropriate to talk to their counselors about gathering information on colleges and universities. More than 89% of the boys and girls combined checked either *strongly agree* or *agree* in response to that question. Similarly, students felt comfortable in asking their counselors for help with other school-related administrative concerns in the following descending order: graduation requirements (89.1%), registering for classes (89.0%), assistance in changing a class (87.3%), information regarding career opportunities (83.5%), scholarships and financial aid (81%), interpretation of test results (74.6%), deciding on a career (68.8%), assistance in job hunting (62.2%), conflicts with teachers (61.3%), orientation to a new school (60.9%), discipline problems (55.8%), and truancy problems (47.0%).

But students seemed to be less comfortable in sharing personal problems with their counselors. The more personal the nature of the problem, the less likely these students were to perceive the counselor as a person they could talk to about it. Fewer than half of the students (45.6%) felt that they could talk to a counselor about feelings and values. Other personal problems in descending order as selected by students included: alcohol or drug education (41.6%), conflicts with peers (39.6%), general personal problems (39.5%), how to get along in life (34.2%), alcohol or drug problems (33.3%), sexual, physical, or emotional abuse (32.2%), conflicts with parents (30.7%), relieving tension (26.5%), boy-girl relationships (19.5%), and a question about sex (11.1%).

It is also interesting to note in Table 1 (see rank orders in parentheses) that boys and girls were in nearly identical accord regarding the kinds of problems for which they would seek help from their school counselors. A more detailed account of problems for which senior boys and girls combined would seek help from their school counselors is included in Table 2.

Table 1
Rank Order[a] Comparison of Problems for Which High School Seniors Would Request Help from School Counselors

Question number	Boys	Girls	Boys & Girls combined
6. Info. about college, etc.	(2.0) 88.2	(1.0) 91.0	(1.0) 89.6
21. Graduation requirements	(3.0) 87.3	(2.0) 90.9	(2.0) 89.1
7. Registering for classes	(1.0) 88.3	(3.0) 89.7	(3.0) 89.0
4. Assistance in changing a class	(4.0) 86.8	(4.0) 87.9	(4.0) 87.3
23. Info. about career opportunities	(5.0) 80.4	(5.0) 86.9	(5.0) 83.5
8. Scholarships/financial aid	(6.0) 77.8	(6.0) 84.3	(6.0) 81.0
10. Interpretations of test results	(7.0) 72.5	(7.0) 76.8	(7.0) 74.6
22. Deciding on a career	(8.0) 65.6	(8.0) 72.2	(8.0) 68.8
5. Assistance in job hunting	(11.0) 58.7	(9.0) 65.8	(9.0) 62.2
13. Conflicts with teachers	(10.0) 59.6	(10.0) 63.1	(10.0) 61.3
9. Orientation to a new school	(9.0) 60.1	(11.0) 62.0	(11.0) 60.9
1. Discipline problems	(12.0) 54.7	(12.0) 57.1	(12.0) 55.8
18. Truancy problems	(14.0) 46.1	(13.0) 47.0	(13.0) 47.0
2. Awareness of feelings and values	(13.0) 46.7	(16.0) 44.6	(14.0) 45.6
16. Alcohol or drug education	(16.0) 38.7	(14.5) 44.8	(15.0) 41.6
15. Conflicts with peers	(17.0) 34.6	(14.5) 44.8	(16.0) 39.6
3. General personal problems	(15.0) 39.3	(17.0) 39.6	(17.0) 39.5
20. How to get along in life	(19.0) 31.0	(18.0) 37.6	(18.0) 34.2
17. Alcohol or drug problems	(18.0) 32.3	(20.0) 34.7	(19.0) 33.3
24. Sexual, physical, or emotional abuse	(20.0) 29.6	(19.0) 34.9	(20.0) 32.2
14. Conflicts with parents	(21.0) 27.3	(21.0) 34.3	(21.0) 30.7
12. Relieving tension	(22.0) 25.9	(22.0) 27.1	(22.0) 26.5
19. Boy/girl relationships	(23.0) 18.9	(23.0) 20.1	(23.0) 19.5
11. A question about sex	(24.0) 12.0	(24.0) 10.0	(24.0) 11.1

Note. The numbers in parentheses are rank orders. All others are percentages.
[a]Rank order indicates the percentage of students checking either *Strongly Agree* or *Agree* to each question.

Discussion and Conclusions

Our results are in concert with previous studies in that these Indiana students obviously felt more comfortable talking to their counselors

Table 2
Problems for Which High School Senior Boys and Girls (Combined) Would Request Help from School Counselors (*N*=1734)

Question number	Strongly agree	Agree	Undecided	Disagree	Strongly disagree
1	215 (12.3)	756 (43.5)	438 (25.2)	211 (12.1)	114 (6.5)
2	181 (10.4)	612 (35.2)	486 (28.0)	303 (17.4)	152 (8.7)
3	216 (12.4)	470 (27.1)	431 (24.8)	373 (21.5)	244 (14.0)
4	977 (56.3)	539 (31.0)	91 (5.2)	74 (4.2)	53 (3.0)
5	414 (23.8)	666 (38.4)	436 (25.1)	137 (7.9)	81 (4.6)
6	1031 (59.4)	524 (30.2)	100 (5.7)	45 (2.5)	34 (1.9)
7	924 (53.2)	621 (35.8)	114 (6.5)	43 (2.4)	32 (1.8)
8	764 (44.0)	642 (37.0)	224 (12.9)	62 (3.5)	42 (2.4)
9	435 (25.0)	624 (35.9)	548 (31.6)	81 (4.6)	46 (2.6)
10	586 (33.7)	710 (40.9)	284 (16.3)	95 (5.4)	59 (3.4)
11	61 (3.5)	132 (7.6)	545 (31.4)	393 (22.6)	603 (34.7)
12	108 (6.2)	353 (20.3)	606 (34.9)	387 (22.3)	280 (16.1)
13	297 (17.1)	767 (44.2)	321 (18.5)	213 (12.2)	136 (7.8)
14	146 (8.4)	388 (22.3)	507 (29.2)	403 (23.2)	290 (16.7)
15	165 (9.5)	523 (30.1)	479 (27.6)	344 (19.8)	223 (12.8)
16	185 (10.6)	539 (31.0)	528 (30.4)	263 (15.1)	219 (12.6)
17	166 (9.5)	414 (23.8)	536 (30.9)	315 (18.1)	303 (17.4)
18	190 (10.9)	626 (36.1)	533 (30.7)	238 (13.7)	147 (8.4)
19	115 (6.6)	225 (12.9)	492 (28.3)	440 (25.3)	462 (26.6)
20	141 (8.1)	454 (26.1)	578 (33.3)	357 (20.5)	204 (11.7)
21	937 (54.0)	610 (35.1)	93 (5.3)	48 (2.7)	46 (2.6)
22	531 (30.6)	664 (38.2)	321 (18.5)	126 (7.2)	92 (5.3)
23	729 (42.0)	721 (41.5)	173 (9.9)	63 (3.6)	48 (2.7)
24	186 (10.7)	374 (21.5)	565 (32.5)	257 (14.8)	352 (20.2)

Note. Figures in parentheses are percentages; all others are frequencies.

about school-related administrative concerns than about personal problems. Ironically, students do have many personal problems, and it seems that they would need the most help in those areas. This becomes especially critical when one considers the types of problems with which high school students struggle and the ones that receive so much attention from the media. These problems would obviously include those for which fewer than one-third of the students in this study would seek help from counselors: alcohol or drug problems; sexual, physical, or emotional abuse; conflicts with parents; relieving tension; boy-girl relationships; and questions about sex.

Both our personal observations and a review of literature spanning two decades indicate that there are several probable reasons for students not approaching their counselors for help with personal problems. Many counselors are not sure of their role; often the colleges and universities from which they received their training have not clearly communicated this professional identity to them. Counselors, in turn, fail to communicate to administrators and students who they are and what they do. This often results in their being bogged down with administrative duties. Thus, students identify counselors by the functions that counselors actually perform and do not perceive clear role distinctions between their principals, teachers, or counselors. Consequently, students might not perceive counselors as safe or confidential sources of help.

Students face tough decisions that can drastically alter their lives, and they need a safe place in which to explore choices available to them. Counselors must decide whether or not they are going to meet this challenge and provide such a service. If so, they must clearly define their role to both students and administrators and avoid being paper oriented instead of people oriented.

References

Arbuckle, D. S. (1972). The counselor: Who? What? *The Personnel and Guidance Journal, 50,* 785–790.

Benedict, A. R., Apsler, R., & Morrison, S. (1977). Student views of their counseling needs and counseling services. *Journal of College Student Personnel, 13,* 110–114.

Bradley, M. K. (1978). Counseling past and present: Is there a future? *The Personnel and Guidance Journal, 51,* 42–45.

Cole, C. (1986). Obstacles to excellence in counseling. *The School Counselor, 34,* 85–86.

Cox, H. C. (1969). The relative standing of the high school counselor as perceived by students, parents, teachers, and counselors. *Dissertation Abstracts International, 30,* 3776–3777A.

Crampton, R. B. (1981). The adequacy of counseling as perceived by academically superior adolescents in rural Alabama schools. *Dissertation Abstracts International, 42,* 547A.

Fullerton, J. S., & Potkay, C. R. (1973). Student perceptions of pressures, helps, and psychological services. *Journal of College Student Personnel, 14,* 355–361.

Gelso, C., Brooks, L., & Carl, N. J. (1975). *Perceptions of "counselors" and other help givers: A consumer analysis.* College Park: University of Maryland, Counseling Center.

Gibson, R. L., & Mitchell, M. H. (1986). *Introduction to counseling and guidance* (2nd ed.). New York: Macmillan.

Gladding, S. T. (1988). *Counseling: A comprehensive profession.* Columbus, OH: (Charles E.) Merrill.

Haughey, J., & Bowman, J. (1980). *Counseling and guidance services in selected junior high schools: Utilization and identified need.* Winnipeg, Canada: Manitoba Department of Education, Winnipeg Planning and Research Branch.

Hollis, J. W., & Wantz, R. A. (1986). *Counselor preparation 1986–1989.* Muncie, IN: Accelerated Development.

Hutchinson, R. L., Barrick, A. L., & Groves, M. (1986). Functions of secondary school counselors in the public schools: Ideal and actual. *School Counselor, 34,* 87–91.

Hutchinson, R. L., & Bottorff, R. L. (1986). Selected high school counseling services: Student assessment. *School Counselor, 33,* 350–354.

Ibrahim, F. A., Helms, B. J., & Thompson, D. L. (1983). Counselor role and function: An appraisal by consumers and counselors. *The Personnel and Guidance Journal, 61,* 597–601.

Kramer, H. C., Berger, F., & Miller, G. (1974). Student concerns and sources of assistance. *Journal of College Student Personnel, 15,* 389–393.

Leaverton, W. W. (1976). *The counselor's roles as perceived by the students and counselors.* Ft. Collins: Colorado State University, Department of Vocational Education.

Leviton, H. S. (1977). Consumer feedback on a secondary school guidance program. *The Personnel and Guidance Journal, 55,* 242–244.

Lundt, M. L. (1981). An evaluation of high school counseling as perceived by mentally gifted, special education, and regular high school students. *Dissertation Abstracts International, 42,* 552A.

Peterson, S., & DeGracie, J. (1983). *Secondary counseling services as perceived by selected publics* (Mesa Public Schools Report). Mesa: Arizona Department of Research and Evaluation.

Tinsley, H. E. A., & Harris, D. J. (1976). Client expectations for counseling. *Journal of Counseling Psychology, 23,* 173–177.

Tinsley, H. E. A., Workman, K. R., & Kass, R. A. (1980). Factor analysis of the domain of client expectancies about counseling. *Journal of Counseling Psychology, 27,* 561–570.

Tryon, G. S. (1980). A review of the literature concerning perceptions of and preferences for counseling center services. *Journal of College Student Personnel, 21,* 304–310.

Van Riper, B. W. (1971). Student perception: The counselor is what he does. *School Counselor, 19,* 53–56.

Wells, C. E., & Ritter, K. (1979). Paperwork, pressure, and discouragement: Student attitudes toward guidance services and implications for the profession. *The Personnel and Guidance Journal, 58,* 170–175.

Appendix A
Questionnaire

Directions: Do not put your name on this questionnaire. Please read each statement carefully. There are no right or wrong answers. The following is a list of activities for which the high school counselor might be responsible. Please circle the response that most nearly reflects your feelings about the importance of the statement. Please respond to each item whether or not you have had direct experience with a school counselor.

1. *Strongly agree* (SA)
2. *Agree* (A)
3. *Undecided/no opinion* (?)
4. *Disagree* (D)
5. *Strongly disagree* (SD)

1. Discipline problems	SA A ? D SD
2. Development of awareness of feelings and values	SA A ? D SD
3. General personal problems	SA A ? D SD
4. Assistance in changing a class	SA A ? D SD
5. Assistance in job hunting	SA A ? D SD
6. Current information about colleges, universities, or technical schools	SA A ? D SD
7. Registering for high school classes	SA A ? D SD
8. Obtaining scholarships or financial aid	SA A ? D SD
9. Orientation to a new school	SA A ? D SD
10. Interpretations of test results	SA A ? D SD
11. A question about sex	SA A ? D SD
12. Relieving tension	SA A ? D SD
13. Conflicts with teachers	SA A ? D SD
14. Conflicts with parents	SA A ? D SD
15. Conflicts with peers	SA A ? D SD
16. Alcohol or drug education	SA A ? D SD
17. Alcohol or drug problem	SA A ? D SD
18. Truancy problems	SA A ? D SD
19. Boyfriend-girlfriend relationships	SA A ? D SD
20. How to get along in everyday life	SA A ? D SD
21. Graduation requirements	SA A ? D SD
22. Deciding on a career	SA A ? D SD
23. Information regarding career opportunities	SA A ? D SD
24. Sexual, physical, or emotional abuse	SA A ? D SD

Please circle one: **Male**   **Female**

Enhancing the School Climate: New Opportunities for the Counselor

Leslie S. Kaplan
Kevin E. Geoffroy

A number of prominent educators (Dorman, Lipsitz, & Verner, 1985; Furtwengler, 1985; Saphier & King, 1985) have recently called for a change in American education that emphasizes meeting students' and teachers' affective needs in addition to their cognitive needs. The professional literature in educational administration and instruction is now recognizing what school counselors have long known and advocated: Frustrated or unhappy teachers and students can neither teach nor learn effectively. School climate variables can positively affect the teaching and learning in a school. The school climate literature addresses the perspective and expertise of school counselors and offers a viable leadership role for counselors in their schools.

Michaels (1988) stated that current philosophy about teaching, learning, and human nature needs to be re-examined and that we must create a new environment that makes growth possible for both students and teachers. According to Michaels, the newly adopted first wave of educational reform focused on raising academic standards (e.g., lengthening the school day, making courses more rigorous, and increasing accountability for teachers and students). He proposed a second wave of educational reform for the 21st Century, which includes affective dimensions such as individual decision making, a participatory environment for students and staff, and an increased personalization of the school environment through an atmosphere of trust, high expectations, and a sense of fairness.

Arthur Combs (1988) wrote that new educational reforms should focus on students and professional educators as opposed to methods. He sees helping students explore and examine their belief systems as education's major thrust. The atmosphere for exploring beliefs requires openness, confrontation, and experimentation. These elements should be familiar to school counselors. William Glasser (Brant, 1988b; Glasser,

1986) advised that students must achieve a sense of belonging and control within their classrooms. He proposed that students work in teams in which they identify their own personal needs and establish the skills to make and carry out choices in a supportive school climate. Choice making has long been a productive arena for the skilled school counselor. Paulo Freire, author of *Pedagogy of the Oppressed* (1970) and an international literacy figure, and Theodore R. Sizer, professor and chair, Department of Education, Brown University, both advocated a counseling point of view when they suggested changing the classroom climate to one of cooperative involvement (Brant, 1988a; Timpson, 1988). With this continuing interest in school reform and its focus on altering the school climate, this article explores the role of the school counselor as an influencing factor and potential leader in this movement.

What is School Climate?

School climate may be defined as how people feel about the qualities of a school and the people in that school. "Climate" includes the total physical and psychological environment to which people respond. Climate further reflects how students, teachers, administrators, and the community feel about their school.

Schools with positive climates are affectively healthy places where people care, respect, and trust each other. These are people-centered systems in which beliefs, values, procedures, rules, regulations, and policies show respect for the students, faculty, and staff who work there. People in such schools feel a high sense of pride and ownership, which comes from having the opportunity to make decisions and choices about their lives in the school. Furthermore, positive school climates change as the needs of people within the schools change, reshaping to meet new needs.

In a recent article, Childers and Fairman (1986) stressed the importance of a productive school climate when they stated,

> Schools have an obligation to provide a healthy organizational climate that is conducive to optimal personal-social and academic learning. Environments that provide individuals with a feeling of significance, a sense of competence, and a belief that they have some control over important aspects of their environment will enable these individuals to feel more comfortable, feel greater self-worth, and consequently take more risks. The lack of these

elements in the public schools is a predominant cause of student failure...In addition...[it] is a major cause of burnout among professional staff members.... (p. 332)

School Climate *Is* the Guidance Curriculum

Recent literature on school climate, as well as the most recent school reform reports, have ignored the school-enhancing role of counselors. The authors of these works focused primarily on the traditional basics of schools: the principal's leadership, teaching, curriculum, and students. Guidance services and school counselors were either overlooked or designated an "aside" in recommendations for creating positive school climates.

Educators are shortsighted when they view school counselors and guidance services as being on the periphery of education. Guidance and counseling are not outside the American educational mainstream. The interface between cognitive and affective dimensions now recognized by supporters of positive school climates has long been the realm of school counselors. School administrators risk bypassing those very professionals who have been advocating this reality for many years. Counselors have important professional knowledge, attitudes, and skills essential to building positive school climates.

Reviewing the literature on effective schools and positive school climates, authors should look anew at the school counselors' traditional curriculum, which already advances the following 10 broad goals:

1. Treat each student as an individual who can learn and be successful in school.
2. Respect student and teacher self-esteem as important factors in the learning process.
3. Make opportunities for student self-exploration and self-definition to help the students find meaning and relevance in their school experience and future lives.
4. Teach students and help them use decision-making and problem-solving strategies.
5. Develop open and effective communication skills.
6. Provide regular and appropriate feedback to students as a means to help students monitor their own progress.

7. Provide opportunities for student and teacher participation in the learning process, as well as in the entire educational enterprise, to promote ownership and investment in their own growth.
8. See problem solving as focusing on solutions rather than victims.
9. Consider discipline as focusing on helping students learn more appropriate behaviors to meet their needs.
10. Value prevention rather than remediation.

These 10 climate variables regard the school's affective dimensions as vital qualities that influence student learning. Here, in the educational literature on positive school climate, is "the guidance point of view" (Edgemon, Remley, & Snoddy, 1985) without any overt recognition of either its guidance origin or its presence in today's guidance program.

School counselors are school change agents. School counselors see themselves as change agents in individual and group behavior. They have specialized professional training in developmental psychology, learning theory, personality theories, group processes, and program evaluation. They have professional expertise in human relations and communications skills.

School counselors have the potential to become organizational change agents as well. They hold a unique organizational position and perspective in the school. The staff authority that counselors hold is advisory and supportive. Counselors also interact regularly with all relevant school populations: students, teachers, administrators, and parents, as well as with community groups and agencies. These populations freely discuss private concerns and seek advice from the counselor. As a result, counselors become aware of information not available to the larger system. They become "system problem-sensing" agents (Podemski & Childers, 1980, p. 172), able to identify the needs and potential problems of each group and the resources each brings to the school. Moreover, counselors have a systems perspective as they interface with the entire school program, curricular and cocurricular, and with the individuals and data functioning within the program.

Counselors' perspective and expertise in a variety of affective and cognitive areas, already effective within the guidance office, can contribute to the entire school's climate. Counselors with personal knowledge of students' familial, personal, or social barriers to learning can help the students identify and resolve many issues that prevent effective learning. Counselors understand and can design appropriate interventions for students with special needs, including students who are handicapped, gifted, acting out, dropouts, underachievers, and procrastinators. Ongoing educational planning helps students tie coursework to personal meaning, because students' interests, abilities, priorities, and goals contribute to not only course selection but also student ownership of their educational experiences. Likewise, counselor consultation provides indirect service to students through direct services to teachers, parents, and community agencies (Reschly, 1976).

Eight Roles for Counselors in Creating a Positive School Climate

For counselors to take an active role in building a positive school climate, they can focus on the following roles suggested by Lippitt (1973).

1. *Advocate.* The counselor, with a background of professional knowledge and experiences, may view a school's practice as unworkable and may attempt to offer the school a more effective strategy. In addition, with a full understanding of each student as an individual, counselors can work to find the best fit between the student's needs and the school's program. This occasionally means "lobbying" for justifiable exceptions to accepted practices to meet valid student needs.

2. *Expert.* Counselors can become resources for technical questions related to student growth and development, career development, educational measurement as assessment, educational and career planning, problem solving, decision making, communication skills, stress management, crisis management, and other educational and mental health issues relevant to students and faculty.

3. *Trainer.* Counselors can provide staff development activities on topics that will help teachers and administrators work more effectively with students. These topics include knowing oneself better, crisis intervention, anger management, communication skills, and problem-solving skills. In addition, counselors can assist staff in working with students who have experienced difficulties outside school, such as a death, a family divorce, a single parent or a stepfamily living arrangement, substance abuse, and stress management.

4. *Alternative Identifier.* Counselors' unique role and perspective in the school means possibilities for alternative solutions not ordinarily considered by administrators or classroom teachers. School counselors

speak with so many diverse and interacting populations outside and within the school that counselors many times become aware of alternatives not readily apparent to regular school staff.

5. *Collaborator.* Counselors, who are used to working closely in a problem-solving mode with a wide range of individuals from varying backgrounds and of varying ages, work well with others as part of a team. Counselors see themselves as a vital support service, capable of leadership and teamwork, depending on the task.

6. *Process Specialist.* Counselors are able to help problem-solving groups of fellow professionals, students, or community agencies work more effectively through their individual and group facilitation skills honed by training and experience in group counseling and guidance activities.

7. *Fact Finder.* Counselors are knowledgeable about data-collecting methods through interviews, surveys, observations, or questionnaires. With these techniques, counselors are able to gather data about the school, the community, its persons, and its needs.

8. *Reflector.* Counselors can serve as catalysts to the school. As listeners, they can clearly summarize others' deliberations and ask focusing questions to help set the direction for problem-solving actions.

School counselors are relevant to the achievement of a positive school climate. By virtue of their professional knowledge, attitudes, and skills, they should play a major role for the entire school system in creating and expanding positive school climates.

References

Brant, R. (1988a). On changing secondary schools: A conversation with Ted Sizer. *Educational Leadership, 45*(5), 30–36.

Brant, R. (1988b). On students' needs and team learning: Conversation with William Glasser. *Educational Leadership, 45*(6), 38–45.

Childers, J. H., & Fairman, M. (1986). The school counselor as facilitator of organizational health. *The School Counselor, 33*(5), 332–337.

Combs, A. W. (1988). New assumptions for educational reform. *Educational Leadership, 45*(5), 38–40.

Dorman, G., Lipsitz, J., & Verner, P. (1985). Improving schools for young adolescents. *Educational Leadership, 42*(6), 44–49.

Edgemon, A. W., Remley, T., Jr., & Snoddy, H. N. (1985). Integrating the counselor's point of view. *The School Counselor, 32*(4), 296-301.

Furtwengler, W. J. (1985). Implementing strategies for a school effectiveness program. *Phi Delta Kappan, 67*(4), 262-264.

Glasser, W. (1986). *Control theory in the classroom.* New York: Harper & Row.

Lippitt, G. L. (1973). *Visualizing change: Model building and the change process.* Fairfax, VA: NTL Learning Resources Corporation, Inc.

Michaels, K. (1988). Caution: Second wave reform taking place. *Educational Leadership, 45*(5), 3.

Podemski, R. S., & Childers, J. H., Jr. (1980). The counselor as change agent: An organizational analysis. *The School Counselor, 27*(3), 168–174.

Reschly, D. L. (1976). School psychology consultation: Frenzied, faddish, or fundamental? *Journal of School Psychology, 4*, 104–113.

Saphier, J., & King, M. (1985). Good seeds grow in strong cultures. *Educational Leadership, 42*(6), 67–74.

Timpson, W. M. (1988). Paulo Freire: Advocate of literacy through liberation. *Educational Leadership, 45*(5), 62–66.

Role Statement:
The School Counselor

American School Counselor Association

The American School Counselor Association recognizes and supports the implementation of comprehensive developmental counseling programs at all educational levels. The programs are designed to help all students develop their educational, social, career, and personal strengths and to become responsible and productive citizens. School counselors help create and organize these programs, as well as provide appropriate counselor interventions.

School counseling programs are developmental by design, focusing on needs, interests, and issues related to the various stages of student growth. There are objectives, activities, special services and expected outcomes, with an emphasis on helping students to learn more effectively and efficiently. There is a commitment to individual uniqueness and the maximum development of human potential. A counseling program is an integral part of a school's total educational program.

The School Counselor

The school counselor is a certified professional educator who assists students, teachers, parents, and administrators. Three generally recognized helping processes used by the counselor are counseling, consulting and coordinating: (1) Counseling is a complex helping process in which the counselor establishes a trusting and confidential working relationship. The focus is on problem solving, decision making, and discovering personal meaning related to learning and development; (2) Consultation is a cooperative process in which the counselor-consultant assists others to think through problems and to develop skills that make them more effective in working with students; (3) Coordination is a leadership process in which the counselor helps organize and manage a school's counseling program and related services.

School counselors are employed in elementary, middle/junior high, senior high, and post-secondary schools. Their work is differentiated by attention to age-specific developmental stages of growth and related interests, tasks, and challenges. School counselors are human behavior and relationship specialists who organize their work around fundamental interventions.

Counselor interventions have sometimes been referred to as functions, services, approaches, tasks, activities, or jobs. They have, at times, been viewed as roles themselves, helping to create the image of the counselor. In a comprehensive developmental counseling program, school counselors organize their work schedules around the following basic interventions:

Individual Counseling

Individual counseling is a personal and private interaction between a counselor and a student in which they work together on a problem or topic of interest. A face-to-face, one-to-one meeting with a counselor provides a student maximum privacy in which to freely explore ideas, feelings, and behaviors. School counselors establish trust and build a helping relationship. They respect the privacy of information, always considering actions in terms of the rights, integrity, and welfare of students. Counselors are obligated by law and ethical standards to report and to refer a case when a person's welfare is in jeopardy. It is a counselor's duty to inform an individual of the conditions and limitations under which assistance may be provided.

Small Group Counseling

Small group counseling involves a counselor working with two or more students together. Group size generally ranges from five to eight members. Group discussions may be relatively unstructured or may be based on structured learning activities. Group members have an opportunity to learn from each other. They can share ideas, give and receive feedback, increase their awareness, gain new knowledge, practice skills, and think about their goals and actions. Group discussions may be problem-centered, where attention is given to particular concerns or problems. Discussions may be growth-centered, where general topics are related to personal and academic development.

Large Group Guidance

Large group meetings offer the best opportunity to provide guidance to the largest number of students in a school. Counselors first work with students in large groups wherever appropriate because it is the most efficient use of time. Large group work involves cooperative learning methods, in which the larger group is divided into smaller working groups under the supervision of a counselor or teacher. The counseling curriculum, composed of organized objectives and activities, is delivered by teachers and/or counselors in classrooms or advisory groups. School counselors and teachers may co-lead some activities. Counselors develop and present special guidance units which give attention to particular developmental issues or areas of concern in their respective schools and they help prepare teachers to deliver part of the guidance and counseling curriculum.

Consultation

The counselor as a consultant helps people to be more effective in working with others. Consultation helps individuals think through problems and concerns, acquire more knowledge and skills, and become more objective and self-confident. This intervention can take place in individual or group conferences, or through staff-development activities.

Coordination

Coordination as a counselor intervention is the process of managing different indirect services which benefit students and being a liaison between school and community agencies. It may include organizing special events which involve parents or resource people in the community in guidance projects. It often entails collecting data and disseminating information. Counselors might coordinate a student needs assessment, the interpretation of standardized tests, a child study team, or a guidance related teacher or parent education program.

The Preparation of School Counselors

School counselors are prepared for their work through the study of interpersonal relationships and behavioral sciences in graduate education courses in accredited colleges and universities. Preparation involves special training in counseling theory and skills related to school settings. Particular attention is given to personality and human development theories and research, including career and life-skills development; learning theories, the nature of change and the helping process; theories and approaches to appraisal, multicultural and community awareness; educational environments; curriculum development; professional ethics; and program planning, management, and evaluation.

Counselors are prepared to use the basic interventions in a school setting, with special emphasis on the study of helping relationships, facilitative skills, brief counseling; group dynamics and group learning activities; family systems; peer helper programs; multicultural and cross-cultural helping approaches; and educational and community resources for special school populations.

School counselors are aware of their own professional competence and responsibilities within the school setting. They know when and how to refer or involve other professionals. They are accountable for their actions and participate in appropriate studies and research related to their work.

Responsibility to the Profession

To assure high quality practice, counselors are committed to continued professional growth and personal development. They are active members of the American Association for Counseling and Development and the American School Counselor Association, as well as state and local professional associations which foster and promote school counseling. They also uphold the ethical and professional standards of these associations.

School counselors meet the state certification standards and abide by the laws in the states where they are working. Counselors work cooperatively with individuals and organizations to promote the overall development of children, youth, and families in their communities.

The Role of the Secondary School Counselor

Doris Rhea Coy

Introduction

Knight-Ridder Newspapers' (1989) recent collection of statistics from the Children's Defense Fund, the 1985 Census data, annual crime reports and other information dating from 1985 to 1988 tell the story of how "it's not easy being a kid" in America. In just one day, an average of:

- 2,795 teenagers become pregnant
- 1,027 babies are born drug-or-alcohol-exposed in utero
- 211 children are arrested for drug abuse
- 135,000 children bring a gun to school
- 1,512 teenagers drop out of school
- 1,849 children are abused or neglected
- 6 teenagers commit suicide (Chauvin, 1990)

Within the confines of the school's walls, the individual trained to develop strategies to deal with this range of challenges, is the school counselor.

Goal of School Counseling

The major goals of counseling are to promote personal growth, prepare pupils to become literate and motivated workers, caring family members, and responsible citizens. Professionals concerned with education recognize that in addition to intellectual challenges, pupils encounter personal, social, educational, and career challenges. It is the role of the school counselor to develop strategies to address these challenges and to promote educational success.

Role of the School Counselor

Secondary school counselors, whose original purpose was to assist high school students in choosing appropriate courses and applying to colleges, are now a more integral part of students' daily lives. By practicing preventive and developmental counseling—helping students cope with stressors and pressures that can have momentous effects on their academic performance—the school counselor has taken on a role and function which are necessary components of the educational process. In addition, counselors who once spent more of their time working with students individually, today are more likely to reach a wider range of students through group counseling, classroom and group guidance.

The secondary school counselor is concerned with and accepts responsibility for assisting all students and has as her/his major concern the developmental needs and concerns of youth. The secondary school counselor is the person on the school staff with the professional competencies, understanding of behavioral science, philosophical orientation and position within the school necessary to provide such help to students.

The scope of practice of the secondary school counselor is influenced by several factors: state certification standards, counselor education programs, the nature of the school system, the counseling program within the school, professional organizations and school administrators. Among these factors, the school principal may be the most influential in determining the role of the secondary school counselor (Coy & Sears, 1991).

Principals are generally instrumental in formulating both the philosophy and goals of their school. If the administrator favors a quasi-administrative role, then the counselor may count credits, fill out college references, keep track of attendance and do scheduling. If, however, the administrator values prevention or counselor involvement with student development, the counselor will counsel, guide, consult and coordinate a developmental outcome-based program and will function as a team member in the educational process (Coy & Sears, 1991).

ASCA Statement on the Role of the School Counselor

The American School Counselor Association adopted a role statement for the school counselor in July of 1990. The statement applies to all school counselors, pre-K to postsecondary, yet the term that determines the role played by the counselors at the various levels is the term "developmental." The statement clearly states that the school counseling program is an integral part of a school's total educational program, that it is developmental by design, focusing on needs, interests, and issues related to the various stages of student growth. There is a commitment to individual uniqueness and the maximum development of human potential. There are objectives, activities, special services and expected outcomes, with an emphasis on helping students to learn more effectively and efficiently. The role of the secondary school counselor is differentiated by attention to age-specific developmental stages of growth and related interests, tasks and challenges of high school age students (ASCA, 1990).

Developmental Based Programs

The counselor who designs and implements a successful developmental outcome based program is capable of having a positive influence on the philosophical and goal oriented directions of the school as defined by the principal. According to Norman C. Gysbers (1990), "a comprehensive developmental program, by definition, leads to activities and structured group experiences for all students. It de-emphasizes administrative and clerical tasks, one-to-one counseling only, and limited accountability. It is proactive rather than reactive. For counselors there is a program to implement and, therefore, counselors are busy and unavailable for unrelated administrative and clerical duties" (Gysbers, 1990).

Through a comprehensive developmental school counseling program the emphasis is on the developmental stages of the students with whom the counselor works and the implementation of a school counseling program that is determined primarily by concern for meeting students' developmental needs. One of the first steps in developing a program involves conducting a comprehensive assessment of the student's needs and requests for services.

A comprehensive developmental school counseling program does not just occur. Counselors, students, parents, staff, and administrators must be willing to give time and effort to achieve a workable program for their community. The program must be built on the developmental needs of the students in the school, the needs of the students, and the demand for the service.

Through a comprehensive developmental school counseling program, the emphasis is on the developmental stages of the students with whom the counselor interacts and the implementation of a school counseling program that is determined primarily by concern for meeting students' developmental needs.

School Counselor Responsibilities

In a developmental school counseling program, the counselor has the following responsibilities:

1. To **design** the content of the program.
2. To be involved in the **delivery** of the developmental program content or curriculum.
3. To **counsel** students both individually and in small groups.
4. To provide classroom **guidance** or group guidance to students on issues dealing with prevention and remediation.
4. To **consult** with parents, teachers, other educators, and various community agencies.
5. To **coordinate** the efforts of the program and collaborate in the delivery (Coy & Sears, 1991).

Strategies for Delivering Service

School counselors employ four strategies in delivering their services: **Counseling** (individual and group), **Guidance** (group and classroom), **Consultation**, and **Coordination** (ASCA, 1990). A detailed definition of these strategies can be found in the ASCA Role Statement published in 1990.

Scope of Practice of the School Counselor

Personal/Social Domain

In addition to providing structured activities (guidance) for all students, counselors are expected to do personal and crisis counseling. Through such programs, many issues prevalent in society and in schools (drop-outs, substance and chemical abuse, suicide, irresponsible sexual behavior, eating disorders, pregnancy) can be addressed within the context of prevention. If however, the prevention focus is not successful, the counselors must rely on their counseling skills, crisis intervention skills, and a knowledge of referral sources (consultation).

Career Domain

In January, 1990, the results of a survey were released in the publication "Work in America: A Survey of U.S. Adults on Jobs, Careers and the Workplace." Among the findings of the survey were:

> Fifty-three percent said public high schools are not teaching job-seeking skills to students who are not going to college; and 40% said high schools are not helping students enough in the area of career choice.

From this data, it is clear that secondary school counselors must develop strategies to assist students in making career decisions. Forming a career identity, planning for the future, combating career stereotyping and analyzing skills and interests are but a few of the developmental goals students need to develop. Students cannot prepare for a career that will not exist when they graduate. Current updated information must be available to students, and individuals from business and industry must work closely with the school and the school counselor in preparing students for the world of work.

It should be noted that students and their parents consistently place career needs among their highest priorities. The secondary school counseling program should reflect this by placing a high emphasis on career development.

The NOICC guidelines are a valuable resource for school counselors to use when developing the career component of the developmental school counseling program.

Educational Domain

Students must develop skills that will assist them as they learn. The secondary school counselor through classroom guidance activities, individual counseling and group counseling can assist students in developing effective study skills, setting goals, and learning test-taking skills. The counselor who includes discussions on note taking, procrastination, time management, memory techniques, mnemonic devices, relaxation techniques, test anxiety, developing listening skills and others that will be useful to the student extends their skills to the total educational curriculum.

Advisory Committee

A valuable component to any school counseling program is an advisory committee. They can inform the community about the services available in the school and they can provide input into the development and revision of counseling services. They lend support to the counseling services, provide advice and support to the program and can be instrumental in identifying the goals and priorities of the program and communicating them to the community.

The formation of an advisory committee should be considered carefully. A nucleus of interested persons can assist in generating interest in and enthusiasm for the committee. The composition of the committee will vary with each school district but it should include representatives from all major groups in the school community.

The coordinator of the committee is an important member of the committee. This should be a counselor with a commitment to building strong communication ties between the advisory committee and the school.

Job Description and Counselor Evaluation

Each school counselor should have a board-adopted job description based on their board-adopted developmental school counseling program. The school counselor should be evaluated by an instrument created from the job description and the school counseling program.

Program Evaluation

The evaluation of the counseling program should be an ongoing process. Each phase of the development of the counseling program needs to be evaluated as does each activity. As a result of this process, the developmental program will grow as strengths and weaknesses are reviewed and appropriate adjustments made in the program.

Summary

Administrators can make a valuable contribution toward assuring effective developmental school counseling programs by:

1. Providing leadership for an ongoing competency/outcome based program.
2. Hiring competent, well trained, certified school counselors.
3. Understanding the needs of the school's student population.
4. Working with school board, faculty, administrative staff, and community to secure support for developmental school counseling programs.
5. Encouraging counselor accountability and evaluation of their progress toward goals, objectives and developmental student outcomes.
6. Basing school counselor evaluation on the board-approved job description which is based on the board-approved developmental school counseling program.

The schools of today are constantly changing and we must have programs in the school that address the developmental needs of the students that are served. The school counselor is the developmental specialist in the school who has the training and skills for providing such a program. However, the effectiveness of the school counseling program is greatly influenced by the leadership of the school principal. The program must be built around the needs of the students being served. This includes a commitment by a team of individuals devoted to meeting the needs of students, sons, daughters and citizens of our country.

References

American School Counselor Association. (1990). *The role of the school counselor*. Alexandria, VA: Author.

Chauvin, S. L. (1990, February). Startling statistics about children. *American Bar Association Journal, 8*.

Coy, D. R., & Sears, S. J. (1991). *The scope of practice of the secondary school counselor* (an ERIC/CAPS Digest). Ann Arbor, MI: ERIC Counseling and Personnel Services Clearinghouse.

Gysbers, N. C., & Henderson, P. (1988). *Developing and managing your school guidance program.* Alexandria, VA: American Association for Counseling and Development.

Gysbers, N. C. (1990). *Comprehensive guidance programs that work.* Ann Arbor, MI: ERIC Counseling and Personnel Services Clearinghouse.

Knight-Ridder Newspaper. (1989). *Children's Defense Fund.*

Sears, S. J. (1989). *Student competencies: A guide for school counselors.* Alexandria, VA: American Association for Counseling and Development.

Chapter 5

The Scope of Practice of the Secondary School Counselor— Personal/Social Counseling

Adolescents are growing up in a complex, fast-paced and fast-changing society. Often they don't understand what is happening or what to do about it. The demands of living in such a world hit young people harder because they have fewer adaptive mechanisms and strategies and are less in control of their world. Consequently, school counselors today, and in the foreseeable future, will be faced with more students burdened with social and emotional problems. These children experience problems in their families and at school as well as with stress, sexuality, substance abuse, suicide, physical and sexual abuse, eating disorders, peer group pressure and interpersonal relationships. School counselors are concerned with the total needs of all students and have the skills to intervene effectively. Furthermore, personal/social concerns are congruent with the educational mission of most schools and can be addressed through a comprehensive developmental counseling program.

Stress in school-age children is the result of a variety of factors (stressors). In assisting students to learn to manage stress, many skills taught in a developmental counseling program come into play. For example, decision-making, problem-solving, time management, assertiveness training, relaxation training, goal setting, conflict management, interpersonal skills and positive health care are all life skills which can reduce stress by increasing the competence, effectiveness and satisfaction of students. The article by Omizo, Omizo and Suzuki examines stressors and their symptoms and offers suggestions of ways in which counselors can assist students to manage stress.

Divorce promises to remain a fact of life for teens, and it is a crisis ranked by experts as second only to the death of a parent. Most children do not receive any outside help during their parents' breakup; therefore, school counselors must be prepared to respond to the urgent needs of these youngsters. Coffman and Roark describe a group counseling model for use by secondary school counselors to help students cope with the issue of divorce.

Suicide continues to be the second leading cause of death among adolescents. The May 1990 issue of *The School Counselor* includes a special theme section on "Suicide and the School Counselor." This volume contains many thought-provoking articles which address identification, prevention, intervention and postvention. Kalafat's article, reprinted here, reviews suicide statistics, warning signs, and goals for a school-based program. The author describes the role of the school in a comprehensive response program to adolescent suicide and lists the necessary program elements. Although the program includes a crisis intervention component, it is developmental in nature and attempts to identify, to respond to and to refer potentially suicidal adolescents.

Teenage sexuality issues, including intimacy, pregnancy, and sexual orientation present a challenge of immense magnitude with staggering personal and social costs. Many schools have sex education programs which address "plumbing" and disease prevention, and a few even provide birth control information and curricular alternatives for pregnant students. Issues that are currently being "hushed up" such as the neglected needs of homosexual young people, may soon be addressed as a result of our national concern about AIDS. Huey's article describes a program designed to intervene from the male perspective and addresses the "forgotten half" of the teenage pregnancy problem.

Drug use among adolescents, according to Oetting and Beauvais, is a symptom or reflection of the same personal and social problems that counselors have been confronting for years—lack of self-esteem, peer pressure, family problems, and emotional problems. The authors' suggest that rather than being addicted to drugs, adolescents are experiencing emotional and developmental problems which have made them susceptible to drug use. Since counselors are trained in these areas, the authors suggest that counselors can provide assistance. This proposal is in line with other studies suggesting that developmental group counseling seems to have promise for preventing drug use.

The dropout rate continues to command national attention. The negative consequences of dropping out of school are well documented and effect all of society in a negative way. Bearden, Spencer and Moracco examine the affective components of the decision to leave school, concluding that school is an unfriendly place for the potential dropout. The authors explore how the school counselor can intervene as a change agent in improving school climate, as well as providing more traditional interventions which include counseling (individual and group) and peer programs.

This chapter barely scratches the surface of the many personal/social needs of adolescents; consequently, secondary school counselors must continue their professional development in these areas. Through developmental, preventative programs which include the personal/social realms, counselors can help students learn to live as well as learn to learn.

Children and Stress: An Exploratory Study of Stressors and Symptoms

Michael M. Omizo
Sharon A. Omizo
Lisa A. Suzuki

Children today are living in a hectic and constantly changing world, one that is quite different from what it was a few decades ago. They are growing up much faster and must live up to the expectations and demands of parents, teachers, peers, and society. Children are often forced to adjust to numerous adverse situations such as divorce, death, and abuse without much assistance. These situations can be extremely confusing and frustrating. Many circumstances, including the unfortunate Shuttle disaster, kidnapping of hostages, airport bombings, and world hunger increase anxieties (Arent, 1984; Elkind, 1986; Medeiros, Porter, & Welch, 1983). These conditions create much stress among school-age children.

Many adults believe that children do not experience much stress because they are not expected to be responsible for many things in their lives, they have others to depend on, and they can do a variety of acceptable things to relieve stress. In fact, the opposite is true partly because they don't understand what is happening and partly because they don't know what to do about it.

Arent (1984) discusses children and stress in relation to the common or nontraumatic stressors, which may include family problems and some school problems. The severe stressors include divorce, death, abuse, violence, and accidents. All stresses have negative effects on the physical, emotional, social, and psychological development of children, which are similar to the negative effects of stress on adults. Children under stress experience a variety of serious problems (Chandler, 1982). Several researchers have revealed that children who are unable to relieve their high levels of stress have become depressed, impulsive, aggressive, antisocial, self-destructive, and irritable (Arent, 1984; Kuczen, 1982;

Price, 1986; Seyle, 1976; Tolman & Rose, 1985). These symptoms contribute to difficulties at school and at home.

There are a few studies that have investigated stress and children. These studies have either presented positions advocating stress management or evaluated intervention strategies to cope with stress. No study has provided data on stressors and symptoms from studying school-age children. The purpose of this exploratory study was to investigate stressors and symptoms in elementary, intermediate, and high school students. In order for school counselors, teachers, and parents to assist children in coping with stress, we believe it is important to have a better understanding of what events are stressful to them and what the indicators are that they are under stress.

Method

Sample

The sample included 60 children from grades 1–12. Twenty children were from the elementary level (Grades 1–6), 20 were from the intermediate level (Grades 7 and 8), and 20 were from the high school level (Grades 9–12). Participants from the three levels were selected to determine whether or not there were differences among the levels in stressors and symptoms. The sample was selected from one school district, which basically consisted of lower- to middle-class families. The participants were from various racial backgrounds.

Procedure

Initially, we randomly selected 50 students each from an elementary, intermediate, and high school to participate in the study. The participants were divided into smaller groups of 10 children of the same level (i.e., elementary) and a counselor met with each group for two sessions (1-1/2 hours each) to discuss the concept of stress, stressors, symptoms, and coping mechanisms. At the end of the second session, all of the participants rated themselves on a Stress Scale developed by the senior author. The scale ranged from 0 to 100 in intervals of 10, with zero indicating no stress and 100 the highest level of stress. The 20 participants from each school level who scored the highest were interviewed for approximately one hour about stressors and symptoms. Teachers of the 60 participants also provided characteristics of these children. We believed that the teachers' perceptions would provide valuable data on the symptoms of the children who scored high on stress. The teachers were unaware of the purpose of the study and the reason for the information they were providing.

Stressors were analyzed by the three school levels. To make sense of the overwhelming amount of data, we classified the stressors into categories. For example, stressors such as relationship problems with parents, difficulty with siblings, and pressures from parents were placed in the category of family problems. For each of the three levels, the five highest or most often mentioned stressors are listed. For the symptoms, four classifications (psychological, physiological, behavioral, and emotional) were used. These are not presented in any particular order.

Instruments

A Stress Scale developed by the senior author was used to measure stress among the children. This scale has been used in the past by Omizo, Kornfeld, Hammett, and Omizo (1986). They report reliability coefficients in the .70s to .80s for various school-age populations. Scores from the Stress Scale have been correlated with activity levels on biofeedback equipment and the Anxiety Subscales of the Dimensions of Self-Concept (Michael & Smith, 1978) and the 16 Personality Factor Questionnaire (16 PF) (Cattell, Eber, & Tatsuoka, 1970), with coefficients in the .40s to .50s. Although this Stress Scale uses one self-report score, we viewed it as appropriate and acceptable because: (a) it has been used successfully in the past, (b) the study was exploratory in nature, and (c) no other instrument was available. We interpret and discuss the results of this study in light of the possible limitations of the scale.

Data Analysis

We tabulated the data collected from the interviews with the participants and the information from the teachers by classifying the stressors into categories and then listing the categories in order of the most number of times mentioned. Symptoms were classified into psychological, physiological, behavioral, and emotional indicators.

Results

The following five stressors were cited most by the elementary *(n=20)*, intermediate *(n=20)*, and high school students *(n=20)*. They are presented in order of the number of times mentioned.

Stressors for Elementary School Children

1. *Family problems*. Parental disapproval, feeling unloved and abandoned, guilt feelings about parents' divorce, parents' fighting, competing with a sibling, not spending much time with parents (both parents working, latchkey situation), adjusting to stepparents and two households when parents are divorced.

2. *Feeling different*. Feelings of inferiority, not having the same material things as others, lack of awareness of self (strengths and weaknesses), and not accepting self.

3. *School-related problems*. Teachers not liking them, fear of failing, not getting homework done, failing to meet expectations of parents in regard to academic achievement, and not having friends.

4. *Discipline*. Afraid of being punished, unfair punishment, inconsistent discipline, and parents and teachers being too critical.

5. *General concerns*. Doing something wrong, feeling insecure, feeling that something is going to happen, feeling that something is scary.

Stressors for Intermediate School Children

1. *General adolescent problems*. Adjusting to developmental changes, not having enough autonomy, having different expectations from those of parents and teachers, being different, being part of a group, not accepting themselves, and not understanding things in their lives.

2. *Peer pressure*. Wanting to be accepted by friends, participating in things they don't feel comfortable with (i.e., drugs, sex, smoking, drinking), and not having the resources to be part of the "in" group.

3. *Family problems*. Dealing with stepparents, problems with siblings, and parents not understanding them.

4. *Not feeling in control*. Others telling them what to do, lack of resources (money, cars), not being allowed to think on their own and make decisions, and feeling that no one is listening to them.

5. *School-related problems.* Not doing well academically, not seeing the relevance of school, problems with teachers, and adjusting to the different teachers and students.

Stressors for High School Students

1. *Future.* Career decisions, accepting responsibilities, relationship problems as they affect future decisions, higher education, dealing with the many uncertainties in life, and not understanding themselves enough to make decisions about the future.

2. *School-related problems.* Getting good grades, taking courses to get into college, and teachers not understanding them.

3. *Peer pressure.* Not being accepted, being afraid of doing and saying the wrong thing, and doing things that they don't approve of.

4. *Substance abuse.* Use of cigarettes, drugs, alcohol.

5. *Family problems.* Having different goals from those of parents, lack of parental support, parents not understanding them, and conflicts with stepparents.

The symptoms of stress that were discussed by the participants and their teachers were classified into four areas: psychological, physiological, behavioral, and emotional.

1. *Psychological.* Anxiety, depression, lack of motivation, withdrawal, mood swings or changes, difficulty in paying attention, being unhappy, thoughts of suicide, lack of risk-taking behavior, unrealistic goal setting, low self-efficacy, and having nightmares.

2. *Physiological.* Headaches, stomach aches, tension headaches, tight muscles, dental problems, diarrhea, constipation, hives, fatigue, hypertension, and ulcers.

3. *Behavioral.* Unable to sleep, restlessness, interpersonal problems, maladaptive and inappropriate behaviors, fighting, acting out, overeating, smoking, substance abuse, lower achievements, escape or running away, regressed behaviors (tantrums, wetting pants), verbal and physical aggression, use of denial and avoidance, daydreaming, impulsive behavior, loss of memory, self-destructive behaviors, truancy, and juvenile delinquency.

4. *Emotional.* Fear of failure and success, overreactions or inappropriate reactions or both, irritability, low self-esteem, insecurity, feeling inferior, and feeling guilty.

Discussion

In this section we: (a) discuss the stressors for the various levels separately, (b) compare the stressors, (c) discuss the symptoms, and (d) present implications and suggestions for school counselors. The results indicate that children at different levels in the schools have similar and yet different kinds of stressors. One should keep in mind that the stressors overlap and some of the stressors could fall in several categories. The categories were developed to organize, understand, and make better use of the data.

For children in the elementary school, the stressors, in order of frequency, were family problems, feeling different, school-related problems, discipline, and general concerns. Many of the family problems involved relationships with parents and siblings. Difficulties that the families were having such as divorce, both parents working, and stepparenting were commonly mentioned. The children did not seem to not have a clear understanding of the problems but just did not feel comfortable with the situation. Many children felt guilty about the situation and somehow felt responsible. In situations that involved divorce, the majority of the children also felt abandoned and that they were not loved.

Stressors related to feeling different from the other children were mainly feelings of inferiority. In most instances, the children did not seem to be aware of their strengths and weaknesses. They seemed to have low self-esteem in that they did not accept some characteristics of themselves.

The children also mentioned school-related stressors, with many of the children reporting that it was important that their teachers like them. Some of the stressors involved performance in school, such as not doing as well as their parents and teachers expected and not getting their homework done. It seems that there were many pressures from a variety of sources to do well in school.

Discipline was the next category of stressors most commonly mentioned. The children were fearful of punishment and felt that, at times, the punishment that they received was unfair and inconsistent. Some children did not seem to understand why they had been punished in the past.

The last category of stressors (general) included nonspecific stressors. Among these were general anxiety, being confused about things that were happening, and the uncomfortable feeling of not being in control over things in their lives.

Children in the intermediate grade levels mentioned general adolescent problems most frequently, followed by peer pressure, family problems, not feeling in control, and school-related problems. General adolescent problems included many of the developmental changes that occur during this stage of life. Some of these stressors were related to feeling different and not comprehending things in their lives.

The stressors that were placed in the peer pressure category were mentioned the second most frequently. Friends were very important to children in this age group, and being part of a group was highly desirable. There was also some stress from conflicts in values, behavior, and feelings with others in their peer group.

Family problems were also mentioned by the intermediate school children. These stressors included problems with parents, stepparents, and siblings. The children felt that adults did not understand them.

Intermediate school children also revealed many stressors related to not feeling or being in control over important things in their lives. These included not having the resources to do what they want, others telling them what to do, not being allowed to make decisions, being treated like a child, and not having anyone pay attention to them.

School-related problems were other sources of stress. They sometimes did not see the relevance of school, were not doing well, had problems with the teachers, and had some difficulty with adjusting to all the different teachers and children. Some of the difficulties related to the different structure of the intermediate school.

For high school students, stressors related to the future predominated, followed by school-related problems, peer pressure, substance abuse, and family problems. Career and occupational decision making were frequently mentioned stressors for this age group. Dealing with the uncertainties and responsibilities after high school also provoked anxiety.

School-related problems included feeling that teachers did not understand them, getting good grades, and which courses to take to get into training programs or colleges. Many of the stressors were linked to future educational or career goals.

Peer pressure stressors basically were related to being accepted by their peers. High school students were concerned with not doing or saying things that their peers would disapprove of. The stressors in this category were related to the stressors in the substance abuse category, particularly the use and abuse of various substances. The students frequently mentioned peers who used and encouraged the use of cigarettes, drugs, and alcohol.

Family problems was the last category of stressors for high school students. Conflicts with parents and stepparents in relation to goals, careers, friends, and extracurricular social activities were mentioned. The students also felt that their parents did not understand them and were not supportive.

Although numerous similar stressors were mentioned across the three school levels, the frequency and kinds of stressors within the categories differed. Family problems and school-related problems cut across the three levels. The most often mentioned category for the elementary school children was family problems; however, this category was ranked third for the 7th and 8th graders and fifth for the high school students. Although problems with stepparents and siblings were mentioned at all levels, younger children were more anxious about feeling abandoned and unloved. Older participants were more concerned about parents understanding and supporting them. Types of school-related problems were also different for the three levels. Elementary school children were fearful that their teachers did not like them, they had no friends, and they would not meet the expectations of their parents. The older students were concerned about the relevance of school and getting good grades for future training or education.

Some of the stressors were directly related to cognitive, emotional, and developmental changes of the participants. Elementary school children could not understand many things in their lives (i.e., divorce) that were sources of stress. This lack of understanding probably increased the frequency with which they mentioned general and vague fears. This is also a time in life when they need to feel good about themselves; thus, many stressors were related to understanding themselves.

For intermediate school students, the predominant stressors were related to general adolescent development. Because friends and peers are important to this age group, it is not surprising that stressors related to peer pressure ranked second. This early adolescent period is also one in which the child is not old enough to do many things, a situation that should increase his or her feelings of not being in control of things.

Concerns about the future were mentioned most often by high school students. Because academic achievement is closely related to future education and jobs, school-related problems became more frequent. Peers are still important to high school students, but stresses from peer pressure were ranked third. Stressors related to substance abuse were ranked fourth. This category did not appear in the other two levels.

The symptoms of stress included a variety of indicators that were classified into four categories—psychological, physiological, behavioral, and emotional. Once again, many of the symptoms are interrelated and may fit in more than one category. One needs to also keep in mind that other factors such as diet, genetic makeup, support systems and so forth are important elements that influence the indicators of stress. There were no apparent differences in the symptoms of stress among the three school levels.

The psychological symptoms included anxiety, depression, and being unmotivated. The participants provided many examples of symptoms that were interpreted using psychological concepts (i.e., low self-efficacy). Most of the symptoms listed in the physiological category were mentioned by the participants. The majority of them did not realize the role that stress might have on their bodies. The teachers were extremely helpful in providing behavioral indicators. Symptoms classified in the emotional category were interpreted for the participants from their examples of stressors and stressful situations.

The following are limitations of the study:

1. This is an exploratory project that provides some data for understanding stress among children in the various levels in schools. The results should not be overgeneralized.
2. The participants may not be a representative sample; thus, generalization of the results needs to be done carefully.
3. The definition of stress we used when selecting the participants might differ from other definitions.
4. The Stress Scale we used may have limitations in its validity.
5. The classification of the stressors and symptoms was difficult because of the many overlaps. Although the researchers tried to remain objective, subjective judgments may have influenced the classification.

Implications for School Counselors

Counselors in the schools need to and should be involved in assisting students to manage stress. With a better understanding of stress based on the results of this study, the following suggestions are offered as implications for school counselors:

1. Counselors should serve as consultants to teachers, parents, and administrators in understanding stress among children and being aware of the indicators of stress.
2. Counselors should conduct workshops for parents and teachers to provide training in managing stress for their children and classes.
3. Children can be taught to manage stress in group and individual sessions.
4. Because many stressors involved a lack of understanding or confusion about important events (i.e., divorce), counselors should facilitate groups for not only increasing understanding but coping with these events.
5. Counselors can facilitate groups to enhance self-esteem because many stressors are related to negative evaluations of the self. Because self-esteem is related to so many variables such as academic achievement, not giving in to peer pressure, and motivation (Coopersmith, 1967), the enhancement of self-esteem should relieve other stressors.
6. Counselors should initiate groups to increase students' internal locus of control orientation. Increasing feelings of being in control should have an impact on other variables (memory, success in school, attention span) (Lefcourt, 1976) that are related to stress.
7. Counselors could do family counseling to alleviate some of the stressors related to family problems.
8. Counselors should conduct guidance classes to increase awareness (strengths and weaknesses). This should help in alleviating the stressors that are related to lack of self-understanding and not accepting the self.
9. Initiating parent groups could help to eliminate the problems related to conflicts and misunderstanding between students and parents.
10. Counselors should be able to manage their own stress, so that they can be good role models.

The following are recommendations for future research:

1. This study needs to be replicated with other school-age populations.
2. Intervention strategies need to be developed to assist the children.
3. The effects of stress management need to be researched.

References

Arent, R. P. (1984). *Stress and your child*. Englewood Cliffs, NJ: Prentice-Hall.

Cattell, R., Eber, H., & Tatsuoka, M. (1970). *Handbook for the 16 PF*. Champaign, IL: Institute for Personality and Ability Testing.

Chandler, L. A. (1982). *Children under stress*. Springfield, IL: Thomas.

Coopersmith, S. (1967). *The antecedents of self-esteem*. Palo Alto, CA: Consulting Psychologists Press.

Elkind, D. (1986). Stress and the middle grade. *School Counselor, 33*, 196–206.

Kuczen, B. (1982). *Childhood stress*. New York: Delacorte Press.

Lefcourt, H. M. (1976). *Locus of control: Current trends in theory and research*. Hillsdale, NJ: Lawrence Erlbaum Associates.

Medeiros, D. C., Porter, B. J., & Welch, I. D. (1983). *Children under stress*. Englewood Cliffs, NJ: Prentice-Hall.

Michael, W., & Smith, R. (1978). *Dimensions of self-concept: User's Manual*. Los Angeles: Los Angeles Unified School District.

Omizo, M. M., Kornfeld, A. S., Hammett, V. L., & Omizo, S. A. (1986). *Children and stress*. Paper presented at the annual convention of the American Association for Counseling and Development, Los Angeles.

Price, J. H. (1986) A model for explaining adolescent stress. *Health Education, 16*(3), 36–40.

Seyle, H. (1976). *Stress without distress*. New York: J. B. Lippincott.

Tolman, R., & Rose, S. D. (1985). Coping with stress: A multimodal approach. *Social Work, 30*, 151–158.

Adolescent Suicide and the Implications for School Response Programs

John Kalafat

The Suicide Phenomenon

Between 1960 and 1980 the suicide rate for youths between age 15 and 19 increased from 5.6 to 13.8 per 100,000 for boys and from 1.6 to 3.0 for girls (National Center for Health Statistics, 1987). This increase has led to the implementation of many school-based suicide intervention programs throughout the country (Shaffer, Bacon, Fisher, & Garland, 1987; Smith, Eyman, Dyck, & Ryerson, 1987). Most of these programs have been developed in applied settings, such as community crisis centers, in response to requests from school systems prompted by suicidal behavior among their students. The result is that, although many of these programs are grounded in solid crisis intervention principles, there are widely varied contents, formats, and goals (Kalafat & Garland, 1988a, Perlin, 1988), and questions about the impact of such programs remain unresolved (Kalafat & Garland, 1988b; Shaffer, Bacon, Fisher, & Garland, 1987).

Although empirically-based information about adolescent suicide is slowly accumulating and still somewhat fragmentary, suicide response programs should make use of this information as well as concepts from crisis intervention and adolescent development. This article draws on current understanding of these areas to provide an outline and rationale for comprehensive, school-based suicide response programs.

Among the first questions raised by many school officials who are considering adolescent suicide response programs is whether the incidence of teen suicide has actually increased, or is it just more likely to be reported today.

It is true that adolescent suicide is receiving more media attention and is likely to be reported today rather than covered up. But the increase in incidence cannot be accounted for solely by increased reporting. In addition to the figures previously cited, some of the relevant facts about the incidence of adolescent suicide include:

- Overt suicide alternates with homicide as the second leading cause of death in the 15–24 age range. This may be an under-estimate, because many suicides still go unreported and because accidents are the leading cause of death in this age group (40% percent of these are auto accidents); some accidents, particularly single-car accidents, are likely to be suicides.
- To put these statistics in another perspective, health officials divide the population into age groups such as 15–24, 25–34, 35–44 and so on. The 15–24 age group is the *only* group that actually has a *higher* mortality rate today than it did 20 years ago.
- The current overall adolescent suicide rate is about 12 per 100,000 (about 17 per 100,000 for male adolescents) with variations across states and regions (e.g, higher in Western states; higher in rural than in urban areas).

Although a single adolescent suicide is, of course, a tragedy that affects entire communities, these statistics do indicate that the likelihood that a given school system may experience a suicide is comparatively low. But there are facts about adolescent suicide *attempts* that must be considered.

- Suicide attempts seem to be increasing at an even greater rate than are completions; and attempts seem to be occurring in increasingly younger adolescents. Surveys in a variety of schools throughout the country consistently find 10–15 percent of students reporting that they have made a suicide attempt (Boggs, 1986; Bowers & Gilbert, 1987; Shaffer, Garland, & Whittle, 1988).
- For every completed adult suicide, there are an estimated six to seven attempts. For every completed adolescent suicide there may be 50 to 100 attempts (Smith & Crawford, 1986).
- Girls attempt suicide about 9 times more often than boys, but boys complete suicide about 5 times more often than girls. This difference is partly accounted for by the fact that boys tend to use more violent, hence lethal, means, such as guns and hanging, than girls. The availability of firearms may also contribute to the higher rural suicide rates.

It is extremely important to keep in mind that these attempts often result in serious injury including paralysis and brain damage (Kleiner, 1981). Because such effects have received less media attention, adults and more importantly, adolescents tend to think of suicide as an either-or act: one either dies or one survives and is okay. This is clearly not the case.

Moreover, the risk of a completed suicide among adolescents who have made serious attempts is extraordinarily high. Approximate figures from varied sources summarized by Shaffer, Garland, and Bacon (1987) have indicated that:

1. The ratio for boys who have made an attempt serious enough to be admitted to a psychiatric inpatient facility is 1 in 13.
2. The ratio for girls who have made an attempt serious enough to be admitted to a psychiatric inpatient facility is 1 in 340.

These attempt figures mean that the probability of a given school system experiencing suicide attempts is quite high. These data also indicate that schools and communities must be prepared to deal with a youth who is returning after she or he has made an attempt and is at much higher risk for completion.

Thus, it is clear that adolescent suicidal behavior cannot be ignored. The next question that has particular relevance for school programs is: What is known about teen suicide that can guide school officials' responses to it? Are there known causes, or can suicidal youths be identified reliably?

There is considerable speculation about the possible causes for the rise in suicide among adolescents. At this point, however, researchers have not identified specific conditions, situations or stressors that we can say cause adolescent suicidal behavior. (Blumenthal & Kupfer, 1987; Sudak, Ford, & Rushforth, 1984).

There are some preliminary data (Shaffer, Garland, & Bacon, 1987) indicating that certain characteristics seem to be more common among suicide victims than among the general adolescent population, including:

1. Drug and alcohol use.
2. A history of impulsive and aggressive behavior; depression without behavior problems is less common and mainly found in girls.
3. Learning disorders.
4. Perfectionism, rigid and anxious behavior by some before tests and other major events.
5. Incidence of suicide in the family, though it is not known whether this is because of example, common stressors, or genetic factors.
6. Previous attempts.

Again, these are preliminary data and it is not yet known why some adolescents who have these characteristics commit suicide and some do not, and why some adolescents who do not seem to have these characteristics commit suicide. The point is that characteristics that reliably distinguish between suicidal and nonsuicidal youths have yet to be identified.

This current state of knowledge means that long-range programs that reduce known causes of suicide or teach adolescents and children how to cope with such conditions or stressors cannot yet be established. This is not to say that such preventive programs may not affect suicidal behavior. Suicide does seem to represent an inappropriate attempt to solve problems; thus, programs that teach self-esteem, problem solving, communication skills, and the like may prove to be important components in suicide prevention.

In the meantime, however, the suicidal behavior that is currently prevalent among adolescents must be addressed. That is, there is a need for an immediate plan for responding to suicide attempts and completions. There is additional information about adolescent suicide that can guide educators' efforts in this area.

First, most adolescent suicides seem to be impulsive acts carried out by youths who are in a state of *crisis*. The crisis state is characterized by "tunnel" thinking in which (a) the problem can only be seen in a one, all, or none manner; (b) the person becomes increasingly blind to other options besides suicide; and (c) she or he feels increasingly isolated from others.

Second, although the tunnel may end in a suicide attempt or completion, along the way the youth has often given some warning signs, has directly or indirectly told someone of his or her intent, or both. Although the warning signs are not foolproof predictors of suicide, they do indicate that a youth may be troubled. And today, troubled youths may be more likely than in the past to consider suicide.

These warning signs, as with other characteristics that seem to be associated with youth suicide are what Shaffer, Garland, and Bacon (1987) have referred to as "sensitive, but not specific" (p. 1) in that they may accurately describe suicidal individuals, but also would include extremely large numbers of persons who are not suicidal. Such information may still be used to identify youths who are at risk for suicide, because school officials may take the conservative approach of tolerating false positives, more than false negatives (Grob, Klein, & Eisen, 1982). Table 1 lists warning signs that may be associated with suicidal behavior.

Table 1
Suicide Warning Signs

Warning signs can be organized around the word *FACT*

Feelings:
- Hopelessness—*"It will never get any better," "There's nothing anyone can do." "I'll always feel this way."*
- Fear of losing control, going crazy, harming self or others
- Helpless, worthless—*"Nobody cares," "Everyone would be better off without me."*
- Overwhelming guilt, shame, self-hatred
- Pervasive sadness
- Persistent anxiety or anger

Action or Events:
- Drug or alcohol abuse
- Themes of death or destruction in talk or written materials
- Nightmares
- Recent loss—through death, divorce, separation, broken relationship, or loss of job, money, status, self-esteem
- Loss of religious faith
- Agitation, restlessness
- Aggression, recklessness

Change:
- In personality—more withdrawn, tired, apathetic, indecisive, or more boisterous, talkative, outgoing
- In behavior—can't concentrate on school, work, routine tasks
- In sleep pattern—oversleeping or insomnia, sometimes with early waking
- In eating habits—loss of appetite and weight or overeating
- Loss of interest in friends, hobbies, personal grooming, sex, or other activities previously enjoyed
- *Sudden* improvement after a period of being down or withdrawn

Threats:
- Statements, for example, *"How long does it take to bleed to death?"*
- Threats, for example, *"I won't be around much longer."*
- Plans, for example, putting affairs in order, giving away favorite things, studying drug effects, obtaining a weapon
- Gestures or attempts, for example, overdosing, wrist cutting

Third, experience with both known suicide attempters and completers, as well as surveys of youth, indicate that *peers* are most likely to be told (Boggs, 1986; Bowers & Gilbert, 1987; Shaffer, Garland, & Whittle, 1988). Often, peers are sworn to secrecy or hesitate to take any action for varied reasons. This experience with suicidal youths and the surveys also indicates that a disturbing minority (up to 25%) would tell *no one* of suicidal feelings in themselves or friends. In the actual situation, an even greater percentage may be hesitant to take action.

Fourth, although definite causes of adolescent suicide have not been identified yet, some common *precipitants* have been identified. Precipitants are events that, like the "straw that breaks the camel's back," can push a vulnerable adolescent into an attempt. These events may not seem great in themselves—they simply have particular meaning to a youth who may already be at risk for suicide. Some of the phenomena that seem to be associated with suicide in adolescents include the following (Shaffer & Gould, 1987):

1. Getting into trouble with authorities (e.g., school, police); not knowing and being afraid of the consequences.
2. Disappointment and rejection, such as a dispute with a boyfriend or girlfriend, failure in school, failure to get a job, or rejection from college.
3. Anxiety over impending change.
4. Timing shortly before or after the anniversary of the death of a friend or relative.
5. Knowing someone who committed or attempted suicide.

Thus, certain factors seem to be emerging about adolescent suicidal behavior including the following:

1. Although some problems may be long-standing, the decision to attempt suicide is often an impulsive act carried out by a person in crisis.
2. There are often warning signs and specific precipitants.
3. Peers may be the first to know about a suicidal teen.

These factors indicate that the goals for a school-based program addressing adolescent suicide might include the following:

1. Provide mental "slowdowns" or buffers (Smith, 1988) for suicidal youths who are in that tunnel described earlier. This includes clear, immediate options or alternatives, including responsive, continuously available supports and a consistent message to use them.
2. Increase the effectiveness of those who might come into contact with suicidal youths. This means that students, faculty members, and parents must know the warning signs and how to respond,

have professional supports immediately available, and have a consistent message to use them.

3. Provide responsive supports to suicide attempters as well as to survivors in the community after a completion.

School Concerns

Recommendations for a comprehensive school-based response that carries out these goals will be presented shortly. Before this, however, another concern of school officials must be addressed.

A comprehensive suicide response program that addresses these goals must include the provision of classroom sessions on suicide for students. In this regard, the question has been raised as to whether discussion about suicide might give some vulnerable students the idea to try suicide. This concern must be addressed, particularly in light of the evidence for "copycat" suicides or contagion and the possible effects of the media on suicide.

There is some evidence that television programs depicting factual or fictional suicides, as well as television or newspaper coverage of suicide completions, have been associated with increases in suicide attempts and completions in the areas reached by the media (Berman, 1988; Gould & Shaffer, 1986; Phillips & Carstensen, 1986). Also, there is some evidence that a suicide completion or serious attempt may promote subsequent attempts among vulnerable youths (Coleman, 1987).

The concerns raised by these data can be addressed in several ways in suicide education. First, some of the research on television programs indicates that when they are accompanied by educational components that stress responsible behavior and publicize local services such as hotlines, no increases in suicidal behavior occur (Gould & Shaffer, 1986). This research is supported by the experience of some of the established suicide educational programs that have been provided in many schools, where associated increases in suicidal behavior in these schools have not been experienced after such television programs (Boggs, 1986; Kalafat & Underwood, 1989; Ross, 1988). Berman (1988) noted that although evidence for the general effects of television programs on suicide rates is equivocal, there seems to be evidence that depiction of a suicide may result in imitation of the particular *method* by suicidal youths. These data suggest that media programs depicting suicide attempts should not be used in educational programs. In any case, such depictions miss the point of the educational programs, which is to focus on appropriate *preventive* actions and the *consequences* of failure to act.

Another important factor is that students have been consistently exposed to media programs dealing with suicide and their knowledge about suicidal phenomena has increased over the past decade (Boggs, 1986; Ross, 1980). I have found that in a variety of high school classes, when students are asked if they know someone in the school or community who has attempted suicide, about 70% consistently indicate that they do. Given this consistent exposure to suicide, classroom discussion will rarely be the students' introduction to the topic of suicide. It may, however, be the first balanced, grounded exposure to the topic that emphasizes coping and appropriate actions and resources (Ross, 1980).

In regard to the contagion phenomenon, there seem to be specific factors that promote contagion, which can be controlled for in carefully developed programs (Sowers, 1988). These factors include:

1. A highly charged emotional context.
2. A problem in an already vulnerable youth that is perceived to be similar to that of the model.
3. Consequences of the act are perceived to achieve certain desirable goals.

When programs are presented in a carefully developed, low-key educational context without presentation of media that depict models for suicide, there is no evidence of suicidal behavior associated with such programs. In fact, an important component of comprehensive programs is specifically aimed at attenuating imitation after attempts or completions.

The School's Role and Program Elements

Having been apprised of the relevant facts about adolescent suicide and the general goals of a comprehensive response program, many school officials have asked what the appropriate role of the school is in responding to adolescent suicide. Responsible school personnel acknowledge the need for a program, but are concerned about the limitations presented by overburdened school systems (Grob, Klein, & Eisen, 1982; Wise, Smead, & Huebner, 1987; Sandoval, 1985). In response to this real concern, the role of the school is perceived as crucial but is limited to the following three specific areas:

1. *Identification*. School personnel see students in a relatively structured environment for more of their waking hours than do their parents or other adults. In this context, changes in students that may indicate that he or she is experiencing some trouble may be more easily detected. Examples include drops in performance, excessive (for that student) misbehavior, fatigue, or ceasing to care about appearance.

2. *Support and response*. Teachers and staff members may have contacts with students, particularly outside of classes, that may allow these adults to more readily notice and respond to troubles or be approached by the student for help. School personnel need not provide counseling—a supportive initial response and assistance and encouragement for the student to obtain additional help is all that is called for. Also, a structured, planned and coordinated response in the aftermath of a suicide or a serious attempt is necessary to attenuate the distressing effects on students and adults and to prevent contagion phenomena.

3. *Education*. This is, of course, the basic role of the school, and an important response can be provided as part of the school's overall mandate. Students, staff members, and teachers must learn how to identify and respond to a troubled student, and troubled students must know about available resources and preferable options.

To carry out these functions, there is an emerging consensus (Barrett, 1980; California State Department of Education, 1987; Perlin, 1988; Kalafat & Underwood, 1989) that comprehensive programs need to include the following elements:

1. *Administrative policies and procedures*. These include specific, written guidelines for dealing with at-risk students, attempts, completions, and students returning to school after an attempt. Such procedures should detail exactly what school personnel are to do and to whom they can turn in each of the above situations. Many schools have developed such procedures, and models are available (Kalafat & Underwood, 1989).

2. *Informed faculty and staff members*. All school personnel, including support staff, should be given an overview of relevant facts about adolescent suicide, the rationale for, and details of the school's response program, their specific roles and responsibilities; basic guidelines for responding to troubled students; and, the appropriate school and

community resources. This can be accomplished through a 1- to 2-hour in-service training program with supporting handouts. Often, external presenters add to the interest and (perceived) credibility of this component.

3. *Informed parents*. Parents should be apprised of relevant information about adolescent suicide, the school's program, their responsibilities, and school and community resources. Again, a 1- to 2-hour presentation, plus materials, should suffice for this. This may have to be repeated to reach more parents.

4. *Informed students*. Students can be provided with specific lessons presented within a health or family life curriculum. These lessons can address basic information, appropriate resources, and most important, the need for and a discussion of their concerns about taking appropriate action (i.e., telling an adult) in the event of suicidal feelings in themselves or their peers. The mode among various programs includes two to four classroom sessions (Smith, Eyman, Dyck & Ryerson, 1987).

5. *Community liaison*. Schools are not expected to deal with adolescent suicide on their own. Ideally, the implementation of all the elements of a response program should be carried out along with consultants from local health, mental health, or crisis services. Also, solid working relationships need to be established with such local providers who will be receiving referrals from the school and who must work closely with school personnel in managing the return of a suicide attempter to school.

The goal, then, of a comprehensive suicide response program, is to establish the school-based expertise, backed by local providers, for responding to adolescent suicidal behavior. The objectives of such a program are to increase the probability that:

1. Persons who may come into contact with potentially suicidal adolescents can more readily identify them, know how to initially respond to them, and know how to refer them rapidly for additional help.
2. Troubled adolescents are aware of, and have immediate access to, helping resources and may be more inclined to seek such help as an alternative to suicidal behavior.

The basic thrust of such a program follows the tenets of crisis intervention, which emphasize practical, action-oriented interventions that prepare individuals and systems to respond effectively to situations through the possession of information, supports, and understanding of one's role (Golan, 1978; Hoff & Miller, 1987).

It is also important that such programs be adapted to the realities of the school system or, put in another way, are cost effective. Several features can be incorporated into programs to facilitate this.

Class schedules. Schools have complex scheduling issues and over-burdened curricula as the amount of material that must be taught continually expands. For this reason, the suicide lessons must fit into a regular class period and course framework without requiring time outside of class. Special group sessions outside of regular classes can be a popular format with students and may serve to highlight the important nature of this topic. But suicide should be addressed in an ongoing manner, and incorporation into regular class schedules makes this more feasible. Moreover, adolescent suicide is correlated with other phenomena, such as substance abuse and teen pregnancy, that are usually addressed in health or family life courses. Each of these may represent inappropriate solutions to problems that can be addressed within a complementary context.

Educational focus. As with any lesson, suicide classes are best presented with an educational focus that avoids mental health jargon and "clinical" concepts such as *depression*. Also, established instructional principles (Knowles, 1973) can be used in the lessons including:

1. Lessons are problem versus content centered in that material is organized around issues that students are currently dealing with, such as adolescent stresses and peer relationships.
2. General manuals or guides should be eschewed in favor of detailed, explicit, and sequential lesson plans that include specific time lines for each component.
3. Lessons should include exercises and (carefully chosen) media that promote participatory learning.
4. Each lesson should be limited to about three basic points, which is the most that students (teens and adults alike) will retain in a 45-minute period.

Teacher provided. The lessons should be presented by regular classroom teachers (or other school personnel who are consistently available to students) rather than by external consultants. This is not only more cost effective but also is consistent with the goal to enhance school-based student supports. That is, research has shown that when students have particular concerns, they are more likely to talk about them with an adult who has demonstrated some interest and expertise in that area. Therefore, when regular school personnel cover material on suicide, students may perceive them as concerned, responsive adults who are available during school hours. Because of this, instructors should receive additional special training and should be involved on a purely voluntary basis. For varied reasons, not everyone can discuss this topic, and students should be instructed by individuals whom they can approach and who will not convey discomfort with the topic.

Developmentally grounded. This concept is being used in two ways. First, it is important to teach the material at a level that is appropriate for the age and sophistication of the students. This not only means that essentially the same points must, of course, be presented in a different manner to 8th and 12th grades. It also means that different issues must be addressed for 7th-grade students who may not yet grasp the permanence of death; or for high school seniors, who may need to learn how to find help on a college campus. Second, it is important for educational material to address adolescent developmental issues, including the struggle toward autonomy from adults, which makes it difficult for teens to turn to adults for help; and the importance of developing and maintaining peer relationships, which makes it difficult to betray a confidence from a peer who may be considering suicide.

These attitudes about help seeking have so far been resistant to change through suicide education programs. To date, program evaluations indicate that for the 25% minority who said they would tell no one of a suicidal peer, only the reported willingness to call a hotline has increased after the programs (Kalafat & Garland, 1988a; Spano, 1988).

The increased incidence of adolescent suicidal behavior has presented a serious challenge to school systems. There is sufficient information available to implement efficient, comprehensive, conceptually grounded suicide response programs. In New York, a State Senate Committee on Mental Hygiene published a thorough report reviewing the issues in providing school-based suicide response programs and concluded: "In the Committee's view, no convincing evidence warrants any further hesitation in establishing statewide school-based suicide prevention programs addressed to students" (Spano, 1988, p. 46). These programs must, however, remain flexible and responsive to new data about adolescent suicide, as well as about the specific impacts of various program components.

References

Barrett, T. C. (1980). *The self destructive behavior of adolescents. Seeking solutions: Inservice and resource guide*. Denver: Cherry Creek Schools.

Berman, A. L. (1988). Fictional depiction of suicide in television films and imitation effects. *American Journal of Psychiatry, 145*, 982–986.

Blumenthal, S. J., & Kupfer, D. J. (1987). Overview of early detection and treatment strategies for suicidal behavior in young people. *Journal of Youth and Adolescence, 17*, 1–23.

Boggs, C. (1986). *Project lifesafer: Child and adolescent suicide prevention in two school systems*. Dayton, OH: Suicide Prevention Center, Inc.

Bowers, C. & Gilbert, J. (1987). *Survey of effectiveness of suicide education program in Richmond schools*. Richmond, VA: Richmond Crisis Center.

California State Department of Education. (1987). *Suicide prevention program for California public schools*. Sacramento: Author.

Coleman, L. (1987). *Suicide clusters*. Boston: Faber and Faber, Inc.

Golan, N. (1978). *Treatment in crisis situations*. New York: The Free Press.

Gould, M. S., & Shaffer, D. (1986). The impact of suicide in television movies: Evidence of imitation. *New England Journal of Medicine, 315*, 690–696.

Grob, M. C., Klein, A. A., & Eisen, S. V. (1982). The role of the high school professional in identifying and managing adolescent suicide behavior. *Journal of Youth and Adolescence, 12*, 163–173.

Hoff, L. A., & Miller, N. (1987). *Programs for people in crisis*. Boston: Northeastern University Custom Book Program.

Kalafat, J., & Garland, A. (1988a, April). *Evaluation of school-based suicide programs*. Paper presented at the annual conference of the American Association of Suicidology, Washington, DC.

Kalafat, J., & Garland, A. (1988b, August). *The development and evaluation of a school-based adolescent suicide curriculum*. Paper presented at the 96th annual convention of the American Psychological Association, Atlanta, GA.

Kalafat, J., & Underwood, M. M. (1989). *Lifelines: A school-based adolescent suicide response program*. Dubuque, IA: Kendall/Hunt Publishing Co.

Kleiner, A. (1981, Summer). How not to commit suicide. *The CoEvolution Quarterly,* pp. 89–111.

Knowles, M. (1973). *The adult learner: A neglected species.* Houston: Gulf Publishing.

National Center for Health Statistics, 1985. (1987). (DHHS Publication No. PHS-87-1120). Hyattsville, MD: U.S. Public Health Service.

Perlin, S. (Chair). (1988, April). *Tackling the tough issues in school-based suicide awareness programs.* Symposium conducted at the annual conference of the American Association of Suicidology, Washington, DC.

Phillips, D. P., & Carstensen, L. L. (1986). Clustering of teenage suicides after television news stories about suicide. *New England Journal of Medicine, 315,* 685–689.

Ross, C. P. (1988, April). *The California model for a curriculum on suicide.* Paper presented at the annual conference of the American Association of Suicidology, Washington, DC.

Ross, C. P. (1980). Teaching children the facts of life and death: Suicide prevention in the schools. In M. L. Pech, N. L. Farberow, & R. E. Litman (Eds.), *Youth suicide.* New York: Springer.

Sandoval, J. (1985). Crisis counseling: Conceptualizations and general principles. *School Psychology Review, 14,* 257–265.

Shaffer, D., Bacon, K., Fisher, P., Garland, A. (1987, January). *Review of youth suicide prevention programs* (Report). New York: New York State Psychiatric Institute.

Shaffer, D., Garland, A., & Bacon, K. (1987, July). *Prevention issues in youth suicide* (Prepared for Project Prevention). Washington, DC: American Academy of Child and Adolescent Psychiatry.

Shaffer, D., Garland, A., & Whittle, B. (1988, March). An evaluation of youth suicide prevention programs. *New Jersey adolescent suicide prevention project* (Final project report). Trenton: New Jersey Division of Mental Health and Hospitals.

Shaffer, D., & Gould, M. S. (1987). *A study of completed and attempted suicide in adolescents* (Progress report). Bethesda, MD: National Institutes of Health.

Smith, K. (1988, April). How do we know what we've done? Controversy in evaluation. Panel presentation in S. Perlin (Chair), *Tackling the tough issues in school-based suicide awareness programs.* Symposium conducted at the annual conference of the American Association of Suicidology, Washington, DC.

Smith, K., & Crawford, S. (1986). Suicidal behavior among "normal" high school students. *Suicide and Life Threatening Behavior, 3,* 313–325.

Smith, K., Eyman, J., Dyck, R., & Ryerson, D. (1987, October). *Report of the school suicide programs questionnaire.* Albuquerque, NM: The Menninger Clinic.

Sowers, J. (1988, April). Who, what and how: Curriculum development and program content. Panel presentation in S. Perlin (Chair), *Tackling the tough issues in school-based suicide awareness programs.* Symposium conducted at the annual conference of the American Association of Suicidiology, Washington, DC.

Spano, N. A. (1988, June). *Adolescent suicide: A statewide action plan.* Report by New York State Senate Committee on Mental Hygiene.

Sudak, H. S., Ford, A. B., & Rushforth, N. B. (Eds.). (1984). *Suicide in the young.* Boston: John Wright, PSG Inc.

Wise, P. S., Smead, V. S., & Huebner, E. S. (1987). Crisis intervention: Involvement and training needs of school psychology personnel. *Journal of School Psychology, 25,* 185–187.

Likely Candidates for Group Counseling: Adolescents With Divorced Parents

Shirley Gwinn Coffman
Albert E. Roark

It is imperative that secondary school counselors stop the whirlwind of paper shuffling and come to understand the psychological needs of adolescents from single-parent families. The students involved in this crisis situation require immediate attention. The 1981 nationwide census bureau sampling indicated that there was a 356% increase in single-parent families headed by unwed women (from 234,000 in 1970 to more than 1 million in 1980); the number of families headed by divorced women rose 181% (from 956,000 to 2.7 million) ("Homes Headed," 1982). It is projected that by 1990, 75% of all Black children and 33% of all White children will reside at some time in a single-parent family (Testa & Wulczyn, 1980). The net result is that 45% of all children born in any given year will live with only one of their parents before reaching their 18th birthday (Francke et al., 1980).

The secondary school counselor faces the reality that many students have needs that go beyond the selection of appropriate academic courses and a prestigious university or an area vocational school. For adolescents whose parents are divorced or about to be, it is a time of crisis that teachers, pediatricians, and mental health workers rank second only to death in the family as requiring the greatest amount of adjustment for the student (Coddington, 1972). Fundamental to the crisis theory of Aguilera and Messick (1974) is the belief that a temporary state of crisis can result in either an elevated or a lowered level of functioning for the student. The strength with which a person emerges from a crisis situation depends on the appropriateness and flexibility of his or her coping strategies.

Developmental Issues

When designing a treatment model for an adolescent in crisis because of divorce, the counselor should keep in mind the adolescent developmental issues. The presenting problems should be considered as they relate to the normal developmental stages of adolescence (Jacobson, 1978). It is important that children whose parents are divorcing not be regarded as a homogeneous population and that the divorce not be regarded as a singular uniform event (Prinz, Bella, & Oppenheimer, 1983).

The normal onset of adolescence spans 6 years, during which children of the same age and sex show a continuum of adolescent growth spurts and secondary sexual characteristics. At a time when every young person has a need to feel "average," to be exactly like peers, it seems to some that they are always too tall or too short, too fat or too thin, too early or too late. Understandably, issues of self-image are abundant (Lipsitz, 1983).

Erikson (1968) contended that the stage of life known as adolescence is a pivotal time; its nature is determined by preceding events and foreshadows those to follow. Lipsitz (1980) stated that one task of this developmental stage is the person's exploration of his or her uniqueness and relatedness to others. Adolescents depend on their external world to offer a positive, realistic self-image and a believable set of purposes and expectations for eventual self-evaluation. Gradually, the separation from parental authority and the strengthening of personal autonomy must occur.

Elkind (1967) identified a critical task of adolescence as breaking through a characteristic form of egocentrism labeled as the "personal fable." This self-written script of the normal adolescent speaks of uniqueness, immunity and immortality. The bubble of belief characterized by such statements as, "Me, I'll never get pregnant" and "Sure, I do pot, but I'll never get hooked" are not rationalizations, but reality to the adolescent. Students who are not equipped with the developmental tools necessary to make the gigantic leap from immunity to vulnerability dismiss the messages of standard prevention programs as irrelevant. If school counselors are to effectively facilitate growth in their adolescent population, they must understand the students' unique developmental level.

Impact of Divorce

A review of the literature reveals that nearly all conclusions concerning the impact of divorce on children are drawn from Wallerstein and

Kelly's (1980) landmark research project "California's Children of Divorce." Major psychological adjustment is demanded of youths who are in a divorce situation that is likely to stretch from the time of separation through the period of adolescence. The youth uses six coping tasks during this adjustment period. These hierarchical tasks are initiated with the separation of the parents, and, if resolved, reach closure during late adolescence or early adulthood. They are as follows:

1. Likely to be optimally resolved within the first year after marital rupture:
   a. Acknowledging the reality of the marital rupture.
   b. Disengaging from parental conflict and distress and resuming customary pursuits.
2. Likely to be resolved (continually reworked) during adolescence:
   a. Resolving the loss.
   b. Resolving anger and self-blame.
   c. Accepting permanence of the divorce.
3. Likely to be resolved during adolescence and at times, early adulthood:
   a. Achieving realistic hope regarding relationships (Wallerstein, 1983).

It remains clear that Task 3a, achieving realistic hope regarding relationships, must be mastered before the young person can enter the stage of psychologically well-adjusted adulthood (Wallerstein & Kelly, 1980).

McPhee (1983) offered two school-related competencies that are closely related to positive adjustment after divorce:

1. Those children who went into the divorce with "solid developmental achievements, including the capacity to make use of their resources within the present [SIC] (particularly intelligence, the capacity for fantasy, social maturity, and the ability to turn to adults and peers for support), coped more successfully than those who did not have these qualities.
2. The availability of support systems both within and external to the home" (pp. 4–5).

Exploratory studies by Bonkowski (cited in Bonkowski, Bequette, & Boomhower, 1984) revealed that only 25% of the children in divorce situations received any type of outside help during their parents' breakup. In contrast, 90% of the parents involved in divorce sought assistance from at least one outside source, with many using several sources. To whom can adolescent children of divorcing parents turn? Secondary school counselors, persons having professional training to facilitate growth in their students, have access to these adolescents 6 hours per day for the academic year. The counselor may become the first to provide the necessary support to these adolescents from transitional families through the development of counseling groups. Because it is not always apparent that a student is going through a divorce situation at home, the initial task is to identify those students. Though procedures for doing this will vary, it is important that the task be accomplished.

Group Counseling

Group counseling is often the most satisfactory method of providing support to students identified. The counselor in a guidance department for Grades 10–12 met with each sophomore English class with the cooperation of the English department chairperson. The counselor gave each class a 5-minute synopsis of the small-group counseling process and a statement of the unique needs of the adolescent in a divorce situation. Each student completed a brief questionnaire indicating: (a) if he or she would or would not be interested in group participation, and (b) the class period during which the student could participate in a group. By the close of the day, 80 students had expressed interest in becoming a member of a counseling group for adolescents in divorce situations. Because counseling groups should ideally be made up of 5 to 10 students, 8 to 16 groups were formed as a result of one day spent in the sophomore English classes.

The response of the faculty members involved was equally encouraging. Repeatedly, teachers supported the counselor's effort with positive remarks and numerous suggestions for additional counseling groups (adolescents who are abused, study skill groups, etc.). The school administration was an active partner in the organizational process and remained supportive and encouraging during the time when the counseling groups met.

The second task involved forming the counseling groups. When each student volunteers to become a group member, the counselor can expect high enthusiasm. In the initial session, it is important that the counselor explain to the students how the group process can be beneficial, why punctuality and regular attendance are important, and the number of sessions to be held. For this purpose, when working with 5–10 adolescents, 5 or 6 sessions is ideal. However, the number of sessions can be extended (Roark & Roark, 1979).

An awareness of the conceptual model first drawn by Ruth Cohn (cited in Shaffer & Galinsky, 1974) can offer direction to the counselor in facilitating expression of group members' concerns. Cohn's "It, We, and I" can be assigned to stages of development of the group process as shown in Figure 1.

The Divorce:
Extrapersonal Issues the Group Has Formed to Address

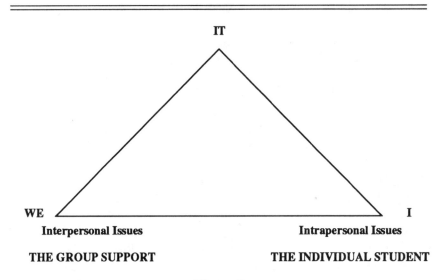

Figure 1
Conceptual Model

The first session is wisely spent dealing with the "IT," "THE DIVORCE." Information provided by the group leader about the effects of divorce helps to reassure the student that he or she is certainly not alone in the dilemma. Emergence of self-statements characteristic of the "I" can be anticipated, as well as statements of emerging group cohesiveness involving the "WE." The group leader should respond to "I" and "WE" statements at this time by simple reflections and clarifications and continue the emphasis on information about the effects of divorce. The reflective responses by the group leader will lead to some discussion by all members as well as the person the leader is addressing. These discussions should not be discouraged, but they should not be allowed to dominate until all members of the group have been provided with enough information to correct most of the erroneous information that is creating problems for them. As soon as the students begin to share their particular problems, and as soon as their concepts of the effects of divorce are relatively accurate, the leader should begin to emphasize "I" and "WE" interaction.

When "I" and "WE" interaction is being emphasized, the group leader's responses should remain primarily facilitative and he or she needs to provide information only to correct blatantly inaccurate concepts or to help students with their questions of fact. Counselor responses, therefore, tend to be primarily reflections, clarifications, linking, and redirections. Reflections serve to help students feel understood and to facilitate deeper self-understanding. Clarifications serve the same function as reflections; in addition, they help students to express themselves clearly and to clarify their thoughts. In the process, the counselor aids group interaction and encourages all members to carefully examine their circumstances and feelings.

Linking serves to show the similarities among students. When it is done "historically" it allows the students to see how what they said at one time is different from what they are now saying. This may draw attention to changes that have taken place or to growth that has been experienced. The redirecting shifts from one student to another or from one topic to another. For example, if one student is dominating the group and not allowing others time for expression, a counselor might say, "Joe, quite a few other members need to talk and have not had time. Would you mind if we switched to Jane?" Or, if the group has been emphasizing the negative aspects of divorce, the leader might say, "Perhaps we should also look at the opportunities divorce has provided us." Facilitation of a group, once the information needed at the beginning has been provided, is primarily a matter of helping members express themselves and occasionally providing needed support. Basically, the groups run themselves when members are at the "WE" stage of interaction.

The flow of group concerns cannot be expected to remain fixed at any point. Instead, the flow from the "IT" to the "I" to the "WE" will be continually experienced during the process. A secondary emphasis when working with groups of adolescents in divorce situations may be the need to provide individual counseling for the members who remain fixed in the "I" stage of intrapersonal expression. Often, the only way to determine whether a student needs additional individual counseling is to simply ask, "Would you like to be in individual counseling concerning this issue?" Other times, it is quite obvious that a student is not able to work out feelings or concerns sufficiently in the group. For example, issues surrounding legal problems may need individual work and issues concerning sexual preference of the parents may be too sensitive to be addressed in the group. The counselor needs to be alert to when he or she should contact students individually for additional help. Obviously, these students can remain in the group in almost all cases while they are being counseled individually.

An extensive review of the literature revealed few articles offering group therapy models for the target population of secondary school students in divorce situations. Secondary school counselors, however, may wish to refer to Kalter, Pickar, and Lesowitz's (1984) "School-Based Developmental Facilitation Groups for Children of Divorce: A Preventive Intervention." This provides one of many available models of group therapy intervention designed for elementary students in divorce situations.

Conclusion

The many secondary-school students who are experiencing the effects of divorce deserve to be supported by the efforts of their counselors. Research (Francke et al., 1980) reveals that these students can better cope with the psychological issues of divorce when they experience the hope, appropriate information, and support that can emerge from group counseling. The model of group counseling that has been provided here can easily be implemented by counselors and is likely to be supported by the administrators, the faculty, and the parents. Secondary-school counselors are encouraged to respond to the urgent need for help of this unique and identifiable population of adolescents.

References

Aguilera, D. C., & Messick, J. M. (1974). *Crisis intervention: Theory and methodology.* St. Louis: Mosby.

Bonkowski, S. E., Bequette, S. Q., & Boomhower, S. (1984). A group design to help children adjust to parental divorce. *Social Casework: The Journal of Contemporary Social Work, 65,* 131–137.

Coddington, R. D. (1972). The significance of life events as etiologic factors in diseases of children. *Journal of Psychosomatic Research, 16,* 205–213.

Elkind, E. (1967). Egocentrism in America. *Child Development, 38,* 1025–1034.

Erikson, E. (1968). *Identity: Youth and crisis.* New York: Norton.

Francke, L. B., Sherman, D., Simons, P. E., Abramson, P., Zabarsky, M., Huck, J., & Whitman, L. (1980, February 11). The children of divorce. *Newsweek,* pp. 58–63.

Homes headed by unwed mothers up 356%. (1982, June 18). *The Washington Post,* p. A8.

Jacobson, D. S. (1978). The impact of marital separation/divorce on children: 1. Parent-child separation and child adjustment. *Journal of Divorce, 1,* 341–361.

Kalter, N., Pickar, J., and Lesowitz, M. (1984). School-based developmental facilitation groups for children of divorce: A preventive intervention. *American Journal of Orthopsychiatry, 54,* 613–623.

Lipsitz, J. S. (1980). The age group. In J. Soltis, (Ed.), *Toward adolescence: The middle-school years. Seventy-ninth Yearbook of the National Society for the Study of Education, Part 1* (pp. 7–31). Chicago: University of Chicago Press.

Lipsitz, J. S. (1983). *Making it the hard way: Adolescents in the 1980s.* Testimony prepared for the Crisis Intervention Task Force, House Select Committee on Children, Youth, and Families. (ERIC Document Reproduction Service No. ED 248 002).

McPhee, J. T. (1983). *Children at risk: Vulnerability/resiliency to psychopathology after parental separation/divorce.* West Lafayette, IN: Purdue University. (ERIC Document Reproduction Service No. ED 243 060).

Prinz, R. J., Bella, B. S., & Oppenheimer, K. C. (1983). *Children of separating parents: They are not all alike.* Paper presented at the Annual Convention of the American Psychological Association, Anaheim, CA. (ERIC Document Reproduction Service No. ED 241 854)

Roark, A. E., & Roark, A. B. (1979). Group structure: components and effects. *The Journal for Specialists in Group Work, 4,* 186–192.

Shaffer, J. B. P., & Galinsky, M. D. (1974). *Models of group therapy and sensitivity training*. Englewood Cliffs, NJ: Prentice-Hall.

Testa, M., & Wulczyn, F. (1980). *The state of the child* (Vol. 1). Chicago: University of Chicago, The Children's Policy Research Project.

Wallerstein, J. S., & Kelly, J. B. (1980). *Surviving the breakup*. New York: Basic Books.

Wallerstein, J. S. (1983). Children of divorce: The psychological tasks of the child. *American Journal of Orthopsychiatry, 53,* 230–243.

Counseling Teenage Fathers: The "Maximizing a Life Experience" (MALE) Group

Wayne C. Huey

The pervasiveness and magnitude of the teenage pregnancy problem has been well documented in the literature (Meredith, 1985; Miller & Miller, 1983; Wallis, 1985). American adolescents are maturing physically and initiating sexual activity at an earlier age than did previous generations, resulting in more than one million pregnancies annually. In contrast to previous patterns, 94% of unmarried mothers now keep their babies (Saed, 1979); moreover, 50% of these young women will become pregnant again within 3 years (Foster & Miller, 1980).

Numerous polls have indicated that American adults regard teenage pregnancy as a serious national problem (Kennedy & Orr, 1984; Wallis, 1985). Although teenage pregnancy is no respecter of race, culture, or ethnic background, the negative impact seems to be most critical among the economically deprived and "is widely viewed as the very hub of the United States poverty cycle" (Wallis, 1985, p. 79). Black leaders have joined other concerned citizens in calling for programs to end this national disgrace (Rousseve, 1985; Wallis, 1985). In one response to the crisis, in November 1985 Governor Anthony Earl of Wisconsin signed a law addressing many facets of the problem, such as making both sets of grandparents responsible for the financial support of babies born to their teenage children.

Teenage pregnancy is not new, and many programs have been developed and implemented to address the problem; however, the emphasis has been primarily on the teenage mother and her child (Cohen & Rose, 1984; Eddy, McCray, Stilson, & DeNardo, 1983; Wallis, 1985). In most instances, teenage pregnancy has been viewed solely as a woman's issue, with the adolescent father regarded as a shadowy, unknown figure—more a culprit than a potential contributor to either the mother or his offspring (Parke, Power, & Fisher, 1980).

School and agency counselors must continue to offer programs to support young mothers and their children, but the forgotten half of the teenage pregnancy problem cannot continue to be overlooked. Recently, the plight of the unwed, teenage father has begun to gain attention (Meredith, 1985; Robinson & Barret, 1985; Stengel, 1985). Why has it taken so long to recognize the needs of the teenage father? Young men in American society generally are expected to have it all together or to pretend that they do. Too often, unwed teenage fathers have been stereotyped as callous, "macho studs" who are interested only in their own pleasure. Because of these stereotypes, counselors, educators, and others did not believe that the young men recognized their need for help or that they would participate in programs designed to assist them. Studies now show that most teenage fathers do not have it all together and are just as confused, afraid, and anxious as the young women they impregnate (Jensen, 1979; Robinson & Barret, 1985; Saed, 1979). The reality is that, Black or White, rich or poor, being an unwed father often means a lifetime of frustration.

Most teenage fathers care about what happens to their children (Barret & Robinson, 1981; Earls & Siegel, 1980; Parke, Power, & Fisher, 1980; Stengel, 1985) and need to be given the opportunity to explore their concerns and feelings; however, they do not usually ask for help on their own (Coleman, 1981). Little has been reported in the literature about the counselor's role in providing support for unwed fathers. Articles on teenage pregnancy occasionally will include a paragraph suggesting that the young man also should be helped, but specific programs designed to assist the adolescent father are still relatively rare (Foster & Miller, 1980; Stengel, 1985; Tegtmeyer, 1980; Wagner, 1980). The purpose of this article is to describe a group counseling program that was developed to provide support and assistance for unwed teenage fathers in the school.

The eight group participants were enrolled in a suburban high school with a student population that was primarily Black and from lower socioeconomic levels. The young men, two of whom were expectant fathers, were between 15 and 18 years old and had academic averages that ranged from a B to a D. About half of them hoped to continue their education after high school graduation. The average age of first sexual activity was 12, which is consistent with reported data for Black men (Earls & Siegel, 1980). Two of the young men still dated the mothers of their children; they all maintained regular contact with their children.

Program Rationale and Objectives

Recognizing that unwed teenage fathers had feelings, questions, and concerns about their situation and needed as much care and counsel as unwed mothers, I developed the Maximizing a Life Experience (MALE) program to focus on a different set of the three Rs: Rights, Responsibilities, and Resources. The general goals were to help the young men understand their emotional rights (to express feelings and concerns and receive emotional support) and responsibilities, as well as their legal rights and responsibilities, and to learn about available resources. The specific objectives for the program were to help the teenage fathers:

1. Learn more about themselves and better understand their feelings about their present situation.
2. Understand their legal and emotional rights and responsibilities.
3. Recognize that pregnancy cannot be dismissed as an accident.
4. Obtain factual information about reproductive biology, contraception, and sexually transmitted diseases.
5. Identify and explore their present and future options.
6. Learn how to solve problems and make sound decisions.
7. Realize what resources are available and how to use them.

The Male Group

Recruiting participants for this program required a more involved referral process than the one used for identifying pregnant girls. Leads were solicited from teachers, coaches, administrators, other counselors, and unwed teenage mothers. Initial contact with several teenage fathers produced additional names, and eight prospective participants were identified. I interviewed each young man individually to explain the goals of the program, determine his level of interest, and obtain a commitment to participate. A parental consent form was required of all participants. Each group member then completed a questionnaire designed to obtain personal background information and took a pretest to evaluate his attitudes, values, and knowledge about human sexuality. A group counseling approach was selected for this particular population, because most adolescents turn to their peers for understanding and support, especially if those peers have similar experiences (Thompson, 1984).

One of the group leaders was a school counselor (myself); the other was the school principal. Both had worked in the school for more than 10 years and were readily accepted by the students as receptive, understanding adults who cared about them and wanted to help. Although I had background knowledge in anatomy, physiology, and human sexuality, we used outside resource persons to teach portions of the program about reproductive biology, contraception, and sexually transmitted diseases. Neither leader was knowledgeable about legal issues; consequently, we relied on assistance from another agency to present that aspect of the program.

The MALE group met once a week for 8 weeks in 1-hour sessions during the school day and took one 3-hour field trip on a teacher workday. The meetings were scheduled on a rotating basis so that group members did not miss the same class more than twice. They were required to obtain assignments ahead of time and to keep up in their course work.

Session 1

The first session included four primary tasks: program overview and logistical information, a get-acquainted activity, setting group and individual goals, and development of ground rules.

The program overview and logistical information provided the leaders with an opportunity to review the topics to be covered and to describe the specifics of the program, such as the number of sessions, meeting dates, and times. The introductory exercise provided an opportunity to establish several commonalities among participants and to initiate group interaction on a level that was minimally threatening.

A review of the general goals of the group allowed the leaders to review their reasons for initiating the program and to establish agreement on the importance of group objectives. Before stating individual goals, each group member was asked to share personal background information about his situation, such as his relationship with and feelings for his child and its mother, how each felt about the situation, what options the couple had considered after learning of the pregnancy, how both sets of parents had reacted, and what the young men had learned from their situation. This background information helped group members and leaders to understand individual goals. Some sample goals selected by group members were to learn the legal rights of unwed fathers, to decide whether or not to quit school and go to work to better help support the child, and to receive help in handling feelings of guilt.

The development of group ground rules allowed the participants to structure the setting so that they felt safe and comfortable as they dealt with their concerns and feelings. Guidelines pertaining to honesty, respect, confidentiality, and equality were among those adopted by group consensus.

Session 2

The second session began with a film, *Teenage Father* (Hackford, 1978), which followed a teenage couple from the time they learned that the girl was pregnant until a decision was reached as to what action to take. Filmed from the young man's perspective, it served as an excellent stimulus for discussion of values and attitudes regarding teenage sexual activity. The leaders continued to focus on values during this session by using a values continuum to encourage exploration and clarification. Sample items included such statements as: "Having a baby proves you are a man," "Even if a girl says 'no,' she means 'yes,'" and "Because the girl is the one to get pregnant, it is her responsibility to take precautions." Group leaders helped the members to compare the values they expressed in response to the items on the continuum with those they had shown through their behaviors. Confronting the discrepancies between the values they expressed and their actions provided a challenge to personal growth.

Session 3

The third session also began with an audiovisual presentation. Titled *His Baby Too: Problems of Teenage Pregnancy,* the filmstrip "defines and highlights the role of the unwed father, and stresses the importance of his active role in solving the problems of an unplanned pregnancy" (Vanderslice, 1980, p. 4). Discussion questions, suggested activities, and a bibliography, combined with the audiovisual presentation, made this an excellent resource and stimulated further discussion of options available to the teenage father or prospective teenage father. The remaining time in this session was used to allow group members to prepare a list of questions on legal issues in anticipation of the next session's topic.

Session 4

Learning the legal rights and responsibilities of unwed teenage fathers was one of the primary reasons some of the members joined the group. An attorney from the Legal Aid Society was provided with a copy of the group's questions before the fourth session and came prepared to respond to those and any additional questions. Sample questions included: "Can I get the baby if she doesn't want it?" "Can they make me pay child support when I don't have a job?" "Can she make me marry her?" "Can I make her let me see the baby?" Although laws vary from state to state, the general legal position of unwed fathers, whether adolescents or adults, is that they have all the responsibilities of fatherhood but none of the rights. That status remains unchanged, unless they take steps to legally acknowledge paternity.

Sessions 5 and 6

Sessions 5 and 6 were designed to provide information on reproductive biology, contraception, and sexually transmitted diseases. In Session 5, a speaker from Planned Parenthood presented basic information on reproductive processes and contraception. Because teenage fathers are sexually active earlier and have more frequent sexual activities than do their peers, they are often assumed to be more knowledgeable than are other teenagers. Studies show, however, that the unwed, adolescent father is as uninformed as the mother, because teenagers receive approximately 90% of their information on sexuality and birth control from their peers (Barret & Robinson, 1981). There is good evidence that the decision to become sexually active is unrelated to contraceptive concerns. Studies of adolescent contraceptive use have found that 80% of sexually active teenagers do not use contraceptives regularly (Lewis, 1980; Rienzo, 1981) and that some young women blame their pregnancy on their partner's objections to using contraceptives (Phipps-Yonas, 1980). Sessions 5 and 6 were, therefore, aimed at providing contraceptive information and services for the teenage fathers and encouraging them to assume more responsibility for contraception than they had in the past.

In Session 6 we included a field trip to a Planned Parenthood center, where a staff member reviewed information on reproduction and contraception and presented information on sexually transmitted diseases. The young men were then given a tour of the center, which had a library and reading room, a bookstore, and a clinic where free contraceptives were available. Services available for their sexual partners were also discussed.

Sessions 7 and 8

The ability to analyze and solve problems and make sound decisions is essential for adolescents if they are to become responsible, independent individuals. Most young people become sexually active without making informed and responsible decisions about their own happiness and future goals; thus, they create problems for themselves, their partners, their offspring and society. Teenagers who lack the necessary skills for effective problem solving become doomed to one crisis after another and live lives of frustration. Phipps-Yonas (1980) reported that teenagers who use contraception effectively seem to be better problem solvers. Session 7 was designed, therefore, to teach effective problem-solving and decision-making models and to give group members the opportunity to use their new skills in simulated situations.

After these practice activities, in Session 8 we gave each member an opportunity to use the group resources and his new skills in selecting and working through a personal problem related to being a teenage father. Some sample issues to be resolved were: "Should I take the football scholarship or get a job to support my child?" "Should I still join the military even though I'll be transferred away from my baby?" "Should I take steps to legally acknowledge paternity?" Throughout these sessions, it was emphasized to the adolescent fathers that what they did and what they became depended on their own concerted efforts. The group provided support for each member to move toward self-sufficiency and active decision making about future alternatives.

Session 9

Session 9 included three primary tasks: reviewing and summarizing the group experience, providing information about the availability of resources and completing a group evaluation and posttest. The first task was to review and summarize the group experience. This included a review of the rights and responsibilities covered in all phases of the program as well as an opportunity for group members to express feelings

about their experiences. New friendships, new skills, and a new awareness of supportive male relationships were acknowledged.

The second task for the leaders was to provide additional information
about resources. We showed group members the beginnings of a special
library section that contained books and other printed materials related to
teenage fathers, child rearing, and sex education. We reminded them of
community resources and assured them that even though the group
would no longer meet, the leaders would remain available for individual
assistance. Finally, each of the young men completed a written evaluation of the group experience and a posttest designed to evaluate any
changes in attitudes, values, and knowledge about human sexuality.

Program Evaluation and Follow-Up

The group evaluation form contained items such as, "Did you learn more
about yourself? About others? About birth control? How to solve
problems and make decisions? Where to go for help?" On a 10-point
scale, with 10 being the most favorable rating, the members gave the
group experience an overall rating of 9.5. Group members also answered
questions on what they liked best about the group, what they would
change, and what was the most important thing they learned. Their
responses indicated that they liked the supportive atmosphere and a
chance to discuss their situations with others who had similar problems.
Most of them had not been aware that they shared the unwed father role
before joining the group. The most commonly suggested change was to
have longer and more frequent sessions. Some of the responses listed as
the most important things learned were: "That we don't have many
rights," "To keep myself protected," and "It is a problem that has to be
faced and dealt with." One of the senior members wrote: "I had been
having headaches because I felt so guilty and frustrated and did not
know what to do. I thought I was all alone. Now I know my rights, what
my options are, and how to keep from getting in this situation again. I
can work on my problems and make the decisions I have to. It's nice to
know you are still there when I need help."

Changes also were noted on several posttest items. For example,
seven members reported that they: (a) now consider the possibility of
pregnancy before having sexual relations and (b) would now consider

abortion as an option, compared with five positive responses to these two items on the pretest. All eight group members agreed that the man should share contraceptive responsibility, compared with four on the pretest; and, seven members reported that they now used contraceptives consistently, compared with three on the pretest.

In a follow-up of the eight group members one year later, four were in college or technical school, two were in the military, and two were still in high school. None were married or had a second child, and all were continuing to contribute toward the support of their first child. The only change in the follow-up two years later was that one young man had dropped out of college, and one had graduated from high school. Both of them were working full time.

Conclusion and Implications

The personal and social costs of teenage pregnancy are staggering. Additional prevention programs need to be developed, but counseling must also be available for young people who are already parents. Unwed teenage mothers and their children should continue to receive adequate assistance, but helping professionals cannot continue to overlook their frustrated, confused, anxious, and frightened partners. The experience of fatherhood is a life-changing event. School counselors must overcome the prevalent myths about teenage fathers and assume a more equitable position in providing services for these young men. They need help in understanding their feelings, their legal and emotional rights and responsibilities, their alternatives, and the possible consequences of these choices.

The MALE group program was an attempt to provide unwed teenage fathers with knowledge, resources, care, support, and counsel so that they could cope more effectively with their quickly changing lives and become productive citizens who could compete successfully with their peers.

Becoming a father during adolescence has serious consequences for individual development, and teenage fathers are not psychologically prepared for their new role. School counselors must become more active in responding to the silent cries of the forgotten half of the teenage pregnancy problem.

References

Barret, R. L., & Robinson, B. E. (1981). Teenage fathers: A profile. *Personnel and Guidance Journal, 60,* 226–228.

Cohen, D., & Rose, R. (1984). Male adolescent birth control behavior: The importance of developmental factors and sex differences. *Journal of Youth and Adolescence, 13,* 239–252.

Coleman, E. (1981). Counseling adolescent males. *Personnel and Guidance Journal, 60,* 215–218.

Earls, F., & Siegel, B. (1980). Precocious fathers. *American Journal of Orthopsychiatry, 50,* 469–480.

Eddy, J., McCray, E. H., Stilson, D., & DeNardo. N. (1983). Pregnancy counseling for teenagers. *School Counselor, 30,* 398–402.

Foster, C. D., & Miller, G. M. (1980). Adolescent pregnancy: A challenge for counselors. *Personnel and Guidance Journal, 59,* 236–240.

Hackford, T. (Producer and Director). (1978). *Teenage father* [Film]. Los Angeles: Children's Home Society of California.

Jensen, J. D. (1979). *Youth and sex: Pleasure and responsibility* (2nd ed.). Chicago: Nelson-Hall.

Kennedy, A. M., & Orr, M. T. (1984). Sex education: An overview of current programs, policies and research. *Phi Delta Kappan, 65,* 491–496.

Lewis, C. C. (1980). A comparison of minors' and adults' pregnancy decisions. *American Journal of Orthopsychiatry, 50,* 446–453.

Meredith, D. (1985, June). Mom, dad and the kids. *Psychology Today,* pp. 62–67.

Miller, E. K., & Miller, K. A. (1983). Adolescent pregnancy: A model for intervention. *Personnel and Guidance Journal, 62,* 15–20.

Parke, R. D., Power, T. G., & Fisher, T. (1980). The adolescent father's impact on the mother and child. *Journal of Social Issues, 36,* 88–106.

Phipps-Yonas, S. (1980). Teenage pregnancy and motherhood: A review of the literature. *American Journal of Orthopsychiatry, 50,* 403–431.

Rienzo, B. A. (1981). The status of sex education: An overview and recommendations. *Phi Delta Kappan, 63,* 192–193.

Robinson. B. E., & Barret, R. L. (1985, December). Teenage fathers. *Psychology Today,* pp. 66–70.

Rousseve, R. J. (1985). Unwed adolescents with babies: A grim American reality. *School Counselor, 33,* 85–87.

Saed, W. W. (1979). Counseling the adolescent parent. *School Counselor, 26,* 346–349.

Stengel, R. (1985, December 9). The missing-father myth. *Time,* p. 90.

Tegtmeyer, V. (1980). The role of the school counselor in facilitating sexual development. *Personnel and Guidance Journal, 58,* 430–433.

Thompson, R. A. (1984). The critical needs of the adolescent unwed mother. *School Counselor, 31,* 460–466.

Vanderslice, C. (Ed.). (1980). *His baby too: Problems of teenage pregnancy.* [Filmstrip]. Pleasantville, NY: Sunburst Communications.

Wagner, C. A. (1980). Sexuality of American adolescents. *Adolescence, 15,* 567–580.

Wallis, C. (1985, December 9). Children having children. *Time,* pp. 78–80.

Adolescent Drug Use and the Counselor

Eugene R. Oetting
Fred Beauvais

During the summer of 1987, a member of our staff visited one-third of the alcohol and drug treatment centers in Colorado. It was notable that in every center visited, treatment was based on the Alcoholics Anonymous (AA) 12-step model, and that each treatment center provided essentially the same treatment for everyone who entered its door. Our experience suggests that we would find this same pattern almost everywhere in the United States, that almost every treatment program is based on the explicit or implicit assumption that anyone in treatment for drug use is addicted, and that every client needs a treatment that is at least philosophically based on breaking an addiction by following these 12 steps.

There are, of course, differences between treatment settings in staffing and program, but the influence of the concept of addiction and the 12-step model is pervasive. This influence also occurs in the literature. Guydish (1982), for example, wrote about substance abuse treatment for youth, but, except for a few sentences, he focused almost entirely on the AA model. There is, however, another traditional model for treatment, one that we do not hear much about when we look at drug treatment programs, and one that we believe may be particularly appropriate for treatment of adolescent drug use. It is called counseling.

Origins of Youth Drug Abuse

Although the use of illicit drugs is not solely an adolescent problem, it is clear that the majority of use occurs during this critical time period (Kandel, Kessler, & Margulies, 1978; Johnston, O'Malley, & Bachman, 1986).

What are the roots of this adolescent drug abuse? Following is a list of the variables that we have found to be correlated with drug use among youths (Oetting & Goldstein, 1975, 1978; Oetting, Goldstein, Beauvais,

& Edwards, 1980; Oetting, Beauvais, & Edwards, 1988; Oetting & Beauvais, 1987a, 1987b): (a) family structure—is it intact; does the family care; are they antidrug? (b) peers—do they encourage use, or will they directly and strongly discourage use? (c) general deviance—is there high tolerance of deviance; are there other deviant behaviors? (d) school—are feelings negative; is performance poor? (e) expectancy—is there hope, or despair for the future? (f) drug attitudes—do drugs lead to harm; are there perceived benefits?

Most of these characteristics have also been related to drug use in other studies, for example, the work of Donovan and Jessor (1978), Jessor (1987), Kandel et al. (1978), and Newcomb, Maddahian, Skager, and Bentler (1987). In our own studies, these characteristics have been significantly related to drug use in many different large samples, including three different cultural groups: Native Americans, Hispanics and Whites. These relationships are, therefore, probably generalizable; these same characteristics are likely to be related to drug use in any school and in any part of the country.

There are, in addition, some personality characteristics that may engender drug use. The evidence in the literature that deep personality problems lead to drug use is not consistent, but there are some links. Spotts and Shontz (1984a, 1984b) have shown, for example, that in a heavy drug user, the preference for a particular drug may be related to how the drug compensates for, or balances against, deep-seated Jungian personality traits. Other studies have shown that a positive self-concept can, in some circumstances, be a factor in protecting children against using drugs, and a negative self-concept can make them more susceptible to peers who encourage drug use (Segal, 1975; Norem-Hebeisen, 1975).

Emotional problems can also be related to drug use, but the interpretations are not simple. Variables such as anxiety, depression, alienation, and anger have been related to drug use. Swaim (1987) reviewed this literature. Depression is only slightly related to drug use among younger children, but is not related at all in those students who are beyond the 10th grade. The relationships between the other personality variables are inconsistent and rarely large enough for one to draw meaningful conclusions, although Swaim found that anger does have a significant correlation with drug use. In contrast, when we ask children why they use drugs, the more seriously drug involved will say that, in addition to taking drugs for social reasons and because drugs make them feel good, they take drugs when they are feeling anxious, depressed, or alienated

(Binion, Miller, Beauvais, & Oetting, 1988). The distinction is subtle, but important—personality variables do not necessarily lead to drug use, but children who are heavily involved with drugs may self-medicate with drugs when they encounter the normal range of negative feelings experienced by nearly all adolescents.

The problems discussed above should be familiar to counselors. Nearly all of these problems are the same personal and social problems that counselors have been dealing with for most of their professional lives—family conflicts, feelings of lack of self-esteem, peer influence, feelings of anger, and so forth. Considering this list of the factors that seem to underlie drug involvement, there is a good chance that this problem is not an entirely new one needing a brand new set of *tools*. Drug abuse is probably just a new reflection, a new symptom, of the same old problems, the kinds of problems that counselors have been treating for the last half century.

Effects of Drugs on Personal and Social Problems

Drug use does, unfortunately, exacerbate those problems. Every one of the above correlates of drug use can be seen as an underlying cause of drug use but, at the same time, every one of these problems can also be perceived as a result of drug involvement. For example, peers influence drug use, but drug-using children also select peers who will support a style of drug involvement that they want to engage in (Oetting & Beauvais, 1986). As another example, family discord creates conditions that make a child susceptible to drug use, but drugs can also create family conflicts. The cycles feed on themselves and become self-sustaining.

Once a pattern of drug use has been initiated, the effects of the drug itself can add to the self-sustaining cycle. It is possible that a few young people find the physiological effects of drugs so powerful that they have extreme difficulty in stopping use and then develop a dependency. Although there are alcohol-, "downer-," or inhalant-dependent youths, they are extremely rare exceptions. A slightly more common pattern may be a form of psychological dependence that occurs for youths who just do not feel right unless they are a little high, for instance, on marijuana. Again, however, this does not characterize the majority of adolescent drug users. Johnston et al. (1986), for instance, reported that less than 5% of high school seniors are daily users of marijuana and would, therefore, be considered dependent on this drug.

Table 1 shows what percentage of 8th- and 12th-grade youths are involved in various types of drug use and at which levels. (For a description of the development of this typology see Oetting & Beauvais, 1983.) The data are from the American Drug and Alcohol Survey™ (1987), an instrument used to provide schools with local data on drug use. The sample is from 17 junior high schools and 20 senior high schools (many of them small schools) that used the survey early in the 1987-88 school year. Table 1 makes it clear that even relatively heavy drug users among adolescents do not take drugs every day and are not really using drugs often enough to be physiologically addicted.

We try to avoid using the term *addiction* in describing drug effects in adolescents, both because it does not really describe their drug use and because it tends to obscure the much more potent social and psychological underpinnings of drug use. Unfortunately, descriptions of "addicted" children get most of the publicity, partly because they are dramatic, but also probably because constant talk about the addictiveness of drugs allows people to place the blame for drug abuse on the drug itself. Parents, students, and counselors can then avoid looking at some of the other reasons for drug use. The most recent example of this attitude is the extreme concern being expressed about the addictive potential of cocaine—especially when it is smoked in the freebase form known as "crack." Though reports on use of "crack" suggest that it may, indeed, create severe dependency problems, it is still true that a person must try "crack" before it can exert a physiological or psychological effect. It would be inane to say, "She wouldn't have taken crack at all if she was not addicted to it." Though drugs can have an effect on the continuation of drug use among adolescents, the root causes of drug use are not the drugs, themselves, but the conditions leading to use. Those conditions are largely social and psychological factors. We have, for example, found that more than half of the variance in drug use can be explained by psychosocial factors (Oetting & Beauvais, 1987b).

In summary, most adolescent drug use is not rooted in the addictive properties of drugs. In the words of one recent writer in the field, "...addictive behavior is no different from all other human feeling and action in being subject to social and cognitive influences" (Peele, 1985, p. 2).

Table 1
Percentages of 8th- and 12th-Grade Youths in Each Drug-Use Type

Drug-Use Type	Percentage 8th grade (n=2651)	Percentage 12th grade (n=2074)
Multidrug and chronic users: Use any drug daily (almost always marijuana) or used several different drugs during the past month.	2.2	2.0
Stimulant users: Use marijuana most weekends and sometimes during week; use amphetamines or cocaine, usually 1–10 times a month.	0.5	1.2
Heavy marijuana users: Use marijuana on weekends and during week, but not daily; seldom use other drugs.	0.2	0.6
Heavy alcohol users: Get drunk most weekends; some may use marijuana about once a month.	0.5	4.8
Occasional drug users: Use a drug other than marijuana once or twice a month.	18.7	14.3
Light marijuana users: Use marijuana, but only a few times a year.	3.6	10.7
Drug experimenters: Have tried a drug, but are not using now.	12.7	22.2
Light alcohol users: Use some alcohol but rarely, if ever, get drunk.	12.0	21.9
Negligible or no use: May have tried alcohol, but don't use now; never tried a drug.	49.6	22.3

Drugs and the Adolescent Lifestyle

Adolescent drug use takes place in a psychosocial context that is probably the dominant force determining why, where, how, and what drugs are used (Oetting & Beauvais, 1987a, 1987b). Walters (1980) presented a dramatic model that illustrates how closely these social and personal forces tie in with drug use. He divided suburban students into "rowdies," "straights," and "cools." Rowdies are public in their display of anti-authority activity. They use drugs openly and use "downers," and combinations of drugs in large amounts so that they become publicly wild or crazy. Straights are "jocks" and "brains" and may drink some but do not use drugs much. Cools are into marijuana and perhaps "uppers" and use them in small groups, privately, and while listening to music. The type of drug and the way it is used is an integral part of the whole lifestyle. Walters' model is appealing partly because everyone knows rowdies, straights, and cools. It is, however, somewhat simplistic—there are more than three drug-use styles (Oetting & Beauvais, 1983).

The general concept that drug use of a particular type is maintained by social context and lifestyle is, nevertheless, an important one for the counselor to understand. Unless the counselor can break the chains to that lifestyle and help the young person find a new way of living, an hour in the office will have little potency compared with 100 hours in the real world; an hour with a counselor will have little effect in countering 25 to 30 hours spent with drug-using friends.

Implications for Counseling

Drug use by young people is rooted in personal attitudes and values and in the youth's relationships with the family and peers. Drugs are an integral part of a chosen lifestyle. Today's counselor must, therefore, be knowledgeable about drugs. If the counselor fails to consider the impact of drugs on students, a major area of adjustment is being avoided, and one that may be a potent force in the adolescent's life. On the positive side, however, the use of drugs is rooted in those problems that are the counselor's specific domain—family troubles, the influence of peers, and feelings about the future. This is familiar territory for counselors.

Why, then, have counselors tended to avoid drug problems or believed that they are the domain of a specialist? Perhaps this is true because drug use provides a great opportunity for externalizing blame or guilt. The adolescent can focus on drug use and avoid looking at other problems. Parents can blame the drug for what has happened to their child. The counselor can point to the drug as the reason why therapy is not progressing. Everyone is right— drugs are the source of many of the difficulties everyone is experiencing, but the counselor would not think of letting any other single factor dominate a case and prevent working on all dimensions of the case. Why, then, let drugs play that role?

The counselor may, in fact, be better equipped to deal with the typical drug-using adolescent than a drug counselor from Alcoholics or Narcotics Anonymous. The drug counselor is often someone who was dependent on drugs and who did, because of personal history and personal characteristics, happen to benefit from AA or NA treatment. That counselor approaches the youth with the idea that addiction to the drug is the primary problem. But most children are not "hooked" on the drugs they are using, they are instead experiencing emotional and developmental problems that have made them susceptible to becoming involved in lifestyles that include drug use. Overemphasizing the role that "addiction" plays in adolescent adjustment, which is quite likely to occur if every drug user is placed in a special program for "addicts," distorts the situation as much as ignoring the impact of drugs. In contrast, the counselor is trained and has years of experience in dealing with adjustment problems that young people encounter. Special problems are created because every correlate of drug use is also a result of drug use, so that the cycles become self-maintaining. Counselors, however, are familiar with such self-destructive cycles in other contexts and have learned how to break them. In dealing with the drug-using teenager, the counselor needs to assess all of the psychosocial elements of the case; then, drugs can take their place as only one part of the problem. The counselor and the adolescent can then work together to resolve basic conflicts and find a new lifestyle that places the youth on a more positive developmental track.

References

American Drug and Alcohol Survey.™ (1987). (Available from Rocky Mountain Behavioral Science Institute, Inc., P.O. Box 1066, Fort Collins, CO 80522.)

Binion, A., Miller, D. C., Beauvais, F., & Oetting, E. R. (1988). Rationales for the use of alcohol, marijuana, and other drugs by eighth grade Native American and Anglo youth. *International Journal of the Addictions, 23,* 47–64.

Donovan, J. E., & Jessor, R. (1978). Adolescent problem drinking: Psychosocial correlates in a national sample study. *Journal of Studies on Alcohol, 39,* 1506–1524.

Guydish, J. (1982). Substance abuse and alphabet soup. *Personnel and Guidance Journal, 60,* 397–401.

Jessor, R. (1987). Problem behavior theory, psychosocial development, and adolescent problem drinking. *British Journal of Addiction, 82,* 331–342.

Johnston, L. D., O'Malley, P. M., & Bachman, J. C. (1986). *Drug use among American high school students, college students, and other young adults.* Rockville, MD: National Institute on Drug Abuse.

Kandel, D. B., Kessler, R. C., & Margulies, R. Z. (1978). Antecedents of adolescent initiation into stages of drug use: A developmental analysis. In D. B. Kandel (Ed.), *Longitudinal research on drug use: Empirical findings and methodological issues.* New York: Wiley.

Newcomb, M. D., Maddahian, E., Skager, R., & Bentler, P. M. (1987). Substance abuse and psychosocial risk factors among teenagers: Associations with sex, age, ethnicity, and type of school. *American Journal of Drug and Alcohol Abuse, 13,* 413–433.

Norem-Hebeisen, A. A. (1975). Self-esteem as a predictor of adolescent drug abuse. In D. J. Lettieri (Ed.), *Predicting adolescent drug abuse: A review of issues, methods, and correlates* (Research Issues No. 11). Rockville, MD: National Institute on Drug Abuse.

Oetting, E. R., & Beauvais, F. (1983). A typology of adolescent drug use: A practical classification system for describing drug use patterns. *Academic Psychology Bulletin, 5,* 55–69.

Oetting, E. R., & Beauvais, F. (1986). Peer cluster theory: Drugs and the adolescent. *Journal of Counseling and Development, 65,* 17–22.

Oetting, E. R., & Beauvais, F. (1987a). Common elements in youth drug abuse: Peer clusters and other psychosocial factors. *Journal of Drug Issues, 17*(1 & 2), 133–151.

Oetting, E. R., & Beauvais, F. (1987b). Peer cluster theory, socialization characteristics, and adolescent drug use: A path analysis. *Journal of Counseling Psychology, 34,* 205–213.

Oetting, E. R., Beauvais, F., & Edwards, R. W. (1988). Alcohol and Indian youth: Social and psychological correlates and prevention. *Journal of Drug issues, 18,* 87–101.

Oetting, E. R., & Goldstein, G. S. (1975). *Drug abuse among American Indian adolescents: A final report* (NIDA Grant No. DA-01054-01-S1). Fort Collins: Colorado State University, Western Behavioral Studies.

Oetting, E. R., & Goldstein, G. S. (1978). *Native American drug use* (Final Report, NIDA Grant No. 2R01-DA-01054). Fort Collins: Colorado State University, Western Behavioral Studies.

Oetting, E. R., Goldstein, G., Beauvais, F., & Edwards, R. (1980). *Drug abuse among Indian children* (Interim Report, NIDA Grant No. 1R01-DA-01853). Fort Collins: Colorado State University, Western Behavioral Studies.

Peele, S. (1985). *The meaning of addiction.* Lexington, MA: Lexington Books.

Segal, B. (1975). Personality factors related to drug and alcohol use. In D. J. Lettieri (Ed.), *Predicting adolescent drug abuse: A review of issues, methods, and correlates* (Research Issue 11). Rockville, MD: National Institute on Drug Abuse.

Spotts, J. V., & Shontz, F. C. (1984a). Drug induced ego states I. Cocaine: Phenomenology and implications. *International Journal of the Addictions, 19,* 119–152.

Spotts, J. V., & Shontz, F. C. (1984b). The phenomenological structure of drug induced states II: Barbiturates and sedative hypnotics. *International Journal of the Addictions, 19,* 295–326.

Swaim, R. (1987). *Links from emotional distress to adolescent drug use: A path model.* Dissertation, Colorado State University, Fort Collins.

Walters, J. M. (1980). Buzzin': PCP use in Philadelphia. In Feldman, A., Agar, M., & Beschner, G. (Eds.), *Angel dust.* Lexington, MA: (D. C.) Heath & Co.

A Study of High School Dropouts

Lisa J. Bearden
William A. Spencer
John C. Moracco

Concern over the national high school dropout problem continues to grow as increasing attention is being focused on retaining marginal students. Historically, the public has measured school success by standardized test scores. This definition of success bypassed marginal students because of their inability to perform well on such tests. As a consequence, school systems may not have emphasized their holding power because of the likelihood of poorer performing students contributing to a less favorable evaluation of schools (Bateman, 1985).

In an effort to keep the dropout issue before the public, much research has been conducted on identifying the characteristics of potential dropouts. Characteristics typically designated as descriptive of this at-risk population include larger numbers of boys than girls, lower socioeconomic levels, previous failures, poor grades, monetary difficulties, behavior problems, boredom, problems with school staff, poor attendance, and substance abuse (Klein, 1977; Peng & Takai, 1983; Presholdt & Fisher, 1983).

Some research on dropouts analyzes the process of leaving school, with particular attention paid to the affective component of why a student chooses to leave school prematurely. Such studies can be helpful in understanding the complex nature of the problem, because it is not helpful to regard dropping out as a single, impulsive decision (Garni, 1980). How students perceive themselves in conjunction with the school experience has been found to be particularly important. Students' motivation may be decreased by the school process, not by learning (Self, 1985). Dropouts seem to subscribe to a self-concept as loners, sometimes rejecting both the school and self (Hedman, 1984). Many at-risk students feel little respect and interest from school administrators and teachers. Consequently, the potential dropout may be more a victim of a lack of understanding than a student with a learning problem

(Pittman, 1986). An example of this is when students' cultural experiences conflict with school norms (Schwabach, 1985).

Dropout intervention programs have been developed out of descriptive studies. Typical components of these programs include tutorial activities, alternative classes, counseling and advising, and work-related activities (Balfour & Harris, 1979; Cox, Holley, Kite, & Durham, 1985). To be more effective, the implementation of programs should include parental involvement, referral and outreach systems, staff commitment, environmental support, and systems of evaluation (Crawford, Miskel, & Johnson, 1980; Keller, 1977).

How to confront the issue of the dropout effectively is still not known. There seems to be little doubt that the affective component of the decision to leave school must be addressed. To examine the issue of the high school dropout in Alabama, the Governor's Education Reform Commission contracted with the Auburn University Center for School Effectiveness and Evaluation to conduct a comprehensive study within the state. One purpose of the study was to describe the dropout phenomenon from the student's point of view. This article will discuss some of the findings from that study.

Method

Participants

The study consisted of two phases. Phase 1, the pilot phase, included 40 high school students who withdrew from school during the previous three school years. Information from the pilot study aided in constructing the interview schedule used in Phase 2. In Phase 2, the main sample included 400 dropouts, 75 from the 1984–1985 school year and 325 from the 1985–1986 school year. Emphasis was placed on selecting a geographic cross section of dropouts to ensure representation proportionate to dropout percentages previously observed across the state.

Procedure

The 40 dropouts included in the pilot phase were interviewed, using open-ended questions to assess demographic data and perceived reasons for withdrawing from school before completing a high school diploma.

From the responses, a standard interview schedule was developed for use with the main sample of 400 dropouts. Each participant was given the option to be interviewed in person or by telephone, with most choosing the latter. The responses were recorded on the standard interview schedule form, coded, and tabulated for computer analysis. In addition to overall frequencies, means, and variances, the results were analyzed for sex and race differences using chi square. Although space limitations preclude a full analysis here, an examination of the perceived reasons for dropping out is presented below.

Results

In many respects, the profile of the dropouts reflected an all-too-familiar pattern: mostly unemployed or underemployed since leaving school (61%), mostly male (63%), average age (16.9 years) just over the legal minimum, and having failed at least one grade (60.1%). In other respects, however, they were somewhat atypical compared to other dropouts as reported in the literature, particularly studies conducted in large, inner-city school systems. Almost half (43%) came from families in which the father had completed high school or more, and more than half (51%) came from families in which both original parents still lived together. Most of the dropouts had participated in extracurricular activities (60%), primarily athletics, and almost 80% said they used no drugs at all, not even alcohol, while in high school. On the face of it then, many of these students were not judged to have been "high-risk" students when they were in high school. Yet, they dropped out. Why? The answers to this question will probably be of interest to counselors, because obvious problems such as broken families and drug addiction are less prominent features of the problems of these dropouts.

To answer this question, several strategies were used. First, each respondent was given 16 factors found in past research to be related to dropping out of high school and asked to rate each in terms of its importance in his or her particular case. The 10 factors rated highest are shown in Table 1.

Subsequently, each participant was asked to name the one factor perceived as the most important reason why he or she left school early. As might be expected, and as has been found to be the case in other dropout studies, there is no single factor or reason why students say they

Table 1
Ten Highest Reported Reasons Given for Dropping Out Selected
from a List of 16 ($N = 401$)

		Means			
Reason given	All	Men	Women	Whites	Non-Whites
1. Absent for too many days	1.94	1.84	2.07		
2. Bad grades	1.74	1.80	1.64	1.85	1.53
3. Preferred work to school	1.72	1.81	1.59		
4. Could not get along with family	1.70	1.84	1.50		
5. School was boring	1.68				
6. Unable to keep up with school work	1.65				
7. Had to work because of financial problems	1.43				
8. Teachers did not care	1.35				
9. No one helped me	1.31				
10. Got pregnant	1.29	1.08	1.59	1.17	1.50

drop out of high school. The nine most often mentioned reasons are summarized in Table 2.

Finally, each respondent was asked to suggest ways in which the school could help students remain in school longer. The five suggestions that were most often mentioned were: (a) talk or counsel with students, (b) have more respect for students, (c) be more lenient and understanding with students, (d) provide students more help with their academic work, and (e) improve teaching (see Table 3).

Discussion

Dropping out of school has enormous economic impact on students. Over a lifetime, the dollar amount for a person may be as high as $200,000 (Catterall, 1986). Yet, this is only a part of the loss due to non-completion of high school. The personal and social consequences extend to all sectors of society. Taken to an extreme, the failure of schools to educate students may well promote a two-tier class system, in which the low end is permanently locked into poverty (Finn, 1987). The social consequences related to this scenario are sobering and far-reaching. The

Table 2
Ranking of Reasons Named as Most Important for
Dropping Out of School ($N = 401$)

Reason	n	Percentage
1. Problems with faculty	47	11.7
2. Pregnancy	46	11.5
3. Preferred work to school	45	11.2
4. Bad grades	42	10.5
5. Finances	31	7.7
6. School was boring	28	7.0
7. Absenteeism	27	6.7
8. Expelled or suspended	20	5.0
9. Teachers did not care	15	3.7
10. Miscellaneous	100	24.9

dropout phenomenon is correlated to poverty levels, out-of-wedlock births, crime rates, and drug abuse.

In many respects, the dropout problem, like other social concerns, can be so complex that serious reflection should be initiated before commencing with remedial programs. A broad perspective on the problem can be extremely helpful in coming to resolution. Although there is a crisis, the dropout problem has always been a part of American education; there is no reason to believe that it will be resolved soon or easily.

If programs are to be successful, rethinking of the problem is necessary. The perception that the roots of the dropout problem lie

Table 3
Suggestions Made by Dropouts for Reducing the Dropout Rate

Suggestion	n	Percentage
Talk or counsel with student	82	20.5
Have more respect for students	55	13.7
Be more lenient and understanding	49	12.2
Provide more assistance with academic work	48	12.0
Improve teaching in the high school	32	8.0

primarily in the student provides a rationale for research focusing on profiles of dropouts as well as descriptions of schools. Although this approach is popular, it may prove to be ineffective. It is more likely that the problem lies in society, because teenage pregnancy, low motivation, drug abuse, and the like (traditional predictors of dropping out) are symptoms more of social dysfunctions than they are of inadequate schools. Thus, trying to change either students or the school when social policy needs changing is akin to instituting changes in delivery room techniques to reduce rates of out-of-wedlock pregnancies (Finn, 1987).

Given the above precautions, what can schools do generally and what can counselors do specifically, based on the results of this study?

The Counselor's Role

Counselors can assume a leadership role in reinforcing the perspective that the quality of interpersonal relationships makes a positive difference to youth at risk. Counselors collaborating with administrators, teachers, parents, and students can coordinate a comprehensive plan to improve the school climate.

Effective dropout prevention programs begin as soon as the child enters school. One strategy counselors can use is to be an assertive advocate in promoting the idea that raised expectations of students can result in increased school achievement. Effective school communities operate on the premise that students can learn despite adverse conditions existing in schools. Counselors have a role to play in encouraging teachers, students, and the community to expect students to achieve. Studies by Beck and Muia (1980) suggested that the most effective dropout prevention programs are those in which teachers were open and approving to students in the early grades.

Larsen and Shertzer (1987) stated that "many dropouts have a history of academic and social problems that began in elementary school" (p. 167). Early identification of potential dropouts seems crucial. Gadwa and Griggs (1985) suggested that school counselors play an integral role in identifying potential dropouts and in working with parents, teachers, and administrators to develop strategies, interventions, and policies that are responsive to the characteristics and needs of students.

Counselors can expand their services as a resource for classroom teachers to include working on the dropout problem. They can provide in-service training for groups of teachers on recognition of early signs of risk and strategies for helping students learn to cope in school environments. Staff training that is designed to increase awareness of the relationship between cognition and affect ultimately benefits not only the potential dropout but also all students, by providing students with a rationale for their behavior.

Counselors, as a liaison between the student and the community, can coordinate with juvenile court judges and community agencies willing to work with school personnel in an effort to keep students in school. Business leaders and civic groups may provide support for dropout-prevention programs and serve as resources for work-study programs. Uhrmacher (1985) described how community members joined forces with three neighboring school systems in Colorado to form a dropout prevention "commission." The group established the following goals:

> Seek funding for dropout prevention programs, develop links with community service agencies, identify and work with organizations that can help schools improve their academic environment, and prepare research and position papers on how schools, homes, and the community can fight the dropout problem. (p. 40)

Using Groups

Many schools are involving parents in dropout-prevention efforts. Group work with families can be helpful when families are in crises such as those caused by unemployment, divorce, and physiological or psychological abuse (Gadwa & Griggs, 1985). Parent training workshops aimed at teaching effective discipline techniques and mobilizing family resources are offered by many school counselors and school psychologists. Some programs have grown to include the parents as trainers, and small groups have formed in churches, community agencies, and private homes (Mauer, 1982).

Larsen and Shertzer (1987) suggested that support groups be started for identified at-risk students consisting of 6 to 10 members, with 2 to 3 of the group members identified as not likely to drop out. This arrangement allows for the positive effects of modeling, as well as providing support, suggestions for problem solving, and so forth. Groups can be structured to provide guidance on time management, study skills, decision making, stress reduction, assertiveness training, social skills, survival skills, rules for participation in meetings, and training as peer helpers (Larsen & Shertzer, 1987).

Groups may meet to discuss issues of concern to students. Chesapeake Junior High School (Virginia) used the Education for Employment Program, which focuses on seventh and eighth graders who say they do not want a college preparatory program of study. These students spend half of each school day in classes and then meet together in groups of 10 to have discussions. Bateman (1985) reported that these groups help students to work out their fears and problems and help them develop positive feelings about themselves. Since initiating this program and others aimed at keeping kids in school, Chesapeake's school dropout rate has been reduced by almost half.

Peer-tutoring and peer-support groups may prove effective in letting students know that someone cares about them. Student Advocates Inspire Learning (SAIL) uses such an approach. Project SAIL was designed in 1975 for high school students in a middle class suburban community in Minnesota. Project SAIL serves both potential dropouts and students who have dropped out once and wish to return to school. Students in SAIL attend regular academic classes and participate in intensive peer counseling groups as well as individual sessions with staff members (Balfour & Harris, 1979).

Students who have dropped out more than once may need help in overcoming problems associated with the traditional educational system. Counselors could establish re-entry groups for these students that focus on helping students identify strategies for coping with school-related concerns. In this way, counselors can assist students with immediate problems while working toward improving the educational climate (Gadwa & Griggs, 1985).

Establishing and maintaining effective counseling groups for potential dropouts, re-entry students, or both, is not without obstacles. Some administrators may believe that students should not be taken from class for counseling sessions. Dropout-prone students may frequently be absent. Frequent absences by group members may demoralize the group, weaken cohesiveness, and delay productive group work. Students may perceive sharing personal feelings in a school setting as a threat to confidentiality and therefore be fearful of self-disclosure.

These obstacles, while considerable, need not be insurmountable. Schools can change policies and practices, and educators, including counselors, can begin to examine the organizational structure of school to improve the school climate. Counselors need to emphasize that standardized test scores are not the sole measure of a successful school. School counselors can help administrators and teachers learn to recognize the school's responsibility to take direct action to address each student's need for success, approval, challenge, and meaning (Knowles & Barr, 1987).

There are no simple answers to the dropout questions. This article has focused on the interaction between school personnel and students rather than on student correction. It encourages school personnel, especially counselors, to learn more about students at risk and to assume responsibility for improving the school climate. Students as consumers of education need to perceive school as relevant to their lives; they need to feel respected and to experience a sense of belonging. Students want to know that someone notices them when they withdraw, and school personnel should be aware that students often leave psychologically long before they drop out physically. If the assumption is accepted that all members of society should finish school and that the only way into the world of work is through schooling, then educators can no longer afford to construct profiles of only students at risk. Although educators must not ignore the problems that students bring with them to school, they must concentrate on how to make the system more responsive to student needs. Counselors can be the catalyst for the development of an educational climate that recognizes the dignity and worth of each individual. By recognizing the social context in which learning takes place and the influence that teachers, counselors, and other school personnel can have on students' lives, a small step has been taken toward preventing dropouts.

References

Balfour, M. J., & Harris, L. H. (1979). Middle class dropouts: Myths and observations. *Education Unlimited, 1,* 12–16.

Bateman, C. F. (1985). In the rush toward excellence, don't let your schools "holding power" slide. *American School Board Journal, 172,* 39, 47.

Beck, L., & Muia, J. A. (1980). A portrait of a tragedy: Research findings on the dropout. *The High School Journal, 64,* 65–72.

Catterall, J. S. (1986). Dropping out: The cost to society. *Education, 4,* 9–13.

Cox, J. L., Holley, J. A., Kite, R. H., & Durham, W. Y. (1985). *Study of high school dropouts in Appalachia*. Washington, DC: Appalachian Regional Commission.

Crawford, G. J., Miskel, C., & Johnson, M. C. (1980). An urban school renewal program: A case analysis. *The Urban Review, 12*, 175–199.

Finn, C. E., Jr. (1987, Spring). The high school dropout puzzle. *The Public Interest*, pp. 3–22.

Gadwa, K., & Griggs, S. (1985). The school dropout: Implications for counselors. *The School Counselor, 33*, 9–15.

Garni, K. F. (1980). Counseling centers and student retention: Why the failures? Where the successes? *Journal of College Student Personnel, 21*, 223–228.

Hedman, C. G. (1984). Promoting the autonomy of another person: The difficult case of the high school dropout. *Educational Theory, 34*, 355–365.

Keller, A. J. (1977) Career education: Success for the potential dropout. *The Clearing House, 51*, 70–72.

Klein, W. P. (1977). The continuing education center: An alternative that is working. *The High School Journal, 61*, 111–118.

Knowles, G. W., & Barr, R. B. (1987, April). *The 1984-85 school leaver and high school diploma participant attitude study*. Paper presented at the annual meeting of the American Educational Research Association, Washington, DC.

Larsen, P., & Shertzer, B. (1987). The high school dropout: Everybody's problem? *The School Counselor, 34*, 163-169.

Mauer, R. E. (1982). Dropout prevention: An intervention model for today's high schools. *Phi Delta Kappan, 63*, 470–472.

Peng, S. S., & Takai, R. T. (1983). *High school dropouts: Descriptive information from high school and beyond*. Washington, DC: National Center for Education Statistics Bulletin.

Pittman, R. B. (1986). Importance of personal, social factors as potential means for reducing high school dropout rate. *The High School Journal, 70*, 7–13.

Presholdt, P. H., & Fisher, J. L. (1983, March). *Dropping out of high school: An application of the theory of reasoned action*. Paper presented at the annual meeting of the Southeastern Psychological Association, Atlanta, GA.

Schwabach, D. (1985). Here's why your board must throw a lifeline to foundering kids. *American School Board Journal, 172*, 28, 33.

Self, T. C. (1985). *High school retention: A review of literature.* Monroe: Northeast Louisiana University, Project Talent Search.

Uhrmacher, P. B. (1985). Use this step-by-step approach to reduce the student dropout rate. *American School Board Journal, 171,* 40-1, 40.

Chapter 6

The Scope of Practice of the Secondary School Counselor— Career Counseling

During the last decade many school reforms have been proposed in the name of achieving excellence in public schools. While talk of reform has brought with it demands for new requirements, longer school hours, and more tests, little attention has been paid to how students make educational and career choices. This lack of attention is particularly surprising considering predictions that the work force in the 21st century will grow more slowly, the pool of young workers will shrink, and more women and minorities will be needed to fill increasingly complex jobs.

Thoughtful analysts such as Harold Hodgkinson, experts at the Hudson Institute in their report entitled "Workforce 2000," and researchers at the College Entrance Examination Board maintain that the nation's economic future depends upon higher levels of educational attainment among those at the bottom of the economic ladder. Students must set career goals earlier in their school lives. Setting goals implies making choices and engaging in thoughtful educational and career planning, developing aspirations, and learning to sustain motivation. School counselors should renew their efforts to improve the career decision-making skills of their students. This chapter suggests ways that counselors can assist students in making appropriate career choices.

The article by Wood advocates group career counseling as a way for the counselor to make contact with all freshmen in an efficient and effective manner. This approach also permits the counselor to introduce herself to the students, get to know them, and to remind the staff that the counselor is an integral part of the school setting. Wood urges careful planning and involvement of teachers in a career unit which she carefully describes for the reader.

One of the major problems facing society is the number of students who drop out before they finish high school. Some researchers speculate that 15.2% of students drop out of school while other estimates range as high as 29%. Using career counseling to reach potential dropouts is the theme of the second article in this chapter. The National Career Information System undertook a study to identify successful programs in schools and agencies using the Career Information System. (The National Career Information System is an organization located in the Center for the Advancement of Technology in Education at the University of Oregon. It provides software, occupational and educational information, and technical assistance to various states). In this article, Bloch reports the results of the study, describes successful career planning programs, and suggests six guidelines that can be used to improve career planning programs.

Career myths are irrational attitudes about the career development process. Irrational career attitudes can result in dysfunctional cognitive schema when individuals are thinking about career decisions. For example, exaggerating the negative or underplaying the positive aspects of a career event (magnification or minimization) is irrational and can lead to faulty career decision-making. Herring, author of the third article in this chapter, discusses several factors that influence the presence of career myths among Native-American youths. The author advocates for better qualified counselors to address the career needs of minorities, the teaching of decision-making and problem-solving skills, and increased research regarding the career development of Native Americans and other minorities.

The fourth article focuses on an innovative "delivery" of career counseling. Whiston, using a family systems approach, describes a group for parents with the goal of maximizing their involvement in their children's career development. The group focuses on a blend of traditional career exploration and family dynamics techniques. Some parents even reported that the group led to better relationships with their children.

Using a Job Club model to help disabled students find jobs is suggested in the final article in the chapter. Research indicates that individuals who participate in Job Clubs enjoy higher rates of employment than individuals receiving traditional job search counseling. Elksnin and Elksnin describe the major principles and activities of the Job Club model and encourage counselors to expand their counseling services to disabled students.

Initiating Career Plans with Freshmen

Sally Wood

By the time students complete their freshman year, it is necessary for them to begin making some definite career plans. Yet ninth graders often perceive their career decisions as being far into the future—too far even to consider. The school counselor can play a major role in helping freshman students realize the importance of making at least tentative general career plans. Far too often, however, counselors find individual career counseling too time consuming to attempt. Taking every student out of class may not prove feasible for the students, the counselor, or the teacher. There, counselors who already have full schedules may find themselves offering career counseling to only those students who come to them asking for information. Obviously, few students—especially ninth graders—are likely to do so.

An alternative to such a haphazard, student-initiated approach is group career counseling, in which the counselor is able to make contact with all freshmen in a time-efficient, effective capacity. A career-preparation unit is one such means. Not only does conducting such a unit allow the counselor a chance to get to know the freshmen and vice versa, but also "borrowing" the students during class time reinforces for the classroom teachers the idea that the counselor is an integral part of the school setting, with goals and objectives similar to their own.

Making Arrangements

Vital to the success of the career unit is careful early planning, first with the classroom teachers. The teachers are more likely to be receptive if they have an overview of the unit and a list of objectives and materials used, and if they know the amount of time involved.

It may be feasible to borrow freshmen from one teacher or one department all day for 4 consecutive days. For example, if all freshmen are required to take English I, then the counselor might conduct the unit in English I classes all day for 4 days. However, an alternative to this schedule involves contact with more classroom teachers as well as more daily scheduling ease for the counselor.

The counselor may plan to set aside a certain class hour for freshman career planning. For instance, the second period of the school day might be the most workable for this activity. Then would come contact with each teacher who has freshmen during that class time. If upperclassmen are in the class too, the counselor may want to arrange to take the freshmen to a different setting—ideally a classroom that is not in use that hour if one is available. Using a teacher-contact sheet acknowledging the importance of the teachers' plans and time schedule, the counselor may allow the teachers to select the dates—within a specific time frame—that would be most convenient (see Appendix A).

Once a time schedule has been established and arrangements have been made for the counselor to "borrow" each class of freshmen for 4 days, the counselor is ready to begin the unit with the students (see Appendix B).

First Day: Completing an Interest Survey

The first day serves as a time for the counselor and the students to get to know one another; often, this time may be the first for the ninth grader actually to have contact with the counselor. If the groups can be kept to no more than 20 students (25 at most), the counselor can quickly learn the students' names and get to know something about each of them, simply by observing them and reacting with them in a classroom setting. A brief explanation of the career unit and discussion of the importance of early career plans can show students at least one area in which the counselor can assist them. After initial discussion, the students should complete a career interest survey, such as the *Kuder-E* (Kuder, 1985).

Second Day: Survey Results and Counseling Services

On the second day, the students should finish the career interest survey if they have not already done so. If it is a self-scoring instrument, then scoring should be completed. The results of the survey can serve as an excellent means of helping the students realize the relationship between their career choice and their likes and dislikes. The counselor's filing of the results of the survey in the student's file may be useful for later reference by the counselor or the student.

At this point, the counselor may also want to discuss things to consider in career selection (e.g., setting, salary, educational or vocational preparation). Time should be allowed during the class hour for the counselor briefly to let the students know about other services available through the counselor's office, in addition to those involving career preparation. By the time students come to class the following day, they each should have in mind two careers that interest them.

Third Day: Researching a Career

The third day is devoted to having each student research at least one career. Available sources might include occupational guides, career encyclopedias, microfiche materials, and brochures—any material available in the counseling office and the media center. If possible, the counselor might want to bring all the materials to the classroom so that they will be easily accessible for the day's work. Telling the students where the different materials are normally kept will help them realize where they can obtain career information on their own. And letting them know that the counselor will help them get additional information encourages them to use counseling services.

In completing their individual research, the students answer questions on a research sheet concerning specific aspects of the career they have selected. They are asked to look at obvious areas as well as some they might not ordinarily consider. Then they rate each aspect as to the degree they like or dislike what they have discovered about the job. If they have more "dislikes" than "likes," they are encouraged to weigh the importance of each aspect. For example, if they like the salary but dislike the hours, they need to consider the importance of these two areas as well as other aspects of the job. Could they put up with the hours if they were paid enough, or is their time more important than money? A general class discussion may help the students realize the importance of each aspect; then individuals may need additional help after filling out their sheets.

The counselor needs to emphasize that the work the students do during this unit is aimed at helping them put serious thought into their career choice. It is not, however, intended to make them come to definite, inflexible decisions about their future. The students do need to realize that by the end of their freshman year, they need to have some tentative, yet specific, ideas about their future (e.g., postsecondary education or not, general career area, etc.) (see Appendix C).

Fourth Day: Planning a High School Schedule

On the fourth day, the students look at their tentative high school schedule for the next 3 years. Ninth graders typically have mostly required classes and have not yet had to be concerned with selecting electives, meeting graduation requirements, and planning for the future. Filling out a tentative schedule will help them to realize what choices they have and will give them time to put some thought into their schedule. The counselor's, having already completed part of their schedules by filling in required classes (e.g., English I, II, and III) at the appropriate levels, will help ensure that the students understand how they will meet graduation requirements. The students may complete their individual schedules, using written and oral assistance that the counselor provides.

Before the students begin preparing the tentative schedule, the counselor should have checked the students' research sheets. In addition to other comments on each student's sheet, recommendations may be included regarding high school classes that might be useful to that student's career preparation. The schedule plan should allow room for the student to fill in a tentative class schedule and should list graduation requirements as well as a list of electives from which students may choose (see Appendix D).

In addition to the schedule sheet the students must complete, also helpful are other recommended schedules and already-developed course lists (e.g., in curriculum guides or in student handbooks, if available) for those who plan to attend college, for those who want to enter the business field, for those who want to go to vocational-technical school, and so forth. Such guidelines will help the students see what studies will be necessary and may help them decide if they really want to go into the field they are considering. Seeing the actual schedule of studies necessary for entry into a career field can help determine what is and is not a realistic choice.

When the counselor has checked and returned the schedules, the students should be encouraged to show the schedules to their parents and to discuss them. Individual conferences may be set up for students who want additional help or information. If possible, keeping a copy of each tentative schedule for the individual's file will be useful for future reference by the student, the counselor, and perhaps even the parent.

When the students return to their regular class, it may be helpful to the classroom teacher if the counselor assigns "grades" to each student for the unit. For example, each student might be able to earn a possible total of 25 points per day, based on attendance, cooperation, and completion of the work (interest survey, research sheet, schedule). A total of 100 points possible for the 4-day unit would be easy for the teacher to adapt to almost any type of grading scale.

Conclusion

This relatively simple career unit serves several purposes. It helps the counselor get to know the ninth graders—associate names with faces, get to know something about their personalities and classroom behavior, and learn about their career interests and plans. Likewise, the students become familiar with the counselor and with available counseling services. Such familiarity makes it easier for the student to come to the counselor when help is needed. Conducting a unit during class time and having objectives and a scoring system reinforces for the teachers the fact that the counselor—an educator—is integral to the school system and has goals and objectives for the counseling department, just as they have for their academic areas. Thus, such a freshman career unit proves effective and beneficial for the counselor, students, and the classroom teacher.

Reference

Kuder, G. F. (1985). *Kuder-E: General interest survey*. Chicago: Science Research Associates.

Appendix A
Teacher-Contact Sheet

I am planning a career-exploration unit for freshmen. If possible, I would like to borrow each second-hour freshman class, one per week, until I have reached all of the freshmen.

Would it be possible for me to take your second-hour freshmen for 4 days? I realize that my doing so would cause you some inconvenience and I will do all that I can to help minimize any problems that might result (for example, in the past I have given them points on cooperativeness, and so forth, to compensate for the points that they might have missed in regular classwork.)

Please indicate below if I may have your second-hour freshmen for 4 days for this purpose. (Note: I will be taking freshmen only.)

Yes _____ No _____

I will be scheduling this unit during the following weeks: (Indicate weeks planned for unit.)

Would any particular week be more convenient than others?_____

How many freshmen do you have sixth hour?

Thank you!
(Counselor's signature)

Appendix B
Overview

The following overview helps classroom teachers understand how students will spend class time and the amount of time involved:

Plans for Freshman Career Exploration Unit

Prepared by: (Counselor's Name)

Overview: As the freshman counselor, I am planning a 4-day unit on career exploration. I have sent a notice to each teacher who has freshmen during second hour, explaining my objectives to them and requesting that they allow me to borrow their second-hour freshmen for 4 days.

Dates: (Indicate dates)

Objectives: By the end of the unit, the student will be able to:

1. Identify one or two interest areas as indicated.
2. Identify jobs related to major interest as indicated by the survey.
3. Identify and evaluate qualifications related to the career(s) being considered.
4. Identify attitudes and skills conducive to an effective work situation.
5. Obtain pertinent information relative to careers and occupations of interest.
6. Plan a high school schedule as preparation for at least one career or occupation of interest.

Materials:

1. Career interest survey (e.g., *Kuder–E*).
2. Handout sheets:
   a. Suggested programs of study (related to career and educational goals).
   b. List of required classes and class electives.
   c. Four-year high school plan for each student.
   d. Exercise on discovering requirements and pertinent information on specific jobs.
3. Occupational and career information in counseling and media center.

Appendix C
Research Sheet

Your Name _____

Career or Occupation _____

For some of the information required below you will need to refer to sources; for some you will need to use your own knowledge or assumptions.

Answer each of the following questions. Be thorough.

Rate each aspect of the career or occupation, based on the information you have written in the first column. A 5 means "This aspect suits me just fine"; a 1 means "I don't like this about the job at all"; 2, 3, or 4 means a reaction somewhere between "just fine" and "dislike."

What does this job involve (What does one do in this career or occupation)?	1 2 3 4 5
What training, education, or experience is required?	1 2 3 4 5
What is the salary range in this career or occupation?	1 2 3 4 5
What are some disadvantages of this career or occupation?	1 2 3 4 5
What type of work setting does this career or occupation involve? (For example, is it indoors or outdoors? What type of place? Describe it.)	1 2 3 4 5
If you enter this career or occupation, will you be working with others or alone? Explain.	1 2 3 4 5
Will you be supervising others or will someone be supervising you, or both? Explain.	1 2 3 4 5
Will you have to dress in any special way? Explain.	1 2 3 4 5
What hours of the day will you probably be working? Explain.	1 2 3 4 5
What days of the week will you probably be working? Explain.	1 2 3 4 5
If you enter this career or occupation, will you be doing the same thing every day, or will each day be different? Explain.	1 2 3 4 5
Will the work be mostly physical or mental? Explain.	1 2 3 4 5
What courses could you take in high school or what experiences could you get during high school, in order to prepare for this career or occupation?	1 2 3 4 5

Appendix D
Tentative High School Schedule

Name _____

Career or job that you plan to enter after high school _____

Requirements for Graduation:
  English I, II, III
  World History-Geography
  American History
  Modern American History-Government
  Physical Science
  Second year of science
  Two math units
  One fine arts unit
  One practical arts unit
  Two units of physical education
  Health
  Additional electives to total 24 units

Freshman (this year)	Sophomore	Junior	Senior
English I	English II	English III	
World History	American History	Modern American Government	
Physical Science	Health		
P.E.			
Math:			
Elective:			
Elective:			

Total number of units you have scheduled: _____

(24 units required for graduation)

See attached sheet for list of electives and recommended course schedules.

Using Career Information With Dropouts and At-Risk Youth

Deborah Perlmutter Bloch

A survey of sites using the Career Information System identified successful career development programs for dropouts and potential dropouts. Model programs and program development guidelines are described.

Both the education community and the public believe that schools in the United States are facing problems in their efforts to provide universal education—education that helps every student become an adult who functions effectively as a family member, a citizen, and a member of the work force. One measure of the extent of the problems facing schools is the number of students who drop out before they finish high school. Rumberger (1987) estimated that between 15.2% and 29.1% of high school students in the country leave before graduation. Other reports show "some urban high schools with dropout rates as high as 85% for Native Americans and between 70% and 80% for Puerto Ricans" (Institute for Educational Leadership [IEL], 1986, p. 8). Evidence of the widespread concern for the dropout problem may be seen in the number of articles in professional and popular publications, in proposed and passed "dropout prevention" legislation in a number of states, and in the efforts of such groups as the National Governor's Association (1986).

Because of the concern about the many young people who leave school without constructive plans for their futures or the skills to make and carry out these plans, and because of informal "success stories" from counselors who were using the computerized career information program, the National Career Information System undertook a study to identify successful programs in schools and agencies using the Career Information System (Bloch, 1988).

The National Career Information System is an organization located in the Center for the Advancement of Technology in Education at the University of Oregon. This organization provides software, occupational and educational information, and technical assistance to operating entities in 16 states. Each operating agency then localizes the information and offers the program and associated training to schools and agencies in that state. The schools and agencies, in turn, provide the program to their students and clients. The final users, clients and students, use this microcomputer program and associated printed material for interactive exploration of occupational choice, occupational information, secondary and postsecondary educational information, financial aid information and job-seeking and entrepreneurial skills development. The software, information, and training approaches are known collectively as the Career Information System (CIS). Generically, CIS is a computer-based career information delivery system (CIDS).

The goal of the study was to identify successful strategies for using the Career Information System with at-risk youth, young people who had dropped out of high school or were in danger of doing so. The remainder of this article presents a brief review of the literature on the elements of successful programs for at-risk youth and a summary of the study procedures and results. The article concludes with some ideas that can be gleaned from the study results to increase the number and improve the results of programs and practices.

Elements of Successful Programs

Despite limited consensus concerning the causes of student drop out (Ekstrom, Goertz, Pollack, & Rock, 1986; Rumberger, 1987; Sewell, Palmo, & Manni, 1981; Wehlage & Rutter, 1986), there are a number of educational programs in place that appear to be successful. Some efforts have been made to identify the elements that characterize those programs that are successful. Although little evidence has been gathered to substantiate the efficacy of the programs and services, several observers have identified qualities that contribute to successful outcomes.

Mann (1986) identified four elements of successful educational programs: cash, care, computers, and coalitions (the four Cs). The first, cash, means that students are involved in programs in which they see the link between earning money and their school subjects. The second, caring, means that students get the concern they need from teachers and other adults because they experience smaller institutions, lower pupil to teacher ratios, and, at times, the involvement of adults outside the school. Computers, the third element, are both for teaching and for the management of records, to identify those students who are at risk of leaving school. The final C is for coalitions of schools, businesses, and local educational foundations. These four Cs can be used as a framework to outline the findings of other researchers regarding the components they have found common to successful programs for at-risk youth.

Cash

A number of studies cite the necessity for enabling at-risk youth to see the connections between going to school and future earning power. There is an experiential work-related or community-service component in the educational program (Donnelly, 1987; Peck, Law, & Mills, 1987; Institute for Educational Leadership, Inc., 1986; Wehlage, 1983). Work programs are related to learning and curriculum is related to skills needed in the workplace. Job-seeking skills are taught when they are needed, not as the central element of a program (Hahn, 1987). Intensive, individualized, basic skills training in school is combined with work-related projects out of school (Hodgkinson, 1985). Each student is helped to establish and progress toward life-career goals (Walz, 1987).

Care

The need to communicate a sense of caring by school personnel for at-risk students, and the ways to do so, appear in several studies. School districts begin with early childhood programs for disadvantaged children. They reduce teacher workloads so that teachers can have more contact with students and parents (Institute for Educational Leadership, Inc., 1986; Walz, 1987). There is a school-wide attitude that every student can be successful if given appropriate instructional and support services (Grossnickle, 1986). Possible needs of the students in the retention program are met through administrative flexibility, such as individualized student scheduling, including leaving early in the day for work programs (Donnelly, 1987; O'Connor, 1985). Supportive services associated with the educational program are intensive and the high school provides "an array of social services, including health care, family planning education, and infant care facilities for adolescent mothers" (Hahn, 1987, p. 260). Classes are small and have a low student-to-teacher ratio. There is personalized, individualized attention to student needs, and remedial instruction is available to develop basic reading and mathematics skills for those who need it. Students receive immediate feedback and rewards for achievement (Peck et al., 1987). Teachers in the program are unafraid of the students and exhibit empathy for them despite the fact that at-risk students "tend to be among the most 'unlovable' members of the student body" (O'Connor, 1985, p. 9).

Computers

There are also authors who discuss the use of computers for record-keeping as a means of reducing the number of dropouts. Program development comes from an assessment of dropout statistics and an analysis of why students drop out of high school. Students at risk of leaving school prior to graduation are identified early in their school careers (Grossnickle, 1986; O'Connor, 1985). Daily attendance is strongly encouraged; those who are absent are contacted immediately to communicate concern and interest. Where needed, computerized records are used to facilitate attendance-taking and attendance-reporting (Walz, 1987). Other studies cite the use of appropriate teaching technologies in reaching at-risk youth. For example, Hahn (1987) emphasized teaching by caring teachers and the use of teaching technology to meet the individual needs of students. Similarly in an IEL (1986) report, one of the characteristics of successful programs identified was intensive, individualized training in basic reading and mathematics skills, along with concrete projects related to the world of work. Delivery of individual math and reading remediation and the implementation of concrete projects require appropriate teaching technologies.

Coalitions

Successful education programs for dropouts and those at risk of dropping out are planned carefully, using a full knowledge of community resources. Counseling is integrated into the academic program since teachers are on the alert to identify students who have emotional or behavioral problems and to refer them to school counselors. Team teaching and mentoring are integral parts of the program. There is community involvement in the program in its planning (O'Connor, 1985). Resources in the school and community are identified to help students with special needs and problems (Grossnickle, 1986; Walz, 1987). Parents, as well, are involved in school learning activities (Walz, 1987). Parents, local government, higher education, business and industry, civic groups, and community agencies are brought together by the schools to develop programs for at-risk youth (Donnelly, 1987; IEL, 1986).

Method

Participants

The survey measure, "Strategies for Helping At-Risk Youth" (Bloch, 1988), was used to identify ways in which schools and agencies using the Career Information System were successful in working with at-risk youth. In spring 1987 the survey instrument was distributed to 11 operating agencies providing CIS to schools and agencies in their states. The operators, in turn, mailed the survey instruments to those individuals identified by participating schools or agencies as CIS site coordinators. In all, the survey instrument, "Strategies for Helping At-Risk Youth" was mailed to 1,584 sites in 11 states. There were 307 or 19.4% useable responses. Although the composition of the respondent pool is a relatively small percentage of those surveyed, it does include a diverse, although not necessarily representative, group of schools and agencies serving young people.

The responding sites were extremely varied in size, as measured by enrollment for schools or number served in a year, in the case of agencies. The mean site size was 992 students enrolled or clients served in a year, but the standard deviation was 2,119 students or clients enrolled. The smallest site responding, a rural high school, had three students. The largest site responding, a school district, had 21,750 students. A total of 302,700 clients and students are served by these sites; 305 sites responded to this question. (The unusually high standard deviation is clearly due to large differences in the size of the sites, differences in the types of sites, and how sites define themselves.)

Similarly, sites varied greatly in their estimates of the number of at-risk youth in their populations. The minimum percentage estimated was 0, and the maximum 100. The mean percentage was 17, with a standard deviation of 25; 281 sites responded to this question.

Of the 307 CIS site coordinators who responded to the survey, 186 (60.6%) identified themselves as counselors; 66 (21.5%) as administrators; 7 (2.3%) as teachers; 22 (7.2%) as other professionals; 6 (2.0%) as career aids or technicians; and 20 (6.5%) did not respond to the question. It should be noted that the CIS site coordinator usually had many other responsibilities in addition to the coordination of the use of CIS. For example, site coordinators who are counselors have a caseload of students; those who are teachers also teach classes; and those who are administrators serve as assistant principals or principals. Coordinating the use of CIS within a school or agency is thus only a portion of the site coordinator's job.

Instrument

The survey instrument, "Strategies for Helping At-Risk Youth," was developed for this project. Items were sought from operators, those who manage the delivery of CIS in their states. A draft of the instrument was written and reviewed by the operators, by a State Occupational Information Coordinating Committee Chairperson, by a counselor educator, and by others at the Center for the Advancement of Technology in Education at the University of Oregon.

In addition to identifying information, the survey asked the respondents to describe the at-risk youth in their schools or agencies, to discuss the factors or conditions that cause the problems of those at-risk youth, to describe any programs specifically designed for or successful in serving at-risk youth, to explain how CIS was used in those programs, and to describe the results they saw from the programs or activities. The survey also asked the respondents to identify "the ways in which CIS was most helpful to at-risk youth."

A number of the items in the survey instrument were deliberately open-ended. For example, a definition of "at-risk youth" was not provided. This was done so that the site coordinators could interpret the question to mean those the school or agency had identified and, therefore, chose to provide with needed services. It was also followed by two questions, one asking how the institution identified at-risk youth and another asking for the factors causing the problems of at-risk youth. Examination of these answers showed that, in general, common definitions were in use. The definitions of at-risk youth may be summarized as those who were not achieving in school, those who may be expected to drop out before completing high school, and those who had dropped out of high school. In addition, the site coordinators were asked to identify programs and practices that they found successful in working with at-risk youth. The criteria for success were not defined because it was felt that many site coordinators would not report programs that seemed to be working but which had not been formally evaluated. Since many school-designed programs do not undergo formal evaluation, specifying criteria for success might have unduly limited the programs and practices that would be described.

This article focuses on the model programs that were identified through the survey and through telephone and written correspondence follow-up with the site coordinators whose answers identified successful programs. It also presents an analysis of the responses to the question of the helpfulness of the CIS.

Results

The Model Programs

Based on the literature of successful programs outlined above and on the statements of the respondents to the survey, 13 model programs were identified for follow-up and description. It may be noted that there were more than 13 identified by site coordinators, but the follow-up was limited to those that seemed most fully developed and varied, in terms of student population served and approaches to serving that population. All of the identified programs shared certain characteristics.

The first set of characteristics related to Mann's four Cs (1986). The programs all had components that emphasized *cash*, in that they used career development activities, including the delivery of career information to help the clients see the relationships between their current status, their planned occupational futures, and their educational needs. All of the programs used *computers* as a means of instruction, specifically in the delivery of career information. None of the programs, however, identified recordkeeping as a computer function. It was difficult to measure *caring* in the written description of a program, but all of the programs had elements that individualized the approach for each student. In addition, all of the site coordinators who were called for follow-up information were responsive, both on the telephone and in the materials they sent. They seemed both caring and enthusiastic about their programs and clients. Four of the programs showed evidence of *coalitions* beyond their schools or agencies, and eight others indicated cooperative work between counselors and teachers.

Other programmatic characteristics emerged in examining the programs. First, they are all integrated career development programs, in contrast to one-shot approaches to the delivery of career information in which a school puts all of its resources into working with juniors or seniors on college choice. For example, several of the school programs had multiyear career development components and the agency programs had a clear sequence of activities. Second, they offered career development activities that were age and stage appropriate. Third, they all incorporated a variety of media, materials, activities, and approaches. Therefore, in some programs the CIS was the linchpin, but in others it was one of the several equally-used resources. Among the resources cited by the respondents, in addition to the CIDS, were videotapes that promoted self-examination and job-seeking skills; textbooks about career development and careers; interest inventories; aptitude tests; commercial, printed occupational information; state Department of Labor and Department of Education materials; and counselor-made worksheets and booklets.

Summaries of the key elements of three of the model programs follow. Full descriptions of the programs with samples of their materials, as well as brief descriptions of 40 additional successful programs or practices, may be found in Bloch (1988).

A rural California high school instituted a program for ninth graders who had failed two or more courses during the year. It has both a summer and a year-long component. At the end of the school year, counselors meet the parents of identified students at home or at school, at which time they provide the parents with: (a) the student's schedule of classes for the following term, (b) a transcript of completed course work, (c) a printout of the student's attendance for the year, (d) material on school requirements and registration information, and (e) booklets describing the homework policy of the school district and study skills. In addition, the counselor brings a contract, "Future Goals as Related to Education and Employment." Through discussion, the contract is completed and signed by the parent, the student, and the counselor. It includes the student's individualized short-term and long-term goals and the actions that the student, the parent, and the school will take so that the student achieves her or his goals.

During the following school year, the student receives individual counseling and uses CIS. The use of CIS begins with a brief introduction to its resources, then it moves to a discussion with students of their interests, activities, hobbies and goals. From that discussion, students move to general concerns in selecting a career and then to the use of the computer system. Once students have printouts of the description of occupations that interest them and of the statements concerning preparation for those occupations, the counselors work with the students relating the career information to courses available at the high school, and, if appropriate, to postsecondary study. An evaluation of the first year of the program showed that 43 of the 53 students involved in the program were still in school after 1 year. The remainder had moved out of the district or transferred to other high schools. The average failure rate had dropped from 2.7 courses per student in the ninth grade to 1.5 courses per student in the tenth grade.

In a junior high school in Minnesota, all students participate in a career education program that includes specific learning activities in the seventh, eighth, and ninth grades. The overall goals of the program include: (a) the development of self-awareness, (b) the development of decision-making skills, (c) increased knowledge of how careers affect lifestyles, and (d) the development of interpersonal skills, with an emphasis on communication in the work setting. The range of activities for each year may be seen by examining those of the eighth grade.

Activities in the eighth grade include: (a) aptitude testing and inter-pretation, (b) orientation to CIS, (c) use of QUEST (a 21-question interactive exploratory portion of CIS, which yields a list of occupations related to self-reported interests and ability levels), (d) interviewing an adult about her or his job, and (e) completing an interest inventory. A career planning activity record is maintained by each student for the 3 years of junior high school. It includes space for recording all of the career activities completed, the results of interest inventories and apti-tude tests, paid or unpaid job experiences, and changes in career choice, interests, favorite subjects and goals. The experiences of this program are integrated with developmental group counseling for at-risk students. Counselors report that the program captures and maintains student interest and encourages future planning.

At a Nebraska center for juvenile delinquents, students pursue an "independent living course." The course includes the exploration of students' values, as well as practical issues in job planning and living skills. CIS is used as a primary tool as students explore their near-term futures. Using CIS, each student "chooses a career" for the duration of the course. All the budgeting and planning exercises take that career into consideration. Student evaluations of the course suggested that their awareness of adult responsibilities had increased. Teachers in the program observed that students developed more realistic ideas about the jobs they qualified for and the pay they expected to receive.

Evidence of Program Success

Although this survey did not request numerical data concerning the results of the programs, each of the respondents provided information concerning program success. Among the client outcomes observed (formally and informally) by the site coordinators were the following:

- Promotion to the next grade in school.
- Reduction in course failures.
- Increased retention in school, as compared to similar students in similar schools who were not in the program.
- Greater understanding by parents of academic requirements and resources.
- Increased knowledge of the relationships between self and future plans, between future plans and school courses, and between school courses and training needed for specific jobs.
- Increased knowledge regarding which businesses and industries may be potential employers.
- Increased understanding of the relationship of mathematical and verbal skills to job skills.
- Increased desire for and independent use of career information, including occupational information, educational information and job-seeking skills information.
- Discovery of new occupational and educational options.
- Increased motivation to pursue education.
- Increased and improved goal-setting, including narrowing of the gap between fantasy and reality.
- Increased self-awareness.
- Increased self-esteem.

Another way to explain the success of the programs is to examine the responses to the open-ended question that asked: "What is the best thing about CIS in helping at-risk youth?" Of the 307 survey respondents, 111 site coordinators answered this question. Answers were grouped into seven categories with some respondents reporting more than one type of benefit. The greatest number (39.6%) cited the motivational aspects of CIS. The next most frequently cited benefit was realistic goal setting (33.3%). Following this was the delivery of factual information (27.0%) and other facilitation of career development (25.0%). The remaining responses dealt more with how the system was used rather than with outcomes. Ease of use and attractiveness were cited by 17.1%; 14.4%

cited user control and interactivity; and 9.0% cited individualization as benefits of the CIS program.

These responses are particularly interesting, since the goal of the computerized CIDS is to deliver information, not to exhort students into action. Yet, the two most frequent benefits observed by people working with at-risk youth were the motivational and goal-setting effects.

Summary and Conclusion

The importance of career development programs at all school levels has been well documented by the national career guidance and counseling guidelines project of the National Occupational Information Coordinating Committee (1988). The findings of the survey, "Strategies for Helping At-Risk Youth," reported in this article, suggest that career education and development programs can play a vital role in schools and agencies that work with young people at-risk of dropping out of high school, as well as with those who already have dropped out.

Six guidelines for educational program design emerged from the results of this study:

1. The content of the program helps the students understand relationships between their current status, their planned occupational futures, and their educational needs. This idea was discussed in the review of the literature as the C which meant *cash*. Furthermore, in citing the effects of CIS and in describing their programs, site coordinators repeatedly identified the development of the ability to make connections between the present and the future as a critical outcome.

2. The programs are not only delivered by caring individuals, but they have individualization built-in to ensure the communication of this caring. Again, the importance of caring and of individualization as an aspect of caring were factors cited by Donnelly (1987), Grossnickle (1986), Peck et al. (1987) and others. Individualization can be seen in a number of the model programs in this article.

3. Coalitions of schools and agencies, of institutions and businesses, and of counselors, teachers, and parents are fostered in developing and delivering the programs. Four of the programs showed evidence of coalitions beyond their schools or agencies, and eight others indicated cooperative work between counselors and teachers. Mann (1986), O'Connor (1985), and Walz (1987), among others, have cited coalition

formation as an important factor in the development of successful educational programs for at-risk youth.

4. The programs include an integrated sequence of career development activities. In too many situations, schools offer one-shot approaches to career development, which focus on college selection. The successful programs described by the site coordinators all had many activities, including self-exploration, information gathering, and decision-making components.

5. The career development activities offered are age and stage appropriate and provide opportunities for individuals to proceed at their own pace.

6. The activities incorporate a wide variety of media and career development resources, including computer-based CIDSs with up-to-date, locally relevant information.

Counselors and administrators can use the guidelines to initiate programs designed to meet the particular needs of their populations and the resources of their institutions. They can also use the guidelines to examine and improve programs already in place. In addition to providing directions for program development, the study findings suggest a number of areas for evaluation and research.

In carrying out future educational programs for at-risk youth and dropouts, it would be helpful if evaluation designs were incorporated so that the body of knowledge on successful programs could include more detailed and, therefore, more helpful information. For example, it would be helpful to know *which* activities or combinations of activities are particularly successful with students of specific ages or with particular problems. It would also be helpful to know *why* the programs are successful. For example, what interactions between schools and students contributed to students dropping out and which interventions successfully overcame these problems? Responses by the site coordinators suggested that the programs and the computerized CIDS increased student motivation, self-awareness, self-esteem, and internal locus of control. Too little is known, however, about the part these personality factors play in students staying in school and achieving, or how the identified approaches work in bringing about improvement.

While the research that will contribute to long-range change for all students in all educational settings is being designed and implemented, it is important that work continues for those young people currently at-risk. Career information as delivered in these programs seems to do that.

In the words of one site coordinator, "It helps them dream realistic dreams."

References

Bloch, D. P. (1988). *Reducing the risk: Using career information with at-risk youth.* Eugene, OR: Career Information System.

Donnelly, M. (1987). *At-risk students.* (Eric Digest Series, 21). Eugene, OR: University of Oregon, ERIC Clearinghouse on Educational Management.

Ekstrom, R. B., Goertz, M. E., Pollack, J. M., & Rock, D. (1986). Who drops out of high school and why? Findings from a national study. *Teachers College Record, 87,* 356–373.

Grossnickle, D. R. (1986). *High school dropouts: Causes, consequences, and cure.* (Fastback 242). Bloomington, IN: Phi Delta Kappa.

Hahn, A. (1987). Reaching out to America's dropouts: What to do? *Kappan, 69,* 256–263.

Hodgkinson, H. L. (1985). *All one system: Demographics of education, kindergarten through graduate school.* Washington, DC: Institute for Educational Leadership, Inc.

Institute for Educational Leadership, Inc. (IEL). (1986). *School dropouts everybody's problem.* Washington, DC: Author.

Mann, D. (1986). Dropout prevention—Getting serious about programs that work. *NASSP Bulletin, 70,* 66–73.

National Governors' Association. (1986). *Time for results: The governors' 1991 report on education.* (Labor Notes, Number 10). Washington, DC: Author.

National Occupational Information Coordinating Committee. (1988). *The national career guidance and counseling guidelines.* Washington, DC: Author.

O'Connor, P. (1985). Dropout prevention programs that work. *OSSC Bulletin, 29*(4).

Peck, N., Law, A., & Mills, R. C. (1987). *Dropout prevention: What we have learned.* Ann Arbor, MI: ERIC Counseling and Personnel Services Clearinghouse.

Rumberger, R. W. (1987). High school dropouts. *Review of Educational Research, 57,* 101–122.

Sewell, T. E., Palmo, A. J., & Manni, J. L. (1981). High school dropouts: Psychological, academic and vocational factors. *Urban Education, 16,* 65–76.

Walz, G. R. (1987). *Combating the school dropout problem: Proactive strategies for school counselors.* Ann Arbor, MI: ERIC Counseling and Personnel Services Clearinghouse.

Wehlage, G. G. (1983). *Effective programs for the marginal high school student.* (Fastback 197). Bloomington, IN: Phi Delta Kappa Educational Foundation.

Wehlage, G. G., & Rutter, R. A. (1986). Dropping out: How much do schools contribute to the problem? *Teachers College Record, 87,* 374–392.

Attacking Career Myths Among Native Americans: Implications for Counseling

Roger D. Herring

Native-American youths of today are unlike their ancestors in career aspirations. Today's Native-American youths aspire to a lifestyle in which the Native American will represent a greater percentage among the employed and will play a more viable role in society. The move is toward a lifestyle in which Native Americans will provide adequate financial and emotional support to their children. This trend is also reflected in a lifestyle that presents more options for the Native American than ever before. This new lifestyle is possible, however, only if Native Americans can overcome the many barriers—a major one being career myths—that have prevented and continue to hinder occupational success.

What Are Career Myths?

Career myths can be defined as irrational attitudes about the career development process. These irrational attitudes most often are generated from historical, familial patterns of career ignorance and negative career-development experiences.

Irrational career attitudes—or career myths—generally result in dysfunctional cognitive schema when individuals are contemplating career decisions. Examples of dysfunctional cognitive schema include drawing conclusions where evidence is absent (arbitrary inference), making important career decisions on the basis of one incident (overgeneralization), exaggerating the negative or underplaying the positive aspects of a career event (magnification or minimization), overly self-attributing negative career occurrences (personalization), and perceiving career events only in extreme terms (dichotomous or absolutistic thinking) (Beck, 1970).

The link between career myths and irrational attitudes is supported in studies such as Alden and Safran (1978) and Dryden (1979). Other research has also substantiated the relationship between irrational cognitions and indecisiveness in a student's career-development experiences (Haase, Reed, Winer, & Bodden, 1970). In addition, irrational thinking has been found to be the basic component of minority students' career myths (Slaney, 1983).

Common Influences on Career Myths

Several factors influence the presence of career myths among Native youths. Contributing significantly to the uninformed status of Native-American students regarding career knowledge is the limited research available on the psychological, philosophical, and career needs of Native Americans. In addition, much of the available research emphasizes the reservation Native Americans from historical and sociological perspectives.

A second variable affecting American career myths is the continuation of Native-American stereotypes. Stereotypes concerning Native Americans that are popular with non-Native Americans depict many negative images. Native Americans continue to be stereotyped by current media and, more importantly, by the educational systems of this nation. These negative images have now overlapped into career-development areas and need to be addressed more appropriately by counselors than in the past.

A third influence is the Native-American youth's lack of career awareness and weak understanding of a particular career area or the training and duties required. Research has shown that most minority students display less satisfaction with program choices and give lower ratings on receiving help with job choice and career decisions (Richmond, Johnson, Downs, & Ellinghaus, 1983). These weaknesses contribute to students' lack of self-awareness when contemplating career choices (Newlon, Nye, & Hill, 1985).

Research has indicated that the average minority student is different from the average non-Native American, middle-class student in background experience, values, and orientations. These differences occur even though the minority student's aspirations may equal or exceed those of the middle-class non-Native-American student (Williams, 1979). These differences also tend to restrict a minority student's awareness of available careers or of the skills required. As a result,

Native Americans continue, in disproportionate numbers, to enter traditional career areas or to become unemployed (Burris, 1983).

The American Council on Education's studies of bachelor's degrees among minorities indicate that minorities tend to earn degrees in selected areas (National Center for Educational Statistics, 1978). For example, one-third of Native-American students earned degrees in either education or social science. By contrast, Native Americans earned only .1% of all engineering degrees. Out of 5,403 master's degrees granted in the physical sciences during the 1975-1976 year, Native-American students received only nine. Out of the nearly 2.2 million scientists and engineers surveyed in 1974, .025% were Native Americans. A similar survey of doctoral scientists and engineers in the United States in 1975 revealed that Native Americans made up .2% (National Science Foundation, 1977).

Native-American students are plagued with problems of anxiety, racism, employment, and education. These problems complicate career development and appropriately identify cogent areas to unfold self-sufficiency skills. It is also imperative that education personnel sincerely understand that Native Americans' tribal characteristics vary significantly. Yet, a tendency to erroneously globalize certain attributes to all Native Americans still persists.

Implications

Three basic implications can be derived from the previously presented rationales for the existence of a Native-American career mythology. The first implication involves the need for both enlargement and enhancement of research literature on Native Americans and career development. Existing research related to Native Americans, as a rule, emphasizes the western-reservation Native American and may not be directly applicable to other Native-American groups. Also, most of the studies have been contributed by non-Native American researchers. Such research may lack both cultural and ethnic perspectives. A more substantial research base can only be attained through the increased desire to expand the current literature.

A second implication is related to the continued existence of stereotypes. All levels of the educational system must be involved if negative images of the Native American are to be eradicated. School materials (e.g., textbooks and media materials) need to be purged of any inadvertent illustrations, photographs, and references that inaccurately depict Native Americans. This accomplishment would greatly facilitate the erasure of the negative image of Native Americans.

Subtle and inadvertent biases in counseling materials can convey many hidden messages to students. Are different minorities displayed in the posters, charts, and photographs? Are the careers of doctor, lawyer, and other professional worker illustrated with different ethnic groups? Or, are minorities being portrayed in the nontraditional jobs? These kinds of displays convey the impression that the heights to which minority students can aspire should fit into neat categories (Gunnings & Gunnings, 1983). Such examples reflect career stereotyping found (hopefully innocently) in many counseling departments and career-exploration settings.

A third implication that would have effects on employment, job satisfaction, career knowledge and decisions, and other weaknesses of Native-American students involves the counseling profession. Counselor bias pertains to ethnic, cultural, and educational discrimination in the counseling process, or a combination of these. Cultural bias generally reflects both ethnic and socioeconomic background prejudices. Caution must be used to prevent these biases, whether overt or subtle, from spreading. Counselors must be informed even to the point of re-education, if necessary, to assure themselves of competency and appropriateness when counseling with Native Americans. The career and generalist counselors have the responsibility to determine and to correct student misconceptions that lead to career choice difficulties and negative career aspirations.

Wilbur, Roberts-Wilbur, and Jefferson (1983) suggested additional and better qualified counselors to address the career needs of minority students. Recent studies have shown that counselors can adapt a student's irrational beliefs to become positive factors in the career decision process (Dorn & Welch, 1985; Gerler, 1980). These mental imageries can be incorporated into useful goal-setting strategies rather than remaining as irrational career attitudes.

A skillful, cross-cultural counselor functions to help Native-American students understand the parameters of careers in realistic terms, not through negative mythologies. The goal for implementing a comprehensive career program would be to present Native-American role models from nontraditional career clusters. The intent should be to provide the Native-American student with general career information such as career titles, where people work and what they do, and the skills and abilities needed to perform certain jobs. The counselor must avoid unwittingly signaling the assumed superiority of any one value system, thereby alienating the Native-American student.

The unique value system of the Native American must be recognized in the identification and elimination of career myths. Both readable and informative studies of Native-American values and world views are available. I suggest that counselors would be more competent in crosscultural counseling if they became familiar with the research and information available in studies such as those by Herring (1989, 1990), Sue and Sue (1977), and McDavis and Parker (1981).

Decision-making and problem-solving skills are of extreme value to the ending of career myths. Minorities lack good problem-solving skills and need more expertise if they are to cope in the world. Aspirations, which are highly influenced by career myths, have a direct relationship to problem solving, career development and planning, and career indecisiveness. Effective cross-cultural counselors can reduce these weaknesses.

Research has demonstrated that the traditional theorists of career development (i.e., Holland, Roe, & Super) have neglected to include ethnicity in their career concepts (June & Pringle, 1977). Consequently, many researchers believe a reform of the entire educational system is required before any minority can be incorporated into the mainstream of career education (Hoyt, 1983). Others call for the increased use of labor market information, career awareness workshops, equal opportunity programs, and intensive re-evaluation of the current occupational literature to remove any ethnic bias that may exist (Coelho & Williams, 1980; Newlon et al., 1985; Wilbur et al., 1983).

The training of cross-cultural counselors to work with Native Americans would be more effective and expedient. The Native-American student offers a direct challenge to the counseling profession. Sue and Sue (1977) noted that 50% of Native-American clients terminate after their initial counseling session compared to 30% for Anglo-American clients. Few Native-American counselors exist, comparatively speaking. Consequently, most counseling relationships have to be cross-cultural ones. Research has established the superiority of cross-cultural counselors in minority counseling compared to traditional Anglo-American counselors (Gunnings & Gunnings, 1983). Native-American students have unique social and emotional needs, diverse family constellations, and historical discrimination influences. These Native-American students require specific strategies to deal with these influences (Herring, 1990).

Conclusion

The existence of career myths among Native-American students needs to be acknowledged and addressed so that the myths can be eliminated. Such barriers to good career thinking as those presented in this article (i.e., lack of research, stereotypes, lack of career assistance, disproportionate employment and educational opportunities, and inappropriate counseling techniques) provide the focal points for counselors.

To attain the desired goal of the elimination of the barriers to successful career development and the subsequent restoration of rational career thinking will require a multifaceted intervention, which will entail improving counseling techniques (individual and family) and improving the current, unequal career opportunity structure and poor educational systems that created the disparity in achievement and the low expectation levels of Native-American students. The reasons a Native-American student chooses to explain or to justify a point of view are inextricably related to that student's assumptions about career knowledge and skills. Native-American students often enter career counseling and career decision making possessing ideas about the career-development process that hinder decision-making ability. The reality that Native-American students do internalize the negative aspects of their historical experiences, resulting in negative career myths, deserves to become a primary concern of counselors who serve Native Americans as well as other helping and service personnel in education.

References

Alden, L., & Safran, J. (1978). Irrational beliefs and nonassertive behavior. *Cognitive Therapy and Research, 2,* 357–364.

Beck, A. T. (1970). Cognitive therapy: Nature and relation to behavior therapy. *Behavior Therapy, 2,* 184–200.

Burris, B. (1983). *No room at the top: Underemployment and alienation in the corporation.* New York: Praeger.

Coelho, R. J., & Williams, D. M. (1980). Evaluation of occupational literature: A guide to use with minorities. *Journal of Non-White Concerns, 9,* 3–9.

Dorn, F. J., & Welch, N. (1985). Assessing career mythology: A profile of high school students. *The School Counselor, 33,* 136–141.

Dryden, W. (1979). RET and its contribution to careers. *British Journal of Guidance and Counseling, 7,* 181–187.

Gerler, E. R. (1980). Mental imagery in multimodal career education. *Vocational Guidance Quarterly, 28,* 306–312.

Gunnings, B. B., & Gunnings, T. S. (1983). A bias review procedure for career counselors. *Journal of Non-White Concerns, 11,* 78–83.

Haase, R. F., Reed, C. F., Winer, J. L., & Bodden, J. L. (1970). Effect of positive, negative, and mixed occupational information on cognitive and affective complexity. *Journal of Vocational Behavior, 15,* 294–301.

Herring, R. D. (1989). Native American families: Dissolution by coercion. *Journal of Multicultural Counseling and Development, 17,* 4–13.

Herring, R. D. (1990). Understanding Native-American values: Process and content concerns for counselors. *Counseling and Values, 34,* 134–137.

Hoyt, K. B. (1983). Career education and educational reform. *Journal of Career Development, 11,* 8–19.

June, L. N., & Pringle, G. D. (1977). The concept of race in the career development theories of Roe, Super, and Holland. *Journal of Non-White Concerns, 6,* 17–24.

McDavis, R. J., & Parker, W. M. (1981). Strategies for helping ethnic minorities with career development. *Journal of Non-White Concerns, 9,* 130–136.

National Center for Educational Statistics. (1978). *Condition of education, 2978* (Statistical report). Washington, DC: Author.

National Science Foundation. (1977). *Women and minorities in science and engineering* (NSF 77-304). Washington, DC: Author.

Newlon, B. J., Nye, N. K., & Hill, M. S. (1985). Career awareness workshops for disadvantaged youth. *Journal of Career Development, 11,* 305–315.

Richmond, L. J., Johnson, J., Downs, M., & Ellinghaus, A. (1983). Needs of noncaucasian students in vocational education: A special minority group. *Journal of Non-White Concerns, 12,* 13–18.

Slaney, R. B. (1983). Influence of career indecision on treatments exploring the vocational interests of college women. *Journal of Counseling Psychology, 30,* 55–63.

Sue, D. W., & Sue, D. (1977). Ethnic minorities: Failure and responsibilities of the social sciences. *Journal of Non-White Concerns, 5,* 99–105.

Wilbur, M. P., Roberts-Wilbur, J. P., & Jefferson, D. (1983). Equal opportunity programs: A case for counseling. *Journal of Non-White Concerns, 11,* 34–42.

Williams, J. H. (1979). Career counseling for the minority students: Should it be different? *Journal of Non-White Concerns, 7,* 176–182.

Using Family Systems Theory in Career Counseling: A Group for Parents

Susan C. Whiston

According to Palmo, Lowry, Weldon, and Scioscia (1984), adolescent career planning has become one of the major problems facing schools and parents. Uncertainty about economic trends and financial constraints often results in families experiencing emotional stress concerning career choices. Many parents look to school counselors for assistance. But counselors often have extremely large caseloads and have difficulty finding the time to work with individual parents on these issues.

There seems to be a growing interest in incorporating family systems theory into school counseling (Wilcoxon & Comas, 1987; Nicoll, 1984; Palmo et al., 1984). Horne and Ohlsen (1982) contended that central to family counseling is the belief that problems experienced by the individual are an indication of difficulty within the social system of that individual, usually the family. Recently there has been an introduction of the family systems perspective into career counseling (Lopez & Andrews, 1987; Bratcher, 1982; Zingaro, 1983), but in these laudable efforts, the authors discussed working with individuals and did not address the issues of working with parents.

Osipow (1983) stated that it is remarkable that so little theorizing has been done to explain the role of the family in vocational behavior, especially when extensive data exist to show how family background influences the kinds of initial choices made and how they are implemented. Schulenberg, Vondracek, and Crouter (1984) found little research on the influence of family interaction patterns on children's vocational development, but contended that, intuitively, it seems that family interaction patterns are a salient component of vocational development. Tinto's (1975) paramount work in college retention included family background in the model and concluded that in this area, the most important factors are the quality of relationships within the family and the interest and expectations parents have for their children's education. Held and Bellows (1983) contended that the most striking characteristic of college students in crisis is their belief that they must achieve or perform for the family. Zingaro (1983) discussed how a client with a low level of differentiation from the nuclear family may be confused because he or she cannot tell the difference between parental expectations and his or her own expectations. Therefore, it is difficult for the client to realistically explore careers when he or she is in a state of confusion.

In general, there seems to be a relationship between family interactions and children's career development. Parents often want to assist their children in career decisions, but frequently do not have the knowledge and skills to encourage effective career decision making. Otto and Call (1985) have found that involving parents is a visible way to respond to the public expectation that schools assist young people in making career plans. Little is written, however, about specific techniques for working with parents on issues related to their children's career planning needs.

This article describes a group for parents with a focus on maximum parental involvement in their children's career development. The group is designed to be a blend of traditional career exploration and family dynamics techniques. Parents who have participated in this group have reported that they gain insight into the complexity of effective career decision making and communication patterns within their families. Often, the parents reported that they felt this group assisted in a better overall relationship with their children.

Formation of the Group

For counselors organizing such a group, the formation must be primarily based on the needs of the community. A major decision a counselor needs to make concerns appropriate scheduling of the group for maximum attendance and participation. If parents are highly interested and motivated, then a more traditional group format can be organized, with weekly meetings for approximately 6 weeks. Time constraints may prohibit weekly sessions, however, and the counselor may select a Saturday workshop or some other appropriate format.

The size of the group will also depend on the needs of the community, but the number of participants should be limited to allow for discussion. For many parents, this will be the first experience with a group, so the counselor needs to do some teaching about group process. Confidentiality needs to be stressed, because topics such as their children's personalities and family values will be discussed.

From the initiation of the group, the focus should be on maximum involvement by parents in their children's career exploration. The parents need a clear understanding that the workshop will not help them decide what the ideal careers for their children are; instead, it will provide techniques for facilitation of the career development process. Another goal of this group is to strengthen interactions within the family; thus, parents need to understand from the beginning that the emphasis will be on parental expectations and behaviors. A good way to initiate this process is to have the participants examine how their parents influenced their present career directions. The counselor may have participants do an exercise dealing with the careers their parents would have liked them to pursue and how their parents encouraged and discouraged their career choices.

Career Exploration Issues

As far back as 1909 and Frank Parsons' *Choosing a Vocation,* career development theorists have stressed the importance of self-knowledge. Zunker (1986) suggested that career-life planning includes discussion, evaluation, and clarification of interests, abilities, achievements, values, and work life experiences. Many parents, however, may not be familiar with a comprehensive career exploration procedure and will want to focus only on information concerning occupations, with the greatest growth projections for the coming decades. The benefits of looking at the person, the world of work, and the interaction between them will provide an introduction to many of the concepts related to career exploration.

Because of the vast number of careers it is possible to be interested in, the use of a classification system can help parents to expedite the exploration process by sorting careers into manageable groups. Holland's (1985) system of typing persons based on interest and work environments into six corresponding categories can be an easily understood organizational system. Using Holland's code to have parents identify their own interests and project what they think their children's interests codes are has proven to be an extremely insightful experience for parents. Parents then need to examine whether or not their career interests are having an impact on their children's career selections instead of allowing them to base the decision on the children's interests.

Bolles (1986) stressed the importance of identifying favorite and strongest skills. In working with parents, the author has found that they often can list only a few skills that their children have developed. Often, the reason is that people perceive skills and abilities from a narrow perspective and do not identify the varied skills they and their children use in everyday life. After the parents have developed a broader view of skills, then methods for assisting their children in developing a comprehensive list of abilities can be explored. While on the topic of skills, the importance of a mathematics background for entrance into many careers can be explained. This topic is particularly important, because research generally indicates that a lack of background in math constitutes one of the major barriers to women's career development (Betz & Fitzgerald, 1987).

Work values have continually been recognized as a critical concept in career planning and development (Pine & Innis, 1987). Mangum, Gale, Olsen, Peterson, and Thorum (1977) suggested that parents provide values clarification experiences, because pursuing a career congruent with one's values releases personal energy. From a family systems orientation, exploration of family values can lead to an analysis of roles and boundaries. Bratcher (1982) contended that rules, boundaries, and homeostasis are perhaps the most influential systemic issues likely to affect career choice. He suggested examining whether or not the client has internalized values from the family without actually integrating them into a philosophy of life and whether or not the client feels constrained by these values. Working with parents provides the opportunity for them to examine family values and traditions and how those messages are affecting their children's abilities to consider career options. This thorough evaluation of values from a family systems theory orientation leads to the parents' assessment of the family's rules, boundaries, and interaction patterns. This intervention will often identify additional difficulties within the family system, and the counselor may need to refer the family for more in-depth family counseling.

Parents need to develop techniques for encouraging their children to gain self-knowledge about their interests, skills, and values. In addition, they also need methods for surveying the world of work. On the topic of imparting occupational information, Crites (1976) suggested that the counselor orient clients to information, including computerized systems, and reinforce the clients in their exploration. These two concepts can be quite helpful to parents. First, the parents need to be oriented to specific information sources (e.g., the *Dictionary of Occupational Titles* [U.S.

Department of Labor, 1977] and the *Occupational Outlook Handbook* [U.S. Department of Labor, 1988]) and where these sources are easily accessible in the community. The second concept of reinforcing exploration for career information is equally important. Parents often want to assume the responsibility for obtaining and evaluating career information to ensure that the correct career is selected. If children are to become autonomous, however, then parents need to leave the responsibility of acquiring the information to the children. They can encourage the process by suggesting specific information sources and then reinforcing information-gathering behaviors.

Parents often become frustrated as a student approaches graduation from high school and has not selected a career. Parents are frequently unfamiliar with the stages of career development and have unrealistic expectations of when definite choices are made. Grites (1981) stressed the benefits of students entering college with an "undecided" major instead of selecting something for which they are unprepared and are inadequately informed. Parents need to explore whether or not they are rushing the children into a premature decision or whether the children are prepared but lack decision-making skills. Parents may be unaware that effective decision making is a learned skill that can be taught. Reviewing an effective decision-making process such as Krumboltz and Sorenson's (1974) systems can prove to be an extremely useful exercise. But a lack of decision-making skills may not be the major difficulty in reaching a career decision. Lopez and Andrews (1987) proposed a family systems perspective on career indecision when an individual's disturbances or symptoms serve important regulatory functions in the family through their influence on family process. From this perspective, the group explores the probable system functions of career indecision. What is often identified is that career indecision serves to postpone the separation of the children from the family.

A constant theme throughout the group process needs to be communication patterns between the parents and children. Both Lopez and Andrews (1987) and Mangum et al. (1977) suggested that parents will need to change the nature of their interactions with the children, and this change may involve maintaining sufficient distance to allow their offspring to do the developmental work. In concluding the group, the counselor must ensure that parents understand they can be facilitative in the career development process, but that sometimes facilitation involves withdrawing and letting the children assume the responsibility.

Conclusion

The school counselor is often responsible for career exploration and development in the school. A group designed for parents can provide a unique opportunity to respond to parents' requests for assistance and information concerning students' career choices. The parents' career group also provides an opportunity to promote effective family communication patterns and more productive family environments. By centering counseling around the topic of careers, counselors can encourage parents to participate who typically would not become involved in family counseling. In addition, the group has helped some parents clarify some of their own career issues (e.g., whether or not to initiate a midlife career change). In conclusion, a parents' career group has shown to be an extremely effective therapeutic intervention, which can address varied issues.

References

Betz, N. E., & Fitzgerald, L. F. (1987). *The career psychology of women.* Orlando, FL: Academic Press.

Bolles, R. N. (1986). *What color is your parachute: A practical manual for job-hunters and career changers* (rev. ed.). Berkeley, CA: Ten Speed Press.

Bratcher, W. E. (1982). The influence of the family on career selection: A family systems perspective. *Personnel and Guidance Journal, 61,* 87–91.

Crites, J. O. (1976). Career counseling: A comprehensive approach. *The Counseling Psychologist, 6,* 2–12.

Grites, T. J. (1981). Being "undecided" might be the best decision they could make. *School Counselor, 29,* 41–46.

Held, B. S., & Bellows, D. C. (1983). A family systems approach to crisis reactions in college students. *Journal of Marital and Family Therapy, 9,* 365–373.

Holland, J. L. (1985). *Making vocational choices: A theory of vocational personality and work environments* (2nd ed.). Englewood Cliffs, NJ: Prentice-Hall.

Horne, A. M., & Ohlsen, M. M. (1982). *Family counseling and therapy.* Itasca, IL: Peacock.

Krumboltz, J. D., & Sorenson, D. L. (1974). *Career decision-making* [Film]. Madison, WI: Counseling Films, Inc.

Lopez, F. G., & Andrews, S. (1987). Career indecision: A family systems perspective. *Journal of Counseling and Development, 65,* 304–307.

Mangum, G. L., Gale, G. D., Olsen, M. L., Peterson, E., & Thorum, A. R. (1977). *Your child's career: A guide to home-based career education.* Salt Lake City, UT: Olympus Publishing Co.

Nicoll, W. (1984). School counselors as family counselors: A rationale and training model. *School Counselor, 31,* 279–284.

Osipow, S. H. (1983). *Theories of career development* (3rd ed.). Englewood Cliffs, NJ: Prentice-Hall.

Otto, L. B., & Call, V. R. A. (1985). Parental influence on young people's career development. *Journal of Career Development, 12,* 65–69.

Palmo, A. J., Lowry, L. A., Weldon, D. P., & Scioscia, T. M. (1984). Schools and family: Future perspectives for school counselors. *School Counselor, 31,* 272–278.

Parsons, F. (1909). *Choosing a vocation.* Boston: Houghton Mifflin.

Pine, G. J., & Innis, G. (1987). Cultural and individual work values. *Career Development Quarterly, 35,* 279–287.

Schulenberg, J. E., Vondracek, F. W., & Crouter, A. C. (1984). The influence of the family on vocational development. *Journal of Marriage and the Family, 10,* 129–143.

Tinto, V. (1975). Dropout from higher education: A theoretical synthesis of recent research. *Review of Education Research, 45,* 89–125.

U.S. Department of Labor. (1977). *Dictionary of occupational titles* (4th ed.). Washington, DC: U.S. Government Printing Office.

U.S. Department of Labor. (1988). *Occupational outlook handbook* (1988–1989 ed.). Washington, DC: U.S. Government Printing Office.

Wilcoxon, J. A., & Comas, R. E. (1987). Contemporary trends in family counseling: What do they mean for the school counselor? *School Counselor, 34,* 219–225.

Zingaro, J. C. (1983). A family systems approach for the career counselor. *The Personnel and Guidance Journal, 62,* 24–27.

Zunker, V. G. (1986). *Career counseling: Applied concepts of life planning* (2nd ed.). Monterey, CA: Brooks/Cole.

The School Counselor as Job Search Facilitator: Increasing Employment of Handicapped Students Through Job Clubs

Linda K. Elksnin
Nick Elksnin

Results of recent studies indicate a need to focus on the career development of students enrolled in special education programs (Cobb, Hasazi, Collins, & Salembier, 1988; Elksnin & Elksnin, 1988). The evidence clearly indicates that handicapped individuals have difficulty securing and maintaining employment. Zigmond and Thornton (1985) reported that 26% of learning disabled (LD) high school graduates and 56% of LD high school dropouts were unemployed. After surveying 459 special education students who exited high school between 1979 and 1983, Hasazi, Gordon, and Roe (1985) reported that 65% were employed and only 37% were employed in a full-time capacity. Employment rates for 54 LD students who dropped out of high school have been reported as high as 73% (Levin, Zigmond, & Birch, 1985). The importance of career development is further supported by the Office of Special Education and Rehabilitation, U.S. Department of Education, which has selected successful transition from school to work as a primary objective for handicapped students (Will, 1984). Although vocational educators teach handicapped students job skills and special educators teach job-related academic skills, school counselors have the expertise to provide job counseling and to improve the job-finding skills of these students.

The school counselor's level of involvement with handicapped students has increased with the passage of Public Law 94-142 in 1975 (Hohenshil, 1983; Leyser, 1988). Counselors also will engage in activities related to the career and vocational development of these students as legislated by the Carl D. Perkins Vocational Education Act of 1984 (U.S. Public Law 98-524). The purposes of the legislation are to improve the quality of vocational training programs and to make vocational programs accessible to handicapped and disadvantaged individuals. Two of four services required by the Perkins Act relate to career and vocational counseling. Specifically, handicapped and disadvantaged students enrolled in vocational education programs must receive the following, as described in Sec. 204(c): (a) assessment of vocational interests and abilities and of special needs; (b) special services, including adaptation of facilities, equipment, instruction, and curriculum; (c) guidance, counseling, and career development activities; and (d) counseling services that will assist transition from school to postschool employment.

In addition to having this legislative mandate, the school counselor is best equipped to provide vocational and career counseling to handicapped students for several reasons. School counselors possess greater knowledge of career development than other members of the special education multidisciplinary team (e.g., special educator, school psychologist, and vocational educator). In addition, counselors at the secondary level who have been providing career and vocational counseling to nonhandicapped students can expand their services to include handicapped students (Levinson, 1987). An important component of vocational counseling focuses on improving the client's job search or job find skills. The purposes of this article are to: (a) compare traditional job search procedures with an alternative approach called the Job Club, (b) briefly review the literature that compares employment rates of individuals undergoing traditional job search and Job Club counseling, and (c) discuss ways in which counselors can implement Job Clubs with handicapped students in secondary settings.

Redefining the Job Search Process

Most individuals who attempt to find a job assume that they need to obtain training and experience and then submit applications for advertised positions. The employer then hires the individual whose skills best match those required by the job. Azrin (1985) has proposed an alternative model of job seeking and hiring. He described job finding and hiring as an exchange of social reinforcers rather than as a matchup between the applicant's skills and the employer's job requirements. Azrin maintained that employers are more influenced by the *personal factors* of the applicant than by that individual's training or experience. The employer is more apt to hire an applicant with whom a bond is established. In addition, data indicate that job seekers find out about jobs through an informal job information network: Jones and Azrin (1973) reported that two-thirds of successful job seekers secured positions after finding out about the job through friends, acquaintances, or relatives. The Job Club was developed to teach job seekers how to gain access to the informal job information network (Azrin, Flores, & Kaplan, 1975).

Efficacy of the Job Club Model

Results of studies that compare the success rate of the Job Club model with more traditional job-finding methods indicate that employment rates of Job Club participants have been 90% or more, whereas employment rates for individuals who used traditional job-finding methods have ranged from 28% to 60%. Azrin, Flores, and Kaplan (1975) compared the employment records of 60 adult Job Club participants and a control group of 60 adults and reported that only 60% of control group individuals secured jobs at the end of a 3-month period. The experimental Job Club group boasted 93% employment rates, and average salaries were one-third higher than members of the control group. A modified Job Club model was adopted by Stude and Pauls (1977) for use with vocational rehabilitation clients. Of employed clients, more than half obtained their own jobs with help of job clubs.

Six self-directed job search approaches were compared by Wesolowski (1981): job interview training, the Job Obtaining Behavior Strategy (JOBS) program, the Job Seeking Skills (JSS) program, a self-instructional package, the Job Seeker Aids program, and the Job Club approach. The Job Club and JOBS (a Job Club approach involving videotape feedback) resulted in the highest placement rates (i.e., 90%), and both models were effective with diverse populations.

Several researchers examined the effectiveness of the Job Club model with handicapped adults who have lower rates of employment than the general population. Garvin (1984) integrated the Job Club model with vocational assessment data and reported that 22 of 56 severely disabled adult participants obtained jobs. In addition to a 73% placement rate for 23 blind adults, Dickson and MacDonell (1982) reported spillover effects of the Job Club model including improved public perceptions of visually handicapped persons and improved relations between a state commission for the blind and the business community. The Job Club program was used with 85 psychiatric patients, resulting in a job placement rate of 76% (Jacobs, Kardashian, Kreinbring, Ponder, & Simpson, 1984). Follow-up data were equally impressive, with over 67% of clients still employed after 6 months.

In summary, results of studies indicate that individuals who participate in Job Clubs enjoy higher rates of employment than individuals receiving traditional job search counseling. Unlike some job search approaches, which are successful only with highly-motivated and well-educated clients, the Job Club is equally effective with diverse populations, including handicapped adults, retired persons, housewives entering the work force for the first time, marginally literate high school dropouts, college students, business executives, and professionals (Azrin, 1985). Finally, follow-up data indicate that high employment rates of Job Club members continue over time.

Implementing the Job Club Model
With Handicapped Students

Recently, the Job Club model has been advocated for use with school-age handicapped students (Brolin, 1982; Frederickson, 1982; Kimeldorf & Tornow, 1984a, 1984b; Sarkees & Scott, 1985). When adopting this model, the counselor: (a) views every individual as employable, (b) assists every member of the group in securing a job, and (c) supports job seekers and stresses each participant's positive personal characteristics. Azrin and Basalel (1980) suggested that the Job Club "uses a very directive approach to counseling. The counselor has a set of specific activities and skills that the job seekers are to learn. The counselor is not viewed as a discussion leader but as a knowledgeable source of encouragement and feedback to the job seeker" (p. 12).

The Job Club Counselor's Manual (Azrin & Basalel, 1980) is a valuable resource for school counselors who wish to design a Job Club for handicapped students. The manual includes a detailed description of the Job Club approach, the conceptual framework of the model, and standardized forms and charts that can be used by the counselor and club members. The major principles and activities of the Job Club model are as follows:

1. Job search skills are broken down into behaviorally defined steps.
2. Job seeking is regarded as a full-time job and the job seeker plans a structured job-seeking schedule.
3. Job leads are systematically obtained through friends, relatives, and acquaintances. Job Club participants are taught how to use the telephone as the primary contact for job leads, as well as how

to gain access to more traditional job lead sources such as the yellow pages and the want ads.

4. Job seekers meet as a group, and members offer support and assistance to one another.

5. Job seekers learn to emphasize their personal characteristics through open letters of recommendation, resumes, and applications.

6. Job seekers learn to emphasize non-employment-derived work skills.

7. Job seekers receive training and practice in traditional job-seeking skills such as interviewing, resume and letter writing, and filling out applications.

8. Job seekers keep progress charts, and data are used to evaluate performance and to determine if job-seeking behavior needs to change.

The school counselor may also wish to examine materials developed by Kimeldorf (1985a, 1985b). Based on the Job Club model, these materials have been successfully field-tested with high school-age students enrolled in special and vocational education programs, as well as with incarcerated youths and vocational rehabilitation clients.

Summary

Employment rates for handicapped students after they exit high school are much lower than rates for their nonhandicapped peers. The need for expanding career development services for handicapped adolescents is further underscored by the passage of the Carl D. Perkins Vocational Act and the emphasis placed on successful transition of these students from school to work by the Office of Special Education and Rehabilitation. School counselors possess the training, skills, and experience that will enable them to provide appropriate career counseling and career development services to students with handicaps. An important component of career development for handicapped students is counseling them to use effective job search strategies. There is empirical evidence to suggest the Job Club approach results in higher rates of employment than other more traditional job search methods. School counselors can combine their skills with this effective job search method to enable handicapped students to become successfully employed.

References

Azrin. N. (Speaker). (1985). *The psychology of job-hunting* (Cassette Recording No. 20207). Washington, DC: American Psychological Association.

Azrin, N. H., & Basalel, V. A. (1980). *Job club counselor's manual: A behavioral approach to vocational counseling.* Austin, TX: PRO-ED.

Azrin, N. H., Flores, T., & Kaplan, S. J. (1975). Job-finding club: A group-assisted program for obtaining employment. *Behavior Research and Therapy, 13,* 17–27.

Brolin, D. E. (1982). *Vocational preparation of persons with handicaps* (2nd ed.). Columbus, OH: Merrill.

Cobb, R. B., Hasazi, S. B., Collins, C. M., & Salembier, G. (1988). Preparing school-based employment specialists. *Teacher Education and Special Education, 11,* 64–71 .

Dickson, M. B., & MacDonell, P. K. (1982). Career club for blind job seekers. *Visual Impairment and Blindness, 76,* 1–4.

Elksnin, N., & Elksnin, L. (1988). Improving handicapped adolescents' job-seeking skills through job clubs: Expanding career development services in the high school. *Career Development for Exceptional Individuals, 11,* 118–125.

Frederickson, R. H. (1982). *Career Information.* Englewood Cliffs. NJ: Prentice Hall.

Garvin, R. E. (1984). Vocational exploration and job search activities in a group setting. *Journal of Applied Rehabilitation Counseling, 15,* 15–17.

Hasazi, S. B., Gordon, R. L., & Roe, C. A. (1985). Factors associated with the employment status of handicapped youth exiting high school from 1979–1983. *Exceptional Children, 51,* 455–469.

Hohenshil, T. H. (1983). Vocational school psychology. In T. R. Kratochwill (Ed.), *Advances in school psychology* (Vol. III, pp. 83–100). Hillsdale, NJ: Erlbaum.

Jacobs, H. E., Kardashian, S., Kreinbring, R. K., Ponder, R., & Simpson, A. R. (1984). A skills-oriented model for facilitating employment among psychiatrically disabled persons. *Rehabilitation Counseling Bulletin, 78,* 87–96.

Jones, R. J., & Azrin, N. H. (1973). An experimental application of a social reinforcement approach to the program of job finding. *Journal of Applied Behavior Analysis, 6,* 345–353.

Kimeldorf, M. (1985a). *Job search education*. New York: Educational Design.

Kimeldorf, M. (1985b). *Job search education: Program guide*. New York: Educational Design.

Kimeldorf, M., & Tornow, J. A. (1984a). Job clubs: Getting into the hidden labor market. *The Pointer, 28,* 29–32.

Kimeldorf, M., & Tornow, J. A. (1984b). Job search education: Meeting the challenge of unemployment. *The Journal for Vocational Special Needs Education, 7,* 7–10.

Levin, E. K, Zigmond, N., & Birch, J. W. (1985). A follow-up study of 52 learning disabled adolescents. *Journal of Learning Disabilities, 18,* 2–7.

Levinson, E. M. (1987). Vocational assessment and programming of students with handicaps: A need for counselor involvement. *The School Counselor, 35,* 6–8.

Leyser, Y. (1988). Let's listen to the consumer: The voice of parents of exceptional children. *The School Counselor, 35,* 363–369.

Sarkees, M. D., & Scott, J. L. (1985). *Vocational special needs* (2nd ed.). Chicago: American Technical Publishers.

Stude, E. W., & Pauls. T. (1977). The use of job-seeking skills group in developing placement readiness. *Journal of Applied Rehabilitation Counseling, 8*(2), 115–120.

U.S. Public Law 94-142. Education for All Handicapped Children Act.

U.S. Public Law 98-524. The Carl D. Perkins Vocational Education Act of 1984. 20 U.S.C. § 2301 (October 19, 1984).

Wesolowski, M. D. (1981). Self-directed job placement in rehabilitation: A comparative review. *Rehabilitation Counseling Bulletin, 25,* 80–89.

Will, M. (1984). *OSERS programming for the transitions of youth with disabilities: Bridges from school to working life*. Washington, DC: Office of Special Education and Rehabilitative Services.

Zigmond, N., & Thornton, H. (1985). Follow-up of postsecondary age learning disabled graduates and drop-outs. *Learning Disabilities Research, 1,* 50–55.

Chapter 7

The Scope of Practice of the Secondary School Counselor— Educational Counseling

School counselors rose to prominence in American high schools in the late 1950s when they received the mandate to guide more students into college, especially into technical careers, following the launch of Sputnik. Today, this aspect of the school counselor's role continues to be important, as educators worry about the increasing dropout rate, the under-educated work force, and the widening gap in society between the "haves" and the "have nots." High school counselors see educational counseling as a key responsibility as they work with underachieving young people planning to leave school; under-aspiring youth who do not see opportunities available to them; high-achieving young people headed toward prestigious, competitive universities; and highly confused, under-informed students who really do not have any idea of what they want to do to gain a successful future.

Educational counseling takes on many dimensions in a school counseling program. Much special counseling is done currently with youth who face obstacles while they are in high school. The need to raise student aspirations is described by Breen and Quaglia, while Downing and Harrison consider how to keep students from becoming dropouts. Special populations receive additional attention: Valerie George explains special needs of young women; Gade, Hurlburt, and Fuqua

313

consider special populations such as American Indians, and Cunningham and Tidwell discuss how to help low-income students who aspire to attend college. "Searching for Solutions" is a packet of information for school counselors prepared for the American School Counselor Association by Doris Rhea Coy and Susan Jones Sears.

Educational counseling requires that a school counselor have counseling skills, information, and a plan for working with students to ensure that each receives the necessary counseling services to enable them to make good educational decisions.

Raising Student Aspirations: The Need to Share a Vision

Dorothy Tysse Breen
Russ Quaglia

The term *aspirations* has been defined in a number of ways. Words—such as *goals, dreams, ambitions, drives*—have all been used interchangeably when discussing student aspirations. We believe that aspirations drive students to be all they can be. As educators, it is our responsibility to provide an environment in our school system that will allow students to do more and be more than they currently are and may be. In our schools it is necessary to help students develop an understanding of how they grow and develop and thus have the ability to make informed choices and have the capacity to adjust to change.

There is a great deal of evidence that student aspirations are low, particularly in rural areas. Research shows that these students have lower levels of academic and vocational aspirations than students from other regions. Although low aspirations are believed to be a national issue, it seems to be more prominent in rural areas (Cobb, McIntire, & Pratt, 1985).

Rationale and Purpose of Study

The purpose of this study is to identify how principals and school counselors can combine their efforts to raise student aspirations. If school counselors and principals develop an understanding of and respect for their roles, as well as a positive communication pattern, they will be better able to work together to meet the needs of the students.

At the Maine Aspirations Conference in April 1987, the keynote speaker, John Elkins, President of Naisbett, a private research organization that monitors major socio-economic trends, said that structural changes in education need to take place in order to take advantage of the structural growth in the economy. The work in rural areas is changing from factory and industrial work to business and professional opportunities. Therefore, educators need to help students broaden their aspirations to include considerations of a business and professional career. Elkins proposed that to help students broaden their aspirations, educators need to structure education to create opportunities for students to: (a) learn to think, (b) learn to learn, and (c) learn to be creative. We believe that a well-balanced developmental guidance program that is integrated into the school curriculum is a step toward structuring education to create opportunities for students to learn to think, learn, and be creative.

A number of states have required guidance in the schools for *all* students in kindergarten through grade 12. A comprehensive, kindergarten through grade 12, developmental guidance program can help students broaden and raise their aspirations because it is designed to help all students with their educational, personal, social, career, and vocational growth and development. Leaders in developmental guidance (Gysbers & Henderson, 1988; Myrick, 1987; Wilson, 1986) agree that human beings have the potential for positive growth, development, and personal achievement. There are, however, obstacles in the environment that may slow down this process and prohibit positive personal growth and development. Within a developmental guidance program, school counselors can help students through the developing process by working on self-concept, motivation, locus of control, and decision making in classrooms, small groups, and with individuals.

For developmental guidance to be effective in the schools, however, cooperation of the entire school staff is required. This study focuses on the importance of the school counselor and the principal working together—*sharing a vision*. A comprehensive developmental guidance program requires a commitment on the part of both the school counselor and the principal (Baker & Shaw, 1987; Gysbers & Henderson, 1988; Myrick, 1987). The purpose of this article is to show how school principals and school counselors can work together in an effort to meet growth and developmental needs of all students in the schools.

Objectives

With the premise that school counselors and principals can work together in an effort to meet growth and developmental needs of all students in the schools, the objectives of this study are as follows:

1. To present selected data comparing the aspirations of rural youths with those of suburban and urban youths.
2. To present the role of the school counselor and how it relates to the fostering of student aspirations.
3. To present the role of the principal and how it relates to the fostering of student aspirations.
4. To offer viable solutions for the principal and school counselor to work collaboratively in the school building that would enhance student aspirations.

Presentation of Data

In order to understand the importance of the relationship between school counselors and principals and how it affects students, data are presented in four sections: (a) presentation and discussion of selected data from the National Center for Education Statistics and the Maine Occupational Information Coordinating Committee, (b) description of the current role of a school counselor, (c) description of the current role of a principal, and (d) presentation of the results of a group meeting between four principals and four counselors in which they analyzed the role of the counselor. After the data are presented, a discussion section follows highlighting conclusions that can be drawn from the data, as well as implications for future research.

Findings

Presentation and Discussion of Selected Data

Cobb et al. (1985) analyzed selected variables from the High School and Beyond (HSB) study (National Center for Education Statistics, 1983). The HSB study compared 58,000 high school students from 1,015 rural, urban, and suburban schools in the United States in order to determine if the educational, vocational, and personal aspirations of rural students differed from those of urban and suburban students. Cobb et al.'s (1985) analysis indicates that rural youths have lower levels of academic and vocational aspirations than suburban and urban youths. Aspirations are influenced by the expectations of parents, teachers, and school counselors. Since rural parents, teachers, and counselors do not hold career and educational aspirations for their youths that are as high as those held by parents, teachers, and counselors of urban and suburban youths, it is not surprising that more rural youths expect to enter the work force right after high school and fewer aspire to continue their education. Furthermore, those rural students who do expect to continue their education aspire to lower levels of higher education, express lower levels of self-confidence in completing the degree requirements, and expect to pursue higher education for a shorter time than urban students.

In addition, rural students do not express the same interest as urban students do in correcting social and economic inequities. This indicates that although some rural youths may be leaders in their own communities, they do not seem to carry this leadership beyond their communities into the rest of the world. Another difference between rural and urban youths is that rural parents do not seek to give their children better opportunities than they currently have. This might lead one to draw the conclusion that rural youths do not aspire beyond the confines of their well-known environment. If their rural environment, therefore, does not begin to provide them with a broad experience and with opportunities to learn about how they would function in different environments, these rural students may continue to have low aspirations. According to the preceding data, at a national level it seems that rural high school students have lower academic and vocational aspirations than urban and suburban students have. The following data describe the academic and vocational aspirations of high school students in Maine, which is characterized as a rural state.

In order to determine the career and lifestyle aspirations of students in Maine, the Maine Occupational Information Coordinating Committee (Thompson & Shannon, 1990) conducted a study with 754 students between the ages of 15 and 17. According to the results, it seems that the majority of the students in Maine perceived themselves to be average or above-average academically; however, less than half aspired to go to college. Because most of the students in Maine live in rural areas, it might be expected, based on the HSB results, that the youths in Maine would have low vocational aspirations. This seems to be the case because a "Realistic" work environment (made up of people who have athletic or mechanical ability; who prefer to work with objects, machines, tools, plants, or animals; or who prefer to be outdoors) was chosen by the highest percentage of Maine students as the most appealing work environment. Also, as one might predict, an "Enterprising" work environment (made up of people who like to work with people by influencing, persuading, or performing; leading, or managing for organizational goals or for economic gain) was chosen by the lowest percentage of Maine students as the most appealing work environment. Additionally, less than 25% of the students in Maine indicated that they liked white-collar work. When one considers the issue of pursuing aspirations beyond high school, it becomes obvious that Maine youths expect to limit themselves to the opportunities available in Maine. The data support that only one-quarter of the respondents would either attend postsecondary educational schools or meet their career plans outside the state of Maine.

These results suggest that, as with rural youths across the nation, Maine youths also aspire only to what they are familiar with and do not intend to broaden their aspirations in order to influence and lead others in a more global world. The data clearly support the hypothesis that rural students have lower levels of aspirations. The next obvious step is to look at the role of the school counselor and principal to show how they can have a positive impact on students.

Role of the School Counselor

The school counselor is concerned with the growth and development of all students, kindergarten through grade 12. Ideally, the school counselor works proactively, with emphasis on helping students master developmental stages and tasks in learning, career, vocational, personal, and social areas while putting less emphasis on remediation. This preventative approach requires the school counselor to provide: (a) classroom guidance units, (b) small group counseling, and (c) individual counseling for all students.

Traditionally, however, the school counselor's days are consumed by working with problem students and helping with crisis situations as they arise. Consequently, there does not seem to be enough time for the counselor to work developmentally with all students. The school counselor may have large student:counselor ratios and may be required to perform tasks that do not allow functioning at a level that involves all students developmentally. For example, the school counselor may have to perform basic clerical tasks (report cards and counting credits), provide disciplinary action, monitor attendance and tardiness, administer and score intelligence and psychological tests, and schedule classes. Because the school counselor may be involved in the preceding tasks, how can there be time to help students with self-concept, motivation, locus of control, identifying personal strengths, understanding feelings and behaviors, understanding others, social skills, communication skills, decision-making skills, problem-solving skills, and preparation for the world of work? How can the school counselor help raise student aspirations? Baker and Shaw (1987) suggested that "there must be a willingness to forego some traditional activities which do not achieve any particular purpose or which can be achieved equally well through other means" (p. 17). This would require a commitment from both the school counselor and the principal.

If some of the traditional activities were relieved, as suggested by Baker and Shaw, the school counselor would be able to function as a counselor, educator, consultant, and resource person with individuals, small groups, and large groups. As a consultant, the school counselor would confer with parents, teachers, administrators. and community members about the needs of students in order to develop and deliver specific units (classroom and small group) to meet those needs. As a resource person, the school counselor would coordinate faculty- and staff-development programs related to guidance in an effort to help faculty and staff integrate guidance-related concepts into the curriculum. In essence, the school counselor's role is dependent on involvement of the entire school staff, the parents and the community.

Role of the Principal

Studies of factors that contribute to making an effective school conclude that the leadership of the principal is a significant influence. The principal is responsible, among other things, for establishing conditions that support teachers' work.

In this respect, the principal encourages leadership among teachers, counselors, and students. The principal respects the role of each and provides opportunities for critical and meaningful involvement of staff in important decisions. The principal must also organize available resources that will provide maximum support to instruction. It is obvious why the leadership role of the principal in an effective school has become an important consideration in efforts to restructure schools during this period of reform.

The actual list of a principal's duties is a long list indeed. The report of the National Commission on Excellence in Educational Administration (1987) addressed a number of significant issues for administrators. Areas that were highlighted as being characteristic of good schools with effective principals include those that: (a) demonstrate they are learning communities, (b) foster collegiality, (c) individualize instruction, and (d) encourage involvement.

The question is how an administrator can foster such characteristics. Before answering this question, one must first understand the daily hurdles principals need to address. Factors such as budgets, politics, legal issues, student test scores, teacher unions, management styles of school boards, and special interest groups consistently dictate the principal's role. In short, the school principal is more of a crisis manager than educational leader.

It becomes obvious that in order for principals to have a positive impact on schools, they will have to use more resources. Principals must have a vision, not only in the sense of looking toward the future and making educated predictions but also in which they can see the whole picture. They must be driven by the need to understand the problems around them, while constantly striving to look for solutions.

In this light, administrators need to match needs with resources, aware of when to intervene and when not to. Educational decisions must be based on a broad perspective of academic choices. This again requires the use of others from both within and outside the school building. A principal must not only create a climate of involvement but also be an advocate of participation from students, teachers, counselors, staff, and parents for day-to-day operations and long-term planning. The overall goal of all these participants, one may say, is to acquire the necessary resources to meet the needs of the entire school system.

Results of the Group Meeting

A group meeting was conducted with four school counselors and four school principals from different school districts in Maine. These particular school counselors and principals were chosen because they worked collaboratively and their students were considered to have high aspirations. The group represented two high schools, one middle school, and one elementary school in various socio-economic environments. The meeting began by separating the groups into two rooms: counselors in one room, principals in the other. Both groups were given the same questionnaire and asked to: (a) rank order a list of activities that school counselors *should do* and (b) rank order the same list of activities identifying what school counselors *actually do*.

Realizing that the counselors and principals selected for this activity were considered to be successful and that their students were considered to have high aspirations, it was not surprising to find that there was a great deal of consensus between the two groups. The top four activities of both groups regarding what counselors do and should do were: (a) help students individually with personal problems; (b) help students have greater self-understanding and show how it relates to future life; (c) work with small groups of students regarding issues of decision making, problem solving, communication skills, and interpersonal skills; and (d) participate as a member of pupil evaluation teams.

The two groups also agreed on certain suggestions that need to be adhered to if school counselors and principals are to work successfully together. The suggestions were that: (a) school counselors should not be overburdened with paper work, (b) the perception that school counselors do not work very hard needs to be changed, (c) there is a need for school counselors to be more active regarding parental involvement, and (d) the role of the principal in relation to the school counselor should be that of support and assistance.

It is interesting to note that the principals and counselors were in total agreement as to what counselors do and should do and what needs to be done to create a more effective counseling program.

These findings support our hypothesis that a successful relationship between the principal and school counselor creates an environment in the school that will foster high aspirations. We believe that the successful relationship between counselors and principals is due to the fact that they share a vision. A shared vision exists if values, beliefs, and behaviors regarding the welfare of the school and students are the same for principals and for school counselors. A shared vision exists if the school counselors and principals are willing to take the time to communicate regarding the welfare of the school and students. If compatibility does not exist between counselors and principals, uneasiness, resentment, lack of respect, and uncooperativeness will prevail, thus creating an educational environment that stifles student aspirations.

Discussion

The issue of student aspirations is not only a rural concern but also a national one. There has been one study after another identifying that students have low aspirations in our schools (Barringer, 1984; Cobb et al., 1985; McIntire & Pratt, 1984; National Center for Education Statistics, 1983). It is time to ask the following questions: What needs to be done? What should be done? What *must* be done? It is time for a solution. In this article we offer just that. Our solution includes two key actors in the school system: the principal and the school counselor. It is our belief that these two actors can work together—involving staff, parents, and community members—to have a positive impact on students, thus raising their aspiration levels.

The next logical question to ask is how school counselors and principals can positively influence their relationship with one another. And how can a good, working relationship between a school counselor and principal affect student aspirations? To answer the first question, a description of what school counselors can do to enhance the relationship between themselves and principals is provided. First of all, school counselors can inform principals about the role of the school counselor in order to provide a foundation from which the counselors and principals can work together. Second, school counselors can consistently inform the principals about the specific needs of the students, the strategies used to meet those needs, and the effectiveness of those strategies. On the other hand, principals must provide leadership and support for the guidance program. Support can come in two forms, administrative and psychological. School counselors must be given the necessary resources not just to get the job done but to do it well. Principals must also provide encouragement; a pat on the back can go a long way. Above all, principals must consult with the guidance staff regarding special issues, concerns, or problems that may exist in the school. The emphasis for both the principal and school counselor is that there is a need to open channels of communication. Without communication, there is little or no chance that the two groups could ever share a vision.

This study brings to attention a number of areas that need to be addressed by future research. There is obviously a need for future research related to the continued critical examination of the basic question: How can schools raise the aspirational levels of students? Specifically, there needs to be a larger knowledge base in the following areas:

1. A definition of high aspirations that will be representative of various socio-economic, political, educational, and age groups.
2. The change process regarding the introduction of a comprehensive developmental guidance program that will use the skills and resources of school counselors and administrators.

3. The relationship between the school counselor and the principal and how they work together to foster an environment conducive to raising student aspirations.
4. The role of all types of school personnel and how they influence student aspirations.
5. The types of staff development necessary to create a school climate that will promote higher student aspirations.

We believe that until there is a strong relationship between principals and counselors, raising student aspirations will fall short. If all students are to be provided the opportunity for positive growth and development, it is essential that a comprehensive developmental guidance program be in place. We believe that a comprehensive developmental guidance program cannot exist unless there is support, respect, and communication between the school counselor and principal.

References

Baker, S. B., & Shaw, M. C. (1987). *Improving counseling through primary prevention.* Columbus, OH: Merrill.

Barringer, R. E. (1984). *Presentation of the Maine State Planning Office.* Bangor, ME: The Conference on Raising Aspirations of Maine Youth.

Cobb, R. A., McIntire, W. G., & Pratt, P. A. (1985). Where are the dreamers? Aspirations of Maine's rural high school students. *Explorations: A Journal of Research, 2*(1), 6–11.

Gysbers, N. C., & Henderson, P. (1988). *Developing and managing your school guidance program.* Alexandria, VA: American Association for Counseling and Development.

McIntire, W. G., & Pratt, P. A. (1984, November). *Demographic, motivational and aspirational characteristics of UMO's 1983 freshman.* Paper distributed at the Conference on Raising Aspirations of Maine Youth, Bangor, Maine.

Myrick, R. D. (1987). *Developmental guidance and counseling: A practical approach.* Minneapolis, MN: Educational Media Corporation.

National Center for Education Statistics. (1983). *Contractor report: Data file user's manual for High School and Beyond 1980 sophomore/senior cohort first follow-up.* Washington, DC: U.S. Department of Education.

National Commission on Excellence in Educational Administration. (1987). *Leaders for America's schools*. Tempe, AZ: The University Council for Educational Administration, Arizona State University.

Thompson, S., & Shannon, M. (1990). *A study of work family integration issues*. Augusta, ME: Maine Occupational Information Coordinating Committee, Maine Department of Labor.

Wilson, P. J. (1986). *School counseling programs: A resource and planning guide*. Madison, WI: Wisconsin Department of Public Instruction.

Talented Adolescent Women and the Motive To Avoid Success

Valerie D. George

This study was designed to determine whether talented Black and White adolescent women differ in their expression of the motive to avoid success (MAS). This question is explored among a sample of talented Black and White tenth-grade women.

Black and White women express similar educational and occupational aspirations and expectations but realize different outcomes because of several socialization factors (i.e., their perceptions of the possibility of success, sex-role stereotyping, the different experiences of Blacks and Whites in the educational and economic areas and the expectations of significant others [Burlew, 1977]). According to Burlew, when Black women are confronted with situations in which they believe the achievement of success is contrary to societal expectations, they display avoidance behaviors typical of those described by Horner (1968) in studies of high-achieving women.

The negative impact of socialization factors on the occupational choices of Black women attending traditional Black colleges in the South is illustrated by findings from several studies: Gurin and Katz (1966), Gurin and Gaylord (1977) and Gump (1975). In these studies Black women aspired to occupations that were traditional for women and also traditional for Black women. These findings were not supported in Mednick and Puryear's (1975) study of the relationship between need achievement, fear of success, and level of occupational expectations of Black women attending colleges in the southeastern and middle Atlantic states. They reported that these women expressed preference for more nontraditional occupations.

Authors who have explored the effect of race on the incidence of the MAS among Black and White college women have consistently reported lower incidences for Black women (Mednick & Puryear, 1975; Weston & Mednick, 1970). Findings on the incidence of MAS among Black women from different socioeconomic groups have been inconsistent.

Fleming's (1978) report of a significant difference in the occurrence of MAS for working-class and middle-class Black college women attending Radcliffe College disputes the findings of Weston and Mednick (1970), who found no difference in the MAS response of Black college women from upper and lower middle-class subgroups.

Lavach and Lanier (1975) explored the incidence of MAS among high achieving, Black and White adolescent women and found no significant differences between the two groups. Winchel, Fenner, and Shaver (1974) studied the impact of coeducation on the MAS response and reported that young women attending Jewish, coeducational elementary schools wrote significantly more stories depicting MAS imagery.

The paucity of studies related to the occurrence of MAS among talented Black and White adolescent women attests to the need for exploring this construct with this group. Furthermore, studies that have explored the incidence of MAS among Black and White college women (Fleming, 1978; Gump, 1975; Mednick & Puryear, 1975; Weston & Mednick, 1970) have not produced consistent findings that can be generalized to talented Black and White adolescent women.

The purposes of this study were to explore the extent to which talented Black and White adolescent women express MAS and the effect of socioeconomic status (SES) on the expression of negative imagery.

Method

Sample

During the fall 1976 semester of their sophomore year in high school, the 64 adolescent women in this study were identified as talented by Project Choice (Fleming & Hollinger, 1979). These young women consented to participate in the project, which was designed to help talented adolescent women actively explore career options. These participants were from a group of 289 talented young women who attended six high schools in the Cleveland Area (i.e., two large, coeducational public schools; two private, all girls' schools; and two Catholic, all girls' schools).

Before being identified as talented, each young woman completed a self-report questionnaire and identified activities in which she was engaged. The categories being assessed were: (a) home-related activities,

(b) athletics, (c) community involvement, (d) employment, (e) achievement in literary, visual, and the performing arts, and (f) extracurricular activities.

Each adolescent's unique pattern of talent was evaluated from her self-assessment along with her academic performance, achievement test scores, and aptitude scores. She was identified as talented if she achieved a rating of 4 or 5 on one or more of the criterion measures used by the project.

Socioeconomic Status

Hollingshead's Two-Factor Index of Social Position (Hollingshead & Redlich, 1958) was used to determine the SES of the adolescent's father. This tool is used to differentially weigh educational level and occupational level and to derive a designation of social class. If the adolescent resided in a single-parent family, or if data were not available for either the father's education or occupation, then data for her mother or the person with whom she lived were used to calculate her SES.

The SES scores for the Black parents in the sample (n=33) were compared with those of the White parents (n=289) by the two-sample t test. Although the means of the two groups were not significantly different at the .05 level, a significant difference between the variances was found, indicating violations of the assumptions of homogeneity of variance. In an attempt to obtain two samples that did not violate the assumptions, persons with extreme scores were dropped from the analysis. The SES scores for the Black parents ranged from 22 to 66; scores for White parents ranged from 11 to 77. The Black adolescents were then matched with a computer generated sample of White adolescents based on SES scores. The median score for the Black adolescents was used to partition the SES scores into upper and lower middle-class subgroups. The upper middle-class group consisted of 14 Black and 17 White adolescents; the lower middle-class group consisted of 18 Black and 15 White adolescents.

Procedure

Data were collected in spring 1977. The battery of questionnaires was administered to participants after regular class sessions in the two private schools and during release-time periods in the other four schools. The respondents completed a self-report questionnaire that assessed occupational aspirations and demographic data. This was followed by instructions for completing the verbal cues.

I gave written instructions for the verbal cues to each participant and also read them aloud. The procedure for completing the verbal cues followed the standard Thematic Apperception Test (TAT) format with the exception that respondents were given 6 minutes to write a response to each cue rather than 5 minutes. In addition, they were asked to imagine what was going on in the story, what the situation was, what led up to the situation, what people were thinking and feeling, and what they would do. They were directed to write a complete story, one with plot and characters.

The young women wrote stories to three cues that were arranged randomly, and they were not aware that at any given time their peers were responding to a different cue. The following cues were used: (a) "Half of Anne's classmates in medical school are women, and after first-term finals, Anne finds herself at the top of her class"; (b) "After first-term finals, Judy finds that she is the top child psychology graduate student"; and (c) "Nancy and the boy she has been dating for over a year have both applied to the same highly selective university."

Only responses to the first two cues are reported because those cues were designed to measure fear of success imagery from a success-specific verbal lead. The third cue is a neutral cue.

The first cue was developed by Lockheed (1975) to offset the deviancy of Anne's behavior in the original Horner (1969) cue that involved competition with men in an area of traditional male achievement. Reference to the fact that half of Anne's classmates were women placed Anne's behavior in perspective; she was not the only woman or one of a few women who was engaged in a nontraditional area.

In the second cue, developed by Hoffman (1974), the medical school setting of Horner's (1969) cue was replaced with a career field that is viewed as more neutral. Its use was intended to determine if the MAS response would be aroused in adolescents if the participant in the cue achieved success in an occupation that had an equal representation of men and women (the ratio of men to women in child psychology is approximately 60 to 40).

A respondent was identified as expressing MAS when each story that she wrote was assigned a score of 1, resulting in a total score of 2. The respondent was classified as MAS absent when she was assigned a total score of 1 or 0 for responses to both verbal cues.

Scoring

Each verbal cue was scored for negative imagery with the criteria developed by Horner (1970). A verbal cue was scored for the presence of negative imagery if it indicated any of the following themes:

1. Negative consequences because of success.
2. Anticipation of negative consequences because of success.
3. Activity away from present or future success, including leaving the field for more traditional female work such as nursing, teaching, or social work.
4. Negative affect because of success.
5. Any direct expression of conflict about success.
6. Denial of effort in attaining the success (also cheating or any other attempt to deny responsibility or reject credit for the success).
7. Denial of the situation described by the cue.
8. Bizarre, inappropriate, unrealistic, or nonadaptive responses to the situation described by the cue.

Horner's (1970) scoring system was used because it was designed to measure MAS imagery from a verbal lead that was related to success in a specific activity (Fleming, 1978). Furthermore, its use facilitated comparisons with findings from previous studies with high-achieving, Black and White adolescent women (Lavach & Lanier, 1975) and Black college women (Fleming, 1978; Gump, 1975; Gurin & Gaylord, 1977; Mednick & Puryear, 1975; Weston & Mednick, 1970).

The new empirically derived, fantasy-based scoring system to measure MAS (Horner, Tresemer, Berens, & Watson, 1973) was not used because of researchers' questions regarding its validity. Its construct validity has been questioned because of the significant, positive correlation with instruments used to measure fear of failure (Griffore, 1977; Jackaway & Teevan, 1976; Pappo, 1972), and its inability to differentiate between pure MAS themes and negative antecedent themes (Tresemer, 1977). According to Tresemer, two additional factors limit its use: (a) its theoretical derivation from situations threatening to women negates its usefulness for determining MAS among men, and (b) differences in the arousal-setting situation required by this tool and that are present in Horner's original work in 1968 increase its propensity for measurement error.

All responses were scored by women: two doctoral candidates and an experienced high school counselor. Interrater agreement was 88% for the two cues (Anne, 87%; Judy 90%). These scores differ from the 96% reported by Winchel et al. (1974) for a male and female rater but are higher than the 80% required for TAT.

Data were analyzed by the Michigan Interactive Data Analysis System (MIDAS) (Fox & Guyre, 1976); 2 x 2 chi-square designs. The established level of significance for all analyses was .05.

Results and Discussion

Talented Black and White adolescent women did not differ in their expression of MAS ($x^2 = .322$, $df = 1$). This finding was consistent with that reported by Weston & Mednick (1970) for their sample of college women and by Lavach and Lanier (1975) for high-achieving, Black and White adolescent women. There was no significant difference in the occurrence of MAS between upper middle- and lower middle-class Black and White adolescents or between upper and lower middle-class Black and White adolescents. This finding was consistent with that reported by Weston and Mednick (1970) but contradicted that reported by Fleming (1978).

Post hoc analysis revealed a significant difference in the responses of these talented women as a function of cues and SES. The Judy cue yielded significantly more stories expressing negative imagery than did the Anne cue ($x^2 = 9.31$, $df = 1$, $p < .002$); Judy's status as the "top child psychology graduate student" might have been perceived by these talented young women as being more deviant than Anne being "at the top of her class" in a medical school in which half of the students were women.

Furthermore, when responses to the Judy cue were analyzed in relation to SES, respondents in the upper and lower SES subgroups differed significantly in their responses ($x^2 = 4.91$, $df = 1$, $p < .026$). Lower middle-class participants experienced MAS to a significantly greater extent than did upper middle-class respondents. In this study, Black adolescents constituted 54% of persons in the lower middle-class subgroup. This finding seems to indicate that when MAS is measured by the Judy cue SES makes a significant contribution to the expression of negative imagery.

Because of the possible impact of SES on the achievement strivings of talented adolescent women, there is need for continuous support from teachers (Pallone, Rickard, & Hurley, 1970), and significant others (Astin, 1974) to encourage pursual of nontraditional career options. The adolescent subculture is a potent factor in the educational and occupational behavior of high school students. Conformity to peer group norms is particularly prevalent in large metropolitan high schools (Boyle, 1966) and can be mediated by interactions of parents, faculty members, and counselors that are based on mutual respect and sharing.

One career counseling strategy might be helping young Black and White women to deal effectively with the anxieties and uncertainties involved with leaving friends behind as they become socially mobile. Another strategy might be assisting these young women to set goals for future achievement. These adolescents might have to be convinced that putting forth the effort to set goals will result in worthwhile outcomes. In the initial goal-setting endeavors, adolescents might have to be helped to internalize the desired objectives and to set realistic and achievable goals (Harvey, 1975).

Talented adolescent women must surmount several barriers (i.e., racial, socioeconomic, occupational, and societal). They need support from significant others to pursue personal goals related to achievement in career fields that are viewed by them as being nontraditional either because of sex, race, or SES. Talented adolescents should be encouraged to explore nontraditional fields of study and work through reading, volunteering, observing persons at work in career fields that interest them, and through mentorships and paid employment. These experiences will provide the adolescent with a working knowledge of career fields and facilitate informed decision making.

Lower middle-class adolescent women seem particularly vulnerable to anxiety about success and require continued support and acceptance by peers and significant others. Parents and significant others might be asked to state their occupational expectation for their daughters, or the adolescent might be asked to state her parents' occupational and educational preference for her. The latter method elicits the adolescent's perceptions of her parents' expressed or implied expectations which may or may not be an accurate perception. Both adolescent and parent might be assisted in exploring their expectations in relation to the adolescent's ability and interest and to set goals for attaining these objectives. Specific guidance regarding available resources and strategies for gaining access to them should be explored.

Summary

The findings from this study indicate that talented Black and White adolescent women do not differ in their expression of the motivation to avoid success. There was a significant difference in the responses of participants as a function of the cues and also as a function of SES. Implications for career counseling of talented adolescent women were explored.

Further research should explore: (a) the incidence of the MAS response in a larger sample of talented Black and White adolescent women, (b) the effect of SES and type of school on the occurrence of MAS, and (c) MAS response of adolescent women who exhibit different types of talent.

References

Astin, H. S. (1974). Sex differences in mathematical and scientific precocity. In J. C. Stanley, D. Keating, & L. H. Fox (Eds.), *Mathematical talent: Discovery, description, and development* (pp. 70–86). Baltimore: Johns Hopkins University Press.

Boyle, R. P. (1966). The effect of the high school on students' aspirations. *American Journal of Sociology, 71*, 628–739.

Burlew, K. A. (1977). Career educational choices of Black females. *Journal of Black Psychology, 3*, 89–106.

Fleming, J. (1978). Fear of success, achievement-related motives and behavior in Black college women. *Journal of Personality, 46*, 694–716.

Fleming, E. S., & Hollinger, C. L. (1979). *Realizing the promise of female adolescents: A diagnostic prescriptive model* (Final Report). Cleveland: Case Western Reserve University, Department of Education.

Fox, D., & Guyre, K. (1976). *Documentation for MIDAS.* Ann Arbor: University of Michigan Press.

Griffore, R. J. (1977). Fear of success and task difficulty: Effects on graduate students' final exam performance. *Journal of Educational Psychology, 69*, 556–563.

Gump, J. P. (1975). Comparative analysis of Black women's and White women's sex-role attitudes. *Journal of Consulting and Clinical Psychology, 43*, 858–863.

Gurin, P., & Gaylord, C. (1977). Educational and occupational goals of men and women at Black colleges. *Monthly Labor Review, 99*(6), 10–16.

Gurin, P., & Katz, D. (1966). *Motivation and aspiration in the Negro college*. Ann Arbor: University of Michigan, Survey Research Center, Institute for Social Research.

Harvey, A. L. (1975). Goal setting as compensation for fear of success. *Adolescence, 10*(37), 137–142.

Hoffman, L. W. (1974). Fear of success in males and females 1965–1971. *Journal of Consulting and Clinical Psychology, 42*, 353–358.

Hollingshead, A. B., & Redlich, F. C. (1958). *Social class and mental illness: A community study*. New York: Wiley.

Horner, M. S. (1969). Sex differences in achievement motivation and performance in competitive and noncompetitive situations. *Dissertation Abstracts International, 30*, 407B. (University Microfilms No. 69–12, 136)

Horner, M. S. (1970). Femininity and successful achievement: A basic inconsistency. In J. Bardwick, E. Douvan, M. S. Horner, & D. Gutmann (Eds.), *Feminine personality and conflict* (pp. 45–74). Belmont, CA: Brooks/Cole.

Horner, M. S., Tresemer, D. W., Berens, A. E., & Watson, R. I., Jr. (1973). *Scoring manual for an empirically derived scoring system for motive to avoid success*. Unpublished manuscript, Harvard University, Cambridge, MA.

Jackaway, R., & Teevan, R. (1976). Fear of failure and fear of success: Two dimensions of the same motive. *Sex Roles: A Journal of Research, 2*, 283–293.

Lavach, J. F., & Lanier, H. B. (1975). The motive to avoid success in 7th, 8th, 9th and 10th grade high-achieving girls. *Journal of Educational Research, 68*, 216–218.

Lockheed, M. E. (1975). Female motive to avoid success: A psychological barrier or a response to deviancy? *Sex Roles: A Journal of Research, 1*, 41–50.

Mednick, M. T. S., & Puryear, G. R. (1975). Motivational and personality factors related to career goals of Black college women. *Journal of Social and Behavioral Sciences, 21*(1), 1–30.

Pallone, N. J., Rickard, S. S., & Hurley, R. B. (1970). Key influences in occupational preference among Black youths. *Journal of Counseling Psychology, 17*, 498–501.

Pappo, M. (1972). Fear of success: A theoretical analysis and the construction and validation of a measuring instrument. *Dissertation Abstracts International, 34,* 01B (University Microfilms No. 73-16, 235)

Tresemer, D. W. (1977). *Fear of success.* New York: Plenum Press.

Weston, P. T., & Mednick, M. (1970). Race, social class and the motive to avoid success in women. *Journal of Cross-Cultural Psychology, 1,* 284–291.

Winchel, R., Fenner, D., & Shaver, P. (1974). Impact of coeducation on "fear of success" imagery expressed by male and female high school students. *Journal of Educational Psychology, 66,* 726–730.

Dropout Prevention: A Practical Approach

Jerry Downing
Thomas C. Harrison, Jr.

The time has come for practical approaches to the high school dropout issue. The problems of high school dropouts in the United States and the resulting difficulties for all concerned have been well documented (Hahn & Danzberger, 1987; Larson & Shertzer, 1987). It serves little purpose to continue the rhetoric or to add to the evidence that, indeed, there is a significant high school dropout problem. It appears that enough is now known about this problem to allow for effective intervention (Hahn & Danzberger, 1987).

Unfortunately, the problem is so complex that it seems to exceed the boundaries of our traditional thinking and produces levels of frustration that tend to be dysfunctional. This article is based on Weick's (1984) view that such overwhelming problems can best be approached via a strategy of gaining *small wins*. This approach suggests that counselors search for small ways in which they may help their students complete high school. Thus, specific tactics of a practical nature are suggested for school counselors engaged in the battle to help potential high school dropouts.

The numbers seem clear: approximately 25% of the 17- and 18-year-old population fail to graduate from high school with their age group (Institute for Educational Leadership, 1986). It is no surprise that dropouts experience more than their share of social problems. These range from a marked sense of worthlessness to extremely high unemployment, poor advancement promise, and a variety of personal problems (Larson & Shertzer, 1987). The price that the American society pays for these problems is enormous (Institute for Educational Leadership, 1986).

It is of interest that the research documenting these problems presents a strangely discontinuous picture. This research points to a large number of high school dropouts with severe problems, while high school graduates experience considerably less difficulties (Larson & Shertzer, 1987). The research does not distinguish the degree of learning required to lessen problems but does emphasize the critical nature of owning a high school diploma. If the high school diploma is so powerful, perhaps school personnel should make certain that every student has one!

In 1982–1983 a series of reports on secondary education in the United States were generally critical of educational practices and demanded change. Most states and local school districts have responded with sweeping changes in high school graduation requirements. The net result has been a dramatic shift from comprehensive high school curricula to a "one program fits all" approach (Aubrey, 1986). This singular program is very clearly a college preparatory curriculum. When viewed against the 1980 U.S. Census Bureau figure of less than 20% of the adult population having earned a baccalaureate degree, that college preparatory curriculum appears highly unrealistic (Axelson, 1985). This one basic curriculum also ignores what is known of the range of academic intelligence (Anastasi, 1988). The curricular reform measures have made the high school diploma even more difficult to obtain for the youngsters with the greatest need (Hahn & Danzberger, 1987) .

The professional literature is reasonably consistent as to the nature of the dropout population (Institute for Educational Leadership, 1986). Students at high risk to leave high school without graduating usually fit one or more of these descriptors: retained in earlier grades, achieving poorly in current school work, having less-than-average academic intelligence, experienced a pregnancy during high school, coming from seriously disrupted families, coming from families of low socio-economic status, suffering the consequences of ethnic bigotry, perceiving themselves to be of low social status in the school setting, and attending schools operating under strong middle-class rule systems (Larson & Shertzer, 1987).

The solutions for the dropout problem most commonly offered in the literature attempt to make schools more hospitable places to learn. Suggestions are frequently made to provide greater personal support for at-risk youth through expanded social services. A popular suggestion is to place the responsibility of solving the problem on dramatic changes in early school experiences (Association of California Urban School Districts, 1985). Remediation programs, summer schools, and extended school calendars are urged to provide additional opportunities for students to repeat again what they have previously failed (Institute for Educational Leadership, 1986). Additionally, suggestions are often made to increase the rigidity of enforcement of compulsory attendance laws (Hahn & Danzberger, 1987). Seldom does the professional literature address the inappropriateness of the predominant high school curriculum or of other barriers placed in the path of high-risk students (Aubrey, 1986).

Hurdles Before a High School Diploma

We contend that a number of inappropriate hurdles have been placed between high school students and a diploma. In the immediate future it seems unlikely that these hurdles will be removed or significantly lowered. If high-risk students are to complete high school, ways must be found to help them past these barriers.

The Hurdles

High school graduation requirements. In many states the current high school graduation requirements are the equivalent of low- to middle-demand college entrance requirements. This means the graduation demands are beyond the capacity of large numbers of high school students (Aubrey, 1986).

The teaching approach. The academic thrust of current educational reform encourages teachers to aim their efforts toward the university-bound students. The vast majority of high school students are left wondering as to the value of school in their lives (Fine, 1986).

Competency/proficiency examinations. Competency exams have recently become a standard hurdle before high school graduation. Such exams are easily passed by 70-80% of the high school population but serve as a major barrier for students who really need the diploma (Anastasi, 1988; Wehlage & Rutter, 1986) .

The good life means a college degree. High school students are buried in propaganda suggesting a good life is attainable only through the college of their choice. Even military recruitment material is based on the opportunity to save money to go to college (Aubrey, 1986).

Rules. All schools must have rules of operation, and these frequently serve as hurdles to the high-risk student (Fine, 1986). It is developmentally appropriate for adolescents to seek a place at center stage (Ingersoll, 1982). For students lacking in academic skills and ability, the testing of rules serves as a means to gain attention.

Isolation. Different value systems, poor skills or abilities, lack of success, limited support, and different interests often result in students who experience a strong sense of isolation in the American high school (Larson & Shertzer, 1987; Wehlage & Rutter, 1986).

Bigotry. Minority students, poor students, students with limited academic skills or abilities, and students with other than middle-class values continue to experience exhibitions of bigotry by both students and staff in our schools (Fine, 1986; Rumberger, 1983).

A Big Problem Calls for *Small Wins*

The hurdles between high-risk students and high school diplomas appear to be overwhelming. The problems are so great as to limit innovative action because the boundaries of most rational thought processes are exceeded (Weick, 1984). When this happens, human emotions are aroused to dysfunctional levels and efforts to attack the original problems are often counterproductive. Application of Weick's small wins strategy helps school personnel to establish reasonable objectives and provides opportunities for success that counter emotional frustration.

A major adjustment called for by a small wins strategy has to do with acceptance of elements of the status quo when the situation cannot readily be changed. School personnel who wish to reduce the high school dropout rate need to accept the existence of the hurdles described earlier. The curriculum reforms of the mid-1980s will probably continue to cause high schools to serve primarily as precollege training centers into the next century (Aubrey, 1986). This is probably a reality, as frustrating as this may be for school counselors with their broader perspective of the nature of high school students. That curriculum focus will also reinforce the academic thrust of the teaching staff and the training of future teachers (Wehlage & Rutter, 1986).

Counselors and other knowledgeable helpers probably need to accept and adjust to this trend in secondary education. Efforts to change the basic curriculum or the academic thrust of many teachers will take too long for thousands of youth and will lead to counterproductive levels of frustration for concerned helpers. Such personnel may find it more rewarding and more effective to adopt a *small wins* strategy (Weick, 1984) .

Other topics of acceptance and adjustment would seem to revolve around the value of high school education. As noted earlier, the research points out the problems of nongraduates and the almost magical differences in terms of life success of graduates (Hahn & Danzberger,

1987). It would seem that one could operate from the position that the ultimate objective with the high-risk group is the obtaining of a high school diploma. The actual acquisition of the knowledge and skills currently dominating high school curricula could be viewed as relatively unimportant in this effort. If the counselors can bring themselves to this conclusion, then reasonable objectives can be established.

Perhaps the greatest adjustment called for to significantly alter the dropout picture involves the attitude of "Why bother!" School staffs tend to see dropout prevention efforts as futile, unrewarding, and receiving only lip service support from management and decision makers (Association of California Urban School Districts, 1985). The parents of high-risk students are not considered to have the political power seen as important by school managers (Hodgkinson, 1985). The hard work involved in helping a potential dropout remain in school may result in criticism from colleagues who might prefer to be rid of resistant learners. A *small wins* strategy may provide the encouragement needed to persevere in dropout prevention.

Small Wins and Dropout Prevention

The following are illustrations of *small wins* tactics that have been used to help potential dropouts. This listing is not intended as a comprehensive tool but rather as a stimulus. The reader can develop other and more effective tactics as part of a personal *small wins* strategy. The counselor needs to keep in mind a basic principle—that no single strategy will always be successful.

Us against them. Student cooperation and increased effort can sometimes be obtained by use of the Weakland collaborative model (Fisch, Weakland, & Segal, 1982). In this approach the counselor verbally takes the side of the student in opposition to the school system. The counselor may agree that the system is "out to lunch" and attempts to enlist the student in efforts to beat the system. When successful, this model sets the stage for collaborative efforts between student and counselor aimed at dodging the school's efforts to prevent this student from graduating.

The goal. The student must have a reason for obtaining the diploma. Extreme counseling measures may be called for to convince the resistant learner that the piece of paper is worthwhile. Frequently, the counselor must first destroy the myth that the only way to a good job is through college. High school counselors have found success with experience-centered learning in countering such propaganda by providing on-the-job learning experiences (Aubrey, 1986).

A local counselor has success by placing high-risk students in contact with selected community persons. The owner of the local refuse collection service cooperates by having the students talk to his drivers and collectors. A high school diploma is required to move from the collecting job to the driving job. This one small bit of firsthand data appears to have a marked impact on the students.

Who are those guys? An obvious need in preventing school dropout behavior involves identification of high-risk students before they are out of school. A *small wins* example in approaching this issue is to ask for potential dropout estimates from referral or feeder schools. Teachers and counselors of these schools often have amazingly accurate ideas of the risk levels of students being referred to secondary schools (Hodgkinson, 1985).

Must kiss a lot of frogs. For high-risk students to complete a high school program, they will need to "kiss a lot of frogs," or put up with a lot of nonsense, as they view the world. Using the collaborative model, the counselor can address these issues directly, attempting to help the student maintain focus on the goal. Philips (1969) provided a number of useful tools that the counselor can teach students to address perceived nonsense. Tools of particular utility are the thought-stopping techniques and the silent-ridicule system. *Thought stopping* provides the person with a way to prevent distracting thoughts from interfering with his or her productive efforts. The *silent-ridicule system* allows the person the opportunity to "strike back" at unfair treatment but without bringing harm to anyone.

Graduation requirements. Where schools offer different levels of diplomas or certificates of completion, students need counseling help in deciding if they possess the abilities and drive to aim toward a specific type of diploma. Once the type of goal is established, the counselor can often manage the student's course of study to meet requirements with a minimum of student effort. The earlier in high school that students acknowledge their need to move toward a goal of less resistance, the greater the likelihood of success. The traditional counselor role of careful selection of classes and teachers for high-risk students remains an important function.

Students often require help in accepting minimum passing grades and ignoring negative teacher feedback. The *small wins* approach can be taught to students, so that they remind themselves that the goal is to pass the course; *a grade of D gets the job done!* Students need frequent reminders that inappropriate responses to poor grades that are used as punishment and for teacher criticism will not help them reach their goal.

The exams. Many states have instituted competency or proficiency examinations to be passed prior to high school graduation. Such exams are a major hurdle for academically marginal students. These tests represent an arbitrary sampling of academic subject matter covering a vast range. The student must either be competent across the scope of the material or be fortunate enough to be competent in those specific areas sampled by the test (Anastasi, 1988).

Research studies indicate that the "need to know" information presented in any course of study is actually limited and relatively specific (Southwest Regional Laboratory, 1986). The so-called pivotal skills can be identified in any body of knowledge. If school personnel carefully study the high school curriculum and the examinations in use, they can determine the pivotal skills for specific subjects. Perhaps high-risk students should be informed of the really important material to be learned. Such coaching can be highly effective in helping students to gain the competency they require to pass both courses and exams (Southwest Regional Laboratory, 1986).

The scholarly teacher. The high-risk student often engages in real power struggles with teachers who have little understanding of the resistant learner. Students can be taught how to win the classroom game. Academic achievers have learned to do this and may be the best sources of information about the classroom game of particular teachers (Downing, 1977). Things such as seating location (if optional), volunteering to answer questions, asking relevant questions, appropriate social behavior, and exhibiting interest are ways students can appear involved in the class. When presented to marginal students as ways to win the classroom game, many students respond favorably to this *small win.*

The rules. Many arbitrary school rules appear to have been established with the purpose of trapping the resistant learner. At times students can be seduced into avoiding rule conflicts by using the "us against them" collaborative model (Fisch et al., 1982). The objective is to help the student beat the system by following the rules.

Isolation. The high-risk student often feels isolated in American high schools because that isolation is real. Marginal academic students have very few opportunities to obtain appropriate attention or affection in the school setting. Efforts to develop more personal, family-style learning centers have proved to be expensive and of limited effectiveness (Wehlage & Rutter, 1986).

Programs that have been effective in relieving feelings of isolation are those that couple academic curriculum with social involvement within a relevant context. Agricultural education programs with Future Farmers of America activities aimed at real-life experience serve as excellent examples. Unfortunately, schools have largely dismantled the vocational education programs developed around this effective and logical system.

A *small wins* approach would include the use of the experience in such programs to develop similar academic models. The basic idea is to couple the academic curriculum to the social needs of adolescents and to focus the learning effort on real-life needs. This is a simple but powerful educational approach.

Bigotry. A *small wins* approach to in-school bigotry involves the power of someone showing interest in a student who has been given a message that he or she is less than desirable. Again, the collaborative model can be used to build a positive "we'll show 'em" approach.

Implications for School Counselors

The dropout problem is so large and difficult to address that many school counselors are overwhelmed by the issue. Our bounds of rationality are exceeded, and as the frustration mounts there is a tendency to give up and move on to other problems (Weick, 1984). This article suggests the need to change our approach to something within our limits of thinking.

The *small wins* approach would have counselors look for those efforts in which they can engage that are limited in scope and promising in outcome. For example, counselors who maintain case study records of their successes in helping students to graduate may feel much better about their work than do those who only develop depressing dropout statistics.

If educational decision makers became enlightened overnight to the need for a comprehensive secondary school curriculum, it would require years to implement. School counselors must throw themselves into the breech and help high-risk students to complete high school despite the existing system. This may require nontraditional and even controversial procedures, but it is a worthwhile cause.

Finally, counselors entering this battle must be prepared for little support and limited rewards. While the professional literature suggests the desirability of holding students in school to graduation, the practical question may well be "Who wants them?"

References

Anastasi, A. (1988). *Psychological testing* (6th ed.). New York: Macmillan.

Association of California Urban School Districts. (1985). *Dropouts from California's urban school districts.* San Francisco: Author.

Aubrey, R. F. (1986). Excellence, school reform and counselors. *Counseling and Human Development, 19*(3), 1–10.

Axelson. J. A. (1985). *Counseling and development in a multicultural society.* Monterey, CA: Brooks/Cole.

Downing, C. J. (1977). Teaching children behavior change techniques. *Elementary School Guidance and Counseling, 11*(4), 237–245.

Fine, M. (1986). Why urban adolescents drop into and out of public high school. *Teachers College Record, 87*(3), 393–409.

Fisch, R., Weakland, J. H., & Segal, L. (1982). *The tactics of change.* San Francisco: Jossey-Bass.

Hahn, A., & Danzberger, J. (1987). *Dropouts in America.* Washington, DC: Institute for Educational Leadership.

Hodgkinson, H. L. (1985). *All one system.* Washington, DC: Institute for Educational Leadership.

Ingersoll, G. M. (1982). *Adolescents in school and society.* Lexington, MA: D.C. Heath.

Institute for Educational Leadership. (1986). *School dropouts: Everybody's problem.* Washington, DC: Author.

Larson, P., & Shertzer, B. (1987). The high school dropout: Everybody's problem. *The School Counselor, 34*(3), 163–169.

Philips, D. (1969). *How to fall out of love.* New York: Bantam Books.

Rumberger, R. W. (1983). Dropping out of high school: The influence of race, sex, and family background. *American Educational Research Journal, 20,* 199–220.

Southwest Regional Laboratory. (1986). *Instructional risk reduction.* Los Alamitos, CA: Author.

Wehlage, G., & Rutter, R. (1986). Dropping out: How much do schools contribute to the problem? *Teachers College Review, 87*(3), 374–392.

Weick, K. E. (1984). Small wins, redefining the scale of social problem. *American Psychologist, 39*(1), 40–49.

Study Habits and Attitudes of American Indian Students: Implications for Counselors

Eldon Gade
Graham Hurlburt
Dale Fuqua

Nationally, 25% of all students fail to graduate from high school (Gardner, 1983). More disturbing statistics indicate even higher dropout rates among certain minority groups. Dropout rates, for example, in many American Indian schools are as high as 40% in the junior high school years and 60% in the senior high school years (Blinkhorn, 1981; Coladarci, 1983). And, for those Indian students who stay in school, absenteeism, disciplinary problems, and poor motivation remain very prevalent (Coladarci, 1983).

Elliot and Wendling (1966) stated that 75% of academic failure in high school is the result of poor study and examination habits. They also pointed out that 75% of students who drop out of high school had the ability to do passing or even superior work.

Many possible reasons for the high dropout rate and for poor achievement among American Indian students have been advanced (Blinkhorn, 1981; Coladarci, 1983), ranging from economic and sociological factors to school policies. Despite the high dropout rate and low achievement, little research has been conducted about the study habits and attitudes of American Indian students using a standardized instrument.

The purposes of this study were: (a) to provide comparison data about the study habits and attitudes of American Indian students; (b) to determine the relationship of scores on the *Survey of Study Habits and Attitudes, Form H* (SSHA) (Brown & Holtzman, 1967), to classroom achievement and classroom behavior; and (c) to consider implications of these findings for counselors.

Method

Participants

Participants in this study consisted of 160 American Indian students enrolled in Grades 7–12 at a reserve school in Manitoba, Canada. This school is controlled by local American Indians, and students are members of the Plains Cree and Saulteaux tribes. In 1985, the school district enrolled 635 students from kindergarten to grade 12. American Indians make up 40% of the faculty. The sample consisted of 160 students in attendance on the testing dates: 71% of the total enrollment of 226 students in Grades 7–12. Daily attendance in these grades averaged 72% of the total enrollment. Participants included 96 students in Grades 7–9 (64 girls and 32 boys) and 64 in Grades 10–12 (32 girls and 32 boys).

Instrument and Procedure

The *Survey of Study Habits and Attitudes, Form H* (SSHA) (Brown & Holtzman, 1967) was administered by the senior author to all students in Grades 7–12 who were in attendance on the day of the examination. The SSHA is one of the most popular study skills instruments, and its norms have been established on the basis of more than 11,000 students in 13 school systems. Relationships of the total score of the SSHA and grade point average range from a correlation of .46 in Grade 12 to .55 in Grade 7. Test-retest reliabilities over a 4-week interval range between .93 and .95 (Morris, 1961).

There are seven scales on the SSHA:

1. *Delay Avoidance*—a measure of the degree to which a student is prompt in completing assignments and efficient in time management.
2. *Work Methods*—a measure of effective use of study skills.
3. *Teacher Approval*—a measure of student opinions about teacher classroom behavior and methods.
4. *Education Acceptance*—a measure of student approval of educational objectives, practices, and requirements.
5. *Study Habits*—a combined score of the Delay Avoidance and Work Methods scales.
6. *Study Attitudes*—a combination of the scores of the Teacher Approval and Education Acceptance scales.

7. *Study Orientation*—an overall measure of a student's study habits and attitudes.

Classroom achievement and behavior were measured by teacher ratings of student academic achievement, cooperation, and work habits. The students were independently rated by 13 classroom teachers on three 5-point teacher rating scales (developed by the authors): academic achievement was rated *poor* (1) to *outstanding* (5), cooperation was rated *very uncooperative* (1) to *very cooperative* (5), and work habits were rated *needs much improvement* (1) to *very efficient* (5). All teacher ratings were averaged to determine final scores on each of the three scales.

Statistical Analysis

Means and standard deviations were computed for each of the seven SSHA scales and for the three teacher-rating scales, and *t* tests were computed comparing boys and girls. An intercorrelational matrix was constructed from all the scales. Finally, SSHA scores for the sample were converted to percentile scores and compared with the normative data reported in the SSHA manual.

Results

Compared to the percentile norms found in the SSHA manual, scores for American Indian girls in Grades 7–9 were at about the 35th percentile on overall study orientation, whereas the boys at this grade level were only at the 15th percentile. The girls' scores ranged from about the 50th percentile on use of good work methods to the 25th percentile on acceptance of educational objectives and practices. The boys at this level scored only at about the 10th percentile on acceptance of educational objectives and practices to about the 30th percentile on use of good work and study methods. In Grades 10–12 girls scored overall at about the 55th percentile whereas boys were at about the 45th percentile. The girls were near average or slightly above average on all scales. The boys were at about the 40th percentile on avoiding procrastination and on acceptance of educational policies and near average on all the other scales.

A comparison of the means of the SSHA scales showed that the girls scored significantly higher than the boys did ($p < .05$) on all seven scales of the SSHA. The girls were also rated by the classroom teachers as being significantly higher than the boys on all three of the classroom behaviors of academic achievement, cooperativeness, and work habits.

The SSHA scales seem to possess adequate internal consistency for use with American Indian students, and the four basic scales (Delay Avoidance, Work Methods, Teacher Approval, and Education Acceptance) correlated between .79 and .93 with the total Study Orientation score.

The final focus of this study was on the relationship of the SSHA scores to the three teacher ratings of student academic achievement, cooperation, and work habits. We found that there was a significant but low correlation of about .30 for each of these three scales and the SSHA scales, indicating some concurrent validity for the use of the SSHA with this type of population and a possible explanation of the study skills factors involved in poor student achievement and classroom behavior.

Discussion

This study is one of the few reported investigations about the study habits and attitudes of American Indian students. The results provide data on American Indians' study habits and comparisons with the normative data found in the SSHA manual. These data may help promote the use of the SSHA or other such inventories with students from minority groups. Although the findings are limited to only one sample, the study can be used in a preliminary way to help counselors and educators analyze the study habits and attitudes of American Indian students. The results indicate that the SSHA possesses adequate concurrent validity and internal scale reliability for use with this population. This study has demonstrated that poor study habits and poor study attitudes, especially in the junior high school years and among boys, are related to teacher ratings of low achievement, insufficient cooperation, and poor work habits.

What can school counselors do to help American Indian youths improve their study habits and attitudes? First, it is important to understand that study habits and attitudes involve the total school faculty—not just classroom teachers. Garni (1980) urged school counselors to assume a preventive role in reducing student attrition by taking a proactive rather than a remedial approach. This is a particularly important role when one considers the much higher dropout rates of American Indian youth. More specifically, Lander (1981) has recommended "intrusive counseling," in which counselors increase their active and collaborative involvement with teachers' classroom efforts. Along these same lines, McKinnon and Kiraly (1984) described strategies, methods, and programs combining cognitive and affective learning in the classroom to produce more relevant student learning, more student self-control, and greater respect toward teachers and classmates.

The low scores on the Teacher Approval Scale of the SSHA at the junior high school level, and particularly among the boys, indicate that these students had poor opinions of teachers and their classroom behaviors and methods. More recruitment of American Indian teachers and counselors may help these students identify with more relevant faculty role models. Counselors can invite back to school former students who can give testimony to junior high students that good study habits and attitudes are valuable tools for success. Counselors can also play a leadership role in promoting multicultural education and human relations training.

The low scores at the junior high school level on the Education Acceptance scale suggest that these students have become "turned off" by school objectives, practices, and requirements. Counselors can use the results of this study to demonstrate to administrators and teachers the continuing need to promote relevance in the school curriculum such as that advocated by the career education movement. Again, affective education strategies and materials can improve student acceptance of cognitive learning.

The below-average scores on the Delay Avoidance and Work Methods scales, particularly at the junior high level, are further indicators that these students need help with time management and study skills. Counselors can use "time budget sheets" (Miller, 1973) to graphically illustrate for students the concept of more effective use of their time. Counselors can also introduce students to the SQ3R (Survey, Question, Read, Recite, Repeat) method of study developed by Robinson (1970).

Presnell (1980) described how counselors can increase teachers' student referrals by stressing better counselor-teacher relations and better feedback to teachers about student needs. American Indian youths are often too shy and reluctant to make self-referrals for counseling, and the teacher-referral process may be the best means of initiating student contacts. A good beginning for counseling with American Indian students is to focus on academic concerns. Academic difficulties are a common experience for many of these students; thus, focusing first on positive study skills and attitudes may help to develop rapport. Later, as Castagna and Codd (1984) described, a counselor can focus on motivational and personal problems that may be interacting with poor study habits and attitudes.

The administration and interpretation of the SSHA by itself can be useful for improving the study skills of American Indian students, especially at the junior high school level. The survey can be administered early in the school year and thus be used as a screening instrument to identify students who may need immediate assistance and counseling. The Diagnostic Profile of the SSHA can be given to each individual student to pinpoint specific areas of skill difficulties. Students can also examine their responses to individual statements that make up each SSHA subscale. A special Counseling Key of the SSHA can be laid over student answer sheets, so that counselors can identify specific statements that represent poor study habits or attitudes that may be contributing to a student's academic difficulties.

It is apparent from the results of this study that many junior high school students can benefit from help in improving their study skills. In addition to its use in individual counseling, the SSHA can also be used in the classroom in semester-long skills courses, brief units in regular subject fields, or during homeroom periods.

Conclusion

American Indian students in increasing numbers are attending postsecondary educational institutions (Chavers, 1982). Good study habits and attitudes seem necessary if these students are to survive academically in higher education. The findings of this study indicate that American Indian junior high school students, especially boys, have poor attitudes about their school and their teachers and also have poor study habits and skills. In this article we have described how counselors of American Indian students can play an important, proactive role in improving study skills in the classroom and through individual counseling strategies.

References

Blinkhorn, K. (1981, October). *Peguis adult high school program, an experiment in local control.* Paper presented at the Western Adult Education Conference, Red River Community College, Winnipeg, Manitoba.

Brown, W., & Holtzman, W. (1967). *Manual: Survey of Study Habits and Attitudes.* New York: Psychological Corporation.

Castagna, S., & Codd, J. (1984). High school study skills: Reasons and techniques for counselor involvement. *School Counselor, 32,* 37–42.

Chavers, D. (1982). False promises: Barriers in American Indian education. *Integrated Education, 19, 1–2.*

Coladarci, T. (1983). High school dropout among Native Americans. *Journal of American Indian Education, 23,* 15–22.

Elliot, D., & Wendling, A. (1966). Capable dropouts and the social milieu of the high school. *Journal of Educational Research, 60,* 180–186.

Gardner, D. P. (1983). A *nation at risk: The imperative for educational reform.* Washington, DC: U.S. Department of Education.

Garni, K. (1980). Counseling centers and student retention: Why the failures? Where the success? *Journal of College Student Personnel, 21,* 223–228.

Lander, V. (1981). Counseling in an educational setting. *NASPA Journal, 18*(4), 37–44.

McKinnon, A., & Kiraly, J. (1984). *Pupil behavior, self-control, and social skills in the classroom.* Springfield, IL: Charles C Thomas.

Miller, L. (1973). *Time budget sheet* (rev. ed.). Laramie, WY: Developmental Reading Distributors.

Morris, F. L. (1961). *The validity of the Brown-Holtzman Survey of Study Habits and Attitudes, 1960 experimental revision for grades 7–12.* Unpublished master's thesis, Wayne State University, Detroit.

Presnell, C. (1980). Counselor-team collaboration in middle and junior high schools. *Clearing House, 54,* 58–59.

Robinson, F. (1970). *Effective study.* New York: Harper & Row.

Cognitive-Developmental Counseling: Preparing Low-Income Students for College

James Virgil Cunningham
Romeria Tidwell

The cognitive-developmental counseling model presented here is designed to promote high school seniors' social readiness for college through the process of "psychological education" (Mosher & Sprinthall, 1971). The explicit objective of psychological education is to give students information drawn from behavioral science research that is relevant to helping them deal with their own personal problems. Psychological education has a further, implicit goal of influencing students' psychological and social development. The program presented below is specifically designed to encourage and support the psychological growth of prospective college students from low-socioeconomic status *(low-SES)* backgrounds.

Several programs have been designed recently to prepare low-income and minority students for advancement to successful college careers. Upward Bound and Talent Search, among others, are specifically designed to ease the transition from high school to college for low-SES students. Adjustment to college is a significant problem for entering students in general, but it is particularly acute for students from low-SES backgrounds. Because such students often come from minority ethnic groups and have limited financial resources, and because the parents of such students often have limited formal education, low-SES students are clearly differentiable from "traditional" mainstream college students.

Low income and minority students drop out of college at a high rate. For example, the attrition rate for Afro-American students at predominately Caucasian institutions was 49.5% during the early 1970s (Astin, 1975). Although the inferior academic abilities of low-SES students are often cited as the explanation for their high attrition rates even when ability is held constant, these students drop out at higher rates than do middle-income students (Trent, 1970).

Several factors contribute to the difficulties low-SES students have in adjusting to the college environment. In contrast with students whose parents attended college, many if not most, low-SES students have not been able to benefit from the implicit preparation of having a college-educated role model in their homes (Reeder & Heppner, 1985). College is an arena in which the individual makes a transition to adult social and emotional responsibilities. Many students are overwhelmed by the change in status implicit in attending college. For minority students, the load is often greater because they are not only unused to their new role, but also they are often unused to the social values and norms reflected everywhere on the college campus.

The simple difference in backgrounds between low-income students and traditional students entering college is a source of considerable stress for the former (Munoz & Garcia-Bahne, 1978). Low-income students, especially those from minority backgrounds, experience so-called "culture shock" upon their entrance to the college environment (Vasquez & Chavez, 1980). They also fall prey to feelings of isolation and alienation (Casas & Atkinson, 1981). In short, low-SES students must make a greater social adjustment to the typical college environment than their peers from higher-SES backgrounds (Gunnings, 1982).

While low-SES students struggle with purely social problems, they are still required to cope with the academic demands of college. Yet, as Fleming (1981) observed, such students frequently spend more time learning coping strategies than acquiring academic skills. Low-SES students are simultaneously trying to integrate socially and achieve academically.

Several current programs address, to some degree, both the academic and social sides of low-income and minority students' adjustment to college life. Some programs focus on academic skills and others on linguistic or social development. It is probably true, however, that efforts in the one domain have positive effects in the other. Students with greater confidence in their academic skills may also have greater confidence in their overall ability to adjust to college. On the other hand, improvements in social skills should facilitate students' greater involvement in all phases of college life, including coursework. Such programs can and have been instituted at both the high school and college levels.

At the high school level, there is a diversity of programs designed to improve the prospects for true social integration in a multicultural environment (Tidwell, 1980). High school programs for minority youngsters often emphasize cultural diversity and, at the same time, expose students to the career possibilities that education makes available. Many of the precollege summer programs, which are often held on college campuses, stress both academic and social skills.

The Linguistic Minority Project at the University of California, for example, helps students, primarily Hispanics who come from non-English-speaking backgrounds to develop the full repertoire of linguistic skills in English (Linguistic Minority Project, 1986). By preparing students for participation in college courses, such a program can also aid students in adjusting to a new cultural setting.

The Professional Development Program (PDP), at the University of California, Berkeley, helps minority students already enrolled at the campus improve their mathematics skills sufficiently to compete in the calculus courses that are a prerequisite for a major in several science-related disciplines. The PDP fosters a workshop environment, in which members of small learning groups work cooperatively to master the necessary mathematical material. Such group work supports these students' adjustment to college and assists them in establishing a network of relationships. In several respects, the Afro-American and Hispanic participants in the PDP outperform their Caucasian and Asian counterparts. The high performance of students in PDP demonstrates to them that, through dedication, they can succeed in the somewhat alien environment of the university. There can be little doubt that for many such students, the experience of their own success enhances their self-image and self-esteem and reinforces the relationship between responsible hard work and high performance. That is, academic success has positive implications for psychological development.

One way to ameliorate the problems low-SES students have in adjusting to college life is to develop counseling interventions that promote their psychological development. Most successful college-level retention programs currently use counseling to encourage the development of personal skills (Beal & Noel, 1980). Mannon and Preusz (1980), for example, have even endorsed mandatory student development courses for freshmen as a way of reducing student attrition. The obvious limitation of retention programs, however, is that they are offered to college students who may already be experiencing adjustment problems.

The implementation of a developmental counseling program in the high schools offers the advantage of preparing students for some of the problems they may face *before* they make the critical passage into college. That is, high school programs aimed at minority and low-income students must go beyond helping them acclimate generally to the social environment of school and actively encourage the social and emotional development necessary to functioning effectively in the college environment.

Psychological maturity seems to be critical to the success of most college students. Unfortunately, it may be especially difficult for low-SES students to achieve the requisite level of maturity to "make it" at college, at least partly because they must often undergo a radical redefinition of their identities (Vasquez & Chavez, 1980). The problem of establishing a mature identity is compounded for minority students attending predominantly Caucasian institutions (Gibbs, 1975; Gurin & Epps, 1975). An intervention like the PDP described above may come too late for freshmen who are already weighted down with personal difficulties. The most effective program for preparing low-SES students for college will, ideally, protect students against the worst emotional effects of transition from high school to college before that transition has actually taken place.

Cross (1971) has noted that low-SES students learn more effectively through direct experience and in environments that presuppose personal attention. Widick, Knefelkamp, and Parker (1975) have identified four institutional strategies that closely address the characteristics of "disadvantaged" students. Such strategies include a high degree of structure, a diversity of instructional methods, direct experiential learning and a high degree of social interaction. Bradley and Stewart (1982) and King and Fields (1980) have called for the implementation of developmental interventions as a means of addressing the needs of low-SES students.

Counseling interventions designed for prospective college students provide them with the opportunity to develop important cognitive and interpersonal skills and, above all, promote their sense of identity and self-esteem (King & Fields, 1980). As we have said above, just as programs that focus on academic skills promote psychological development, programs that focus on psychological development will contribute to the building of academic skills. It is further assumed that such a program is particularly important for low-SES students. The intervention presented below, which uses psychoeducational strategies, includes the use of readings and exercises that address major developmental issues from a general perspective as well as special readings and exercises that reflect the perspective of the low-SES student.

The Program

Chickering (1969) has identified seven *vectors of development* for the college student and has incorporated them into a model for the resolution of identity problems. These vectors are: (a) developing intellectual, manual, and social competence; (b) managing emotions through an increasing awareness and integration of feelings; (c) developing emotional and instrumental autonomy; (d) establishing an integrated, stable identity; (e) freeing interpersonal relationships through an increased tolerance and the fostering of mature relationships; (f) developing a purpose in both work and recreation; and (g) developing integrity through the building of humanizing, personalizing values. Indeed, *identity is* central to the development of an adult system of values and actions (Chickering, 1969; Erikson, 1959, 1968; Havighurst, 1975). The curriculum described below is termed *cognitive-developmental* because it is based on the assumption that psychological development cannot be taught, but only fostered by the presentation of appropriate experiences.

The cognitive-developmental curriculum for low-SES students consists of didactic, experiential, and reflective exercises organized into seven units that correspond exactly to Chickering's vectors of development. Because, on the surface, this counseling program is a course, its successful implementation requires that students get an intellectual grasp of its contents. Beyond that, however, the purpose of the intervention, in accord with the principles of psychological education, is for the students to personalize the information they receive. Therefore, the counselor who delivers the curriculum must interact with each student in a way that emphasizes an *affective* reaction to the course materials (Widick et al., 1975). Moreover, group discussions of the lessons are designed to help students internalize both the intellectual and affective aspects of the coursework in a relatively nonthreatening atmosphere. The requirement that students keep journals further encourages them to reflect on what they have read and heard as it encourages them to use and develop their writing skills.

Each unit of the curriculum is introduced with a definition of the developmental task(s) it addresses, a description of the structure of the unit, a discussion of the procedures involved in the unit's implementation, and a statement of the function of the unit in promoting development. Unit procedures include readings, experiential exercises that are often based on the readings, and a reflective component.

For example, the first part of the unit on Establishing Autonomy begins with a reading, "The Transition From Home to College," which has been taken from *Friends and Lovers in the College Years* (1983). The article introduces such issues as how and why the student's parents influence his or her decisions, how the student's leaving home affects both the student and his or her family, and how autonomy is related to the development of identity. The experiential component for the first part of the autonomy unit requires students to conduct a series of interviews designed to determine the applicability and accuracy of the ideas expressed in the reading. The reflective component of the first part of the unit on autonomy asks students to identify individuals who have influenced their thinking about college and about their careers and to specify how those individuals have influenced them.

The chief instructional objective of the first part of the unit, Establishing Autonomy, is to give students a valid basis for evaluating their goals in attending college and for understanding the sources of those goals: their parents, their friends, their culture, and, above all, themselves. Thus, like all parts of the course, it has a "hidden curriculum"—implicit instructional goals. The implicit objective here was to motivate students to evaluate their own choices by giving them some of the tools for making that evaluation.

The second part of the unit on Establishing Autonomy is organized around an article, "Leaving Home: Is There a Right Time to Go?" by Daniel Goleman (1980), which appeared in *Psychology Today*. The explicit objective of this part of the curriculum is to provide students with the terms and concepts for describing the experience of leaving home. The implicit objective (hidden curriculum) is getting students to apply that knowledge to their own feelings and the feelings of their families about the possibility of their leaving home to go to college.

The last part of the unit on Establishing Autonomy includes a reading by D. P. Johnson (1980), "Counseling Students With Homesick Blues," which appeared in *College Student Journal*. Students need to identify the symptoms and causes of homesickness. They also need to prepare themselves for homesickness if they are ever to establish an existence separate from their families, at college or elsewhere.

In other words, each unit is structured around a set of tightly-defined objectives embodied in a reading that specifically addresses the completion of developmental tasks connected with going to college. Some units and parts of units are organized around the experience of low-SES and minority-group college students.

The readings, which play a central role in the program, have been chosen for their clarity and for the extent to which they illustrate the problems addressed in a given section. Most come from publications aimed at young people.

Evaluation

The program was submitted to a panel of experts for evaluation. The experts were selected on the basis of their educational background and their professional experience in the area of multiethnic counseling. Nine individuals identified as experts were asked to participate in the evaluation of substantial parts of the cognitive-developmental curriculum for low-SES students. Of those nine, five agreed to participate.

Each of the five individuals had an advanced degree in an area related to counseling and education. All were men and all were minority-group members (three Hispanics and two Afro-Americans). They had from 5 to 20 years of counseling experience and all had been involved professionally for many years in both high school and college environments.

The questionnaire developed for the evaluation focused on what were considered the most fundamental issues in the curriculum design. The basic questions concerned the *relevance* of the curriculum's instructional objectives to its intended target population, the *appropriateness* of the instructional materials and strategies to providing meaningful, varied opportunities for learning, and the *congruence* of the content and instructional strategies with the curriculum's stated purposes (Lewy, 1973).

The panel of experts was asked to evaluate the units on Establishing Autonomy and Freeing Interpersonal Relationships. A 5-point Likert scale was used to evaluate the curriculum; the highest rating was 1 and the lowest was 5. In addition, members of the panel were requested to provide feedback in the form of unstructured comments on the curriculum.

Their ratings and comments indicated the following: All but one member of the panel believed the material in the unit on Establishing Autonomy to be relevant and appropriate for students who are thinking about leaving home to attend college, and all but one judged the unit to be fully congruent with its objectives. The same expert gave the unit relatively low marks across the board, primarily because of his objection to one of the readings. All five of the panel members approved of the unit as a whole.

The panel members' judgment of the unit on Freeing Interpersonal Relationships was slightly less favorable than was their response to the unit on autonomy. Although three of the experts believed the content of the unit was relevant to its objectives, two others were less sure. Only two panelists fully endorsed the appropriateness of the unit's instructional strategies; the three others adopted a negative stance. Four panel members were convinced, however, of the congruence of the unit's structure with its objectives. Overall, three panel members were definitely positively disposed toward the unit, and the ratings of the other two reflected some doubts about it. The comments of one expert suggested that because the unit focuses on the experience of Afro-Americans entering college, it might not be appropriate for use in ethnically heterogeneous settings.

The evaluation did provide evidence of the merits of the cognitive developmental approach in helping low-SES students cope with the prospect of entering college. The generally positive evaluation of the two curriculum units by the panel of experts suggests the value of such a proactive intervention.

Conclusion

Because most traditional counseling models are designed to remediate an existing condition, they focus on the resolution of existing problems. Preventative, proactive counseling models are less common. Proactive counseling interventions are designed to decrease the likelihood that a problem will occur and, if the problem is unavoidable, to minimize its impact on the individuals involved. The intervention presented here is of the latter type. It is designed to prepare young people, particularly those from low-SES backgrounds, to cope with the pressures of college *before* they get there.

Psychological maturity is especially important for college students. Students with little sense of their own identities tend to cope poorly with the academic, social, and emotional pressures of college life. Low-SES students are particularly prone to experiencing an identity crisis after entering college, because the pressures on them are greater, for many reasons, than they are on mainstream students. The problems that afflict low-SES students can be kept to a minimum if they are familiarized with the form of the difficulties they may face and with ways of dealing with those difficulties.

The counseling intervention described here emphasizes cultural issues and the specific environment against which students are likely to develop. By acquainting students with the issues that will be critical to them as they make a major transition, the intervention attempts to prepare them for facing an important challenge.

References

Astin, A. (1975). *Preventing students from dropping out.* San Francisco: Jossey-Bass.

Beal, P. E., & Noel, L. (1980). *What works in student retention.* Iowa City, IA: American College Testing Program; Boulder, CO: Higher Education Management System.

Bradley, L. R., & Stewart, M. A. (1982). The relationship between self-concept and personality development in black college students: A developmental approach. *Journal of Non-White Concerns, 10,* 114–125.

Casas, J. M., & Atkinson, D. (1981). The Mexican-American in higher education: An example of subtle stereotyping. *The Personnel and Guidance Journal, 59,* 473–476.

Chickering, A. W. (1969). *Education and identity.* San Francisco: Jossey-Bass.

Cross, K. P. (1971). *Beyond the door.* San Francisco: Jossey-Bass.

Erikson, E. (1959). Identity and the life-cycle: Selected papers [Monograph]. *Psychological Issues, 1*(1), 1–171.

Erikson, E. (1968). *Identity: Youth in crisis.* New York: Norton.

Fleming, J. (1981). Special needs of blacks and other minorities. In A. W. Chickering & Associates (Eds.), *The modern American college* (pp. 393–410). San Francisco: Jossey-Bass.

Gibbs, J. T. (1975). The use of mental health services by black students at a predominantly white university: A three-year study. *American Journal of Orthopsychiatry, 45,* 430–445.

Goleman, D. (1980, August). Leaving home: Is there a right time to go? *Psychology Today,* pp. 53, 55–56, 59–60.

Gunnings, B. B. (1982). Stress and the minority student on a predominantly white campus. *Journal of Non-White Concerns, 11*, 11–16.

Gurin, P., & Epps, E. (1975). *Afro-American consciousness, identity, and achievement.* New York: Wiley.

Havighurst, J. J. (1975). Objectives for youth development. In R. J. Havighurst & P. H. Dreyer (Eds.), *The 74th yearbook of the National Society for the Study of Education.* Chicago: University of Chicago Press.

Johnson, D. P. (1980, Summer). Counseling students with homesick blues. *College Student Journal,* pp. 159–166.

King, P. M., & Fields, A. L. (1980). A framework for student development: From student development goals to educational opportunity practice. *Journal of College Student Personnel, 21,* 541–548.

Lewy, A. (1973). *Utilizing experts' judgment in the process of curriculum evaluation* (CSE Report No. 87). Los Angeles: Center for the Study of Evaluation, UCLA Graduate School of Education.

Linguistic Minority Project. (1986, April). Schooling language-minority youth. *Proceedings of the Linguistic Minority Project Conference, 4.* Berkeley, CA: Author.

Mannon, G., & Preusz, G. C. (1980). Reducing student attrition on urban campuses. *College Student Journal, 14,* 19–23.

Mental Health Materials Center. (1983). The transition from home to school. In *Friends and lovers in the college years* (pp. 33–50). New York: Author.

Mosher, R. L., & Sprinthall, N. A. (1971). Deliberate psychological education: A means to promote personal development during adolescence. *Counseling Psychologist, 2,* 3–82.

Munoz, D., & Garcia-Bahne, B. (1978). *A study of the Chicano experience in higher education* (Grant No. N 24597-01). San Diego: University of California, Center for Minority Group Mental Health Programs; Rockville, MD: National Institute of Mental Health.

Reeder, B. L., & Heppner, P. P. (1985). Personal problem-solving activities of black university students. *Journal of Multicultural Counseling and Development, 13,* 154–163.

Tidwell, R. (1980). Counseling in a multicultural school setting. *Journal of Non-White Concerns, 8,* 84–90.

Trent, J. W. (1970). *The decision to go on to college: An accumulative multi-variate process.* Los Angeles: UCLA Center for the Study of Evaluation.

Vasquez, M. J. T., & Chavez, E. L. (1980). Unique student populations. In W. H. Morrill, J. C. Hurst, & E. R. Oetting (Eds.), *Dimensions of intervention for student development* (pp. 208–301). New York: Wiley.

Widick, C., Knefelkamp, L. L., & Parker, C. A. (1975). The counselor as a developmental instructor. *Counselor Education and Supervision, 14*, 286–296.

Searching for Solutions

Doris Rhea Coy
Susan Jones Sears

As we approach the 21st century, our complex culture is characterized by diverse and ever-changing values in the home, community, and school. Societal-based problems are worse and this is reflected in dramatic increases in substance abuse, suicide, child abuse, teen pregnancy, truancy, school dropouts, and random acts of violence.

School counselors are being asked to assume a greater role in the lives of their students and the students' families. Parents, particularly single parents, want help in improving their parenting skills. Therefore, counselors have begun to conduct parenting groups. Trying to prevent substance abuse, teen pregnancy and suicide, school counselors have devised student support and intervention groups and have involved teachers in counseling-related activities. With legislative mandates for accountability in education, school counselors have helped students learn test-taking skills and have coordinated testing programs. Assisting students in career planning and in choosing appropriate postsecondary education and training continue to be important counselor activities. The challenges facing counselors and demands on their time will continue to grow during the next decade. School counselors must choose where they spend their time and energy carefully. It will be easy for counselors to engage in quasi-administrative activities rather than child-oriented ones. Given the challenges faced by today's students, counselors must focus on students' personal/social, educational, and career needs. **School counselors must be leaders in searching for solutions!**

The public relations folder entitled "Searching for Solutions" is designed to provide counselors with current information about several important topics such as student achievement, teen pregnancy, and career decision-making. Included here is the section on student achievement. Three "Information Sheets" are included, as well as "Tips for Students." During the next two years, ASCA will be developing additional "information sheets" for counselors. Watch for them so you can add to "Searching for Solutions."

Improving Student Achievement #1

Underachieving students are a major problem in schools today. While some students appear to lack motivation, others simply have not learned how to study. School counselors can assist students in improving their study skills by helping them learn memory techniques, notetaking and reading strategies, and test-taking procedures. This is the first of three brochures designed to help school counselors improve their students' achievement.

How Do We Remember?

Scientists still have a lot to learn about the brain. They don't really know how the brain stores or memorizes facts but since we do have memories of previous experiences, scientists do know the nervous system has been able to record these experiences. They call this record in the brain a neural trace. When we forget a fact or experience, scientists do not know whether the neural trace disappears or whether we just can't get to that particular neural trace.

One fact we do know is that "forgetting" occurs very fast. Some memory experts suggest that after one day we remember only 54% of what we learned the day before. One way of combating forgetting is to learn the material thoroughly in the first place. In other words, you must lay down a strong neural trace when you first learn the material. Then it is necessary to reinforce or rehearse what you are trying to remember.

Memory Skills (Written for Students)

Practicing the following principles of learning and remembering will help you "learn to remember."

1. *The Principle of Motivated Interest.* You need to be interested in a subject to do your best learning. If you are naturally interested, it is easy, but most of us are not interested in all of our school subjects. Give the subject a chance to become interesting to you. Once you begin to learn something new, you may find it genuinely interesting.

2. *The Principle of Selectivity.* Pare the job of learning down to a manageable size. Decide which facts to learn and decide what you can ignore. Trying to learn too many facts makes memorization more difficult.

3. *The Principle of Intention to Remember.* Most of us have helped someone else memorize a poem but have not learned it ourselves. That is because we were not intending to learn but just intending to help someone else learn. We must intend to remember if we are to succeed.

4. *The Principle of Meaningful Organization.* When reading or taking notes, you need to first gather your ideas. Then decide how you can categorize them. Look at this example: If you were asked to try to remember the following items at the grocery store—apples, lettuce, ham, bacon, pears, celery, cabbage, chicken, and oranges—you would have a difficult time doing so. However, if you put the items in these categories: fruit, meat, and vegetables, you could remember them more easily.

5. *The Principle of Recitation.* Saying ideas aloud that you want to remember is called recitation. After you read a paragraph in your textbook, test yourself on what you have read, by saying the key ideas aloud. When you recite an idea, it has a chance to move into your long-term memory. (Neural traces need some time to jell and recitation may well provide that time).

6. *The Principle of Distributed Practice.* When you use relatively short study sessions with short rest periods, you can prevent physical and emotional fatigue. Also, motivation is usually higher when you work within short blocks of time.

7. *The Principle of Imagery.* Mental pictures can help you remember. Creating a picture in your mind or sketching the idea you are trying to remember can help you recall the idea when needed. Silly or humorous images are often better because you can remember them easily.

8. *The Principle of Association.* Tying new information to old can help. The U.S. entered World War I in 1917 and your grandmother was also born in 1917. Tie the two together and you remember both.

Remembering Through Mnemonics

Most of us use mnemonics without even realizing it. Mnemonic means "to help the memory." Think of a favorite mnemonic in spelling: Use " i before e except after c," or, "when sounding like a, as in neighbor and weigh." When material is difficult to organize, mnemonics can be helpful as organizers. There are several types:

1. *Associative Mnemonic.* Sometimes you can associate a fact with some other fact you know, but which has no real connection with the first fact. For example, to remember that the Tropic of Capricorn is in

the Southern Hemisphere, you can associate it with the corns on your feet; that is with the southern part of your body.

2. *Make a Sentence Mnemonic.* In this type of mnemonic device, a "made-up" sentence helps you remember key words. Here is an example: You have just learned about eight principles of remembering. How can you remember them? Take a key word from each principle and make a mnemonic sentence like this one: "Motivated selectivity intending to be organized with recited practice and imaginative association will help me remember. This sentence would jog my memory if I were asked to list the eight principles on a test. For shorter amounts of information, words instead of sentences can be used. For example, if you want to remember the Great Lakes, the word "HOMES" becomes a mnemonic: H(Huron), O(Ontario), M(Michigan), E(Erie), and S(Superior).

Increasing Concentration

To make the best use of their study time, students must be able to concentrate during the time they set aside for study. Yet many students report having problems trying to concentrate. Their minds may begin to wander after only five minutes of reading.

What Can Counselors Do?

Counselors can share their suggestions below to help students improve their concentration.

1. **Counselors can** encourage students to keep records of how long they concentrate. When they sit down to read or study, have them write the time they start on a piece of paper. If their mind begins to wander, they should record the time this happens. When they lose their concentration, they should spend a few minutes doing something else. They should walk around the room, look out the window, or get a drink of water. When they are ready to study, they should record the time. If they couple this procedure with some of the other tips below, they should increase their concentration time in just a few days.

2. **Counselors can** encourage students to make a conscious decision to use their study time wisely. Often students do not think seriously about "study time" and allow themselves to be distracted by radio, music or television.

3. **Counselors can** encourage students to set goals whenever they study. Students need to have a clear idea of exactly what they want to

achieve when they study. They need to make lists of what must be accomplished first, second, etc. Students need to learn to estimate the amount of time it will take them to study each subject so they can set aside reasonable amounts of time.

4. **Counselors can** encourage students to accept that they will have to study subjects whether they like them or not. Putting off studying a subject that is not interesting or not liked has no benefits.

5. **Counselors can** remind students that large tasks are completed by doing many small tasks, one at a time. Some students become overwhelmed with the size of their textbooks or the amount of material to be covered and even lose concentration. By helping students learn how to cut down large projects into manageable pieces, counselors can help them keep or increase their concentration.

References

Brown, W. F., & Holtzman, W. H. (1987). *A guide to college survival* (rev. ed.). Iowa City, IA: The American College Testing Program.

Martin, J., Marx, R. W., & Martin, E. W. (1980). Instructional counseling for chronic underachievers. *The School Counselor, 28*(2), 109–118.

Improving Student Achievement #2

Reading Skills

The most common deterrents to fluent reading are regressions, word-by-word reading, and lip movements. Each one is briefly described.

Regressions. With regard to reading, regression refers to the tendency for the eyes to look back at something that has already been read; this is the most common symptom of slow reading among first-year college students. The following sentence includes, in parentheses, the regressions that a students made while reading it. "America seemed like a (like a) paradise to many Eastern Europeans (Europeans) who could (could) know little or nothing of what it was (it was) really like.

Word-by-word reading. The habit of focusing attention on only one-word-at-a-time while reading is called word-by-word reading. This/sentence/is/divided/to/show/you/what/one/word/at/a/time/reading/

looks/like. If you read this way, you need practice thinking in phrases as you read, just as you think in phrases when you speak.

Lip movements. If you read very slowly, check to see if you are moving your lips while you read. Hold your fingertips gently to your mouth as you read silently; if you detect movements of your lips, they may be preventing you from reading faster.

Why Do Students Procrastinate?

Some students delay studying. The reasons for procrastination are many. Sometimes the task seems so large that it is overwhelming to students. They delude themselves into thinking if they postpone doing it until tomorrow they might "have more energy," "have fewer interruptions," or "be able to concentrate better." A second reason is that some students want to avoid unpleasant tasks. If students have the choice of doing something pleasant (even if it is not important) and something unpleasant, they usually choose the pleasant task (don't we all). A third reason some procrastinate is to excuse inadequate or poor work. "I couldn't do it until the last minute" or "If I had more time, I could have done a better job" often are used to camouflage poor work. A fourth reason individuals procrastinate is to get someone else to do the job. In some situations it is important to delegate a job or task, but to intentionally put off your job so that someone else will end up doing it is an immature way of handling an assignment. Protecting a weak self-image and fearing failure are other reasons for inaction. By rationalizing inaction, students do not risk the anxiety and pain of failure. Inaction also can allow students to avoid success and the accompanying responsibilities and problems that can come with it. Improper goals or goals without deadlines can lead to procrastination. Have students review their goals, making certain they are their own, and then have them set deadlines to work against procrastination.

What Can Students Do To Get Started?

1. When students are procrastinators, they must admit it and recognize the problems it causes in their lives.
2. Students must learn to break down overwhelming tasks into small ones. Henry Ford once remarked, "Nothing is particularly hard if you divide it into small jobs." His auto assembly line was based on this concept.

3. Students must face unpleasant tasks with a new resolve. Postponing does not make it pleasant.
4. Students need to recognize that "getting started" is important. Often a little physical action is needed to get going on a big task. For example, if a student has a paper to write, she could take a sheet of paper and make a list of the ten major points she wishes to include and rank them in the order in which she plans to discuss them in the paper. At least, she is "getting started."
5. Students can become aware of and take advantage of their moods. Sometimes they feel more like doing one thing rather than another. Let's use the assignment of writing a paper again. Maybe the student feels more like reading about the topic rather than writing about it. Then, the student should do that part of the assignment rather than postponing the whole thing.
6. Students should learn to reward themselves for completing a task they have been dodging. Once they have completed the task, they should do something for fun such as going to a movie or concert. Of course, they shouldn't reward themselves if they don't finish the task.
7. Students need to learn how to say no or avoid overcommitment and also how to prioritize tasks.
8. Students must learn to set realistic time schedules. Remember, everything takes longer than we think it will.
9. Students with positive and productive attitudes are not procrastinators. With a set of clear goals students can develop positive attitudes and overcome procrastination.

References

Brown, W. F. & Holtzman, W. H. (1987). *A guide to college survival* (rev. ed.). Iowa City, IA: The American College Testing Program.

Shepherd, J. F. (1982). *The Houghton Mifflin study skills handbook.* Boston: Houghton Mifflin.

Improving Student Achievement #3

School counselors, through educational counseling, can help students improve their achievement at school. Educational counseling includes helping students acquire effective study skills. Armed with memory, notetaking, and test-taking skills, student will be better prepared to learn the necessary content in their classes. The following notetaking and study tips have been prepared as a handout for students. Use it "as is" or change it to fit your school situation.

Notetaking Tips

Taking notes in junior high/middle school and high school classes can be a challenge. Yet good note-taking habits can improve your learning and can pay dividends when you are preparing for tests. The following tips should help you take more complete and accurate notes:

1. Be prepared. Read your assignment before going to class.
2. Listen carefully. Be physically and mentally alert.
3. Keep an open and curious mind. While you may not agree with some points your teachers make, you should not reject an idea before exploring it.
4. Take your notes in outline form to help you distinguish between major and minor points.
5. Date and title your notes carefully.
6. Record or write down the examples given to illustrate points because those examples may help you remember.
7. Your teacher may use study aids, i.e., handouts, overheads, maps. Take note of these because they are usually cues that the material is important.
8. Listen for emphasis. Repetition, writing on the board, or extended comments usually mean that the point is important.
9. Leave room on your paper to expand your notes after class.
10. Take time after class to add comments or thoughts to your notes to make them as clear as possible.
11. Take notes in different colored pencils for different subjects. Sometimes the different colors will help you remember your notes better.
12. Watch your teacher as much as possible because it will help you concentrate on what he/she is saying.

Preparing for Tests

Knowing how to prepare for tests can improve your chances of doing well. Below are some tips to help you "get ready" for tests:

1. Keep up with homework/assignments. Effective students keep up with day-to-day assignments. Keeping up with your reading assignments is particularly important. Take notes while you read. Those notes, plus good class notes, help you acquire a deeper understanding of your subjects. Your notes should be dated and notes from each class should be kept together. Being organized saves time later.

2. Make a habit of reviewing your material regularly. Students remember better when they review their material soon after it is introduced. Reviewing old material often makes the new material easier to understand.

3. Plan ahead by writing down the dates the test is scheduled, the type of test it will be, and the material to be covered. Also, begin reviewing several days before the test is scheduled. Usually the more you review, the better prepared you will be on test day.

4. Determine what to study. Try to figure out what the teacher is likely to ask on the test. Review earlier tests and class handouts for clues.

5. Study smart. To be most effective, you should study when you have the most energy and feel the most alert. Study in blocks of time, usually one hour, and then take a break of 5–10 minutes. Minimize distractions and interruptions. A quiet environment lets you concentrate better. Try to figure out what the teacher is going to ask and answer those questions in your own words.

Preparing for Different Kinds of Tests

The tips just suggested for preparing for tests are useful for any test. However, additional tips may be helpful for specific kinds of tests: objective, problem, or essay.

Objective Tests. True-false, multiple-choice, matching, and fill-in-the-blanks are all objective tests. To prepare for these kinds of tests, you should study key facts, dates, and other detailed information. Focus on memorizing the important details. You may want to take notes on important terms and definitions. Some students even find flash cards helpful in preparing for these tests. Also, memory techniques can assist you in memorizing large amounts of information.

Problem Tests. Tests that involve using a formula or applying a specific rule in a systematic manner are called problem tests. These problems are often found on math and science tests. Doing problems is the best way to prepare for these tests. Of course, you must concentrate on learning the formulas, rules, and equations and applying them to a variety of problems. Use the practice problems in textbooks to help you prepare.

Essay Tests. Essay tests are designed to make you interpret, organize, and apply information you have learned. You might be asked to compare the contributions of two U.S. Presidents or evaluate the consequences of a piece of legislation. To do well on essay tests, you need to have "the big picture" in mind and also know details. In other words, you need to know facts and know the implications of those facts. Making up essay questions and even writing out the answers can be helpful in preparing for these tests.

Test-Taking Strategies

Below are a few strategies that you, as a student, can use to help you do your very best on tests:

1. Get a good night's rest before the test day.
2. Eat a good breakfast or lunch.
3. Go to the test room early so you can take a few minutes to take a deep breath and relax.
4. Bring the appropriate supplies with you—sharpened pencils, paper, and watch.
5. When you start the test, clear your mind of distracting ideas and read all of the directions.
6. Plan your time carefully. Divide your time according to the number and difficulty of the questions.
7. Read each question carefully and reread if you do not understand the question. If you can not answer the question, go on to the next one. Put a mark next to the ones you can not answer so you can go back after finishing the remainder of the questions.
8. Take your time. Finishing "first" is not important. Use all of the time available to you. Use time to go back and check your answers.
9. Practice remaining calm during tests. If you begin to feel anxious, take a few deep breaths and let yourself relax. Close your eyes and try to visualize or imagine yourself confidently taking the test. You can practice deep breathing and imagery anytime you feel anxious (not just during tests).

References

American College Testing. (1987). *Study power.* Iowa City, IA: Author.

Brown, W. F., & Holtzman, W. H. (1987). *A guide to college survival* (rev. ed.). Iowa City, IA: The American College Testing Program.

Chapter 8

The Future of Secondary School Counseling

In our fast changing world, how can counselors help to ensure the continued growth and improvement of secondary school counseling? How can we go about creating a plan and—just as crucial—how can we put the plan into action? "Preferred futuring," a technique that merges modern notions about creative problem solving with our ancient desire to catch a glimpse of the future, just may be the answer.

As school counselors and counseling professionals, we must find the best ways to meet the needs of children. Children afflicted with AIDS, crack babies and homeless children can be found all across America. Are we preparing programs to meet their needs before **and** after they hit the school? Or, will we wait until it is time for them to enter school and then ask, "What are we going to do with these children?"

Predicting a probable future world, and then adjusting our lives for what seems to be the inevitable, doesn't empower us to control our future or that of our profession.

We as counselors must become active consumers of the information provided by mainstream forecasting. Rather than postulating a world and then adjusting to the prediction, it may be more productive to ask, "What kind of future for secondary school counseling do I prefer?" It is a subtle shift—from being reactive to being proactive.

Nancy Perry in her article, "Utopia Lifelong Learning Center" describes and visualizes a typical American secondary school in the year

2040. The learning center is divided into three houses: Learning to Learn, Learning to Live, and Learning to Work. The center houses people of all ages because in 2040 learning is seen as a life long process.

Hannah Dixon and Linda Kelly describe secondary school counselors playing vastly different roles with students, parents, administrators, and teachers in their article, "Secondary School Counseling in the 21st Century."

The transformation of secondary school counseling must occur in the 90s and in the 21st century, but it will take a commitment from both those already in the profession and those entering it to change the direction in which we are now headed. School counselors must direct their own fates.

The destiny of school counseling rests in our hands, and not in the hands of others who are not aware of our training, skills and expertise. We cannot permit others to dictate our scope of practice. Personal, social, educational and career counseling with students must become a priority. Individual and small group counseling, combined with large group guidance, must be utilized to the maximum. Counseling, guidance, consultation and coordination must be seen as our areas of expertise and as our primary areas of responsibility.

The secondary school counselor who is a dreamer turns his or her back on the future and sees only the past. The visionary faces only the future and learns nothing from the past. The wise school counselor contemplates the vista that is the history of his or her profession, comprehends the reality of the past, and then says, "What kind of future for secondary school counseling do I prefer?" This *is* preferred futuring.

Counseling Paints a Bright Future: Student Competencies K–12

Doris Rhea Coy

The American School Counselor Association would like to credit the leadership of the Ohio Coalition for the Future of School Counseling for the development of this booklet. The Coalition, composed of practicing counselors and counselor educators from across Ohio has been working for the improvement of school counseling in Ohio for over one and one-half years and has developed these student competencies to help counselors meet the needs of their students in a systematic and developmental manner. Susan Sears, Terri Pregitzer, and Anita Jackson deserve special thanks for the development of the booklet while Tom Davis and Bill Nemec served as editors of the final product. For information about the Coalition, contact Susan Sears at The Ohio State University in Columbus, Ohio

During the development of these competencies, the authors reviewed various state models of counseling and several books. Wisconsin's *Model of Guidance* and *Developing and Managing Your School Guidance Program* by Norman Gysbers and Patricia Henderson were helpful.

Doris Rhea Coy, ASCA President, 1990

Introduction

As we approach the 21st century, our complex culture is characterized by diverse and ever-changing values in the home, community, and school. Societal-based problems are worse and this is reflected in dramatic increases in substance abuse, suicide, child abuse, teen pregnancy, truancy, school dropouts, and random acts of violence.

School counselors are being asked to assume a greater role in the lives of their students and in the students' families. Parents, particularly single parents, want help in improving their parenting skills. Therefore, counselors have begun to conduct parenting groups. Trying to prevent substance abuse, teen pregnancy, and suicide, school counselors have devised student support and intervention groups and have involved teachers in counseling-related activities. With legislative mandates for accountability in education, school counselors have helped students learn test-taking skills and have coordinated testing programs. Assisting students in career planning and in choosing appropriate post-secondary education and training continue to be important counselor activities. The challenges facing counselors and demands on their time will continue to grow during the next decade. School counselors must choose where they spend their time and energy carefully. It will be easy for counselors to engage in quasi-administrative activities rather than child-oriented ones. Given the challenges faced by today's students, counselors must focus on students' personal/social, educational, and career needs.

School Counselor's Scope of Practice

The scope of practice of the school counselor includes educational, personal-social, and career counseling. Counselors help students acquire study and test-taking skills, use educational information and set educational goals. They help students develop healthy self-concepts, learn to respect diverse cultures and resolve conflicts. Counselors assist students to understand and apply interests and aptitudes, use career information and set career goals. As they counsel students individually and in groups, counselors often consult with parents and teachers to develop the supportive network needed to help students.

While some of the counselor's work is remedial or occurs after a problem has developed, many counselors engage in preventative or developmental counseling. That is, they have developed counseling programs and activities designed to assist students to develop the skills necessary to function effectively in today's complex school and society. Developmental counselors design counseling programs that focus on student competencies and student outcomes. The long-range goals of school counseling are to help students become **effective learners, responsible people, and productive workers.** To accomplish these student outcomes, well-planned counseling programs from preschool through postsecondary are needed. The purpose of this booklet is to help counselors design well-planned counseling programs. Student competency statements for prekindergarten through postsecondary are suggested. If you have a written counseling program, now is the time to reevaluate it. If you don't, now is the time to develop one.

Format of This Booklet

Since the scope of practice of school counseling includes personal/ social, educational, and career counseling, the authors of this booklet developed student goals under each of the three areas of counseling (see the next page for a listing of the student developmental goals). Then, they developed student competencies, by grade level, to implement the student goals. Readers are free to use this resource as they choose. You may use it "as is" or you may wish to change a competency to meet a local need.

Doris Rhea Coy, ASCA President, 1990
Susan Jones Sears, ASCA Public Relations Chair, 1990

Student Developmental Goals

Personal/Social Goals

Students will be:

- Gaining self-awareness
- Developing positive attitudes
- Making healthy choices
- Respecting others
- Gaining responsibility
- Developing relationship skills
- Resolving conflicts
- Making effective decisions

Educational Goals

Students will be:

- Applying effective study skills
- Setting goals
- Learning effectively
- Gaining test taking skills

Career Goals

Students will be:

- Forming a career identity
- Planning for the future
- Combating career stereotyping
- Analyzing skills and interests

Grade Nine Student Competencies

Personal/Social Goals	Students Will:
Gaining self-awareness	Value their unique characteristics and abilities.
Developing positive attitudes	Describe and prioritize their values.
Making healthy choices	Demonstrate assertive skills useful in pressure situations.
Respecting others	Value positive qualities of people that are culturally different.
Gaining responsibility	Analyze when they take responsibility for themselves and when they do not.
Developing relationship skills	Identify own biases and stereotypes that interfere with establishing effective relationships.
Resolving conflicts	Analyze how conflict resolution skills contribute toward work within a group.
Making effective decisions	Analyze the importance of generating alternatives and assessing the consequences of each before making a decision.

Educational Goals	Students Will:
Applying effective study skills	Evaluate their study habits and plan for changes if needed.
Setting goals	Identify and utilize community resources that enable them to reach educational goals.

| Learning effectively | Learn strategies for coping with learning style inadequacies. |
| Gaining test taking skills | Analyze test results and plan for improvement. |

Career Goals   Students Will:

Forming a career identity	Describe how values and needs influence career choice.
Planning for the future	Analyze how choices they are making now will affect their lives in the future.
Combating career stereotyping	Discuss nontraditional careers and explore at least one.
Analyzing skills and interests	Describe their skills, abilities, interests, and aptitudes.

Grade Ten Student Competencies

Personal/Social Goals   Students Will:

Gaining self-awareness	Analyze how they can control and direct their feelings.
Developing positive attitudes	Describe decisions they have made that were based on their attitudes and values.
Making healthy choices	Identify resources that will assist them with personal concerns related to their sexuality.
Respecting others	Describe how prejudices are formed and examine their consequences.
Gaining responsibility	Show how they manage their time effectively.
Developing relationship skills	Describe situations at school and at home where their behavior affects others' behavior toward them.
Resolving conflicts	Identify situations in which they need to control their anger.
Making effective decisions	Distinguish between alternatives that involve varying degrees of risk.

Educational Goals	Students Will:
Applying effective study skills	Evaluate how effective study skills can contribute to effective work habits in the future.
Setting goals	Analyze forces working against their goals.
Learning effectively	Recognize how time and circumstances can cause educational goals to change.
Gaining test taking skills	Evaluate reasons why they may not do well on tests.

Career Goals	Students Will:
Forming a career identity	Review their educational plan and set educational goals based on self-assessment and career exploration.
Planning for the future	Evaluate the need for flexibility in their roles and in their choices.
Combating career stereotyping	Analyze the validity of their own stereotypes.
Analyzing skills and interests	Assess their ability to achieve past goals and integrate this knowledge into future planning.

Grade Eleven Student Competencies

Personal/Social Goals	Students Will:
Gaining self-awareness	Specify characteristics and abilities they appreciate most in themselves and others.
Developing positive attitudes	Generate ways to develop more positive attitudes.
Making healthy choices	Continually evaluate the effects their leisure time activities have on their physical and mental health.
Respecting others	Describe strategies for overcoming biases and prejudices toward others.

Gaining responsibility	Assess how avoiding responsibility hinders their ability to manage their environment effectively.
Developing relationship skills	Assess their current social and family relationships and evaluate their effectiveness.
Resolving conflicts	Value the application of problem solving methods in conflict situations.
Making effective decisions	Identify decisions they have made and analyze how those decisions will affect their future decisions.

Educational Goals   Students Will:

Applying effective study skills	Review relationship between time spent on studying and student success.
Setting goals	Collect post-secondary educational information.
Learning effectively	Contact post-secondary institutions for visits.
Gaining test taking skills	Prepare for national college entrance exams.

Career Goals   Students Will:

Forming a career identity	Evaluate the importance of setting realistic career goals and striving toward them.
Planning for the future	Acquire skills for bringing about positive change.
Combating career stereotyping	Discuss some of the role conflicts they may experience in adulthood.
Analyzing skills and interests	Evaluate the importance of having laws to protect workers from discrimination.

Grade Twelve Student Competencies

Personal/Social Goals   Students Will:

Gaining self-awareness	Appreciate their uniqueness.

Developing positive attitudes	Evaluate how their attitudes and values affect their lives.
Making healthy choices	Analyze the personal skills that have contributed to satisfactory physical and mental health.
Respecting others	Demonstrate appreciation and respect for cultural differences.
Gaining responsibility	Assess how taking responsibility enhances their lives.
Developing relationship skills	Understand the value of maintaining effective relationships throughout life.
Resolving conflicts	Evaluate their current communication and conflict resolution skills and plan how to improve them.
Making effective decisions	Evaluate their present ability to generate alternatives, gather information, and assess the consequences of the decisions they make.

Educational Goals	**Students Will:**
Applying effective study skills	Recognize that learning is a lifetime process.
Setting goals	Evaluate their future educational goals.
Learning effectively	Plan for the transition into post-secondary education and training.
Gaining test taking skills	Evaluate the discrepancies between goals and test performance.

Career Goals	**Students Will:**
Forming a career identity	Review their career goals.
Planning for the future	Analyze the relationships between work and family roles.
Combating career stereotyping	Learn strategies for dealing with discrimination and sexual harassment.
Analyzing skills and interests	Conduct an assessment of their current skills, abilities, and career prospects.

Utopia Lifelong Learning Center

Nancy S. Perry

"Is it not ironical that in a planned society of controlled workers given compulsory assignments, where religious expression is suppressed, the press controlled, and all media of communication censored, where a puppet government is encouraged but denied any real authority, where great attention is given to efficiency and character reports, and attendance at cultural assemblies is compulsory, where it is avowed that all will be administered to each according to his abilities, and where those who flee are tracked down, returned and punished for trying to escape—in short, in the milieu of the typical large American secondary school—we attempt to teach 'THE DEMOCRATIC SYSTEM'?"

—Anonymous

Most of us will blush as we read the above quotation because we will recognize the truth of the statement. We teach the responsibility of citizenship within a democratic society while practicing tyranny through suppression and control. We recognize that children learn what they live but are surprised when they live what they learn. We limit their decision-making but expect them to exit the institution with complete responsibility for themselves. We recognize the need for reform of our secondary schools but, so far, have tried to accomplish this mission by doing more of the same. But all is not lost. Educators of vision spoke, and little by little, communities listened. The year is 2040. Come with me to visit a typical American secondary school.

The Utopia Community Center is easily recognized as an inviting environment. The complex of modern buildings blend into the natural landscape. There is a sense of productivity and energy as people of all ages wend their way in and out of the buildings. Groups of young adults are spiritedly working together with intent and purpose. One group is using surveying tools while another seems to be investigating some natural phenomena. The building directly ahead says, "Utopia Lifelong Learning Center." As we enter the hospitality lobby, we are requested to tell the computer what services we would like to access. Since our purpose is to observe the educational system, we ask the computer how we might visit a ninth grade class. After a moment, the computer replies that ninth grade is not part of its vocabulary. Could we clarify our need?

We finally rephrase our request into understandable language—We wish to observe young people in the process of learning. The computer replies:

> *Do you want to limit your observation to young people only? That may be difficult because the Learning Center is open to all ages.*

We agree to be flexible but indicate our basic interest in 14- or 15-year-olds. The computer lights up brightly.

> *Perhaps you would like to visit the Houses of Learning to Learn, Learning to Live, and Learning to Work?*

It sounded good to us so we were directed to sit in a room where we might observe without intruding on the process. The space surrounding us lit up so that we felt as if we were in the midst of a room of mostly young people. The photoelectronic representations were the three-dimensional images of activity in a room in another part of the building.

A voice said:

> *Welcome to the House of Learning to Learn. Do not be afraid to walk around and talk. The images in this room cannot see or hear you. Before young people come to us, they have mastered the basic tools of learning—communicating, computing, etc. It is now time to hone these skills into practical application through critical thinking and investigation. This house is divided into four interrelated rooms: the room of communication; the room of personal and global stewardship; the room of problem solving and reasoning; and the room of the human record. You are in the room of the human record. The study of the human record not only includes the actions and events of the past but also the constructs of human thought and creativity as they have evolved through time. It includes literature as well as scientific theories, concepts of government, economic systems, philosophy and mathematics as symbols of our humanity.*

The man in the center is telling about the Century of Conflict when nations did not understand the need to operate as a global entity. The young people listen incredulously and question the man intently. Finally someone says:

Now what are the lessons we have learned from the events of the last century when competition rather than cooperation was the operative value?

Before we could hear the discussion, the Voice said:

We must move on. These young adults will stay here until they feel that they fully understand how the events of yesterday affect them today. Their community of learners has decided to concentrate on the human record and personal and global stewardship for this segment. They know that all areas are equally important in learning to learn but they may schedule their time according to their needs.

I could stand it no longer:

But who checks attendance? How do you know what grade each should get?

The Voice pauses:

Please explain checking attendance and grade.

Well, what if they don't come to learn?

The Voice replies:

But of course, the community would be concerned and would seek a missing member out to ascertain the reason for the absence. A community does not function well without all of it members. It is a responsibility to participate in the learning for all.

But what about grades—you know, how will you know if they have learned the lesson? How will you compare them?

The Voice hesitated again:

I do not understand, why would they be compared? Each is learning according to his/her ability. They will tell us if the lesson is not clear to their understanding.

The Voice went on to explain:

After acquiring the basic learning tools, young people usually spend about two years in the learning centers. It is necessary to nurture the mind, body, and spirit if intelligence on Earth is to continue. Therefore each young person who is ready for this stage joins a community of learners who will encourage each other in the achievement of each individual's learning plan.

But who makes up this plan?

Why, the mentoring counselor, of course, assists the student in developing the plan. School counselors are an integral part of our educational system. After each member completes his/her plan, the group which forms a community of learners comes together to negotiate for a community plan which can be scheduled.

But who leads that group? Who has the skill to pull off such a task?

The mentoring counselor will act as a resource for the group but the members must make their own decisions. They have all had practice in negotiating, communication, and conflict resolution in the Learning to Live House. In the House of Learning to Live, trained human development experts work with communities of learners as advisors. They provide a forum of human relations skill development as the community sees the need. They counsel the individual to assure that a balance is being maintained in the development of the whole person. You know, we must be equally concerned with the development of the body and spirit. The whole person must experience wellness or the balance of our interdependence will suffer.

But wait a minute, that reminds me, what about the football team? How can you have a high school without a football team?

Oh, we do promote physical fitness and teamwork. That is done in all living and learning areas. We try to emphasize those athletic skills which will be of value for a lifetime. We do have community teams who are constantly trying to improve their skills. However, those are not limited to certain ages. All people participate at the level at which they feel most comfortable. We also have daily opportunities for social gatherings. In this world it is very important that we have the skills to interact in positive ways. The latest fad is nonverbal communication. Young people communicate through extra-sensory perception. Some of them are very good at it. Competition about 'out-of-body experiences' is getting a little out of hand though.

I think I understand the Houses of Learning to Learn and Learning to Live but what about the House of Learning to Work?

That is probably the most intergenerational of all of our houses. People of all ages come here to enhance their skills as wage earners and to learn more about work opportunities. Counselors with specialized training in occupational information systems and careers development assist individuals as they develop their journey of careers. With the recent technological explosion, many older workers are realizing the need to gain new skills. Young people receive their technical skills here but often apprentice to community workers for practice. Sometimes young people come here after they have completed their learning preparation plan. Others might choose to continue to the Institute of Higher Learning. It is a decision that is made at about age sixteen. However, age is not a factor and it is understood that we may change our life pathways as we feel the need. Learning is lifelong, you know.

But do students graduate? What about commencement?

Commencement? That means beginning doesn't it? Certainly all students commence to take their part in the greater community when they leave us. Isn't that what education is all about?

Secondary School Counseling in the 21st Century

Hannah Dixon
Linda Kelly

School counseling at the secondary level will experience drastic changes in the 21st century. Secondary school counselors of the future will be playing vastly different roles with students, parents, administrators, and teachers if they are to survive in the public education system. School counselors will need to adapt quickly to these new roles if they are to meet the needs of a changing society. They will need self-confidence as well as courage and leadership if they are to accept these challenges and survive as an essential part of the educational system. The future for school counselors will require changes in counselor education programs, and the perceptions of school counselors by administrators, teachers and parents. Current school counselors must encourage and fight for positive changes for the betterment of the school counseling profession.

The typical day for a secondary school counselor in the next century will be dramatically different than it is today. A school counselor's schedule will be much more proactive than reactive. Their schedules' must become much more structured. Their daily routine will be determined more by counselor-initiated projects and goals than by external, uncontrollable factors. A school counselor's schedule will begin to look more like that of a classroom teacher or agency counselor than ever before. Time will be set aside for individual and group counseling, consultation with teachers, and planning. Counselors must regain control of their time and manage it effectively to assist students.

Secondary school counselors need to practice effective time management strategies to allow them to set more structured appointments for individual/family counseling, group counseling and consultation as well as set aside time for planning and preparation. The days of a counselor being available at a moments notice will diminish if school counselors are to be effective. School counselors need to make themselves available only during certain time periods to answer general questions, return phone calls and provide general information for students, parents and teachers. We must begin to value our time and let others know it is important. Answering the same questions repeatedly and being available at all times is unnecessary, unproductive and a waste of valuable counselor expertise.

School counselors must let go of some of the tasks they have done for years. Tasks that are of a general information nature (SAT/ACT test information, credit checks, scheduling, G.P.A. calculation, etc.) should be turned over to technicians/clerical staff. This does not exclude counselors from college/career counseling but changes the nature of interaction with students and parents away from that of information giving to focusing on the counseling process. Assisting students with decision-making, problem-solving and test interpretation and/or interventions should be the focus of student-counselor interaction. Counselors need to spend more time using their counseling skills and less time on record-keeping and information services. School counselors need to develop their skills and expertise and let go of tasks that can be done by some other school personnel.

To prepare school counselors for these changes, counselor education programs should reflect and place a high priority on counseling process skills. Courses in counselor education should reflect a strong emphasis on advanced individual and group counseling techniques, family systems and family counseling, consultation services, crisis intervention, assessment/diagnosis/case management, cultural specific counseling, and prevention and remediation interventions. Counselor education programs should reduce their emphasis on record keeping and information services.

Secondary school counselors will become specialists with skills that will be in demand by administrators, teachers, parents and students. These skills must be utilized in such a way as to take full advantage of them and reach the most students. Therefore, school counselors will, out of necessity and cost effectiveness, be asked to serve as consultants for classroom teachers, administrators and parents. School counselors need to become much more involved as consultants training all of these various constituencies. Conducting in-service sessions and seminars will become a major part of a school counselor's responsibility. Counselors will also become more involved with peer-to-peer programs in which they will train students to work with other students in a variety of capacities.

Individual and group counseling will continue to be two of the important specialized services that school counselors will provide. The need for expanded group counseling programs to address the needs of various student groups is vital. These group counseling programs should be incorporated into the school educational program as both preventive and remedial interventions to assist students with issues that may be interfering with the educational process.

Secondary counselors are going to be more knowledgeable and more involved in *career* directions and decisions for students. The technological changes in the 90s and in the next century make it imperative that counselors inventory students' skills and interests so they can make the best, informed decisions regarding their futures. Counselors will also involve families in the student's career decisions with evening hours and appointments a part of the counselor's regular schedule. The counselor will become the liaison and will be knowledgeable and aware of job opportunities and future directions in the community as well as on the State and National level. The counselor will be the "expert" and the "connector" linking student and family, school, business, and postsecondary education opportunities.

Inservices by counselors will become a part of their professional responsibilities. These will be done for administrators and teachers on the following topics: (1) what counseling is and what counselors do; (2) topical concerns (suicide, careers, substance abuse, sexuality issues, conflict resolution, decision making, etc.); (3) networking with agencies and other groups; (4) testing and assessment; (5) special needs; (6) other pertinent topics.

Inservices will also be done for agencies to explain school counseling and the functions of counselors and for parents on specific concerns—educational future, careers, testing, sexuality, etc.

Professional development will be a continuing *must* for secondary counselors. Keeping current and continuing to develop new skills will be an expectation. This will be done through course work, workshops, and professional organizations as counselors learn to be more active professionally and to strive to have an impact on legislation and decisions affecting their profession locally, statewide, and nationally. Counselors will become recognized for their skills and expertise as they continue their professional upgrading and their vocalization of the important factors and needs impinging upon their clientele. In order to survive and to have an impact counselors *must* recognize the foregoing as one of the most vital and necessary components of their continuing existence. Time must be set aside for these opportunities—in the counseling profession stagnation is not permissible. Writing for local newsletters and newspapers will become necessary for counselors; also, writing articles for publication as well as presenting and participating in workshops for other counselors and human development professionals.

The secondary school counselor will be *supervised and evaluated* in the future by a counseling professional who will give support and direction as well as provide skill development and case reviews. This will give counseling a school-advocate, human development emphasis and make it a recognized profession, separate from administration and teaching, achieving parity with other helping professions.

School counselors are underrepresented, highly-trained professionals with skills that at present are not respected or utilized to their fullest extent. It is the school counselors themselves who must step forward to encourage these changes if they are to survive in the education arena. School counselors must unite as a profession and share their knowledge and expertise with others. They must take a stand and become advocates for children and help to change the perceptions, attitudes and systems that are working against a generation of young people who must become empowered if they are to live productive, healthy lives.

School counselors must work to change the attitudes and perceptions of their administrative and teaching colleagues as well as their student and parent constituencies. School counselors must become more involved in determining their schedules, goals and objectives and they must educate others about their special skills and services. School counselors must actively work to influence administrators so they can be more effective in utilizing their skills to impact teachers, parents and students. School counselors must reach out to parents and work with families to facilitate positive change in students, and parents must see school counselors as advocates and partners.